Wartime North Africa

WARTIME NORTH AFRICA

A DOCUMENTARY HISTORY,
1934–1950

EDITED BY
Aomar Boum and Sarah Abrevaya Stein

STANFORD UNIVERSITY PRESS
Stanford, California

STANFORD UNIVERSITY PRESS
Stanford, California

© 2022 by the Board of Trustees of the Leland Stanford Junior University. All rights reserved.

No part of this book may be reproduced or transmitted in any form or by any means, electronic or mechanical, including photocopying and recording, or in any information storage or retrieval system without the prior written permission of Stanford University Press.

Printed in the United States of America on acid-free, archival-quality paper

Library of Congress Cataloging-in-Publication Data

Names: Stein, Sarah Abrevaya, editor. | Boum, Aomar, editor.
Title: Wartime North Africa : a documentary history, 1934–1950 / edited by Sarah Abrevaya Stein and Aomar Boum.
Description: Stanford, California : Stanford University Press, 2022. | Includes bibliographical references and index.
Identifiers: LCCN 2021048241 (print) | LCCN 2021048242 (ebook) | ISBN 9781503611511 (cloth) | ISBN 9781503631991 (paperback) | ISBN 9781503632004 (ebook)
Subjects: LCSH: World War, 1939-1945—Africa, North—Sources. | World War, 1939-1945—Personal narratives, North African. | Africa, North—History—20th century—Sources.
Classification: LCC D766.82 .W37 2022 (print) | LCC D766.82 (ebook) | DDC 940.540961—dc23/eng/20211012
LC record available at https://lccn.loc.gov/2021048241
LC ebook record available at https://lccn.loc.gov/2021048242

Cover photo: German troops, civilians, and Panzer tank, at the Roman amphitheater of Thysdrus, near present day El Djem, Tunisia. The German Archives
Cover design: Rob Ehle

Contents

Note to Readers   ix
List of Illustrations and Maps   xi

Introduction   1

( ) Publication date; [ ] Composition date; { } Time period referenced

PART I. THE RISE OF FASCISM AND NAZISM
AS SEEN FROM NORTH AFRICA, 1934–1940

1. Hitler as Haman [1934]   23
2. A German Agent Poses as a Muslim to Spread Propaganda [1935]   25
3. Mussolini Given a Hero's Welcome by Tripoli's
   Jewish Community [1937]   27
4. A Fantastic, Anti-Hitler Poem Spared from Destruction (1939)   29
5. A Sheikh in Oujda Predicts a Brutal Conquest by Germany [1939]   36
6. A Jewish Adolescent Ponders Her Identity [1939]   38
7. A Manifesto against Racism {1939}   40
8. An Intrafaith Cry to Oppose Racism (1939)   42
9. The Swastika's Looming Shadow—One Woman's Experience
   in Spanish-Occupied Tangier {1939–1941}   46
10. Hitler's Military Is Unmatched—An Anti-French Tirade [1940]   53
11. An Ode to Marshal Pétain {1941}   55
12. Pétain's Portrait [1941]   56
13. Foreign Legion Soldiers Trained at Sidi Bel Abbès {c. Early 1940s}   57
14. A Report on the Poitiers Camp by Léopold Senghor {1940–1942}   63
15. Senegalese Prisoners of War Protest the Release of White
    French Soldiers from a *Frontstalag* Internment Camp [1941]   72
16. Famine in the Anti-Atlas Mountains {c. 1940s}   75

PART II. RACE LAWS, INTERNMENT, AND SPOLIATION, 1940–1943

17. A French Communist's Arduous Deportation
    to North Africa {1940–1945} — 81
18. The Mellah, Revived—Anti-Jewish Residential Laws
    in Vichy Morocco [1941] — 90
19. A Jewish Merchant Strategically Recalls His Family's
    Foundational Support for French Colonialism [1941] — 98
20. Muslim Algerian Doctors Call for the Reinstatement of
    Their Jewish Colleagues [1941] — 101
21. A Photographer's Lens on the Camps [1941] — 103
22. Shoes, Cigarettes, and the Needs of the Interned [1941] — 107
23. An Interned Mother Appeals for Food [1941] — 109
24. Is a French Christian Diva an Algerian Jew? (1941) — 110
25. A Pharmacist's Desperate Appeal [1941] — 112
26. Racist Laws in Action—A French Officer's Boon
    Is a Jewish Merchant's Bust [1941] — 115
27. A Mother's Struggles under Internment [1942] — 117
28. An Influential Psychiatrist Declares Himself Not Jewish [1942] — 120
29. Vichy Law Forces Out a Jewish Shipping Agent [1942] — 121
30. A Jewish Cinema Owner Seeks Restitution of His Business [1943] — 122
31. A Wry Account of Occupation {1942–1943} — 126
32. Six Months under the "Nazi Boot" (1943) — 130
33. Song of the Oppressed—Lyrical Recollections of an Adolescent
    Boy in Tunisia [c. 1943] — 140
34. Controversial Intercession—A Jewish Community Leader's
    Wartime Memoir {1942–1943} — 145
35. Flight, Internment, Annihilation, Defiance—The Many Wartime
    Paths of a Jewish Family from Tunis {1943} — 158
36. "Swept Up in a Monstrous Whirlwind"—The Wartime Diary
    of Albert Memmi {1942–1943} — 162
37. Sexual Violence in the Ḥāra {1942–1943} — 168
38. "Who Is More of a Dog?"—A Radical Poet's View
    of Internment [1942] — 171
39. An Algerian Muslim's Memories of Internment {1940–1943} — 174

40. Daily Life in Djelfa {1940–1945} ... 187
41. A Yiddish Account of a Jewish Burial in the Sahara {1940–1943} ... 191
42. An Internee Seeks Emergency Dental Care [1942] ... 198
43. A Rabbi in Azemmour [1941–1942] ... 200
44. Marking the Days of Awe in Sidi Aziz {1942} ... 202
45. Celebrating Purim in the Bizerte Camp {1942–1943} ... 204
46. Keeping Kosher and Celebrating Shavuot during the War [1942–1943] ... 213
47. After Liberation, Torture {1943} ... 216
48. Surviving the "Tombeau" [c. 1943] ... 217
49. A Correspondent's Wartime Travails [1943] ... 219
50. A German Physician Interned [1942–1944] ... 224
51. A Pianist's Injured Hand, and a Quest for a Visa [1943] ... 233
52. A Doctor in the Bou Azzer Mines [1943–1944] ... 238
53. Shorn of Her Curls—Internment in Giado through a Young Girl's Eyes {1942} ... 241
54. Libyan Jewish Holders of British Passports Languish in Italian Camps {1943–1945} ... 249
55. Refugee Forced Labor in Casablanca [1943] ... 255
56. Muslims Protecting Jewish Neighbors in a Poor Libyan Town {1943} ... 259
57. Internment in Drancy—A Young Algerian Jew's Account {1943} ... 260
58. A "Total Violation of Human Dignity"—Girlhood Interrupted in Auschwitz {1944} ... 266
59. Olympian, Victim, Survivor (1942–1946) ... 271

PART III. THE LATE- AND POSTWAR ERA, 1943–1950

60. Lmirikan (1942) ... 281
61. Hitler's Haggadah (c. 1945) ... 283
62. A Moroccan Adolescent's View of Operation Torch and His American Employers {1942–1947} ... 286
63. The Politics of Cotton and the Postwar Struggle for Power [1943] ... 291
64. A Moroccan Soldier Serves the Colonial, Vichy, Free French, and American Regimes {1906–1942} ... 294
65. Singing the Praises of American Troops in Tunis (c. 1943) ... 296

66. American "Liberators" Perpetuate Sexual Violence [1943] — 299
67. American Power and the Politics of "Seduction" [1943] — 300
68. The Politics of Hunger [1943] — 302
69. The Appeal of an Austrian Lieutenant [1943] — 305
70. An Unequal "Liberation"—Sustained Internment after Operation Torch [c. 1944] — 308
71. A Manifesto of the Formerly Interned [1943] — 315
72. Polish Internee, Political Chameleon [1943] — 317
73. The "Infinite Prolonging of Their Internment"—Forced Labor after Operation Torch [1943] — 319
74. A Moroccan Jewish Community Seeks to Rescue Jewish Children from Occupied Hungary [1944] — 321
75. Director of the Free French Colonial Troops Recommends Deportation of Mixed-Race Couples to Madagascar [1945] — 325
76. A Memorial to the "Martyrs" of Tunis (1946) — 327
77. A Yom Kippur Prayer for Tunisian Victims of the Third Reich (1946) — 331
78. The Long Shadow of Colonialism—Seeking Legal Rights in the Sahara [1948] — 333
79. A Libyan Jewish Rabbinical Student Tries to Emigrate to Palestine (1949) — 334
80. Bearing a "Weird" Tattoo—A Survivor of the Nazi Camps Returns to Tlemcen {1950} — 340

Acknowledgments — 347
Index — 351

Note to Readers

The sources in this volume have been translated from Arabic, French, Hebrew, Italian, North African Judeo-Arabic, Moroccan Darija, Spanish, Tamazight (Berber), and Yiddish, as well as transcribed from English. Some of the selections are plurilingual, containing within them various languages.

North Africa's cities, towns, regions, and peoples are referred to in various ways by the diverse people who inhabited, occupied, or otherwise interacted with them. The Moroccan port city of Eṣawīra, for example, is known as Taṣṣort in Tamazight, rendered as Essaouira in English, and sometimes represented (by Europeans and other foreigners) by its Portuguese, colonial designation of Mogador. The peoples of North Africa, too, are referred to or represented textually with various names and spellings. Thus, sometimes given individuals, when writing in a nonnative language, represented their own name or the name of another person in various forms within a single source (for example, on official French, German, or Italian documents).

In introductions, we use Arabic-language people and place-names, transliterated per the *International Journal of Middle East Studies* system and (in the case of our maps) according to contemporary Arabic-language naming norms. In primary sources, we retain the source's own spelling and designation of proper nouns, and offer Arabic equivalents in the introductions to selections.

For the dates that accompany the selections in this volume, years in parentheses indicate the year of publication, years in square brackets indicate the year of composition, and years in braces indicate the time period referenced in the selection.

Illustrations and Maps

Illustrations

1. German troops pose in front of the Roman amphitheater of Thysdrus, Tunisia — 5
2. German representatives walk a North African street — 6
3. Diverse prisoners of a Vichy labor camp in the Sahara — 12
4. The Bendelac sisters in Morocco — 47
5. French prisoners of war captured by the Germans — 65
6. Al-ḥusin Al-gedari, Moroccan survivor of a terrible famine during the Second World War — 76
7. International Brigade members, now forced laborers, in the Vichy camp of Sidi El Ayachi — 106
8. Refugees Esti and Sophie Freud at a pottery market in Morocco — 118
9. German Air Force soldiers and Italian soldiers threateningly "serenade" a young woman — 129
10. Jewish forced laborers in Tunisia wearing obligatory Stars of David — 149
11. A German soldier extends a cigarette to a local man — 165
12. French Commander Julius Caesar Caboche in front the Djelfa internment camp — 173
13. A guard, seated in front of a forced laborer, at Sidi El Ayachi — 181
14. Watercolor of Mediouna Internment Camp by Edward Bawden — 221

15. Two prisoners at the Im Fout labor camp in Morocco 240
16. Haim Habib, a Libyan Jew, died at just sixteen years
    of age at Italy's Giado internment camp 243
17. Imprisoned men at the Vichy internment camp at Le Kef 258
18. American soldiers sharing cigarettes with locals 293
19. Celebration of former internees at the Djerba internment camp 311

Maps

1. Penal, labor, and internment camps in Vichy-occupied
   Morocco and Algeria 10
2. Penal, labor, and internment camps in German-occupied
   Tunisia and Italian-occupied Libya 14

Wartime North Africa

INTRODUCTION

A rabbi's son in Essaouira, Morocco, writes a scathing, phantasmagorical poem about Hitler's rise to power, only to burn every copy out of fear. An adolescent in Italian Tripolitania ponders the meaning of her Jewishness as fascism gains favor in her community and war threatens the world. A Moroccan Jewish cinema owner is compelled by French Vichy race laws to sell his business to a Christian peer. A Muslim nationalist in Tunisia is hounded, arrested, and interned by the same regime for his political views. A Polish erstwhile volunteer for the International Brigade in Spain is forced to labor on an aspirational trans-Saharan railroad day after day without shoes. Drunken German soldiers and SS officers terrorize the Jewish women of Nazi-occupied Tunis, threatening them with sexual violence. Families across Algeria starve as drought and famine overcome rural communities. A German Jewish photojournalist snaps pictures of the Moroccan infantrymen who guard his internment camp in the desert. A young boy watches Operation Torch, the Allied military campaign to liberate North Africa from the Axis powers, unfold outside his seaside window. A top-ranked Algerian Jewish water-polo player is reported annihilated by the Nazis in the Auschwitz death camp, only to make a shocking return to the competitive stage. The future president of Senegal—a poet, theorist, and anticolonial activist—languishes in a prisoner-of-war (POW) camp in France, incensed at the racial inequities that undergird French military policy. A survivor of the Nazi death camps returns to his native Tlemcen, Algeria, bearing a numerical tattoo on his arm that none can decode. An *ashkeva* (memorial prayer) is composed to memorialize the murdered of Tunisia.

This is wartime North Africa, seen not from the vantage of state policy or military engagements but from the viewpoint of the diverse people who lived it.

During the Second World War, Morocco, Algeria, Tunisia, and Libya witnessed Vichy, Nazi, and Italian fascist rule as well as Spanish control; the implementation of racist and anti-Semitic laws; the theft of property, assets, and businesses; the influx of huge numbers of refugees from Europe; and the mass internment in forced labor and internment camps of women, men, and children of North African, European, and global origin.[1] Some North Africans (Muslims as well as Jews) were deported to Nazi camps from North Africa—in the case of Libyan Jews, by way of internment in Italy.[2] Other North African Jewish émigrés living in France were deported to labor, internment, and death camps by the Nazi regime, with the help of the French authorities.[3] The Nazis also imprisoned North African and West African soldiers who served under the French flag in POW internment camps in France.[4]

Until now, personal histories of wartime North Africa have remained largely inaccessible to English-language readers.[5] To the extent that these stories have been told, they have been narrated separately, which has led to the deceptive perception that the many, varied experiences of wartime North Africa (whether experienced by local Jews or Muslims, European refugees, former volunteers for Spain's International Brigade or France's Foreign Legion, the interned and forced laborers, French "colonial soldiers" from North and West Africa, or others) were discrete phenomena. In this book, these stories are reunited. Here, readers will encounter wartime North Africa in all its diversity, and on a human scale.

To create this book, we have plumbed archives, libraries, and private collections across North Africa and West Africa, the Middle East, Europe, and the Americas. A number of our selections are drawn from published books (memoirs, diaries, collections of poetry, and more), but most have never been published before or translated into English. Translated from French, Arabic, North African Judeo-Arabic, Spanish, Hebrew, Moroccan Darija, Tamazight (Berber), Italian, and Yiddish, or transcribed from their original

English, these sources are like the dots of a pointillist painting. Each is unique and distinct—yet together they form an arresting whole.

Who made up wartime North Africa, that is, the present-day countries of Morocco, Algeria, Tunisia, and Libya?[6] The cast of characters that populate this book is diverse, not only because the Maghrib itself was a region always marked by diversity but also because, in the years leading up to and during the Second World War, its population swelled with officers, bureaucrats, and soldiers foreign and native; émigrés, refugees, and the displaced; internees, prisoners of war, and camp guards; philanthropic representatives; and more.

There was, to begin, an autochthonous Muslim population of roughly twenty million and a smaller Jewish population numbering roughly five hundred thousand in the Maghrib, each of which was multifarious in its own right. These populations shared courtyards and cities, as well as coastal, desert, and mountain towns; they were each, also, internally striated by class, history, language, and religious practice and ritual.[7]

North Africa's Jews lived in distinct, yet porous ethnic quarters or communal spaces alongside Muslims in both the urban and the rural regions of North Africa: the *mellah* (in Morocco and parts of western Algeria) and the *hara* of Algeria, Tunisia, and Tripolitania in northwestern Libya. In rural and mountainous regions of North Africa that were predominantly Berber/Amazigh and Arab, Jews and Muslim tended to live in a more integrated fashion.[8] Increasingly, a segment of North Africa's urban Jews lived in mixed middle- and upper-class neighborhoods, mingling easily with their city's multiethnic and multisectarian bourgeoisie.

Prewar North Africa also housed a population of European settler colonialists. These women, men, and children came from a variety of backgrounds—French, Sicilian, Italian, Maltese—and had been in the Maghrib for different lengths of time: in some cases for generations, in other cases only a few years. In all instances, their arrival in the region was in various respects subsidized and encouraged by the European colonial and "civilizing" project. This so-called colon population was receptive to—and indeed themselves producers of—anti-Jewish and anti-Muslim rhetoric, and the settler colonialists sometimes translated these sentiments into physical violence, as during the Constantine riots of 1934.[9]

The residents of North Africa were spread across the countries and colonies of the prewar era: Morocco, Algeria, Tunisia, and Libya. Subject to a violent colonization that had begun in the early nineteenth century, most of Algeria was integrated into France in 1848, but the state emancipated few Algerian Berber or Arab Muslims, who were categorized as "indigenous subjects of France" rather than French citizens. Since 1870, the bulk of Algeria's indigenous Jews were placed in another legal category by the Crémieux Decree, which granted them citizenship (excepting the small population in the military districts of the Sahara).[10] Morocco and Tunisia, by contrast, were protectorates of France, and here both Muslims and Jews were considered subjects of the sultan and bey (respectively), except for a minority of Jews who obtained French or Italian or other foreign citizenship.[11] The Libyan provinces of Tripolitania and Cyrenaica came under Italian control by treaty in 1912, a year after Italy became embroiled in a war with the Ottoman Empire over the region. Over the ensuing two decades, the Italian army gained control of the remainder of Libya through a brutal conquest overseen, as of 1922, by Benito Mussolini and his National Fascist Party. Fascist Italy granted Libya's residents colonial legal status as "Libyan Italian citizens."[12] Yet there, as across North Africa, a small but powerful percentage of Jewish women, men, and children (and smaller numbers of Muslims) held European or other foreign citizenship, in some cases because they worked for foreign consuls. Under colonialism, such an "extraterritorial" legal status afforded opportunities, but under Vichy, Nazi, and fascist Italian rule it could prove a legal liability.

The European powers had maintained a presence in the Maghrib since the early modern period, but with the colonization of Algeria and Tunisia in the nineteenth century, and Morocco and Libya in the early twentieth, the number of French, Spanish, and Italian people in the region soared. During the Second World War these numbers increased further to encompass military and civilian representatives, including Nazi SS (Schutzstaffel, or paramilitary) officers and German soldiers who occupied Tunisia for six months between November 1942 and May 1943.[13] State power could make itself felt in a violent fashion, of course, but also through pageantry. As sources in this book reveal, the Italian prime minister Benito Mussolini undertook a grandiose visit to Tripoli's Jewish neighborhood in 1937, while in French North Africa, teachers were required to hang portraits of Marshal Philippe Pétain (head of wartime France's collaborationist Vichy regime) in their classrooms.

As Nazism and fascism gained favor and power in Europe and across the

IMAGE 1. Smiling German troops pose in front of the Roman amphitheater of Thysdrus, near present-day El Djem, Tunisia, conjuring Nazi fantasies of the Third Reich as a successor to the Holy Roman Empire. Pictured from the menacing vantage of a Tiger I, a heavy tank used in German wartime incursions into North Africa and the Soviet Union, the photograph captures a group of local boys and men who had gathered as onlookers or had been pressed into service as tour guides. Tunesien, El Djem.-Panzer VI "Tiger I" und Zivilisten vor den Ruinen des römischen Amphitheaters von Thysdrus; KBK Lw 6, c. 1942–1943, Bild 101I-420-2033-33, Das Bundesarchiv, Berlin.

colonial world, the residents of North Africa were watching.[14] But North Africans were not passive observers or hapless victims of these trends. They were, instead, actively caught up in history as oracles, critics, resistance fighters, soldiers, narrators, translators, philanthropists, and religious leaders. As businesspeople and professionals, they maneuvered to keep their places of employment and jobs in the face of racist restrictions. As mothers, they sought the best for children living under duress. As prisoners, they maintained dignity through comradery, reading, writing, prayer, and producing art. As Black and/or colonial soldiers they braved the harshest military assignments and voiced outrage against the racist disrespect of the country whose flag they served.[15] As anticolonialists, they either welcomed or resisted Axis occupation (depending upon their view of French colonial rule) and,

IMAGE 2. The women, children, and men of North Africa were keen observers of the rise of fascism and Nazism in Europe and the unfolding of occupation and war on their own soil. A diverse array of onlookers watch the passage through their town of German representatives accompanied by a heavily laden cart. "Nordafrika.-Belebte Straße mit Torbogen in einer Stadt; KBK Lw6, c. 1942–1943," Bild 101I-418-1832-28A, Das Bundesarchiv, Berlin.

later, the arrival of Allied forces who sought to "liberate" North Africa. As religious leaders, they composed prayers, psalms, and eulogies, helping others to remember, to memorialize, and to heal.

Our first source dates to 1934, a year after Germany's president Paul von Hindenburg appointed Adolf Hitler, leader of the Nazi Party, as chancellor of Germany and a moment when the Nazi leadership was brutally consolidating its power. In Meknes, Morocco, a Moroccan Jewish teacher by the name of Prosper Cohen watched Hitler's rise with horror. Likening the Nazi leader to Haman (the fourth-century enemy of Persian Jewry and the villain of the Purim story), Cohen wrote that the Nazis' rise signaled the precarity of Jews everywhere—even North Africa. Five years later, in 1939, Nazi Germany invaded Poland, initiating the Second World War. Then, another Moroccan Jew from the city of Essaouira (Mogador) echoed Cohen's dark warning. In a fantastical poem that he self-published and distributed (before destroying every available copy in a state of panic), Isaac Knafo presaged ruin for the world.

Writing at the same time, a Muslim sheikh in Oran, Algeria, predicted the German conquest of North Africa and, with it, the defeat of French colonial armies.

Across North Africa, individuals initiated campaigns against the rise of Nazism and fascism, at times bonding into interfaith alliances that called for a boycott of Nazi-sympathizing businesses and settlers in North Africa's cities.[16] For, indeed, German attachés and representatives were using North Africa (and especially the Spanish zone of northern Morocco) as a base from which to spread anti-Semitic, anti-French, and anti-British, Arabic-language propaganda through radio, leaflets, and newspapers, at times with the help of allied Muslims. Meanwhile, in Europe, Jews of North African origin participated in the resistance against Nazi ideology and, later, against German and French race laws.

Other Europeans, too, were enacting their objection to the rise of Nazism and fascism, sometimes by fleeing to North Africa.[17] Whether their origins were humble or notable, these refugees arrived penniless, contactless, and traumatized, with the nature and duration of their time in North Africa unknown. Alegria Bendelac, whose voice and image we encounter in the pages that follow, remembers being an economically privileged Jewish girl struggling to adjust to the influx of desperate European refugees into her native city of Tangier.

Migration could be a political choice, too. As the power of the Nazi party increased, thousands of European Jews (and some Christians, too) volunteered to serve the French Foreign Legion in its fight against Nazism. And a staggering thirty-five thousand volunteers from over fifty countries, including 3,500–4,000 Jews, flocked to Civil War–torn Spain to serve in the Republican Army's International Brigade, fighting on behalf of the fledgling Spanish Republic and against the Nationalist, conservative allies of General Francisco Franco.[18] When Spain fell to Franco and France to Germany, these émigré, volunteer soldiers found themselves vulnerable as political enemies and/or foreigners of the ascendent Francoist dictatorship and Vichy regime.[19] Many International Brigade members fled to France only to be deported to prison, internment, and labor camps in North Africa (a topic we return to momentarily). The same destiny met many of the Jews who volunteered for the French Foreign Legion.

Racist, colonialist, violent legislation and policy had been imposed upon the peoples, cultural fabric, and land of North African since the early nineteenth century. With the expansion of the Second World War, this political foundation was overlaid with Italian fascist, Nazi, and Vichy law. Italian fascist rule took hold in Italy's colony of Libya in 1922, when Benito Mussolini was appointed prime minister by King Emmanuel III. At this time, many Libyan Jews, like their Italian peers, threw in their cause with the fascist project, seeing it as an ambitious, progressive, nationalist endeavor. Their sentiments would shift by 1938, when Mussolini imposed the first anti-Jewish legislation in Italy and Libya. Jews were excluded from schools, the armed forces, and certain sectors of public employment: restricted in their ability to own property and confronted with greatly curtailed economic, social, and cultural activities. Jewish marriages to so-called Aryans were also prohibited by Italy. Watching the unfolding of race laws in her native Libya, the teenager Marie Abravanel mused in 1939 that her Jewishness marked her with "the stamp of shame." Three years later, Mussolini would order the deportation of thousands of Libyan Jews to internment camps in Italy or Libya. Among the deportees were 870 Jewish holders of British passports. When Italy fell to Germany, a portion of that population was deported once again, to the Nazi camp of Bergen-Belsen.

In May 1940, Germany invaded France. But a month later, the aging First World War hero Marshal Henri Philippe Pétain signed an armistice with Germany on behalf of his country. The French-German Armistice of June 22, 1940, established German occupation over a zone in northern and western France, placing southern France under a new, collaborationist regime in the city of Vichy. With Pétain at its head, the Vichy government retained control over France's colonies in Asia and Africa, including the protectorates of Tunisia and Morocco and colonial Algeria.[20] In 1941, the Vichy regime established the Commissariat-General for Jewish Affairs, under the directorship of Xavier Vallat, to craft anti-Jewish legislation.[21] Whatever racist and anti-Semitic laws and policies the Vichy regime would impose upon continental France, it also imposed upon its colonies in North Africa and West Africa: but these laws were implemented variously, as the exigencies of war interacted with the legal and political terrain of the prewar, colonial landscape.

In North Africa, the social and economic changes wrought by these changes were felt acutely. In the coastal city of El Jadida (Mazagan), a young boy by the name of David Bensimon watched his classroom change overnight. Jewish pupils were obliged to recite a poem honoring Pétain as the savior of Greater France. Pétain's image literally looked down upon Bensimon and his classmates, as the French Department of Public Education had ordered schools to display photographs of Pétain in every classroom. Eugene Boretz's wartime chronicles, represented in the pages that follow, describe Tunis as it passed from French to Italian and then German control. Boretz notes how the city was suddenly marked by new sounds and images, and that Jewish girls and women were newly vulnerable to sexual violence by the occupiers.

Beginning in the autumn of 1940, the Vichy regime subjected Jews in French North Africa to a version of the racist and anti-Semitic decrees that had been imposed in continental France. The Statut des Juifs, which had been modeled on Germany's Nuremberg Laws, fixed a racial definition on Jews in France and Algeria, and stripped these French Jews of their citizenship. Other North African Jews were not directly affected by the revocation of citizenship; Moroccan, Tunisian, and Algerian Saharan Jews had been governed as indigenous subjects under French colonial rule and had no citizenship to be taken away. Yet across Vichy-controlled North Africa, quotas were imposed limiting the number of Jewish lawyers, teachers, students, doctors, and journalists. In Algeria, a group of Jewish doctors pleaded with their Muslim friends and colleagues to pressure Vichy representatives to allow them to practice medicine, noting that there was a typhoid epidemic killing Muslims in rural Algeria and their services were desperately required. To no avail.

So that the Vichy economy could be "Aryanized," the state seized Jewish businesses, homes, and property. Jews from across North Africa flooded French bureaucratic agencies with passionate objections to these laws. Appealing from his native Fez, Raymond Bensimhon objected that his family had long supported the French colonial and civilizing mission. Remarkably, his petition was approved; Vichy authorities denied the majority of such requests. In such cases, North Africa's Jews were forced to sell their property at a loss to European settlers and, in cases, to indigenous Muslims.

Soon after the German occupation of France, Pétain ordered the Vichy regime to build a network of penal, labor, and detention camps in West Africa and North Africa. Six detention camps were erected in West Africa and used to intern Allied prisoners of war and the crews of European military or commercial ships. Nearly seventy labor camps were built by the Vichy regime in the Sahara. These were centered on a project of the French colonial

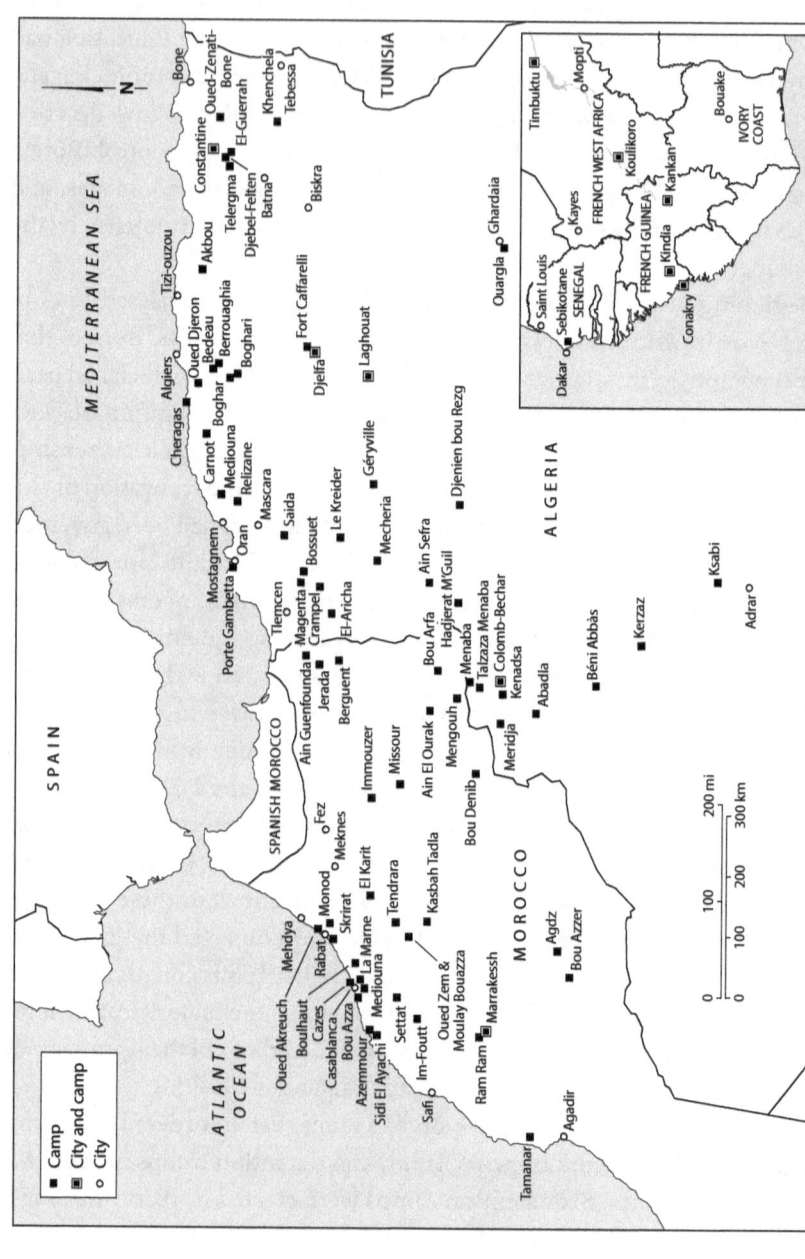

MAP 1. Penal, labor, and internment camps in Vichy-occupied Morocco and Algeria. Map by Bill Nelson.

regime—of building a railroad that would span the Sahara, connecting the Mediterranean and Atlantic coasts. In the colonial era, French authorities imagined a railroad connecting Dakar to the Mediterranean would move valuable goods and resources: the Vichy authorities emphasized that such a rail line could also supply a population of forcibly recruited Senegalese soldiers to the front lines, an ambition the Nazi authorities eagerly backed. To staff this massive infrastructural project, the Vichy Interior Ministry began, in 1940, to deport to the Saharan labor camps so-called undesirables and foreigners from France.[22] Once interned, the political prisoners and internees were organized into groups of foreign workers under the charge of the French Ministry of Industrial Production and Labor. The dizzying mélange of internees in the Sahara included former volunteers for the Spanish International Brigade, former Jewish volunteers of the French Foreign Legion, Muslim and French political prisoners, Algerian Jewish veterans, and more. The interned were allowed access to humanitarian relief and assistance by the Vichy regime, and several organizations, in particular, were important in bettering their fate. Under the leadership of the tireless Moroccan Jewish lawyer Hélène Cazes Benatar, the Refugee Aid Committee in Casablanca cooperated with international service organizations such as HICEM (the Paris-based, combined offices of the Hebrew Immigrant Aid Society of New York and the Jewish Colonization Association of London), the American Jewish Joint Distribution Committee, and the American Friends Services Committee (a Quaker organization) to make life bearable for internees, both before and after the Anglo-American landing.[23]

While the Saharan camps were overseen by soldiers from France, many guards were indigenous Moroccan infantry (*goumiers*), from indigenous tribal Moroccan and Algerian cavalry regiments (*spahis*), and Black colonial soldiers from Senegal, French Guinea, Ivory Coast, Dahomey, Senegambia, Niger, Upper Volta (Burkina Faso), and Mauritania (Senegalese *tirailleurs*), as well as light infantry units of Moroccan, Algerian, and sometimes Tunisian soldiers (also called *tirailleurs*). These soldiers, who served the French flag during colonial military campaigns and the First World War, were in most cases forcibly recruited and scarcely more than prisoners themselves. We follow the fate of some of these young men—including the towering figure of Léopold Senghor, theorist, poet, politician, and first president of the

IMAGE 3. In Vichy camps in the Sahara, prisoners from a wide variety of backgrounds were subjected to forced labor in quarries, mines, and on rail lines. European refugees, Muslim anticolonial activists, erstwhile volunteers for Spain's International Brigade and French Foreign Legion, and forced conscripts from West Africa and North Africa, among others, made up the prisoner population: a diversity that led, equally, to moments of tension and unexpected alliances. Walter Reuter, "Abrazo con pico y pala," Archivo Fotográfico Walter Reuter, Cuernavaca, Mexico.

independent nation of Senegal—to the front lines and German prisoner-of-war camps, unpacking their racist, cruel treatment by France and Germany.

The choice to include within this volume the perspective of West African subjects of the Vichy regime is an intentional one. Vichy-controlled West Africa and its subjects were integrally related to wartime North Africa and its resident, refugees, and prisoners. Senegalese soldiers and their families had lived in North Africa since the interwar period, in cases becoming citizens of Morocco. During the Second World War, Senegalese *tirailleurs* served as guards in Vichy camps across North Africa, and they were dispatched to labor on regional infrastructural projects such as road building. West African soldiers were also dispatched to front lines, becoming among the first military victims of German assaults. Finally, the inclusion of Senegalese voices in this volume helps illustrate the racial logic of the Vichy regime, for which anti-Blackness and anti-Semitism were part of a comprehensive racist, Nazi-aligned logic with roots in European colonialism.

Diverse sources in this documentary history speak to the quotidian experience of life in the Vichy camps of North Africa. From them, we learn of women, children, and men of diverse backgrounds struggling to obtain proper nourishment, shelter, clothing, and shoes: of their struggles with disease, sleep deprivation, severe weather conditions, and pests such as lice, snakes, and scorpions. Drawn from memoirs, poetry, letters, and images, these sources reveal the systematic use of torture within the labor camps, as well as the Vichy strategy of moving prisoners from camp to camp, and between labor and penal camps, in an effort to disorient and rupture solidarities among prisoners. Our selections reveal the crucial importance of philanthropy both during the war and after the Allied victory in North Africa, when the American Friends Service Committee and HICEM managed to facilitate the freedom and emigration of some of the interned. Finally, the sources that follow testify to the resilience of the victims and prisoners of the Vichy, Nazi, and Italian fascist regimes. These individuals leaned on art, poetry, comradery, faith, radicalism, humor, and the written word to retain a grasp on their humanity.

In Tunisia, labor and detention camps were maintained by France, Germany, and Italy, depending on the timing of war. After the Allied landing in North Africa, Germany initiated a six-month occupation of Tunisia (November 1942–May 1943), leaning on the Italians to thwart the Allied advance in Tunisia and Egypt. During its rule of Tunisia, the SS imprisoned some five

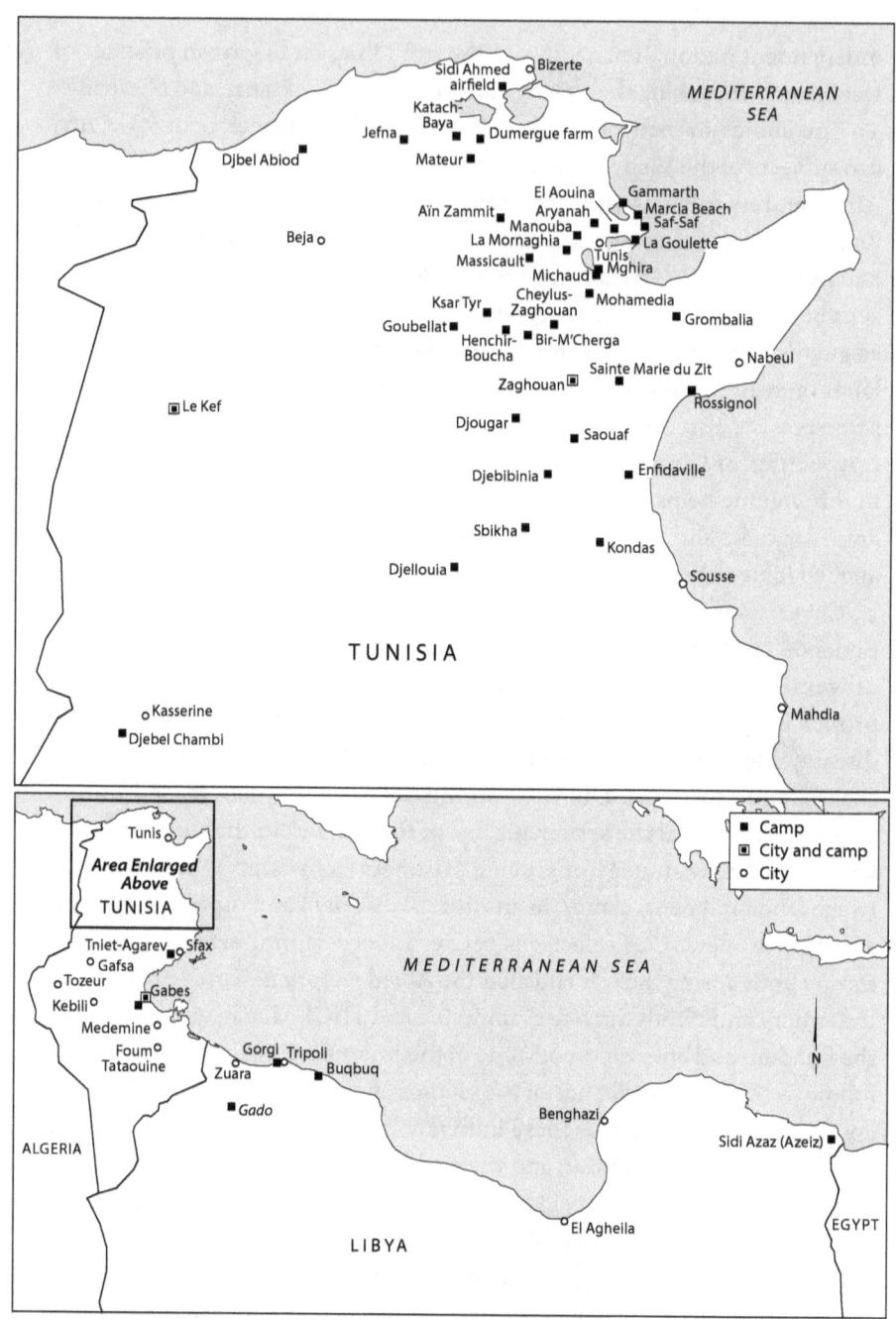

Map 2. Penal, labor, and internment camps in German-occupied Tunisia and Italian-occupied Libya. Map by Bill Nelson.

thousand Jewish men in roughly forty forced labor and detention camps on the front lines and in cities like Tunis, with many of the imprisoned laboring on infrastructural projects. A young Albert Memmi, writing from a labor camp outside Tunis, poured the grief of a man nearly broken by forced labor into his diary: "Sometimes," he wrote, "we ask ourselves if living is worth the pain."

Some North African Jews and Muslims were interned and perished in Nazi internment, labor, and death camps in Europe. Jews of North African origin living in Paris and its environs, for example, were sent to the Drancy internment camp on the outskirts of Paris and, from there, to concentration and death camps in Eastern Europe. Among them were two extraordinary Jewish athletes you will encounter in these pages: the Tunisian flyweight boxing champion Victor Perez, who was annihilated in Auschwitz, and the competitive swimmer of Algerian origin, Alfred Nakache, who survived internment and forced labor in Auschwitz only to make a surprise return to the competitive stage. Smaller numbers of Jews and some Muslims were also deported directly from North Africa or Europe to Nazi labor and death camps in Europe, where some perished.

North Africa served as a militarized zone throughout these years, with violence being experienced not only on the front lines but also by the civilian population and the landscape of North Africa. The fascist Italian and Vichy French authorities, like the German authorities, engaged in the plunder of food from territory under their control, which in the case of North Africa caused widespread starvation and malnutrition. Combined with an acute drought and a typhoid epidemic, the effects were disastrous. Al-ḥusin Al-Geddari recalls how desperate families in his village of Lamḥamid, in the Anti-Atlas Mountains, had to resort to retrieving the shrouds of the buried dead to reuse them for the next deceased in line. Al-Geddari and his neighbors understood that local famine was state engineered, part of a global chain reaction spawned by war and occupation.

In November 1942, Operation Torch marked the Anglo-American defeat of the Vichy powers in Morocco and Algeria, opening a new front from which the Allies could combat the Axis powers and heralding an end to Vichy rule in Morocco.[24] The arrival of the Allies was celebrated by many North Africans, especially North African Jews. Gathering on the streets of Moroccan cities, they welcomed the arriving troops with songs, likening them to a bride approaching her betrothed.

Yet Operation Torch proved a complex and partial victory. To win the alliance of the French, the American leadership accepted that French rule would remain in place in post–Operation Torch Morocco and Algeria, as it would later in Tunisia. Under the command of the French high commissioner General Henri Giraud, this new-old leadership preserved the anti-Semitic legislation of the Vichy regime until it ended in 1944. What's more, Giraud allowed many of the Vichy camps, including labor camps in the Sahara, to continue to operate—in cases, with the same wartime overseers in place. In these untenable circumstances, prisoners' release was delayed for upward of a year. The arrival of Anglo-American troops had the simultaneous effect of heightening American power in North Africa, a show of military and commercial force that many locals viewed with suspicion or outright hostility. As several sources in this book note, American soldiers also brought a renewed threat of sexual violence against North African women, just as had the arrival of European soldiers previously. The Axis powers had been defeated, but neither occupation nor vulnerability had come to an end.

As in Europe and across the survivor diaspora, reckoning with the traumas, memories, and history of the Second World War was a slow and jagged process in North Africa.[25] Arguably this process is unfolding still.[26] This book stands as part of a delayed but surging global interest in the wartime and Holocaust testimonies of North African Muslims, Christians, and Jews. Yet it is also true that this reckoning began in North Africa even before the Second World War came to an end.[27] We conclude this book with a selection of sources, memoirs, testimonies, songs, and prayers that reach beyond the conclusion of the Second World War, speaking to the haunting legacy of occupation and war in North Africa. Some reveal the logistical, legal, and economic challenges wrought by the dénouement of Vichy, Nazi, and fascist Italian control; others point to the tremendous religious and existential angst carried into the wartime era. Perhaps the most haunting of these sources airs the painfully private ordeal of a Tunisian Jewish survivor of Auschwitz struggling to reacclimate to liberation and his home of Tlemcen, where no one—including, it seems, the author himself—is able to grasp the depths of his wartime trauma.

It has been our goal in crafting this book to represent the Second World War as it was experienced in North Africa, on a human scale, giving voice to the diversity of those involved. As the first English-language sourcebook on this topic, it is, inevitably, but a partial effort. Yet this collection does air the perspectives of an astonishing array of actors: women, men, and children; the unknown and the notable; locals, refugees, the displaced and the interned; soldiers, officers, bureaucrats, volunteer fighters and the forcibly recruited, people of a wide variety of ethnic and religious backgrounds. At times their calls are lofty, redolent with spiritual lamentation and political outrage. At times they are humble, voicing yearning for medicine for their children, a cigarette, or a pair of shoes. All told, they shed light on how war, occupation, race laws, internment, and Vichy French, Italian fascist, and German Nazi rule were experienced day by day, across North Africa (and beyond), through warfare, internment and forced labor, racism and race laws, theft, the despoliation of landscape, and the engineering of hunger. These human experiences, combined, make up the history of wartime North Africa.

Notes

1. Aomar Boum and Sarah A. Stein, introduction to *The Holocaust and North Africa*, ed. Aomar Boum and Sarah A. Stein (Stanford, CA: Stanford University Press, 2019), 1–16; Daniel J. Schroeter, "Between Metropole and French North Africa: Vichy's Anti-Semitic Legislation and Colonialism's Racial Hierarchies," in *The Holocaust and North Africa*, ed. Aomar Boum and Sarah A. Stein (Stanford, CA: Stanford University Press, 2019), 19–49; Michel Abitbol, *The Jews of North Africa during the Second World War* (Detroit: Wayne State University Press, 1989).

2. Jens Hoppe, "The Persecution of Jews in Libya Between 1938 and 1945: An Italian Affair?," in *The Holocaust and North Africa*, ed. Aomar Boum and Sarah A. Stein (Stanford, CA: Stanford University Press, 2019), 50–75; Rachel Simon, "It Could Have Happened There: The Jews of Libya during the Second World War," *Africana Journal* 16 (1994): 391–422.

3. Ethan Katz, "Did the Paris Mosque Save Jews? A Mystery and Its Memory," *Jewish Quarterly Review* 102, no. 2 (2012): 256–87; Mitchell Serels, "The Non-European Holocaust: The Fate of Tunisian Jewry," in *Del Fuego: Sephardim and the Holocaust*, ed. Haham Gaon and M. Mitchell Serels (New York: Sepher-Hermon Press, 1995), 129–52.

4. Raffael Scheck, *Hitler's African Victims: The German Army Massacres of Black French Soldiers in 1940* (Cambridge: Cambridge University Press, 2006).

5. Aomar Boum and Sarah A. Stein, eds, *The Holocaust and North Africa* (Stanford, CA: Stanford University Press, 2019).

6. Reeva S. Simon, Michael Laskier, and Sara Reguer, *The Jews of the Middle East and North Africa in Modern Times* (New York: Columbia University Press 2003);

Michael Laskier, *North African Jewry in the Twentieth Century: The Jews of Morocco, Tunisia and Algeria* (New York: New York University Press, 1994).

7. Jessica Marglin, *Across Legal Lines: Jews and Muslims in Modern Morocco* (New Haven, CT: Yale University Press, 2014); Emily B. Gottreich and Daniel Schroeter, eds., *Jewish Culture and Society in North Africa* (Bloomington: Indiana University Press, 2011); Sarah Abrevaya Stein, *Saharan Jews and the Fate of French Algeria* (Chicago: University of Chicago Press, 2010); Maurice Roumani, *The Jews of Libya: Coexistence, Persecution and Resettlement* (Brighton, UK: Sussex University Press, 2008); Paul Sebag, *L'histoire des juifs de Tunisie des origins à nos jours* (Paris: L'Harmattan, 1991); Harvey Goldberg, *Jewish Life in Muslim Libya: Rivals and Relatives* (Chicago: University of Chicago Press, 1990).

8. Pierre Flamand, *Diaspora en terre d'Islam: Les communautés israélites du sud du Maroc: Essai de description et d'analyse de la vie juive en milieu berbère* (Casablanca: Imprimeries Réunies, 1959).

9. Joshua Cole, *Lethal Provocation: The Constantine Murders and the Politics of French Algeria* (Ithaca, NY: Cornell University Press, 2019).

10. Michel Ansky, *Les juifs d'Algérie: Du décret Crémieux à la liberation* (Paris: Éditions du Centre, 1950).

11. Jessica Marglin, "The Extraterritorial Century: Nationality in the Nineteenth-Century Mediterranean," American Society for Legal History Annual Meeting, Houston, TX, November 9–11, 2018; Daniel Schroeter, "Vichy in Morocco: The Residency, Mohammed V, and His Indigenous Jewish Subjects," in *Colonialism and the Jews*, ed. Ethan B. Katz, Lisa Moses Leff, and Maud S. Mandel, 215–50 (Bloomington: Indian University Press, 2017); Sarah Abrevaya Stein, *Extraterritorial Dreams: European Citizenship, Sephardi Jews, and the Ottoman Twentieth Century* (Chicago: University of Chicago Press, 2016).

12. Liliana Picciotto, "Un groupe de juifs libyens dans la Shoah 1942–1944," in *La bienvenue et l'adieu: Migrants juifs et musulmans au Maghreb (XVe–XXe siècle)*, ed. Frédéric Abécassis, Karima Dirèche, and Rita Aouad, 45–56 (Paris: Karthala, 2010); Michele Sarfatti, *The Jews in Mussolini's Italy: From Equality to Persecution*, trans. John Tedeschi and Anne C. Tedeschi (Madison: University of Wisconsin Press, 2006).

13. Daniel Lee, "The Commissariat Général aux Questions Juives in Tunisia and the Implementation of Vichy's Anti-Jewish Legislation," in *The Holocaust and North Africa*, ed. Aomar Boum and Sarah A. Stein (Stanford, CA: Stanford University Press, 2019), 132–45.

14. Dan Michman and Haïm Saadoun, *Les juifs d'Afrique du Nord face à l'Allemagne nazie* (Paris: Perrin, 2018); Michael Laskier, "Between Vichy Antisemitism and German Harassment: The Jews of North Africa during the Early 1940s," *Modern Judaism* 11, no. 3 (1991): 343–69.

15. Ruth Ginio, *The French Army and Its African Soldiers: The Years of Decolonization* (Lincoln: University of Nebraska Press, 2017); Serge Bilé, *Noirs dans les camps nazis* (Monaco: Le Serpent à Plumes, 2005).

16. Ethan Katz, *The Burdens of Brotherhood: Jews and Muslims from North Africa to France* (Cambridge, MA: Harvard University Press, 2015); Aomar Boum, "Partners against Anti-Semitism: Muslims and Jews Respond to Nazism in French North African Colonies, 1936–1940," *Journal of North African Studies* 19, no. 4 (2014): 554–70.

17. Susan Slyomovics, "'Other Places of Confinement': Bedeau Internment Camp for Algerian Jewish Soldiers," in *The Holocaust and North Africa*, ed. Aomar Boum and Sarah A. Stein (Stanford, CA: Stanford University Press, 2019), 95–112; Georges Bensousan, "Les juifs d'Orient face au nazisme et à la Shoah," *Revue d'Histoire de la Shoah* 205 (October 2016): 7–23; Michel Abitbol, "Waiting for Vichy: Europeans and Jews in North Africa on the Eve of World War II," *Yad Vashem Studies* 14 (1981): 139–66; Charles Robert Ageron, "Les populations du Maghreb face à la propagande allemande," *Revue d'Histoire de la Deuxième Guerre Mondiale* 29, no. 114 (1979): 1–39.

18. Gerben Zaagsma, *Jewish Volunteers, the International Brigades and the Spanish Civil War* (New York: Bloomsbury Academic, 2017); Adam Hochschild, *Spain in Our Hearts: Americans in the Spanish Civil War, 1936–1939* (Boston: Houghton Mifflin Harcourt, 2016); Christopher Othen, *Franco's International Brigades: Adventurers, Fascists, and Christian Crusaders in the Spanish Civil War* (New York: Columbia University Press, 2013).

19. Daniel Schroeter, "Philo-Sephardism, Anti-Semitism, and the Arab Nationalism: Muslims and Jews in the Spanish Protectorate of Morocco during the Third Reich," in *Nazism, the Holocaust and the Middle East*, ed. Francis Nicosia and Boğaç Ergene (New York: Berghahn, 2018), 179–215; Isabelle Rohr, *The Spanish Right and the Jews, 1898–1945: Antisemitism and Opportunism* (Brighton, UK: Sussex Academic Press, 2017).

20. Robert Paxton, *Vichy France: Old Guard and New Order (1940–1944)* (New York: Norton, 1975).

21. Joseph Billig, *Le Commissariat Général aux Questions Juives, 1941–1944*, vol. 2 (Paris: Éditions du Centre, 1955).

22. Aomar Boum, "Eyewitness Djelfa: Daily Life in a Saharan Vichy Labor Camp," in *The Holocaust and North Africa*, ed. Aomar Boum and Sarah A. Stein (Stanford, CA: Stanford University Press, 2019), 149–67; Geoffrey Megargee, ed., *The United States Holocaust Memorial Museum Encyclopedia of Camps and Ghettos, 1933–1945*, vol. 3, *Camps and Ghettos Under European Regimes Aligned with Nazi Germany* (Bloomington: Indiana University Press, 2018); Robert Satloff, *Among the Righteous: Lost Stories from the Holocaust's Long Reach into Arab Lands* (New York: Public Affairs,

2006); Jacob Oliel, *Les camps de Vichy, Maghreb-Sahara, 1939–1945* (Montreal: Éditions du Lys, 2005).

23. Susan G. Miller, *Years of Glory: Nelly Benatar and the Pursuit of Justice in Wartime North Africa* (Stanford, CA: Stanford University Press, 2021); Yehuda Bauer, *American Jewry and the Holocaust: The American Jewish Joint Distribution Committee, 1939–1945* (Detroit: Wayne State University Press, 1996).

24. Nicole Cohen-Addad, Aïssa Kadri, and Tramor Quemeneur, dirs., *8 novembre 1942: Résistance et débarquement allié en Afrique du Nord: Dynamiques historiques, politiques et socio-culturelles* (Vulaines-sur-Seine, France: Éditions du Croquant, 2021).

25. Susan G. Miller, "Sephardim and Holocaust Historiography," in *The Holocaust and North Africa*, ed. Aomar Boum and Sarah A. Stein (Stanford, CA: Stanford University Press, 2019), 220–28; Hanna Yablonka, *Les juifs d'Orient, Israël, et la Shoah* (Paris: Calmann-Lévy, 2016); Yochai Oppenheimer, "The Holocaust: A Mizrahi Perspective," *Hebrew Studies* 51, no. 1 (2010): 303–28; Aron Rodrigue, *Sephardim and the Holocaust* (WashingtonDC, DC: Center for Advanced Holocaust Studies, US Holocaust Memorial Museum, 2005); Hayim Azses, ed., *The Shoah in the Sephardic Communities: Dreams, Dilemmas, and Decisions of Sephardic Leaders* (Jerusalem: Sephardic Educational Center in Jerusalem, 2005).

26. Mémorial de la Shoah, "Les juifs d'orient face au nazime et à la Shoah (1930–1945)," *Revue d'Histoire de la Shoah* 2, no. 205 (2016).

27. Lia Brozgal, "The Ethics and Aesthetics of Restraint. Judeo-Tunisian Narratives of Occupation," in *The Holocaust and North Africa: New Research*, ed. Aomar Boum and Sarah Stein (Stanford, CA: Stanford University Press, 2019), 168–84.

PART I

The Rise of Fascism and Nazism as Seen from North Africa, 1934–1940

1. HITLER AS HAMAN [1934]

In March 1934, Adolf Hitler was in his second year as chancellor of Germany and laboring with the Nazi party to consolidate power, marginalize and incarcerate perceived political opponents, and shape a foreign policy moored in his racist and imperialist fantasies. Three thousand kilometers from Munich, the seat of Nazi power, Prosper Cohen recoiled at these developments. With his wife, Laurette, and infant daughter, Cohen lived in in his native city, Meknes, Morocco, home to a thriving Jewish community as well as a European settler colonial population that had appropriated agricultural and vinicultural land nearby. In Meknes, the Cohens worked for the Franco-Jewish educational organization Alliance Israélite Universelle, Prosper as a teacher and administrator, Laurette as a teacher. In the following letter, written to his supervisors in Paris a few weeks after the holiday of Purim, Prosper Cohen condemns the German chancellor as the diabolical "talisman" of the twentieth century whose name provoked even Meknes's children to shudder. Cohen's missive invites a parallel between the assault on the Jews of the Persian Empire in the fourth century BCE—a story told during Purim through the festive, alcohol-fueled reading of the Megilat Ester—and the virulent anti-Jewish sentiment of the ascendant Nazi regime. The villain of the Megilat Ester is Haman, evil adviser to Persia's King Ahasuerus, who seeks to decimate the kingdom's Jews but is foiled by King Ahasuerus's Jewish wife, Esther. In Cohen's eyes, Hitler is Haman's modern-day incarnation; his name (like Haman's during the ceremonial reading of the Megilat Ester) should be drowned out by triumphant jeers. Whether or not he was aware of it, Cohen was among many Jewish writers—from many countries and in a variety of languages—to represent Hitler as Haman in a contemporary riff of the Megilat Ester. Cohen's passionate letter reveals that well before the outbreak of the Second World War, Jews in North Africa were anxiously following the unfolding trauma in Europe and translating it into terms that were evocative and meaningful to them.

January–March, 1934, Hitler in Our Midst

It is quite curious to notice the state of mind that Hitler's rise to the throne of cruelty has created in our average Jew.

The name of the champion of collective and official crime is on everyone's lips. Everything that could be linked to Hitler's Germany, to misfortune, to anything or anyone that might cause material or moral harm, takes the name of Hitler, the Haman of the twentieth century. Even children know this name and it's unfortunate reputation.

The time of Purim was—but is no longer—the celebration of Haman's downfall. We hope that [it is also the celebration] of the imminent downfall of his successor.

In the evening on Purim, in the temples you would hear "Cursed be Hitler" more often than "Cursed be Haman," which amounts to the same thing, for that matter.

In the street, you often hear the Hebrew expression, "May his name be wiped out." They're talking about Adolf.

A person is defined by his maliciousness: he's a Hitler.

During the festivities, Jews raise a glass. Before drinking, they are accustomed to addressing some good wishes to their guests; for a year, they have inevitably added a few prayers for the fall of the enemy of the Jews, for he who—in defiance of law and civilization—made the unique resolution to exterminate Israel, to purify the Aryan race.

Here, we understand very well the bravery of German Jews, and for this reason, we have faith in the future. Time is the best defender of a people whose only reward for the moral and material riches they have contributed to their world is finding themselves shamefully chased and banished on an assassin's capricious whim.

As such, there is no love lost for Hitler, who, in his cruelty, has surpassed even Petliura's most sophisticated imaginings.[1]

A recent invention has just been introduced in Morocco: Russian billiards. One must get his balls into the pockets with the help of a billiard cue. In the middle of the table, there is a pin that, if knocked over, causes everyone to lose. This pin has been baptized "Hitler" because it is an object of bad luck.

Thus, apart from the material and effective wrongdoing with which Jews genuinely charge Hitler Germany, [the name of] the criminal head of this "republik," [which is] more imperialist and Cesariste than the reigns of all the Fredericks and all the Wilhelms of cursed memory [put together], has become synonymous with bad luck, with the devil.

MAROC B 0012 0036: Meknès, March 25–26, 1934, Alliance Israélite Universelle Archives. Translated from French by Rebecca Glasberg.

2. A GERMAN AGENT POSES AS A MUSLIM TO SPREAD PROPAGANDA [1935]

On the eve of and during the Second World War, North Africa was awash with surveillance by states and political parties (local and European) that had a strategic interest in the region. The results of this surveillance were often faulty, based on unsubstantiated rumors and unreliable sources. Yet even if this competing intelligence gathering was flawed, its existence sheds light on the political jockeying, machinations, and apprehensions that reigned in North Africa in the 1930s. The following source points to the intensification in that decade of anti-French and pro-German propaganda by Nazi authorities in Morocco. This propaganda targeted leaders of the nationalist movement through a large network of local associates. Germany's representatives focused their intelligence activity on the Spanish Zone, where they had inroads and connections. For example, they exploited the personal relationship between Iraq-born journalist Yunes Bahri of Radio Berlin, and

1. Symon Vasylyovyc Petliura (1879–1926) was a journalist, poet, Ukrainian nationalist leader, and commander of the united Ukrainian forces during Ukraine's short-lived sovereignty (1918–1921) and the Russian Civil War (1917–1922). Under his rule, mob violence resulted in the murder of tens of thousands—perhaps even hundreds of thousands—of Jews, the wounding of thirty thousand more, and the displacement of half a million Jewish children, women, and men.

Shakib Arsalan, the Beirut-born Druze historian, politician, poet, and writer who was influential among nascent leaders of nationalist movements throughout North Africa. Directly after Arsalan's visit to Spanish-colonized Morocco in 1930, Nazi authorities expanded the reach of propaganda produced by Italy's Radio Bari in Spanish Morocco. Like Radio Stuttgart and Radio Berlin, Radio Bari initiated a number of programs in French and Arabic to North Africa. Using a mixture of local Arabic dialects, these programs included news, religious programs, and even readings of the Quran. At the same time, local Muslim political leaders from the Spanish Zone, including Abd el-Khalek Torres (National Reform Party), Mohammed Hassan El-Wazzani, and Ahmed Belafrej, were maintaining contact with Bahri and Arsalan, even, in cases, visiting Berlin at the invitation of the pair. The following report from the Department of Indigenous Affairs for the French colonial government in Morocco shows how German agents sought contact with the most important and popular leader of the nationalist movement in the region, Allal al-Fassi, in his hometown of Fez (Fès). Fez was a strategic target for Nazi propaganda given the city's importance as a religious center and because it was home to al-Qarawiyīn University. For these reasons, Nazi associates began stirring anti–French colonial sentiment in the city in the early 1930s, hoping to be seen by the local population and Muslim leadership as champions of Moroccan independence.

I.—More than a month ago, a German emissary allegedly conducted an interview in Casablanca with Si Allal El Fassi. It is reported that a second interview occurred a few days later in Sidi Harazene (Harazem) (Fès). In addition to the abovementioned emissary, Si Allal, Ould El Left and Ouled Ben Choqroun attended the meeting. The German agent was reportedly escorted to the secret meeting place by a courier.

The alleged interview lasted a long time, and nothing came of the discussion.

We believe that the foreign agent turned over some money to Si Allal Fassi.

In order the leave the secret meeting place undetected, the German reportedly changed into indigenous clothing which was provided by some Muslim friends.

II.—At the Quaraouiyine Madrasa [Islamic school], a large group of Fassis allegedly gathered together on May 13 to recite the supplication of Al-Latif

[Allah]. At Moulay-Idriss, the moussem Alamiyne was celebrated with distinct gusto.[1] Many people from Salé, Casablanca, Rabat and other regions had gathered there, and it is reported that the "Latif" was recited during the beginning of the pilgrimage ceremony.

As the moussem fell on May 16, the nationalists and party sympathizers reportedly took advantage of this occasion to indulge in their annual protest, even within the sacred city itself.

It is said that attendees took particular note of El Squelli from Salé, whose passionate speech touching on politics was said to have been deeply appreciated.

Petitjean, May 27, 1935, Civil Controller, Chief of administrative constituency.

RG 81.001M, Reel 24, Selected Records from the National Library of Morocco, 1864–1999 (bulk 1925–1945), United States Holocaust Memorial Museum Archives, Washington, DC. Courtesy of the Archives du Maroc. Translated from French by Amber Sackett.

3. MUSSOLINI GIVEN A HERO'S WELCOME BY TRIPOLI'S JEWISH COMMUNITY [1937]

Benito Mussolini, who ruled over the Kingdom of Italy from 1922 to 1943, shaped Italian fascism (and its leading party, the National Fascist Party, or PNF) and defended the territorial expansion of a modern Italian empire as the inheritor of ancient Rome. The Italian fascist movement did not assume a coherent anti-Semitic agenda prior to the 1930s, and many Jews in Italy and its North African colony, Libya, supported the Fascist Party and its colonialist ambition—at least before the regime introduced race laws in 1938. To many Jews living under Italian control, Mussolini and the Fascist Party brought stability and promise, and their support of Il Duce, or "The Duke," and his party was a means of evincing their Italianness. Here, in a report by the Alliance Israélite Universelle, we read of the grand welcome that Mussolini received in the Jewish quarter of Tripoli during a 1937 visit. These reports, similar to those produced by colonial governments, were commonplace at Alliance schools throughout the world and served to keep administrators in France—who frequently were not familiar with the area—informed about the community. Mussolini was met with elaborate pomp and circumstance,

1. The Moussem Alamiyne is a religious festival in honor of the founder of the city.

decorations, a speech by the Chief Rabbi, and ululations from the women present. After the introduction of the 1938 race laws—which applied not only to mainland Italy but also to Libya—many Jews mistakenly believed that they were temporary, implemented only to appease Hitler. Yet while the Italian authorities generally refused to permit the deportation to Nazi camps of Jews from Italy or Italian-occupied territories, Mussolini's race laws did separate Jews economically, professionally, and culturally from Italian and Libyan society. Many of the men who attended this event would have been deported to Italian labor camps in Libya, and some (who were holders of British passports) might have been deported to Europe.

On Wednesday, 17 March 1937, Il Duce visited the Jewish quarter of our city.

In the early morning, our coreligionists, both young and old, did their best to bedeck the principal thoroughfare of the Hara. Portraits of Il Duce, leafy garlands, palm fronds, bolts of silk, flags, and tapestries completely covered the walls, joining together to form a continuous arc of various hues and shades.

From two a.m. on, the neighborhood was teeming with people.

At four thirty, the official procession made its entry into the Hara between two dense rows of Jews clothed in colorful native garb. The president of the community, the members of the commission, and the Chief Rabbi received the arrivals. Cries of joy, cheers, and frenzied acclamation from the crowd mixed together with women's "you-yous" [ululations].

While Il Duce progressed along his path on rolled-out carpets, young girls [dressed] in silk and gleaming jewelry threw orange blossoms at his feet. At the square, where the procession came to an end, was a stage bearing welcome messages. Men were gathered there, surrounded by schoolchildren.

The Great Rabbi of Tripoli gave the following address:

> Duce, it is my honor to convey to your excellency, head of the Italian government and Duce of fasci[s]m, the respectful greetings of the Jewish Community of Tripoli and other Libyan [Jewish] Communities. The Jewish population of Tripoli, whom God has today permitted to welcome into their old neighborhood the Founder of the Empire, now joins together your excellency's name with that of the Great Augustus who protected and defended our ancestors in these same lands. Rome is still the benevolent and pious mother of all her daughters.
>
> Duce, through me, the Jews of Libya wish to express their gratitude to your excellency for the benevolence with which the Italian government has always

treated them. They wish to solemnly confirm their loyalty to Italy and their attachment to the regime that, by having them participate in the Rome's greatness, protects their spiritual heritage and the path of their civil development with kindness. They are proud to stand in the shade of the beautiful Tricolor [flag] and under the aegis of your leadership as modest workers for the grandeur of ever-growing Italy and praying fervently to God that he bestow his infinite treasures and blessings upon your excellency, his majesty the King Emperor.

Il Duce charged the Grand Rabbi with telling the Jews of Tripoli that the expression of their devotion made an impression on him and he departed, once more cheered on by the crowd.

"Visite de Mussolini au quartier juif de Tripoli." LYBIE-I, G. 30, Tripoli, 1937, Alliance Israélite Universelle Archives. Translated from French by Rebecca Glasberg.

4. A FANTASTIC, ANTI-HITLER POEM SPARED FROM DESTRUCTION (1939)

Born in Essaouira (Mogador) in 1912, Isaac D. Knafo (1912–1979) studied in Paris before returning to his hometown in French colonial Essaouira. The son of Rabbi Joseph Knafo, one of the most important religious figures of Essaouira and of Morocco more generally, Knafo was a poet, playwright, and artist who gained a literary reputation among European, Muslim, and Jewish circles in his hometown. He also wrote for many local and national newspapers, founded a theater company, and began directing his own plays. Knafo wrote and published a poem in pamphlet form, Les Hitlériques, *in September and October 1939—just after the German occupation of Poland—to raise concerns about Hitler and the world that could emerge under Nazi German control. He printed only 2,500 copies of the pamphlet, selling them for two and half francs. Given his expansive knowledge of Jewish concerns and European politics, Knafo was able to provide an informed and grim futuristic view—in daringly phantasmagorical form—of the Third Reich's intended conquest of Europe. Knafo's wild poem quickly became a risky document to own. By 1942, the Vichy authorities introduced and implemented anti-Jewish laws in Essaouira, and Knafo felt forced to destroy his work. He recalled all known copies of* Les Hitlériques *in Essaouira and burned them—even the copies he had in his own possession. After the war, Knafo expressed regret for this action. By chance, a sole remaining copy of the work was found in 1995 in the private collection of Meïr Melca, a friend of Knafo's and former president of the Jewish community of Essaouira. Haïm Melca, Meïr Melca's son, has also published an introduction to and the original text of* Les Hitlériques *on his website, which provides extensive genealogical and documentary information on Essaouira. Composed of eleven sections, the feverish work culminates with a lengthy section, excerpted here, written in the form of an "ode to Hitler," which predicts the leader's downfall and Germany's defeat.*

To the Reader

I have seen hatred flourish in the country of the Nazis,
And a whole nation endure the caustic, corrosive acid
Thrown at them like a cruel joke
By the speeches of an insane, vulgar buffoon.
This pernicious clown, seized by fury,
Preaching denunciation, murder, and violence...
Despite my indifference, I felt my face flush
And turn bright red from shame and disgust.
In my feeble hands, the whip of satire
Is too clumsy to excoriate Hitler;
At least it expresses my complete aversion.
And that is why, reader, though I may displease you
In order to release my sorrow and to cry out my anger
I offer you this text filled with indignation.

The Abortus

He's a degenerate, hindered by a clubbed foot,
With an angular profile, a skinny, sickly body,
And the menacing look and furtive laugh
Of a sly criminal, scared but insatiable.
Of the Aryan blond, he has neither symptom nor trace
His progenitor botched him, like a hasty job
And it is this by-product of a fleeting love
[Who calls himself] the ideal regenerator of the race.
He bears the imprint of the disdainful contempt

In which he was held as prodigal nature crafted him,
roughing him out to be uglier than his caricature.
And this is why, incensed like an aggressive, yappy dog,
With each breath, he barks out vile resentment
To spread hatred to the four corners of the earth.

The SAs

Oh Abject Scoundrels, Abominable Slobs,
Accomplished Sleazebags and Aggressive Smooth-talkers,
Acrid Sycophants, Servile Assailants,
Swordsmen Attracted to innumerable crimes.
Sordid Assassins and Asinine Slaughterers,
Starved Slayers, Sanguinary Asses,
Sinister Antics, Scatological Airheads,
[You] who feed your Sanguine Appetites with blood,
Savage Administrators and Sectarians of Atrocity,
Sterile Abortuses, Supreme Absconders,
Remember that one day, the crowd will put an end to your
    ferocious misdeeds
By way of your execution.

Hell

Way over there, somewhere in sad Germany,
Hell has a name: Concentration Camp.
Only for the innocents, this place of detention
Is, as it must be, more inhumane than a penal colony.
Malnourished, eating garbage, laying on pallets
—When not on the floor—in the repugnant barracks,
The exhausted prisoners, tortured and hunted,
Must do battle with rats throughout the night.
Their short breaks are a pointless sham,
Often interrupted by joyous guards
Who shine a ray of light in their eyes,
Finding a bitter pleasure in their torment.

For them, nighttime is nothing if not a total nightmare,
A dream interspersed with horrible visions.
And the daytime holds in store for them a most dreadful fate
Determined by an ingenious and brutal sadist.
Debilitating labor that last for long hours,
Two times the work of an average person,
It shatters their shoulders and wound their hands,
And seems an odious and sinister wager.
The prison guards are there, in the camp,
Specially trained to carry out their vile labor
Of striking bodies and harming souls,
Giving free rein to their perverse excesses.
Their smiles are hideous, and their jokes, sinister,
They wield their clubs as if they were toys,
Striking their batons, cracking their whips,
The only seem happy when giving brutal beatings.
Here the boot is queen, and the kick, king.
Sure to go unpunished, with a cocky demeanor,
They seem to enjoy looking at the whipped faces
Shaking with fear beneath their lashes.
Twenty-five whiplashes for whomever wants a drink,
If he's a blond Aryan. Sixty for a Jew,
When the punishment is not intensified,
To the delight of a merry spectator.
A weak-hearted, exhausted man falls on the path.
So the prison guard tasks his comrades
With pulling the feeble, sick fellow by his feet,
Preferring this method of inhumane torture.
Never entirely satisfied with the supreme delights
That the suffering of others provides their senses,
They know how to bring into the modernity of Today
The various tortures of barbaric times Past.
One day, the object of their cruelty will be gone.
Working for a white-faced death,
Every day the vast camp empties out a bit more,
As its miserable subjects succumb to extinction.

The Hyenas

A sinister showman has taken the power
From the hands of an old dotard, his hypocritical accomplice,
He killed thought and chased away virtue
Along with freedom, taste, and knowledge.
He put a ban on speaking and seeing,
The press became his serf, and the written word
Has since avoided that which irritates him,
Passivity became the only duty.
When the German people took on this distressing appearance,
When, deprived of their souls, they became lifeless,
We saw enraged Nazis crack their whips everywhere.
We saw them attack the people like a pack of howling hounds,
So that from the bleeding nation,
The one could carve out his scrap of flesh, the other, his bone to gnaw.

The Sharks

In the murky waters moves a swarthy spindle,
Silent and insidious, just like a shark.
His cunning walk is that of a little devil
Preparing a sinister dagger for murder.
Neither fife nor drum nor trumpet nor sistrum
Gives rhythm to his work. A miserly silence
Follows his movements, from Hamburg to Peking,
As he, a servile minister, labors for Death.
He goes about shirking followers, his face invisible to others' gaze
Or launching his torpedoes into the sides of steamboats
Breaking laws and regulations without fear.
His role is to kill. What does it matter if a few extra lives are taken,
Fallout from a failed assassination attempt,
Since it is through terror that the Germans prevail.

The Crows

Like a murder of crows, whose whirring liftoff
Desecrates the purity of the sky, the blue of the heavens,
And the serenity of the clear and open space,
A squadron passes by.
Like a rapacious vulture, it delights in carnage
Sowing grief, hatred, and torment,
To impose an insane thought upon the word:
To lock away freedom in the depths of a dark tomb.
Asylums, ambulances, hospitals—all destroyed.
In the midst of the racket, flashes and sounds,
And the artistic treasures that go up in smoke,
Gunned-down civilians and the bodies of deserters,
Cadavers of children and the bones of the old,
Everything says: Swastika-clad airplanes were here.

Ode to Hitler

You want humanity stooped over under your thumb,
Trembling at your speeches, defeated by your words
And, fearing you even more than the worst evils,
You want them to testify to your godliness.
In your abject delirium, so completely beyond the norm,
You wished yourself to be great through the greatness of evil.
And to increase the visibility of your power here on earth,
To seem great, colossal to the extreme,
You piled up your crimes and made them into a pedestal
To your dreadful insanity.
With one word, you unleashed atrocious carnage
Massacre, ruin, and desolation,
You dug mass graves in the middle of nations
To satisfy your hideous hysteria,
Your sadistic appetite for suffering and death,
Your raging instincts of a man who wants to appear strong,
Who believes the stamp of genius to be etched upon his brow,
Who wants to see his excesses finally taken seriously,

When his megalomania has [instead] warranted
The jail cell of a raving madman.
The child opening his eyes in anticipation of life,
The tender newborn, the sweet, innocent angel,
The studious schoolchild, the smooth-faced adolescent,
Those who are pure of heart and rapturous of spirit,
Whose fathers, alas! will die in combat,
Will always remember that "Father died over there."
They will know that you were the only one responsible for
The terrible hardships for which we pity them,
And your name will become forever hated,
Cursed by all fatherless children.
The women in mourning, wearing dark veils,
With dull flowers in their arm and tears in their eyes,
Walking with their eyes on the ground and their heart towards
    heaven,
Whose husbands have now gone to the kingdom of shadows,
And who no longer hope to find happiness
Because their husband "Died on the Field of Honor"
Will recognize the person behind this vile war,
[Who] kills to better steal, murderer and thief.
You will be the accused that their souls will denounce,
And the widows will damn you.
Mothers will mourn the fruit of their wombs,
Their sons, born of their flesh, their only possession,
Their living brightness, their triumphant ray of light,
Mowed down by your bloody machine guns.
And we will never see their eyes free of tears,
With regards to he who brought about their pain.
Their accusatory voices will rise up to the heavens,
Translating up above what is in their hearts,
Finding in their chagrin the words to condemn you.
You will be cursed by mothers.
Fresh like flowers, so many girls of marriageable age
Will be forced to endure lifelong celibacy,
Because death strikes down, cuts down, and slaughters
Strong, passionate, loving, skilled young men.

So many, many betrothed will go off to die,
So many, many futures are going to rot in the ground,
That there will only remain hate, disguised as passion,
In the hearts that are overcome with despair.
Your memory will be cursed in the
Prayers of virgins.
All those who make it back alive from this cataclysm,
Broken down in body and spirit,
Will know that you are responsible,
Having realized the uselessness of the hypocritical logic
Through which you made yourself an angel among demons.
Because they coughed up their lungs in the gas,
Because they were taken down by intense gunfire,
Because, torn up by barbed wire,
And because—thanks to you—they are wounded in body and soul,
The war wounded will condemn you.
You were a cruel shepherd, for you led your flock
Like a passive herd to the bloody slaughterhouse.
But when your last night [on Earth] finally comes,
Their hands will strangle you before you go
Because you will have taken their freedom,
Killed their spirit in favor of brutishness,
And awoken hatred and proclaimed lies,
You people will understand just how much they were mistaken.
And, having swept you away like one sweeps away a dream,
Your people will also curse you.

Knafo, I. D. *Les Hitlériques*. Mogador, September–October 1939. Translated from French by Rebecca Glasberg and Jessie Stoolman.

5. A SHEIKH IN OUJDA PREDICTS A BRUTAL CONQUEST BY GERMANY [1939]

With the rise of fascism and Nazism in Europe and the intentional dissemination of their ideologies throughout North Africa, French authorities became concerned that propaganda would sway popular thought and imagination. French colonial authorities carefully tracked popular understandings of events in Europe and their implications in North Africa, all with an eye toward preventing dissent against France and French rule. This document, gathered in 1939 by the French intelligence, highlights how people in Berkane and Oujda interpreted ongoing events in Europe with reference to a religious will (ouassia, as transliterated in the French-language document, or waṣiyya) left by the sheikh of Mazouna in Oran, Algeria. It is not clear how the French colonial officer reporting the waṣiyya was informed of its existence. During the colonial period, French administrators had complete authority to obfuscate and fabricate information at will. According to the document, the sheikh claimed that North Africa was poised to be conquered by Nazi authorities after years of French colonial modernization, after which a Muslim leader would emerge to defeat the invaders. The account points to the various ways Muslims across North Africa perceived the tumultuous events in Europe, developing popular, religious, and apocalyptic theories about their anticipated resolution.

Martimprey du Kiss, April 7, 1939

It is my pleasure to inform you of the following intelligence that was brought to my attention today.

Many years ago, a Fquih (teacher at an Islamic school) in Mazouna, in the [administrative] department of Oran, named Sheikh Bourab, wrote the following "waṣiyya" (will) and beseeched his students to share it with everyone.

"It is certain that a foreign people will conquer Morocco and remain in power for quite some time until they have brought order to the entire region. They will build roads and bridges. Then, one day these [foreign] people will come into conflict with the Germans and will be forced to leave the country, the latter [Germans] will conquer Morocco in the same manner as did the French and will control everything."

"Then, by the grace of Allah, a valiant Muslim soldier will emerge to massacre the unbelievers—a third of them will die by sword, another [third] from famine and the rest will convert to Islam; having converted, the Christians and the Jews will be the masters [*les maîtres*] and will be able to foresee other conquests."

I have confirmation that this "waṣiyya" is currently circulating in the French Zone of Morocco.

Claverie

Claverie, Chief Inspector of the Security Brigade, to Commissioner Chief of Regional Security, RG 81.001M, Reel 27, Selected Records from the National Library of Morocco, 1864–1999 (bulk 1925–1945), United States Holocaust Memorial Museum Archives, Washington, DC. Courtesy of the Archives du Maroc. Translated from French by Amber Sackett.

6. A JEWISH ADOLESCENT PONDERS HER IDENTITY [1939]

In 1939, Marie Abravanel, resident of Tripoli, was a teenaged student at the local Alliance Israélite Universelle's lycée—one of a network of schools run by the Franco-Jewish organization across the Mediterranean and Middle East. Founded in Paris by members of the Jewish elite in 1860, the Alliance was imagined to provide social and educational opportunity for Levantine Jewish girls and boys, whom it sought to "uplift" through education in French according to the norms of the French bourgeoisie. Alliance schools administered exams to pupils between the ages of thirteen and fifteen to determine particularly promising ones to recommend for its teacher-training program in Paris. It appears that Abravanel was asked to reflect in her exam on what it meant to be Jewish. As might be expected of a young woman trained according to the educational norms of the French bourgeoisie, Abravanel's answers demonstrate all the optimism and anxiety of adolescence, the imprint of her teachers, and the particular climate of late-1930s Libya, where the Italian fascist government had in 1938 extended its racist laws. Notwithstanding the formulaic nature of Abravanel's essay, it is rare to have access to the voice and perspective of a young, Jewish, North African woman of her time.

March 6, 1939
"Being Jewish"

In the past, I rarely thought about the fact that I am Jewish. Reminders would come to me in the course of our holiday festivities, and I considered myself a being just like all the others, blessed with the common capacities of man, sensitive to the pains and joys that are part of life, with the only difference being the religion of my ancestors. I must have fooled myself: to this day, belonging to this faith is a problem; [recent] events have refuted my former convictions and have aroused in me sorrows that only a Jew is called upon to feel. I am Jewish; consequently, in the eyes of some, I am marked by the stamp of shame, unworthy of fulfilling any function in society or of nourishing any lofty aspirations.

By dint of repeatedly hearing these affronts, I have ended up feeling uncomfortable everywhere. In the street, at shows, all these eyes that look at me, do they not reproach me for crimes, do they not seem to banish me from the room, do they not condemn everything about me, down to the way I dress, the way I sit?

I feel as if I must no longer go out, as if I must hide at home to examine my thoughts and behavior. What faults have I committed, because I am less privileged than others? My exam comes to only one conclusion: I am Jewish. Is being so a crime? One could not hold this against me, just as one could not be angry with a Negro for being black [*on ne saurait en vouloir à un nègre d'être noir*],[1] a hunchback for being disfigured, or a mentally deficient [person] for failing to understand.

Following my initial despondency comes a new drive and hope: I look everyone in the eyes, sure of my innocence, of my right to life . . . I am no longer afraid, nor am I ashamed of being Jewish, and I glory in it as others do in their riches or their jobs.

Being part of this dispersed flock, suffering everywhere and at all times, hunted for infinite reasons across time and place, is an honor that in my eyes renews my personal dignity and that of my brothers.

My despondency has vanished, and hope in justice, rooted within us for millennia, is reborn in me, despite all the pain that I may endure.

Marie Abravanel

---

1. In the 1930s, when Marie Abravanel wrote her essay, the terms *Negro* (in English) and *nègre* (in French) were embraced by a global (and especially transatlantic) array of Francophone and Anglophone intellectuals, including Black intellectuals and artists such as Aimé Césaire, Suzanne Césaire, Léon Damas, W. E. B. Du Bois, Paulette Nardal, and Léopold Senghor (and later Frantz Fanon and others). These writers allied themselves with the Négritude and New Negro Movement literary movements, and were also bound by the politics of anticolonialism. While Abravanel's use of the word *nègre* reflects contemporary literature, the spirit of her essay is less anticolonial than Republican in spirit, in keeping with the Alliance Israélite Universelle, whose teachers trained her and assigned and graded the essay.

"Rapport trimestriel, Marie Abravanel, 'Etre juive,'" March 6, 1939, LYBIE-I.E.2, Tripoli, 1939, Alliance Israélite Universelle Archives. Translated from French by Rebecca Glasberg.

7. A MANIFESTO AGAINST RACISM {1939}

In January 1915, in the midst of the First World War, an organization known as the Algerian Committee for Social Science was founded in Algiers. The committee had the goal of defending Algerian Jews against a rise in regional anti-Semitism and was formed in the face of perceived passivity by the French state and its Jewish administrative arm, the Consistory. Among the leading figures involved in the establishment of the committee was the Jewish doctor Henri Aboulker (1876–1957), a professor in the Faculty of Medicine, a renowned surgeon, and an injured veteran of the First World War. Aboulker helped launched a campaign against anti-Semitism: defending Jews' rights in Algeria, advocating for Jewish students' access to the General Association of Students of Algiers, and fighting for Jews' right to own farmland and join municipal and other electoral lists. In 1934, tensions between Muslims and Jews in Algeria eroded after an outbreak of violence against the Jews of Constantine by right-wing French extremists with ties to local political rule. The events helped revive the Algerian Committee for Social Science under a new name, the Algerian Jewish Committee for Social Science. This new body served as a locus for resistance against fascism until its dissolution by the Vichy regime in 1940. This manifesto, signed by Aboulker and his allies, rejects the racist orientation of the Vichy regime, which, the signers argue, denies Jews their human rights. The manifesto is notably silent on the historical roots of Vichy racism, which were deeply impacted in French colonial rule.

Antiracist Manifesto

As Frenchmen—and, thus, as antiracists—assembled without regards to origin or philosophical or religious convictions, we turn to you, men and women from a noble country, to heal the world from a profound wound.

With us, you must refuse loyalty to racial dogma, which generates intolerance, tyranny, crimes and wars.

With us, you must revive the lofty humanist traditions that represent the greatness of French civilization. Among all the betrayals, the most significant betrayal of Vichy was to relinquish—upon foreign orders—these essential traditions and to profess racism. By that act alone, Vichy France definitively dishonored herself.

We disparage and condemn all the doctrines that have, in effect, corrupted the soul of our nation. We disparage and condemn the passivity of spirit that tolerates—and, finally, allows—the establishment and development of racist philosophies, politics, or governmental apparatuses, under whatever form they may take. For racism, in all times and all places, has led, leads, and will continue to lead people into slavery and men to their graves; in all cases, it leads men and peoples to ruin and misery.

The Atlantic Charter, in order to be fully realized and to retain all its symbolic value, must be made reality.

There will be no freedom of conscience as long as people's minds are distorted by racism, even latent racism. There will be no authentic freedom of expression as long as we cannot proclaim and prove that men are free and equal in rights and in duties. The world will not be liberated from misery as long as despotism and its fascinating consequences are not destroyed; the world will not be liberated from fear as long as we refrain from returning to humanity its logical condition, as long as we have not established its free right to development.

For us Frenchmen, it is a question of rebuilding a world battered by years of bloody hatred and, in order to rebuild it, to fully purify it.

France must take back her sovereignty in this rebuilt world and serve as the example of a true resurrection of honor and dignity. It is up to us, freed from the fascist jail, rebelling against traitors, to carry out our motherland's spiritual rearmament by restoring her true face to her.

Because despite Vichy, France was never racist.

For 1,000 years, her kings and her church have granted the right to asylum. For the past 150 years, she has refused tyranny and reassured thinking man of the independence of his soul. The Volunteers of '92 brought liberty to Europe on the tips of their bayonets. They taught her to free herself from fear, to fight misfortune, to express herself and to believe according to her wishes. They brought her hope. Each person was able to merit a life within the limits of her greatness. The Republic, in its essence and purpose, is antiracist. The Republic that is reborn in the ashes of war will be antiracist, or it simply will not be.

Millions of men, women, and children have died, murdered by racism.

The racial hierarchy, instituted as doctrine, codified by the laws of the invader or the usurper, imprisons, deports, and slowly exterminates millions more unfortunate beings through the system of massive migrations and concentration camps. The "Superior Race" and its servants select, sterilize, terrorize, and kill the so-called inferior races: religious peoples or communities, entire nations or parts of nations.

The liability of these racist gangsters is without limits. Their noxiousness is without restraint. They begin with the Jew and do not cease indifferently destroying all those—Catholic, Protestant, Muslim—who have a righteous soul, a pure heart, an independent mind. By destroying the flesh and blood being, they try to destroy faith, spirit, and even the image and essence of spirit and faith.

Racism, the negator of intelligence and gravedigger of morality, is the most extraordinary scientific, intellectual, and political fraud that ever saw the light of day. It abuses the credulity of the poverty-stricken masses through the most shameless breach of trust. It exploits the indignation of the oppressed by diverting it from its natural outlet.

We, undersigned Frenchmen, united today by the motherland's misfortune, appeal to all men and women who have the pride to reclaim a France for whom they express, with their contempt for racism, the desire to fight any and everywhere.

In the name of universal conscience, in the name of the country who declared the equality of men before the law, the abolition of slavery, and the right to live for all, we invite you to join our ranks.

J. Henri Aboulker et al., RG 43.071M, Selected Records from the Collection LIII, Algeria, 1871–1947 (bulk 1939–1946), LIII-21, Centre de documentation juive contemporaine, United States Holocaust Memorial Museum Archives, Washington, DC. Courtesy of the Centre de documentation juive contemporaine, Mémorial de la Shoah, Paris (France). Translated from French by Rebecca Glasberg.

8. AN INTRAFAITH CRY TO OPPOSE RACISM (1939)

A native of Constantine, Algeria, Elie Gozlan (1876–1964) graduated from the city's École Normale with a teaching degree in Arabic. Additionally, Gozlan taught French language and history. After a stint as a journalist, Gozlan cofounded, with Christian and Muslim colleagues, the Union of Monotheistic Believers. With this organization and on his own, Gozlan dedicated the next decades of his life to combating racism, intolerance, and injustice in Algeria. Gozlan was both a dedicated Zionist and an ardent loyalist of the French Republic. Throughout his life he held many positions, including secretary-general of the Jewish Consistory of Algiers and founding editor (from 1936 to 1947) of the Bulletin of the Federation of Jewish Societies of Algeria, the only Jewish periodical whose publication the Vichy regime tolerated. During the Second World War, Gozlan served as the Algerian delegate of the American Jewish Joint Distribution Council: under that organization's auspices, he visited Vichy camps to deliver food and clothing to the interned. By some accounts he also managed to free some 1,600 inmates from Vichy internment. This article by Gozlan, published in an Algerian Jewish newspaper (La Tribune Juive) just after the Nazi invasion of Poland and start of the Second World War, summons Algeria's Jewish, Christian, and Muslim citizens to join together in evincing loyalty to the French Republic and the notion of democracy, and to defend France and Europe against the menace of the Third Reich. Strikingly, Gozlan did not extend his call for unity to Black Algerians, whom he dismisses here with racist terminology.

October 3, 1939

Letter from Algeria
Muslims and Jews stand shoulder to shoulder with democracy

The brutal invasion of Poland by Hitler's Germany brings us back to the first days of the War of 1914 when, to justify the invasion of Belgium and the crushing of the valiant Belgian people, the Krauts—as we have called them since—claimed that the German border had been violated by Belgian patrols who "had shot at German soldiers" and had killed or wounded several of them.

Today, it is yet again the "innocent Germans" who are victims of "Polish brutality," so much so that the Fuhrer's very sensitive heart, and those even more sensitive of Goebels [sic], Goering, Ribbentrop, and other Nazi gangsters, cannot resist flying to the rescue of subjugated German minorities, tears in their eyes and dagger in hand. Poor wolves who persecute the evil sheep!

Who could possibly be fooled by Germany's crookedness and bad faith?

Not even her former and current allies, who hesitate to make themselves complicit.

In all of French North Africa, the same indignation fills the whole population, regardless of origin, race or religion.

The Italians living in Algeria, Tunisia, and Morocco affirm their loyalty with respect to France and their desire to fight in her armies.

The Jews of Tunisia and Morocco who are not French citizens but French subjects ask to be enlisted in the French army and declare their readiness to sacrifice their lives defending democracy.

As for the Muslims, their acts of loyalty and attachment to France and her institutions are affirmed every day in formal declarations addressed to the General Government of Algeria. The Muslim leader, Doctor Bendjelloul, has presented the following proclamation:

> To all Muslims
>
> My dear brothers,
>
> The intent of this message is not to call upon you to do your duty. You have already done so.
>
> Everywhere, in the cities as in the *douars* [villages], you have responded "Present!" to the call of the homeland.
>
> Woken during the night or surprised in the fields in the midst of your work by the mobilization order, serious and resolute, hundreds of thousands of you all immediately left your wives, your homes, your children, and your work in full swing to join together in unity.
>
> These are acts that wrap you in glory and ennoble you, powerful acts that count in the lives of men as in that of the nation. It is with legitimate pride that I note them. You have proven that you stand by your word and that you will loyally execute the declarations made in your name by your elected representatives. By flying to the rescue of a threatened France, you demonstrate that you desire to put yourselves forward in the same way as have the best sons of Europe. In this way, you chart out your life, your future, and your place in the world. Remember that you are the honorable descendants of a noble, brave, and chivalrous race that conquered and civilized continents. Remember as well that your excellent qualities of endurance and status of soldier-warriors are admired. Know that your presence in the military and the willingness with which you respond are possibly of a nature that will make the adversary reflect and withdraw. Through an insidious campaign, he tries to turn you from the straight and narrow path of loyalty, acknowledgment,

duty, and honor. Furthermore, he disputes your status as civilized man and classes you among the Negroids, who can hardly be improved upon, even with training, and well after the Jews—and we know how he treats them.

As did your ancestors in 1870, and as did your brothers and yourselves in 1914, you will fulfill your duty towards France, with the same selflessness and peace of spirit. You will thereby contribute to assuring yourself and your children a better future, to saving the honor and the prestige of France, and to assuring the triumph of peace, Liberty and Democracy. You will thus have rightfully earned your Humanity.

The mobilization of all of France's forces is taking place in the greatest calm and the greatest order.

Each person, whether Christian, Muslim, or Jewish, understands that the fight that has just begun is actually that of Justice against arbitrariness, of Civilization against Barbarism, of right against brutal and aggressive force, and that it is a question of saving humanity, [which is] currently threatened by the diabolical power of a man blinded by pride and unbridled ambition, and whom unfortunately the German people follow blindly.

At this point in time, French Africa is providing the most beautiful example of patriotism and union.

Despite the gold that she has scattered about with both hands, Hitler Germany will certainly not undermine French Africa's goodwill and firm commitment to the Motherland.

Just like Wilhelm II, Hitler will come to realize that the French block is made of granite.

Elie Gozlan

RG 43.071M, Selected Records from the Collection LIII-3, Algeria, 1871–1947 (bulk 1939–1946), Centre de documentation juive contemporaine, United States Holocaust Memorial Museum Archives, Washington, DC. Courtesy of the Centre de documentation juive contemporaine, Mémorial de la Shoah, Paris (France). Translated from French by Rebecca Glasberg.

9. THE SWASTIKA'S LOOMING SHADOW— ONE WOMAN'S EXPERIENCE IN SPANISH- OCCUPIED TANGIER {1939–1941}

Alegria Bendelac was born in Caracas, Venezuela, to émigré Moroccan Jewish parents who returned the family to their native country when Bendelac was an infant. The extended family, Andalusian Jews, lived in Tetouan, the capital of the former Spanish protectorate of northern Morocco, but Bendelac's nuclear family settled in Tangier, giving her a unique perspective on the many cultural, economic, and other differences that divided Morocco's regional Jewish communities. These differences were magnified during the war, when Tangier fell under Spanish colonial rule. In this selection from her memoir, Bendelac writes of the privileged environment of her childhood, the challenges of experiencing adolescence, and pursuing an education in a time of war. Bendelac would go on to earn a PhD from Columbia University and to hold teaching positions at the Lycée Français in New York, Fordham University, and Penn State University, where she was a full professor. She is the author of multiple collections of poetry and various books on the Sephardic Jews of northern Morocco, including a groundbreaking dictionary of Haketia, the Judeo-Spanish language spoken by the Sephardic Jewish community of northern Morocco, published in 1996.

That fall, I started seventh grade and it was a year full of changes. The previous year, when I started secondary school in sixth grade, I had to give up my weekly privilege and go to school on Saturdays.[1] It became too hard to catch up every week on a whole day of missed classes and studies were becoming very important for us. My father fought this change for as long as he could, but ultimately had to surrender. I didn't know it at the time, but our family had just taken another step—an important one—on the path of assimilation.

Seventh grade introduced us to coed classes. Until that point, the French high school had been divided into two buildings, both on the same street— rue Jeanne d'Arc—[that were] about two hundred meters apart: Lycée Regnault, at the end of the rue Goya, took boarders and housed all the boys, boarders or not, from first grade until the baccalaureate; all the girls attended Lycée Saint-Aulaire, on the corner of rue des Vignes, from first grade until the baccalaureate, but only as day students. In autumn 1939, things were reorganized. Lycée Regnault did away with the boarding program and started

---

1. Before the war, Bendelac was allowed to miss school on Saturday in observance of Shabbat.

IMAGE 4. The well-to-do Bendelac family returned to their native Morocco from Venezuela when Alegria (second from right) was an infant. During the war, when Alegria was an adolescent, her hometown—the northern Moroccan city of Tangier—fell from French to Spanish hands, absorbed large numbers of European refugees, and was subject to strict rations: circumstances Alegria details in her memoir and this volume. Alegria Bendelac "Mamé, Clairette, Sol, Alegria & Lea—1940." Courtesy Mercedes Huber.

housing all of the primary classes, both for girls and boys, and the commercial classes. Lycée Saint-Aulaire began accommodating co-ed secondary classes, from sixth grade up to philosophy. For the first time, we shared classes with boys and we sat on the same benches. Some girls began to feel normal attraction [to the opposite sex] and tried their hand at flirting, or even began to develop crushes.

. . . However, the year was marked mainly by the events of the first months of the war. After the first depression caused by the declaration of war, people's minds began to ease; Tangier was far from the theater of operations, no bombing was to be feared and our international status protected us; everyone was optimistic. At school, a merry, patriotic excitement was in the air, as was a strong belief in a quick victory. In chorus class, we were taught all the anthems and military marches of the Allied countries. We sang "La Marseillaise," "Madelon," the "Chant du Depart," "God Save the King," and "Tipperary," with martial spirit; even those who were stateless like myself were an integral part of the group; we were united against the common enemy. Many teachers were mobilized. Some of my classmates had brothers, cousins, uncles or fathers who were mobilized; others were war female pen pals; everyone collected badges, flags, and currency.

We were told that those of us who wanted to knit for the soldiers could dedicate [our] sewing classes doing so, while the others would continue to learn how to embroider. For a year and a half, I had been trying and failing to learn to hem: my stitches were never quite consistent with those of the sewing teacher's model; they bumbled about with difficulty, like little hunchbacks [walking] along a torturous path. When they weren't visible on the front of the piece, it was because they were too big on the back, or too far apart. Every two or three months, I would apprehensively turn in a laboriously finished piece, already dirty gray, to the dreadful Madame M. for inspection. . . . Her cantankerous personality—as well as the marital misfortunes that were its cause—were well known throughout the school. Looking over top of her large glasses, she would examine my hem with a disgusted look, furrowing her brow, and would yap bitterly, "Go and remake it properly." My classmates, having finished with hems long before, were passing quickly from running stitch to backstitch, and from straight stitch to cross-stitch. . . . As for me, I was still working on hems. So I jumped at the opportunity and registered first on the list for patriotic knitting. We were distributed large balls of rough, beigeish wool that skinned our fingers, and we were split into pairs, one knitting the sweater's front and the other, the back.

The work was started with enthusiasm. Based on the measurements we were provided, I imagined that the French army was made up of freezing-cold giants whose glorious bones these sweaters were meant to warm from knee to neck. The rows piled up endlessly, one on top of the other, and the armhole never seemed to get any closer. I knitted, if not as badly, then at least as slowly as I sewed, and when I got to the neckline decreases, it was June 1940: the disaster [i.e., when Nazi forces entered Paris] and the Armistice. "My" soldier, who must have been cold during winter, was now hot; besides, he was going back home; my endeavor had been useless; I put my "front" that nobody thought of claiming anymore back in the storeroom. I wasn't proud of myself and, sometimes, I thought that there was a soldier in French army who had spent the winter shivering because of me, wearing the back and the two sleeves that my classmate had knitted, but with his chest exposed to the bad weather.

Times had changed; no more heroic chants or proud confidence; shame, weariness, and stupor prevailed. A wind of panic was blowing. Such a defeat, so swift, so complete, seemed incredible nightmarish; the future was dark and blocked off; the shadow of the swastika loomed above our peaceful city....

I sincerely believe that I suffered in my heart like my French classmates at the moment of the debacle, and I was more delighted than most of them with General de Gaulle's call to action. But the other side had already organized itself; they were now rolling in humility; the great scission had already begun. The Pétainists had the upper hand, that of legality and official power; they settled into collaboration and disdain of the Jews. From then on, I was no longer the ally, the war buddy. Without even knowing it, I had fallen into the camp of the outcasts. I keenly felt this [change], even though my fate was still extremely enviable.

We settled into a war that had changed shape. We listened feverishly to the radio to hear news of the combat that England was leading in air and sea. Those who had connections in the consulate of England or the United States were invited to film screenings about current affairs that depicted the progress of hostilities. In daily life, rationing started to make itself felt; oil and sugar became rare commodities, imported butter—English, Danish, or Dutch—had disappeared; from the market my father would bring back small clods of farm butter, very white and very fresh, sold inside green leaves, by the country people who had settled in the Gran Socco. My father prided himself on being able to determine at one glance the freshest, least rancid, cleanest clod out of them all, that which had been made by a more conscientious farmer [and] in which we rarely risked finding a strand of hair, a bit of string, or other unappetizing thread. In fact, when well selected, this butter had an extraordinarily fresh and delicate taste.

As the months of war went on, bread became darker and darker, worse and worse, a black dough, heavy, sour, in which we frequently found pieces of string from the [flour] bag or lumps of raw flour. Thus, strange hardship, we would spread a thick layer of good, fresh butter on very thin slices [of this bread].

But just two steps away from a torn, bombed, invaded, abused Europe, we were so terribly privileged that we felt awfully guilty. We were eating enough, we were not cold; we didn't lack clothes; no bombings, no Gestapo, no concentration camps or gas chambers. In this miraculously preserved islet where our parents thanked God every day for their luck, some managed even to build fortunes through unscrupulous speculation; all methods were good, even selling weapons to the Germans. The British consulate's black list periodically got longer; however, the cause came to cancel out the effect, for at the end of the war, a lot of this illicit money was used to erase names from these lists of infamy. Ten years after the end of the war, many speculators who had been despised when war was threatening, were once again welcomed everywhere with open arms, having acquired a newfound innocence in people's forgetful memories.

Shortly after France's defeat, Tangier lost its invaluable international status for a short time. Taking advantage of France's absence, Spain extended its protectorate and its iron rule to the zone of Tangier. From then on, an *interventor* was in charge, *regulares* from the Spanish army filled the streets, often with their distinctive *boinas coloradas*; the Republicans escaped or hid. On Spanish national holidays, the *interventor* organized huge parades in which every male Spanish national of marching age was ordered to participate. [As they] marched behind the enthusiastic and martial formations of young phalangists and troop soldiers, we would watch the clusters of potbellied bourgeois, out of breath, dragging their feet and, depending on the season, taking shelter under a large umbrella or mopping their foreheads under the sun, fulfilling their patriotic duty whether they liked it or not.

My uncle, the husband of my aunt Sultana, who had been jealously guarding his Spanish passport throughout the years and the political vicissitudes, suffered a thousand deaths at this time. He was the most bourgeois man in the world, the biggest wimp, the most attached to his personal comfort, that I have ever come across; he would take a taxi to get to his club (which was two minutes away by foot) if the weather was either slightly too cold or too hot; he would put on his slippers as soon as he stepped over the threshold of his front door in order to not bruise his sensitive feet; the most minor physical ailment wore him out and terrified him, and he had to be endlessly pampered. And thus, on the days of the compulsory marches, [when he was] forced to walk for kilometers, for hours, sometimes under the rain and others under the blazing sun, skipping a meal, fearing chills, heatstroke, and indigestion, with insufficient courage poorly sustained by a lukewarm patriotism, he felt like the most miserable of men, and would search desperately for a medical acquaintance who would excuse him; but the medical certifications were severely scrutinized; and validly excused or not, absences during the parades were noticed, judged with suspicion, and seen badly. In these troubled times, being seen badly by the authorities was particularly hazardous. The poor man resigned himself to his fate. My aunt, who had quite the sense of humor, would spend parade days waving with us from her balcony at the potbellied marchers below, who we knew were doing their patriotic duty whether they liked it or not. At the same time, she would heap pity on her beloved her "sissy" of a husband in a loud and sincere tone, a sly sparkle in her eyes.

In the high school where I was starting eighth grade, the administration, professors, and students were separated by the big political schism: on one side, few but full of panache, there were the assumed and active Gaullists; they constituted a homogeneous core of opposition facing the big organized force of the Pétainists. The new director was a fervent Pétainist; officially, the French consulate, on which the school depended, was Pétainist as well; the remainder of the administration—assistant principal, superintendents, and supervisors—almost all of them followed [the director's] lead out of necessity or conviction. The classrooms were decorated with banners that carried the marshal's mottos: Work, Family, Fatherland; Return to the Land, etc. . . .

For the Jewish students, life became more complicated. It seems barely acceptable to mention these inconsequential problems even in passing, when our contemporaries, two steps away from us, in Europe, were brutalized, decimated, and gassed. We were even privileged in relation to our coreligionists in the south, in Casablanca for instance, where most majority of the Jewish students were expelled from the French high schools. As for us, we were tolerated by the school's Pétainist administration [that] regarded us with a malevolently-tinged neutrality that seemed to say: "we tolerate you, but be careful: behave yourselves, because the slightest infraction or missing work will be severely punished." And as a matter of fact, for the smallest breach, the maximum sanction was applied. Naturally, this situation was never presented to us in these terms, clearly or unclearly, neither by the high school nor by our families; it went without saying, without mentioning, submerged beneath the surface of day-to-day life. But our intuition told us that we were facing an indefinitely suspended sentence, and we adapted to the situation. The year before, my friend Lina and I had been rather unruly, and had willingly participated in most of the disruption. This year, however, we watched our step.

The winds of war helped broaden my horizons concerning Judaism. I have a particularly vivid memory of two boys who joined us in eighth grade. They were part of the innumerable refugees that Nazi persecution had scattered around the world, many of whom poured into Tangier, the last haven, in successive, distressed flights. They came from all over Central Europe: Germans, Austrians, Hungarians, Poles, and Czechs. Soon, Tangier saw the unfamiliar silhouette of the Ashkenazis, with their fitted black coats, large beards and curls the length of their cheeks. Most of women wore wigs and their piety was quite fanatic. Most of them were penniless when they arrived and lived by their wits, trying their hands at any possible trade. Clever and resourceful, as well as courageous, they soon succeeded in amassing real fortunes and, little by little, integrated into Tangier society. Such as the one who survived by making ice-cream and rolls that were resold in a pushcart in the beginning [and] became an established trader with three stores three or four years later.

My two classmates therefore came from somewhere in Central Europe. They were first cousins, thirteen and fifteen years old respectively. The younger one was quite tall and robust, the older one, very tall and athletic. Both had pale skin, brown hair, and hazel green eyes. It was clear that they came from a privileged environment, quite notable, and had had to leave their country before the persecution became too harsh, taking at least part of their wealth with them, as hardship did not mark their faces. They didn't have that tense look, that haunted glaze that many of the later refugees had. With a healthy and well-fed look, they projected a peaceful good mood. Only the maturity of their gaze and the philosophy with which they confronted the various vicissitudes of these troubled school times revealed children who had seen and lived, if not suffered, many things.

Both very intelligent, they learned French with surprising ease. Their flexibility of mind and their ability to adapt enabled them to hold an honorable rank in a class that was totally foreign to them by its program, its methods, and its language. Soon, a very pleasant camaraderie of four was established between them, Lina, and me. They lived right at the end of boulevard Pasteur, very close to my house. We walked back together from school, talking incessantly, debating all available subjects with our newly discovered logic. .

.. All four of us gifted with a solid sense of humor that we applied cheerfully to all that surrounded us, the giggles bent us in two at all the crossroads. We endlessly accompanied one another, unable make ourselves break the thread of an exciting discussion. . . . Unfortunately, the following year, they sailed to other shores and we never heard of them again. . . .

October '41. I'm starting ninth grade. We're living the darkest and most hopeless days of the war. Outside, this translates to further restrictions. The Spanish authorities tighten their hold on the city. We see more and more soldiers. We hear about the scandals of the *interventor*. What reverberates in our ears are the bombings of London, the battles of submarines or battleships, the defeats, the rumors about concentration camps. More and more flights of more and more haggard refugees rain down upon the city. This huge, oppressive cloud is getting darker and darker. The future seems cut short: it shrinks away day after day, just melting away. We quietly contemplated our remaining happy days, which were vanishing irreversibly into thin air.

The Pétainists make up a significant portion of the school. England looks lost, the resistant fighters' efforts seem ridiculous. France sinks with delight into humility: Work, Family, Fatherland, Return to the Land; have children, blindly follow a lost old man down inglorious paths; give in completely to chauvinism's narrow-minded misconceptions and its cruelest prejudices, as if exorcising yourself of all questions, all doubts, and all remorse. Henceforth, this is the watchword, and all the rest is of trifling importance. For us of course, the ostracism deepens. Last year, we were tolerated with a certain kindness; this year, they barely tolerate us. We just have to behave well. We just have to behave well, or else.

Bendelac, Alegria. *Mosaïque: Une enfance juive a Tanger (1930–1945)*. Casablanca: Édition Wallada, 1992. Courtesy of Mercedes Huber. Translated from French by Rebecca Glasberg and Jessie Stoolman.

10. HITLER'S MILITARY IS UNMATCHED— AN ANTI-FRENCH TIRADE [1940]

In June 1940, following the German occupation of France, the French battleship Jean Bart *evaded German capture and was moved to Casablanca with only one functional gun turret. The French military subsequently sought to ferry a second turret to the* Jean Bart *by cargo ship, but that ship was destroyed and sunk by a German submarine. This undated leaflet, collected and translated into French by the Vichy Office of Political Affairs, seemingly produced by a resident of North Africa, derisively rehearses this incident. Written in broken Moroccan Arabic and addressed in a rude tone to General Charles Noguès, France's resident-general in Morocco and commander in chief in French North Africa, its alleged author, a Muslim man by the name of Ben Abbou, mocks France's military weakness. The figure of Ben Abbou is likely fabricated given his unusual name and seeming lack of fluency in Moroccan Arabic. In this likely invented account, Ben Abbou goes on to herald what he sees as the unmatched military power of Adolf Hitler and Nazi Germany, nodding also to the might of fascist Italy and the Soviet Union. Ben Abbou then dares French officials to translate his inflammatory note into French and insults Vichy-controlled Radio Maroc as propaganda. In this fashion, the likely fictitious Ben Abbou questions who the real propogandists were in North Africa and who was more likely to win the war. It is important to note that this source does not detail the author's reasons for supporting the Axis powers (and Soviet Union), even while articulating disdain for the major colonial powers in North Africa: France and Great Britain. As this suggests, anti-Allied sentiments expressed by indigenous inhabitants of North Africa and West Africa could emerge from and inform anticolonial struggles.*

To General Noguès, May God Curse Him

It was me who wrote to you five days ago and you didn't answer me. I am asking you to give me information on the boat that was sunk by Hitler in Casablanca.

Is that a demonstration of the power of the Protectorate government, of its organization and defense?

Long live Morocco, long live Hitler, long live Italy, long live Soviet Russia. Down with France, England, [and] those who love and follow them.

O Germany, inflict a lesson upon France and her ally.

O Germany, I wish for your victory and your success.

Know that it is I who wrote you five days ago. The mailman took the letter and showed it around in several different stores, asking if someone could translate it into French for him, but all the people responded that they didn't know French.

The matter of the second boat destroyed in the Casablanca port on March

23 will make history. It happened in a port defended by nets and other contraptions, by order of France and England; it is the proof that what you diffuse on [the airwaves of] Radio Morocco is nothing but trickery and lies.

Abbou Ben Abbou—Rue Kerkouchi N° 10 890 tel. 0000

Answer without fail. Casablanca, Morocco. Year 1940.

"Abbou Ben Abbou" to Bureau of Political Affairs, March 29, 1940, RG 81.001M, Reel 27, Selected Records from the National Library of Morocco, 1864–1999 (bulk 1925–1945), United States Holocaust Memorial Museum Archives, Washington, DC. Courtesy of the Archives du Maroc. Translated from French by Rebecca Glasberg.

11. AN ODE TO MARSHAL PÉTAIN {1941}

"Maréchal, nous voilà" (Marshal, here we are), was a French song written in honor of Marshal Philippe Pétain, the French general and First World War hero who served as chief of state under Vichy rule in France from 1940 to 1944. The song was composed by André Montagard and its music attributed to Montagard and Charles Courtioux. In fact, it was a plagiarized copy of "La Margoton du bataillon," a song written by the Polish Jewish composer Kazimierz Oberfeld, who perished in Auschwitz at the hands of the Nazis. "Maréchal, nous voilà" celebrates Pétain as savior of France, a hero to all its children. The song was immensely popular during the Vichy era, when it was sung at public and private events. Here, we present an abridged testimony by David Bensimon, a native of El Jadida (Mazagan), Morocco, who currently resides in Montreal. Bensimon was a young child during the Vichy years, and among his most vivid recollections is the sycophantic love that Jewish children (and likely Muslim ones, too) were compelled to show for Pétain, even as the Vichy regime accelerated its assault on Moroccan Jews, their property and possessions, and their sense of belonging.

I was there [in El Jadida] the day when the Americans paraded in Mersane [a modern, mixed Jewish-Muslim neighborhood in El Jadida], passing by the fountain in their beautiful Jeeps, throwing us chewing gum and candy—not to mention the first boxes of "instant" coffee that we threw in the trash not knowing what to make of them.

Some had been injured in clashes with the French Army when they landed near Safi and were proudly wearing their bandages.

When Pétain (*yimakh shemo* [Hebrew, "may his name be destroyed"]) came to power, every Jewish child in Mazagan was forced to buy a photo of him and learn the famous song, "Marshal, here we are before you the savior of France. Marshal, here we are." I can still sing the whole song but I think it's enough to have mentioned his name. Therefore, my family was forced to pay for six copies of his photo; in addition, each classroom had his portrait in the middle.

I also remember that Jews were forced to declare belongings in an effort organized by the French as a prelude to the elimination of the Jewish Community. Overwhelmed by fear, my poor father Messod had what seemed to be the good judgement to throw all his merchandise into the sea in front of the Jewish cemetery, perhaps believing that this would spare us.

French- and English-language interview with David Bensimon by Aomar Boum, April 3, 2019, Toronto, Ontario.

12. PÉTAIN'S PORTRAIT [1941]

Founded in Paris by members of the Jewish elite in 1860, the Alliance Israélite Universelle (AIU) was a philanthropic organization designed to provide social and educational uplift to Jews of the Mediterranean and Middle East. The organization's goals were in keeping with the "civilizing mission" of the French Third Republic: by opening schools for so-called Oriental Jewish children and offering educational training in French according to the norms of the French bourgeoisie, it sought to offer Jewish youth a path to social and economic upward mobility. In the decades that followed, the AIU opened and ran hundreds of schools, offering instruction to thousands of children across North Africa, the Middle East, and southeastern Europe and Anatolia. No fewer than forty-five AIU schools were opened in Morocco. As the Second World War began, AIU schools in Morocco absorbed an influx of refugee children while employees and students threw themselves into the Allied effort—pupils in Fez and Tangier, for example, knit sweaters and gloves for French soldiers. The creation of the Vichy regime proved a disillusioning force for many of the AIU faithful. Because AIU schools were run under the auspices of the French Department of Public Education, the organization's employees were compelled to honor Vichy leadership: their day-to-day experiences, however, made evident that this very regime was eroding the security of AIU students and their families. This poignant internal document details the AIU's intention to distribute portraits of Vichy chief of state Philippe Pétain to meritorious students—a cruel blow to those who fell victim to his regime's anti-Jewish laws, spoliation, and internment centers. One child survivor of this era, whose testimony is offered in the previous source, recalled with pain how his family was forced to buy one such portrait and that another hung in each classroom of his AIU school. The indignity of occupation was felt in such myriad hurtful, daily experiences that too often evade the historical record.

Portrait of Marshal Pétain

I received the following letter from the Central Committee:

"We inform you that we are sending you herewith a package containing a rather large number of portraits of Marshal Pétain. These portraits, which we ask you to distribute to our various schoolmasters, are intended to be given out as prizes to students with either outstanding work or conduct. We thought that in these times which are difficult for France, where each person, from the most humble to the most grand, can and must contribute to France's recovery according to his means and situation, the image of the Marshal's noble face is such as to inspire in our children the finest of thoughts and, at the same time, represents the personification of the concept of Duty."

S. Halff

S. Halff, Casablanca, to Alliance Israélite Universelle, Paris, 22 February 1941, RG 43.117M, "Maroc 1934–1941," Selected Records from the Archives of the Alliance Israélite Universelle, 1860–1976, United States Holocaust Memorial Museum Archives, Washington, DC. Translated from French by Rebecca Glasberg.

13. FOREIGN LEGION SOLDIERS TRAINED AT SIDI BEL ABBÈS {C. EARLY 1940S}

The French Foreign Legion was an early nineteenth-century European colonial creation that originally deployed and united Western European representatives in expeditions for colonial expansion. Only later did the Foreign Legion incorporate colonial troops as secondary soldiers, treating them with suspicion at best, and outright hostility at worse. To be a recruit, forced or otherwise, in the French Foreign Legion in the course of the Second World War was a dubious venture, and depending on one's religion, race, place of origin, political orientation—and, no less, luck and timing—it could prove comfortable or a form of brutal, forced conscription. For Camillo Adler, an Austrian refugee who spent the war years in Switzerland and North Africa, the Legion provided an amiable home. For some time during the war, Adler was stationed in Sidi Bel Abbès. The garrison, located sixty miles south of Oran, had housed a modest depot of the French Foreign Legion since 1843, by which point the Legion was already established as an arm of colonization in North Africa, North America, and Southeast Asia. By the Second World War, Sidi Bel Abbès was a primary garrison of the Foreign Legion in North Africa, with its members split between Vichy loyalists and so-called Gaullists, or supporters of French resistance leader Charles de Gaulle: among the latter were foreign volunteers (the engagés volontaire à la Légion étrangère pour la durée de la guerre) sent to camps in North Africa by the retributive Vichy regime. A certain number of North African Jews and Muslims and Jewish and non-Jewish refugees from Europe were also forcibly recruited (whether by circumstance or order) to train in Sidi Bel Abbès. To Adler, who was among those Foreign Legion recruits favored by the Vichy regime, the garrison at Sidi Bel Abbès felt like a city of its own, with gracious barracks, public squares, tree-lined streets lit with electric lights, a church, prison, cinema, and police station. Those stationed there received basic training and staffed the base's mobile brigade for a symbolic sum; they participated in sporting events, attended concerts and parties, and were allowed to leave the depot for the nearby town of Sidi Bel Abbès, where, according to the following account, they sought out local sex workers. The advantages of life in Sidi Bel Abbès were fleeting. Some Legionnaires were sent from the garrison to labor in camps such as Quargla, which had notoriously poor conditions. Adler's own reminiscences, then, represent Sidi Bel Abbès in its best possible light.

A few days later, we traveled to Sidi-Bel-Abbès. This city was the principal garrison of the Foreign Legion, ancestral seat of the First Foreign Infantry regiment. Here, the new arrivals were once again carefully examined and once and for all accepted into the bosom of the Legion.

How romantic our exotic existence appears when you read the adventure-filled songs and books about the Foreign Legion. "Il était beau, il était fort, il sentait bon, le sable chaud" ("It was beautiful, it was strong, the warm sand smelled good") Madame Dubas sentimentally sang forth in the sultry atmosphere of a nightclub, and the customers were shimmying in their elegant evening clothes, their breasts heaving under silken blouses. Lost in dreams, they sipped from champagne flutes and admired the triumphant, strong, mysterious Legionnaire. Oh, he doesn't exist, this Legionnaire never existed, only in the imagination of the writer, next to the hooker, the pimp, criminals, and other characters of the underworld. Literature.

Legionnaire: synonymous with work—hard, harsh, dangerous work—combat and discipline. *Basic training*: to drill until the poor devil loses every vestige of his individuality and is made into a spineless machine. A robot of the war trade, for whom nothing is too difficult or impossible; who equally well builds streets in the blazing desert as continuing combat against all odds under the command of his fearless officers; who equally finds his way in unrecognizable, unexplored terrain as in the sandy infinity of the desert; who fears nothing, because the drill has erased all fear except possibly fear of his superiors. The enemy can't be worse than the toughness of his own military machine. The daredevil adventure of war is a welcome change from the pressures of rebellious people. And death? Isn't it a deliverance from a failed existence into which only woman and wine offered short escape from a destitute inner life? The Legionnaire is feared. He is stepped on inconsiderately, and inconsiderately he steps on others....

Bunk beds were erected in the sports palace to accommodate the strong influx of recruits. This was where recruits that were not yet undergoing basic training were billeted. Several comrades who had been declared unfit for service after the second examination were now waiting to return to Europe.

The examination was more careful than the one in Sathonay. Nevertheless, the doctors had recently received orders to not be quite as strict in their selections. Man is only matter for the insatiable Moloch of the army. In peace it devours material of the best sort; in war it is satisfied with lesser goods. Except for a few, whose disabilities were obvious, we were declared suitable. A peculiar act of Providence once again called on me to remain civilian. At the eye examination for acuity, I failed again. I lost my patience. I hadn't traveled this far to be turned back. From my pocket, I pulled the note of the Lyon optician from whom I had purchased my glasses and presented the findings. The incompetent aid couldn't come to terms with my two different eye strengths, copied it word for word, and I was declared fit.

Our quarters were afflicted with inadequate security. Our belongings lay in the open and invited outright theft. There was no shortage of pickpockets, and they never passed up lucrative opportunities. One day, I was about to put on clean socks when a fellow spoke to me. I turned around, and we exchanged a few words. The whole thing took less than a minute, plenty of time for the thief to make the socks his. He must have lain in wait for the opportunity.

A thieving raven made off with all of fat Walker's possessions, including his canvas bag. By happenstance, we found the things on another day on a bench, but without discovering the thief. Walter was delighted, but he rejoiced too soon. The thief liked his English electric razor and the hand-knitted full sweater much too much to relinquish them. The next night he repeated his prank, and this time all searches failed. We couldn't count on the help of the superiors; they just laughed when we told them such things. A Legionnaire was responsible for his possessions under all circumstances. It was, by the way, fortunate that we owned so little and didn't have to suffer any great losses. Money we carried on our person and even at night when going to the latrine. The pickpocket fraternity was ever on the lookout, and as soon as someone left his sleeping place, they were sure to ransack his clothes.

Losses made you clever. Walter bought a belt with an inner pocket and carried his cash on his body. I was inadvertently reminded of my Martha's cousin, who as a Czech served in the previous world war in the Foreign Legion. The Legion appears to be an inescapable fate of our family. Now, this cousin owned a valuable gold watch. In 1916, his division was deployed for an assault. The night before, he overheard two of his buddies. "When his lights go out, we inherit his watch," said one of these brave fellows. Fortunately my cousin survived.

All nationalities of Europe were represented in my unit. Half were Jews from Germany, Austria, and Poland; the rest, a polyglot of others. Many spoke only a small smattering of French, as for example the Spaniards. They recently arrived from the internment camp Gurs, a name synonymous with hunger and suffering, where they had spent twenty months after they had fought two years in the civil war in the anti-Fascist brigades. The poor devils were starving, and with animal voracity they attached the food buckets. Besides that, they didn't have a single centime in their sacks and were totally dependent on the penurious pay. We received fifty centimes per day, not even enough for cigarettes. No wonder that many Spaniards couldn't resist the temptation to pilfer. What did they think of a world that treated them this way? Among them were fine and educated humans. They were good to each other, but isolated themselves from strangers. And most of all, they were driven by hunger and need....

We used the first opportunity to acquaint ourselves with African female beauty. My God and Lord! Such filth and excrement, such baseness and depravity, I have hardly ever seen. The love paradise of Bel-Abbès: a snarl of confined, crooked, unpaved lanes, narrow door arches, dilapidated houses, whose walls had been consumed by leprosy, through which open doors and windows a nauseous smell overwhelmed us. In front of these, squatted on bare dirt repulsive creatures, fat matrons in the deepest stuffing of a mat, with puffed up bodies, and young girls hardly past childhood with narrow shoulder and hollow cheeks. Garish red lips, a smile in the made-up face, solicited with spread knees for customers. The places stank more of bitter and neglected poverty than from sweet idleness. And yet many Legionnaires, as long as their pay permitted, sought this scum of hookers. Bartel and I were repulsed; we did not even want to drink a glass of wine in this disgusting place. We hurried back and breathed easier as the nightmare of this sex realm disappeared into the night behind us....

"You hit it just right," said the old Legionnaire. "Christmas in Bel-Abbès lacks nothing." The Legion festively celebrates Christmas—not from devoutness, because the church and priests have no place in the Legion. The men for whom the Legion was their last resort would have rejected an invitation to a church service with scornful laughter. For these displaced, did God exist? Yes, perhaps they believed in a devil who maliciously fractured their lives and cast them here, to have them all assembled when we one day would call them. They knew nothing of divine Providence or of God's goodness.

The Germans, having been well represented in the Legion for eons, transplanted the custom of the Christmas tree to Africa. Once a year even these failed humans remembered that a mother once loved and took care of them and told them about the Christ child. As small children, they looked forward to Christmas, blissful in the light of candles. And so the holy day signified a retrospective moment and melancholy until the light Algerian wine, which goes down so well, numbed their distress.

The Christmas celebration was carefully prepared. Bel-Abbès had an outstanding jujitsu and gymnastics group, who could easily compete with professional athletes. The presentation was a pleasure to watch. Also the orchestra accompanists were artists. Everyone in France remembers well the

Legion Band that on July 14, 1939, scored an intoxicating success. The leader of the Legion orchestra was not at a loss for choices, enough musicians were in the Legion. To be a trumpeter at headquarters was an honor bestowed only on the best.

The midpoint of the program featured a play with patriotic content. An unfortunate set of mistakes, the presumed unfaithfulness of a physician's wife, whom he loved passionately, drove him to join the Legion. Friends investigated his whereabouts, cleared up the misunderstandings, and hatched a plot in association with his wife so that the doctor, who bitterly regretted his rash decision, could make possible his escape from the Legion. The lonely life of the Legionnaire far away in the desert, the toughness of his service, the distress that pursued us, was accurately portrayed. The piece ended with the doctor, after a heavy inner struggle, rejecting the suggestions of his wife and friends. The duty of the given word triumphed over love; the doctor volunteered for the frontlines in France, and as the orchestra played "La Marseillaise," the curtain slowly lowered.

The performance took place in the neighboring movie theater of the Legion. We marched four abreast into the cinema under the command of the corporal, who even on this evening reprimanded us in the usual manner. Even this entertainment didn't spare us the Legion's military coercion. This circumstance rubbed several others and me the wrong way, and we promise each other to forgo next year's celebration and not fall into formation. At least in his free time, man is entitled to escape the pressure of soldiering. No, at least in the evening we wanted to be free and not be surrounded by corporals, whose mere presence spoiled any pleasure.

The giving of Christmas presents took place at midnight. We had to stand for hours in the open un the gifts were distributed, and in the meantime the rain poured down in buckets. The day was tiring, and we were tired and sleepy for the evening: before the celebration we still had to thoroughly clean quarters. One of the fellows suggested forgoing the gifts and going to bed. But that was not possible. Celebration is celebration.

Adler, Camillo. *I Am a Refugee*. Translated by Michel F. Adler. North Charleston, SC: CreateSpace, 2012. Selection from pages 65–66, 68–70, 72–74.

14. A REPORT ON THE POITIERS CAMP BY LÉOPOLD SENGHOR {1940–1942}

Léopold Sédar Senghor (1906–2001) was a towering figure of the twentieth century. A cultural theorist, poet, politician, and first president of the independent nation of Senegal, his home, from 1960 to 1980, Senghor was also among the first to theorize the concept of Négritude promoted by Francophone thinkers and writers across Africa and its diaspora in the 1930s and beyond. Inspired by Marxist political philosophy and the Black radical tradition, Négritude intellectuals promoted the cultivation of Black consciousness, anticolonialism, and Pan-Africanism, as well as the exploration of the ideas of diasporic identity, return to home, and belonging. Like many radical thinkers of his generation, Senghor's ideas were shaped during his captivity. In the summer of 1940, Senghor was among approximately 1.8 million soldiers (including between 120,000 and 200,000 colonial soldiers, tirailleurs [literally, sharpshooters], goumiers, and otherwise) to be captured by Axis powers while serving under the French flag. Most of the tirailleurs (whom Senghor called "black watchdogs of empire") were Senegalese; others were Black Africans conscripted from across West, Central, and East Africa and erroneously called "Senegalese," or they were from French North Africa or Indochina. German representatives divided the prisoners of war by skin color, transferring white prisoners to POW camps in Germany and interning colonial soldiers in Frontstalags, camps in the Occupied Zone of France. In two such camps, Poitiers and Saint Médard, Senghor met with soldiers from North Africa and across French West Africa, inspiring his engagement with West African cultures and languages and his eventual penning of an influential collection of poems called "Hosties noires" (Black hosts). He also wrote a report for the Prisoners of War Diplomatic Service in Paris, the so-called Scapini Mission, which he submitted in June 1942. The short report describes Senghor's experiences in the POW camps during his internment—the deplorable accommodations, food, and conditions—and asserts a loyalty to France, reflects on the receptivity of fellow North African POWs to Nazi propaganda, and puzzles over German culture, with which he had an early and passionate fascination that would endure through his life. Broadly framed, Senghor's words allow us to situate the history of occupation, internment, and racism in Second World War–era North Africa in the context of a longer history of modern colonialism, racism, and violence that was the precondition of the war.

October 1940—February 1942

We arrived in Poitiers around October 10. The first months were difficult. The barracks were not yet assembled, and it was cold. Furthermore, it's a regimen of rutabagas and beatings.

Leadership. Up until the month of February, the camp was controlled by Captain Hahn. He was a very tough officer (Prussian?) whom we called "Captain Achtung!" because he demanded that all commands be issued in German. He had a Senegalese soldier that "made off with" some potatoes shot and killed.

After Hahn came Lieutenant Bayle, a very classy officer who asked us to be worthy of the French Army and our French motherland.

Lodging & Clothing. We didn't move into the barracks until December. In the meantime, we were mostly housed in corrugated tin sheds, without heat of course. Some North Africans who arrived in December will still be here without heat in January.

In the barracks, we had practically as much coal as we wanted, but the barracks were poorly constructed, and didn't protect us well from the cold when the thermometer was below zero.

The area surrounding the barracks was full of sludge to the point where someone could easily sink thirty centimeters. There were neither sinks nor showers in the camp. Only the secretaries took weekly showers at the Kommandantur [German military personnel area] in the camp. The others had to wait until they were infested with lice in order to be deloused. Shower.

Under the command of Lieutenant Bayle, the camp was transformed. When he arrived, he declared that "this pigsty is not befitting the French Army." He ordered the construction of showers, washrooms with running water, stone walkways between the barracks, a sports field, etc. . . . Moreover, soldiers could direct complaints to him that the Arab commander of the camp upheld.

In general, we are well dressed enough. However the constant shortage of gloves and socks should be noted, as many *tirailleurs* fell ill (from frozen feet and frostbite). The Red Cross sent everything they could, but they chose to give us old gear. Where did the rest of it go? . . .

Nutrition. During the first few months, until around February, the food left much to be desired in both quantity and quality. We either had

IMAGE 5. In the course of colonial, First World War, and Second World War military campaigns, the French military relied on forcibly recruited indigenous Moroccan infantry (*goumiers*), indigenous tribal Moroccan and Algerian cavalry regiments (*spahis*), and Black colonial soldiers from Senegal, French Guinea, Ivory Coast, Dahomey, Senegambia, Niger, Upper Volta (Burkina Faso), and Mauritania (Senegalese *tirailleurs*), as well as light infantry units of Moroccan, Algerian, and Tunisian soldiers (also called *tirailleurs*). Whether at the hands of the French military that conscripted them or the German forces who battled them and held them as prisoners of war (as was the fate of the men pictured here), the so-called colonial troops were subject to racist and cruel treatment. "Nordafrika, Tunesien.-Kriegsgefangene, französische Kolonial truppen / Tunesier, Wachsoldaten; KBK Lw 6, c. 1942–1943," Bild 101I-419-1894-38A, Das Bundesarchiv, Berlin.

rutabaga—maybe four times out of five—or rotting potatoes. Every other day, we had only so-called tea or coffee with a tiny, scientifically calculated ration of shortening or jam.

Another development under Bayle—we have a larger variety of vegetables of better quality.

Packages from organizations arrive regularly. Truthfully, during the summer of 1941, we ate pretty well for prisoners, and the Senegalese *tirailleurs* in the German Kommandos ate even better. It is true that they [the *tirailleurs*] ate at the farmer's table, and that practically all of them had a female sponsor [*une marraine*] who spoiled them as much as possible. French women, with their selfless generosity and their courage, were the best propagandists in France.

Letters & Parcels. Services are well organized in Poitiers. Practically anyone can write whenever they want and receive as many packages as desired. A letter from Paris takes two or three days [to arrive], a package takes eight; it is rare for letters and packages to get lost.

Relations between Prisoners. There is close solidarity among the men from different colonies: Caribbean, Malagasy, Indo-Chinese and Senegalese. Only the Arabs sow seeds of discord (aside from the Moroccans). They search to secure the best positions (secretary, cook, house worker, etc. . . .). For this reason, they look down upon the others—the Black intellectuals in particular—portraying them [the Black intellectuals] as Francophiles and Germanophobes (see "Propaganda" below). They have even gone so far as to start an underhanded war with one another: Tunisians against Algerians and vice versa. Later on in Bordeaux, we would see a picturesque fight between the Tunisian Adjoint Officer and the Algerian Adjoint Officer, who argued over the position of camp leader.

Evasions. There were approximately five hundred escapes from Poitiers in one year, mainly North Africans. They are the getaway kings, and we can't help but admire them for it. Sometimes twenty or thirty of them take off from the camp at once, at night or during an errand. They are rarely caught (one out of twenty perhaps). Punishment: one month in prison.

Propaganda. German propaganda was well organized at Poitiers, depending on [what came from the] Office of the "Gestapo" to the commander. The propaganda had very little effect on the Senegalese and Caribbean prisoners. For that matter, in the mornings it was uniquely directed towards the Arabs: Arabic newspapers published by the Germans, favors granted to those of Muslim faith, spies, etc. . . . The Arab "intellectuals," by that I mean those who had some form of education, were the best German agents. They preached to their compatriots and denigrated France in front of the Germans (by comparison, Black intellectuals, specifically those from the Caribbean, were the most resistant [to such propaganda]). When volunteers were needed to deploy to Russia, only the Arabs came forward, most of them well-educated men (by the way, they weren't even sent).

The spies were Arabs, but never Moroccans. The only exception was a Frenchman named Dunonceau. The most dangerous one in the group was Mustapha Messaoudene, a Tunisian. An Arab confirmed to me that it was this same Mustapha Messaoudene who snitched on the Ebone Brothers for being anti-German, simply because they were French.

The Arab noncommissioned officers hit their men, setting a bad example, which the soldiers and German petty officers followed, all the way up to Bayle. This [treatment] caused a great deal of friction between the Arabs and the Senegalese. Naturally this tension served as a pretext [for the Arabs] to accuse Blacks of rebelling against German authority. This is how a Senegalese man who had gotten into a fight with an Arab Sargent and disobeyed a German's orders came to be severely injured from a bullet wound.

I conclude the Propaganda chapter with a particularly interesting fact: I overheard someone say to a prisoner that some Senegalese men were used in a propaganda film on the French campaign. They were required to throw down their weapons, put up their hands and cry out "Comrade" at the arrival of German tanks.

Patients & Doctors. The French doctors' dedication was admirable. I must mention specifically Doctor Cazbilie (Captain), who not only cared for the prisoners [physically] but also supported them psychologically. Their actions were not limited to care and comfort: the doctors tended to so many sick patients that they put their own health at risk.

One exception, however: Captain Dardy (?) who was [stationed] at the infirmary from October-May. He was tough on the prisoners, and eagerly sent a report to the Germans "concerning all the intellectuals of color who wanted to be declared unfit for service."

Bordeaux

We reached Bordeaux—or rather, Saint Médard, on November 5, 1941. We had complained about the Poitiers camp—but in Bordeaux we bemoaned Poitiers as a lost paradise.

Leadership. During my stay at the As Camp in Saint Médard, we had two German lieutenants as camp commanders one right after the other. We barely saw them. Actually, the boss of the camp was a German petty officer. The prisoners had nicknamed him "Misérable," and Misérable lived up to his name.

A German petty officer had encouraged a Senegalese man to report [Misérable], so the Kommandantur was probably unaware of his scheming. Misérable was just as tough as he was corruptible, as we will see later.

Lodging & Clothing. The barracks were better constructed [in Bordeaux] than in Poitiers, and the climate was more agreeable. However, winter's rigors never let up, and firewood was scantily distributed. Only the "barracks" [of the prisoners] who worked in the forest were sufficiently heated. *People froze at the hospital.*

Showering was out of the question and lice proliferated, as there wasn't even an attempt at delousing.

In Poitiers, we typically wore used clothing. Here [in Bordeaux], it was a privilege to get "new clothes" and receive hand-me-downs. You had to be a secretary, police officer, chore-master, etc.! . . . I forgot about the liberated prisoners: they were dressed in new clothes to the extent possible, but they had to leave behind their gloves and all their extra items—what they had on was not taken into account—"for their remaining fellow prisoners." So many prisoners were without gloves and socks. Even I had to wait until January to receive gloves that were sent to me in a care package.

Nutrition. The food was totally inadequate and hardly varied. We had one loaf of bread for five, sometimes for six [people]. In general, we had soup in the morning and in the evening, but what soup! A handful of rice in a somewhat brownish and salty liquid. The proportions were the same as they were in Poitiers. For example, instead of a small bar of chocolate, we received three bars [at a time] whenever we received any. This was because the provisions from the Red Cross, which were considered a supplemental luxury in Poitiers, appeared to be viewed as essential in Bordeaux.

The situation in the hospital wasn't much better. We had, apart from the loaf of bread for five people, one quart—and not a bit more—of rice and vegetables for lunch and dinner, with a tiny morsel of meat the size of your thumb for lunch. To be fair, a mandarin or an orange was thrown in from time to time. By contrast, packages, at least in my personal experience, didn't reach the hospital. I lost two or three because of this.

In the Kommandos, it was worse than at As camp. The men worked from 8:30 to 15:00 and they couldn't eat before 16:00. To tide them over, they received one hundred grams of bread at noon. Their sole job was chopping wood, and there was no question of eating at a communal table in the countryside as in Poitiers.

Besides, the civilians of Gironde [region in southwestern France] generally expressed a perfect indifference [to our presence]. Several civilians complained to me about restrictions and told me that the prisoners weren't the worst off.

Letters & Parcels. A letter from Paris would take *a month and a half to two months* [to arrive]. A package would take about the same time, and often the packages wouldn't arrive at all. It's true that they often got lost. Unclaimed packages were sent to the German Office in the camp with directions to distribute them to the most underprivileged prisoners. "Misérable" gave the Kommandantur a list of prisoners that were awarded the "unclaimed packages." In reality, he would open the packages, take everything of interest to him: cigarettes, chocolate, etc., and send what was left to the kitchen.

When the packages belonged to freed prisoners, they were also be distributed to those remaining in the camp. In this case, the Arab commander would receive them. When I was there, camp commander Bel Aïd pulled a "Misérable," and kept part of the packages' contents [for himself].

Naturally, letters and packages took much more time to reach the Kommandos.

Relations between Prisoners. The situation here was the opposite of that in Poitiers, where the prisoners' solidarity was put to skillful use for propaganda purposes: here the Arabs suffered, and they were a little less selfish. The exception proved the rule, and the camp commander Bel Aïd was a notable exception: he didn't suffer. He had a cook and you'd better believe that his meals weren't the same as the prisoners' [meals], considering he often invited "Misérable." These two partners in crime were thick as thieves.

Before the arrival of the men from Poitiers, there were only two Senegalese-Caribbean barracks. The few "intellectuals" and strong-minded prisoners had been exiled to the Kommandos, and Bel Aïd easily managed the two subdued barracks. The "Poitevins" [men from Poitiers] were another story—we protested the favors granted to the "little buddies" and from that moment on Bel Aïd accused the Blacks [*les Noirs*] of insubordination—high treason in the camp! Admittedly, these men were exasperated, and were ready to react violently to Bel Aïd and the Arab policemen. My suggestions to act with good sense had trouble getting through [to people].

But the commander of the camp also had a bone to pick with the Arabs. Several of them claimed that they had not been liberated on 18 December because they didn't pay off Bel Aïd. Moreover, the French Algerians in the camp owed their liberation entirely to the rivalry that existed between Bel Aïd and the Tunisian staff sargent, Ousseini, because they were hated equally by both.

In any case, the liberated prisoners complained to the Red Cross, whereupon the Kommandantur raided Bel Aïd's residence, where it appears that they discovered supplies and several thousand francs. I was unable to find out the aftermath of this story, because they took advantage of the first opportunity to send me to the Kommandos alongside several other Senegalese and Caribbean people: we were neither sufficiently submissive nor sufficiently blind.

Evasion. Hardly any evasions in Gironde. The camps were surrounded by an intricate barbed wire system, there were German guard posts just about everywhere, and the civilians couldn't have cared less. While at the Kommando, someone told me about an escaped prisoner who was turned in by a foreign woman.

Propaganda. Hardly any propaganda in Bordeaux. They favored the camp commanders and the policemen. They were a bit easier on the Muslims, and from time to time they would distribute Arab newspapers from the German propaganda service; that's about it. The former spies from Poitiers were "back to square one." Surprise: I met numerous Francophile Arabs who shared all the camp's dirty laundry.

To no one's surprise: a Senegalese man wrote to the camp commander to ensure that German and French [language] courses were offered in the Bordeaux camp like they were in Poitiers, one hand washes the other: he was told there were more pressing matters to attend to. Naturally, they stopped distributing issues of *Trait d'Union*.

In sum, the Kommandantur hardly dealt with the prisoners—either to indoctrinate them, listen to their grievances, or to harass them. Even more, the petty officers reigned over us as if they had absolute power and rushed to take advantage of the situation. There wasn't any legitimate oversight. It appears that there was no judicial officer, and a mere police officer—a prisoner just like us—could have thrown us in prison. Welcome to the reign of the arbitrary.

Conclusion: Morale. Naturally, morale varied depending on the day, the circumstances, and also race.

The Indochinese and the Malagasies appeared to react the least and had the hardest time adjusting. The Arabs and the Senegalese were the most readily cheerful. The Caribbean people were equally cheerful, but their spirits were easily shot down.

The hunger was the most demoralizing, and the Bordeaux *Frontstalag* [German prisoner-of-war camp] was the worst in that respect. Truly, the prisoners were half-starved to death. Not to mention the mess halls, which were extremely undersupplied.

Other disheartening factors: metropolitan prisoners in the *Frontstalags* and fathers of large families were liberated, but not colonial prisoners. Well, at least the non-Arab [colonial prisoners]; ten thousand Arabs were liberated in December 1941. A Senegalese prisoner then asked a doctor, "Why do you liberate the Arabs who betray you and not those who remain loyal?" His question echoed what we were all thinking.

Needless to say, the most informed and educated enlightened the others, explaining that the French government wasn't free to do everything it wanted to do. This was why, despite everything, nearly all of them remained loyal to France and attributed France's defeat to its smaller number [of troops] and inferior weaponry.

Among the Arabs, the majority of the Moroccans remained loyal. The Algerians and Tunisians seemed to me far less steadfast and more pervious to propaganda. The German influence clearly made an impression on them, especially with their keen practical nature; they turned to the side with the most power, ready to betray at the first opportunity. Two significant events that happened in Poitiers: (1) a spy took advantage of being on leave so that he could escape. (2) A secretary who gave his word to not escape, disappeared at the first opportunity.

In sum, France could divert attention from its defeat and captivity if it knew how to produce its own propaganda geared [it] toward liberated prisoners. In the camps, rumor had it that Vichy maintained a "reactionary" policy in the colonies. All throughout these same camps, Pétain was the symbol of France, and as such, his portrait was highly revered.

Supplementary Notes. In Bordeaux, everyone who didn't work must do exercises during work hours, even during the winter, or if they were nonhospitalized patients in the infirmary. This measure was all the more unpopular given that those who did not work were kept significantly less nourished and less warm.

In Poitiers prisoners were paid two or four francs a day; in Bordeaux, eight. In Poitiers the prisoners were only able to access a small part of their monthly salary: the rest had to be mailed to their parents.

I remember that in Bordeaux a Tunisian prisoner, who was also the head of the Secretaries' Office, was apprehended for having stolen several thousand francs from money orders that prisoners sent back home to their families. In this particular case, he stole specifically from the Senegalese.

Report by Léopold Sédar Senghor, Poitiers, October 1940–February 1942, enclosed within note by Docteur Bonnaud, 27 July 1942, F/9/2345, Inspection des camps: Dossier général, 1941: Itinéraire des inspections, correspondance concernant les inspections en France, schéma de visite, etc., Affaires militaires, prisonniers de guerre, volume 1 (1940–1945), Archives Nationales, Pierrefitte-sur-Seine, France. Translated from French by Amber Sackett, with help from Rebecca Glasberg.

15. SENEGALESE PRISONERS OF WAR PROTEST THE RELEASE OF WHITE FRENCH SOLDIERS FROM A *FRONTSTALAG* INTERNMENT CAMP [1941]

In the aftermath of the French capitulation to Germany in June 1940, the German military took more than 1.8 million soldiers fighting under the French flag captive as prisoners of war, including between 120,000 and 200,000 men conscripted by France from its colonial territories in North, West, and Central Africa, as well as soldiers from Indochina. The German military divided prisoners according to racist typologies—sending white prisoners to POW camps in Germany and interning soldiers from France's colonies in Frontstalags, *internment camps in the Occupied Zone of France. While all these French POWs found themselves vulnerable to harsh treatment at the hands of German captors, colonial soldiers were at a particular disadvantage. Some French African POWs were chosen for medical experiments by the German military. Others were subjected to racist, dehumanizing anthropological analysis, and mortality rates of Black African POWs were higher than those of the general POW population. In the following letter, a collection of Senegalese men who served the French army and were subsequently interned as German POWs, complain that the treatment of colonial soldiers was blatantly stratified by race—under POW internment as under the French flag. They note that white French soldiers were released from the* Frontstalags *while Black soldiers remained interned, and they argue that all POWs deserve equal treatment: "We are all prisoners." Among the signers of this letter to the French delegate in charge of monitoring the camps is Léopold Sédar Senghor (1906–2001), who later emerged as an influential poet, cultural theorist, and politician, eventually serving as the first president of independent Senegal.*

Prisoners [of War] Camp, May 27, 1941
From all North African and French West African prisoners

To Mr. Seapini, Prisoners of War delegate

Sir—We have the honor of requesting that your great benevolence provide us this Service and grant us the rights that you secured for certain categories of Metropolitan Soldiers: [g]iven the Situation, we address to you the following words.

When war was declared, our commanders called on us, like all Europeans[.] We can tell you that the colonial [soldier]s fought better than all the European soldiers. [Y]ou should know, while we were in Belgium, in the North[,] and at the Somme, these colonial [soldier]s found themselves on the front lines; nearly all the metropolitan French soldiers were stationed at the Maginot Line [France's border in the 1930s with Italy, Switzerland, Germany, and Luxembourg]. [N]ow that there is a provision to be rendered for all of the prisoners of war; meaning that some can be liberated, we see that all of the favors are granted to European solders and none to colonial soldiers.

I.—They [the European soldiers] had leave for four weeks in July 1940, and then all the farmers were liberated, given leave—afterward it was the fathers of eleven children, and the oldest sons of four children, and before long all the veterans of the 1914–1918 war.

But we lowly colonial soldiers, not one of has yet been granted leave, nor liberated, and we see that no one is taking care of us! We are still prisoners, However, Mr. Seapini, we firmly believe that we must be liberated first since we are the ones that that fought the most, and we were the most afflicted.

Back to the European prisoners, they receive news from their parents, their families, packages and event visits from their parents. Here we are going on twelve months of captivity—not a single bit of news, not a single package. What misery and bad blood. We see that we are forgotten, [that's] one thing that we can say: that we are here because of our commander's negligence: because they sold us and betrayed us: finally, Mr. Seapini, do not say that it's not possible to send us on leave. Frankly speaking, we know that France currently possess two zones, and that we can easily be sent to the Non-Occupied Zone. That [would be] to grant us freedom.

After all these explanations, Sir, we believe that you are able to discuss our situation with the German authorities, and don't tell us that there isn't a path to bring us back to our homes, or that [the lack of such a path] is the reason why we are forced to remain in captivity.

II.—All the health workers [were] sent back, even the young ones of maybe twenty-two, twenty-three years old, and we, the lowly colonial solders from the class of 1929–1931 and 1932, not one of us has budged. Why these partial measures? Is it because we are not like all the other European prisoners? We can assure you that after the war, we won't be fools anymore. We will be capable of defending ourselves against your politics and we will exercise all of our rights.

If we may, France needs her colonial soldiers only in dangerous situations or as boots on the ground in deadly military operations.

We look forward to your timely response.

Sincerely, all the colonial prisoners of war, somewhere in France

Prisonniers indigènes, demandes de libération adressées à l'Ambassadeur Scapini, demandes de paiement de l'allocation militaire (liasse gardée à titre de spécimen), F/9/2582, Affaires militaires, prisonniers de guerre, volume 1 (1940–1945), Archives Nationales, Pierrefitte-sur-Seine, France. Translated from French by Amber Sackett.

16. FAMINE IN THE ANTI-ATLAS MOUNTAINS {c. 1940s}

During the Second World War, at least sixty million people died of starvation, malnutrition, and associated diseases such as tuberculosis—a number larger than that associated with military deaths. As it embarked on genocide, the Third Reich implemented policies of exploitation in the territories it occupied, causing local shortages of housing, heating, electricity, and medical supplies across the regions under its control. The fascist Italian and Vichy French authorities echoed these policies, intensively plundering food from places such as Greece and North Africa, which caused widespread starvation and malnutrition. The result was death by famine and related diseases for millions of people living under colonial rule across Europe and from North Africa to Vietnam. Born in the late 1920s, Al-ḥusin Al-gedari is a native of Lamḥamid, a village in Morocco's Anti-Atlas Mountains. In this oral history collected by Abderrahman Aouad and conducted with Al-gedari in 2019, we read of the terrible famine that took root in the region in the course of the war, as the occupying authorities commandeered food supplies, exacerbating the effects of a dreadful drought. As Al-gedari relates, Muslim locals understood the famine to be part of a wartime chain reaction, with Germany's theft of France's foodstuffs resulting in the Vichy regime's plundering of the food supply in North Africa. In Al-gedari's telling, he lays bare the horrific day-to-day experience of state-sanctioned famine.

The year of hunger, otherwise known as the year of rations, killed so many people and destroyed so many communities in our region. A combination of war, typhus, drought, and famine was like a wildfire that struck the southern hinterlands. Palm trees did not yield that many dates ... and the few that did grow were confiscated by tribal lords and distributed between the pasha of Marrakesh El Glaoui and the French colonial administrators. News circulated that Hitler stole the food of France to feed the German population, forcing France to take native North Africa's food shares.... Each family was given a ration of food including just a few grams of wheat and a small portion of sugar and cooking oil.... Not all family were benefactors [even] of this.... Rural areas like ours were not even on the list [for distribution].... Families trekked the mountains of Bani looking for hedgehogs, *mastigure* [spiny-tailed lizards], other lizards, and wild desert animals. I remember people were so hungry that they had to eat their own donkeys and [their] source of farming.

IMAGE 6. During the Second World War, as occupying authorities commandeered food supplies from across North Africa, a terrible famine took place in the region, especially in rural locations. Al-ḥusin Al-gedari, pictured here, a native of Lamḥamid, a village in Morocco's Anti-Atlas Mountains, speaks in this volume of the catastrophic effects of state-sanctioned deprivation, including its impact on the natural landscape, local economy, and health, moral, and religious practices of everyday North Africans. Aomar Boum, photograph of Al-ḥusin Al-gedari, 2021. Courtesy of Aomar Boum.

We could not follow Islamic rules anymore, and many were forced to eat dogs and cats to survive. . . . As the food shortage grew, people started looking for edible grass, especially as the slow supply of American wheat did little to stop hunger. As if that were not enough, typhus struck communities, killing hundreds of families. . . . Clothes were rare. People walked barefoot. Stories circulated that people waited for families to bury their dead and then dug up their tombs to take out the shrouds and use them to cover themselves. Others turned burlap barley bags into garments. . . . The mining companies continued to enlist hungry and weak workers from the village in its mines in the Anti-Atlas. Many local villagers were forced to work in the cobalt mine of Bou Azzer, which was located a few miles from Foum Zguid. Others were enlisted to clear roads between Ouarzazate and Marrakesh.

Interview in Moroccan Arabic with Al-ḥusin Al-Geddari by Abderrahman Aouad, on behalf of Aomar Boum, October 18, 2019, Lamḥamid, Foum Zguid, Morocco.

PART II
Race Laws, Internment, and Spoliation, 1940–1943

17. A FRENCH COMMUNIST'S ARDUOUS DEPORTATION TO NORTH AFRICA {1940–1945}

Paul d'Hérama (the nom de plume of Paul Caillaud) was a French communist, likely of Christian background. Caillaud had spent more than two decades living in Algeria earlier in his life, but the outset of the Second World War found him living and working as a teacher in Surgères, France, where he was an active antifascist and antiwar activist. Caillaud's persecution by the Vichy regime was endless. He was initially interned in a series of prisons in France, then ferried to North Africa, where he worked as a forced laborer for five years in Djelfa, a Vichy prison camp in the Algerian Sahara. Later in this book we read of Caillaud's time in Djelfa, where he was compelled to engage in backbreaking labor on the Trans-Saharan Railway. Here, we encounter an earlier chapter of Caillaud's wartime peregrinations—the disorienting train ride across France; the claustrophobic, interminable journey across the Mediterranean in the waterlogged hull of a ship; the jam-packed train lurching across North Africa, headed toward destinations undisclosed by the prisoners' guards. For all the descriptions of train journeys across Europe that have been offered by survivors of the Nazi concentration and death camps, Caillaud's attention to his journey to Djelfa is unique among memoirs and testimony by survivors of the Vichy, Nazi, and Italian fascist camps of North Africa.

I. The Passengers of the Djebel-Nador

The train raced by, blazing by stations...

From Montauban, we continued to Toulouse, to Carcassonne.

Now, the hypotheses were becoming limited. There were still two plausible ones: either a camp in the Eastern Pyrenees, or North Africa.

In our train cars, strictly watched by mobile guards, we ate our cold meals and smoked. During this leg of the journey, conversations spring up with certain guards. We even share tobacco. None of them know where the journey will end.

I daydreamed... thinking of the good friends that I have just left saddened me. But I suffered above all for my wife. Yet another sorrow she has experienced!

Narbonne... the train, which had progressed at a record-speed worthy of the great express trains, was shunted onto the Port-Vendres line. There is no longer any doubt: it's either the sandy camps of the Roussillon or embarkation.

Night came. Weariness, too. We had been traveling since the morning. The panorama of landscapes had kept everyone occupied. At this time, we allow ourselves give in to sleep.

Despite having taken this line so many times, I dreamed of the past while watching the stars shimmer on the lagoons, from which night birds flew up, frightened by the train. From time to time, the brown silhouettes of fishermen stood out from the dark iridescence of the water while the sea breeze grew stronger.

"Rivesaltes!"

This sudden cry, let out by our comrade, made everyone look up. The big camp, with its multiple lights, is the focal point of everyone's gaze. The train station clock says midnight. And here is the train, which stops exactly across from the camp.

"We're there! This is where we're going!" people cry out, starting to prepare their packages, while the mobile guards put their hands on their gear.

"Nobody move!" proclaims a lieutenant. "Wait for orders."

Only a few officers get off; they come back almost right away.

"Each group must designate a team to get provisions: one cold meal, some bread, a small carafe of wine per person."

"Good!" said Maurice. "They don't want to move us and all our stuff at night. This will make for a lovely bacchanalia! So, we'll eat here, and, at dawn, they will do us the honor of providing housing."

This explanation was acceptable.

After the designated prisoners returned loaded with provisions, we began to eat ... and wait. But for the most part, the only thing that came was sleep.

At two o'clock, the train resumed its journey, waking the sleepers, deceiving everyone.

"North Africa! It's a sure bet, now!" I whispered in Marcel's ear.

Three o'clock ... The train blazes through the Port-Vendres station and goes down to the docks. Despite the darkness, I easily recognize the small port and its pond.

The train stops.

"Everyone must get ready, but no one moves!" yell the mobile unit officers [*les gradés des gardes mobiles*].

After several moments the order comes to get off.

Immediately after stepping on the footboard, and after having slipped between two dark, tunnel-like walls, I suddenly find myself on a dirty, damp, wooden floor, where a sui generis smell tells me that I am in the belly of a ship.

"Caught in a mousetrap!" Maurice says to me. "These bastards pushed us in through the wings!"

Indeed, an entirely enclosed hallway had been constructed across from the footbridge. Each train car took its turn stopping there, and the exiting passengers could do nothing other than sink into the treacherous tunnel and end up on the lower deck.

The government did not dare undertake a diurnal embarkation. And they were secretly abducting deportees.

Maybe they also feared the reactions of the train station and port workers? And maybe even an attempt at revolt by the political prisoners?

The length of the railway journey, the beards of the mobile guards; guys skillfully threw bits of ticket onto the tracks: facts informed people of what was happening. The population of the Midi was surely aware of the events.

Pulled apart by so many emotions over the past twenty-four hours, we were now piled up in the bottom of a cargo ship!

"Deportees! They've made us deportees!"

But, in this narrow and revolting hold—where the cow dung from the previous journey remained, over which they had hastily spread a bit of lime—it was currently a question, for us 275 exiles, of making ourselves a bit of room, of finding a corner to fit our bodies ... and our packages.

Then came the pressing desire to alert our dear, tearful families. An officer indicated that we could give him a letter for them. Nobody refrained from doing so.

The sea was beautiful ...

Many among us had never sailed before. It would have interested them to see the sea, the coasts. But we remained prisoners in the hold. A steep ladder reached up to the deck, with two guards stationed below and two above. Going up there led to the nauseatingly uncomfortable makeshift latrines, which had been constructed outside on the deck of the ship's starboard side.

However, getting a bit of breathable air on this deck was such a temptation when we had spent hours in the foul-smelling atmosphere down below!

At mealtimes, seamen cooks would bring dishes to this ladder, from which the meager fare was distributed among the groups.

The first moments had gripped these men, despite their strong characters. "Deportees! We are deportees!" they repeated to themselves. And sensing their families' hopelessness, they became even more disheartened.

But they regained their energy quickly ... Above the lower deck, they had opened the hatches for ventilation, and sailors, noncommissioned officers, and officers would come and lean on their elbows on the coaming.

The deportees did not want to make a spectacle of their sadness. After the morning meal, an improvised concert spontaneously unfolded. Beforehand, a resounding "Marseillaise" was launched by all, bare headed, eyes lifted towards the square of sky visible through the hatch! Then, singers, stand-up comedians, choristers, everyone took a turn, with a spirit that those in Vichy could never have imagined.

We could feel the emotion that filled the spectators up on the deck as they noticed the admirable moral of these exiles.

In the evening, after the end of the second meal, the concert began again, automatically ... I found this display of never-ending proletarian courage comforting during the hard times.

Thus traveled, from March 1 at 6:00 a.m. to March 2 at 10:30 a.m., the old dual-purpose freighter *Le Djebel-Nador*, bringing with it as livestock an unusual cargo.

II. From Alger to Djelfa

White Alger was shining brightly under a fertile sun when the dilapidated boat entered its port.

The deportees hurried to the latrines in order to have a pretext for approaching the deck, casting a furtive glance at the view that they had so desired to take in!

A clean, azure sky welcomed them. But, apart the ship's masts and some passing seagulls, only this sky was visible to them from the bottom of their moving prison. Nevertheless, this symbolic and promising zenith softened the sorrows of these men, snatched from their loved ones, currently so far behind them!

As soon as the ship entered into the port, they had started loading their bags onto their shoulders.

"Not so fast, comrades," I said to them. "There will be quite some time before the end of operations."

At noon, we were still cooped up in our stifling prison. What were they waiting for before letting us regain dry land? We were excited to see something other than the sheet-metal plates of our cage!

An officer of the mobile guard came to announce that debarkation was delayed due to lack of accurate orders, and that a meal would be served to us.

"What do they want to keep from us?" asked Marcel.

"Dang! . . . This here is the stopover before Guyana!" responded Hucheur.

"Bah!" said another. "Things are without a doubt simpler than that. In their fury to exile us, they didn't fully think things through. I bet they don't even know where to house us!"

The afternoon was long, very long . . . and really nerve-racking, since there was no logical explanation to give about this delay that was keeping 275 men in a fetid cargo hold!

It was only at 7 p.m. that we descended the gangway.

As during embarkation, big dividing walls made of board cladding once again barricaded the quay. And from behind the scenes, we came out into a vast goods shed, where customs officers were waiting to search us.

No firearms? No razors? No knives?

Finally, at 7 p.m., at dusk, they loaded us into cattle cars, behind the goods shed.

Of Alger and her inhabitants, we had seen absolutely nothing. At present, they were going to make us travel overnight.

Twenty-two men per car, plus two guards. No room to lie down or even sit. After having crammed us one against the other, with our packages and suitcases, we receive a cold meal and we settle in to eat . . . then, they give us some bedding straw, that we can only move on top of our blankets, our sparse equipment, our bread and our open cans of sardines, in an indescribable disorder!

No light. The danger of striking a simple match is too high.

Then, the ultimate! They bring us a big latrine bucket, in the middle of the car . . . (Hygiene! Comfort! Decency!)

Then, to round out so many aggravations, train agents come to seal the cars! Treated like convicts! Treated like cattle! Treated like men condemned to die, because if a fire breaks out in a car, we will all roast!

We struggle, yell, protest. The guards rebel just as vehemently. Useless . . . Thusly locked up, we try to sustain ourselves by touch with the bread and cans of sardines that we locate by rummaging around under the straw, thanks to the flashlight of a guard, which he shines every now and again.

It is 8 p.m. and we are still in the same place. Impossible to smoke. Especially since, hunched in unimaginable postures, the majority fall asleep, broken by the fatigue and events of these three days.

Only at midnight do the train cars set off.

Where are we going? Those who are not asleep ask themselves, tortured by cramps. But seeing nothing, hearing nothing apart from the clamor of train cars jolting about on rails, gives no indication.

Two hours. Stop. Right away, employees pass by, unseal the cars and open them.

"Everybody off! Everyone and all equipment on the ground!"

Lovely commotion, in the straw and without light! We must get ourselves out of there with all our gear, however. Several of the train station's pale lamps precariously assist us.

I see that we are in Blida.

"Friends," I say, "if we change trains here, it's because we are going to the Algerian south. Boghari? Djelfa? Laghouat? In any event, I find myself in known territory."

Indeed, we climb into new cattle cars, on a narrower track. These train cars are less wide. But they must still receive their twenty-two deportees, plus the two guards... plus the latrine bucket! It's unbearable!

Cars sealed once again, despite the furious protests. Departure.

6 a.m. They have just blown a fuse. The doors are pushed on their runners. *Oof!* The two guards sit in the opening, legs hanging, carabiners posed on the floorboards.

We can read "Medea" on a sign. I was not mistaken.

The train gets going again. At present, finally breathing, comrades are gathered at the door, to the back of the guards, or at the open shutters, all busy taking in the scenery.

Ben-Chicao... Berrouaghia... The railway runs the length of the Ouarsenis mountain range to the west. Scenic spots appear at every moment, especially to the east, on the mountains of the Titteri, and grandiose landscapes unfold in front of the travelers' amazed eyes.

Boghari, fifteen-minute stopover. Everyone shakes himself off. The disgusting latrine buckets will not be used.

Facing us, about ten kilometers away, is the highly perched fort of Boghar.

Several Arabs have approached us, in spite of the guards and the instructions. An extremely curious attraction for the deportees! A lot of these natives are selling hard-boiled eggs. What a godsend! In the blink of an eye, all the eggs are gone.

Remembering a bit of Arabic vocabulary, I strike up a bit of a conversation.

"Ouaïn touasal tarik el Hadid?" (Where does this railway lead?)

"To Djelfa."

But the train starts up again.

The landscape is no longer the same. We approach the high plains, and for five hours, it is a monotony of flat spaces with stunted vegetation and scattered mastic trees, asphodels, Ampelodesmos, esparto grass, and lavender. Here and there, there are boulders, some corners of land that have been worked by hand or swing plow, and in which meager crops of barley grow. On the horizon, bleak lines, sometimes blocked by the far-off bluish mountain chains of the Aures, south of Constantine.

After numerous stations, we see Sidi Attaïa and the famous, underexploited Salt Rock.

And finally, thirty kilometers later, like a half-civil, half-military city, Djelfa appears between its budding palm grove, its plane trees, and its fortified enclosure.

This time, we know the end of our odyssey: the railway line terminates here....

Accompanied by a guard, we walked quickly to warm ourselves, as all night, an unrelenting glacial wind had been blowing. On route, we were accosted by small native beignet merchants. What a godsend! But the circle of merchants [*deïra*] tried to interfere:

"Là! Là! Ma kaïn che acheter galettes! Diffendi! . . . (No! No! There is nothing to buy! That's it!)."

"Estennâ chouäi. Ranâ djianine! . . . (Wait a little bit! We are hungry!)," I responded, and I took twelve beignets that I divided into fourths, distributing it among the circle.

So, he turned a blind eye to this violation of the rules and ate as eagerly as us, because, at the Caffarelli fort, the general diet of the "belt" reigned supreme.

Each day went like this, from that moment on. And, whether due to tolerance or ignorance of the event, the small vendors were able to help the starving men not to die from hunger, by bringing hundreds of beignets to the fort and the Marabouts camp....

On April 16, the mobile guards finally arrived at the fort. No more doubt! We were going to change camps! We were going to leave Djelfa! It was the first time that the arrival of the "Gallows Swallows," as Maurice, the old sailor called them, made the internees joyful.

The Cow [the nickname given to a Djelfa camp commander], feeling that his prey was escaping him, took advantage of the situation to give only one hundred grams of bread per person on April 17. And . . . no meat!

The embarkation took place on April 18.

During the afternoon of the seventeenth, those who were coming from Bossuet—and whom we were going to replace—got off at the Djelfa train station. What a police presence to make them cross the central path and house them temporarily in the extra tents erected at the other end of the camp! Tents separated from the deportee camp itself by barbed wire, even!

Under threat of the most severe punishment, a total ban on speaking any word whatsoever to the newcomers was instituted! In the evening, however, contacts were established. And the entire French camp found out that the unfortunate replacements were Republican militiamen from Spain, escapees from Franco!

On the eighteenth came the great move: transportation by cart to the train station, with big individual packages; transfer of mats, blankets, bags, cutlery and quarter-liter bottles, etc. . . . For twenty-four hours, we had food: two hundred forty grams of bread and . . . fifty grams of meat! No wine, of course! Combined with the seventeenth, that made for a daily average of 170 grams of bread and 25 grams of meat!

At roll call, on the embankment reserved at the bottom of the Marabouts camp—where the deportees were lined up, duly supervised by the *douaïr* and the mobile guards—a torrential rain began to fall.

Each person waited in the utter silence, with all of his gear on his back and his suitcases and packages in hand.

The captain of the mobile guard took roll himself. Above his head, a guard held an umbrella lent by a detainee, in order to protect the alphabetical lists.

We had to loudly yell out "Present!" and leave quickly to join up with the detachment that was being immediately formed a bit further away, subject to the most vivid and colorful insults.

"Isidore!"

This comrade had a large esparto grass hat on his head, which he had made himself. Without a doubt, the size of this strange headdress did not please these gentlemen, and the captain had the "hat" thrown in the mud. Then, faced with the natural bad mood of the interested party, he gave him eight days in prison!

As my greatcoat dripped on the bottom of my pants, the water soaking into my shoes, I had nothing in mind but the Oranian sky . . . Under this glacial downpour, I reveled in the hope that this departure to Oran generated within me. Destiny was bringing me back to the country that I had left twelve years prior, after having lived there for twenty-three years.

An hour and a half of roll call! With water running streaming down from head to feet!

And under this diluvian downpour, following a waterlogged path of thick, yellowish silt, we proceeded to make our way to the train station. Then it was embarkation in passenger cars—what a pleasant surprise! Then the guard officer's instructions, always the same, which the lieutenant summed up in this terse slogan: "Shoot!"

The deportees, quite familiar with this slogan, only half-listened . . . In this faraway land, why would they have tried to escape?

d'Hérama, Paul [penname of Paul Caillaud]. *Tournant dangereux: Mémoires d'un déporté politique en Afrique du Nord (1940–1945)*. La Rochelle, France: Imprimerie Jean Foucher & Cie, 1957. Selection from pages 81–92, 111, 119–21, 139–41, 150–53. Translated from French by Rebecca Glasberg.

18. THE MELLAH, REVIVED—ANTI-JEWISH RESIDENTIAL LAWS IN VICHY MOROCCO [1941]

In pre–Second World War Morocco and Tunisia, Jews (like their Muslim neighbors) were colonial subjects rather than citizens—but their legal and social rights were generally protected under the Muslim legal principle of dhimma *(covenant of protection). For the most part, Jews were perceived as "native" by most Muslims, but many Jews nonetheless lived in separate neighborhoods (known in Morocco as* mellāḥ *and Tunisia as* ḥāra*) and followed a traditional way of life influenced by rabbinical authority. At the same time, North African Jews' exposure to French, Spanish, and Italian cultures had, since at least the nineteenth century, prompted waves of embourgeoisement, particularly among those from more privileged backgrounds. Evidence of this transformation became clear demographically in the late nineteenth and early twentieth centuries, as elite Jews moved out of traditionally Jewish districts and into new, middle-class neighborhoods. These processes were forcibly reversed during the Second World War, due to the implementation of Vichy anti-Jewish legislation beginning in the autumn of 1940. Even though neither Morocco nor Algeria fell under direct German control during the war, Vichy authorities looked the other way as anti-Semitic settlers attacked Jews (and sometimes native Muslims) and targeted their property and businesses for spoliation. North African Jews who fell under Vichy rule, like the Jews of France, were barred from most sectors of the economy and professional sector, with quotas (*numerus clausus*) limiting the number of Jews who could operate as teachers, lawyers, doctors, journalists, students in non-Jewish schools and universities, and so on. Jewish property was subsequently "Aryanized"—that is, stolen—under Vichy decree, and Jews in Moroccan cities forced to move from outlying neighborhoods into the mellah. Using coded language, this source, a letter from the American consul general in Casablanca to the chargé d'affaires for the American legation in Tangier, documents the unfolding of these events in Morocco and their implications for the local economy and Jewish, Muslim, and Christian relations.*

December 13, 1941

Sir:

With reference to previous correspondence between the Legation and this Consulate with regard to the application of anti-Jewish laws in French Morocco, and with special reference to the Legation's dispatch 437 of November 10, 1941, I beg to report certain new developments which have been occurring with regards to the Jewish question in the French Zone as follows.

Since the publication of the Dahir of August 5, 1941, concerning the status of the Moroccan Jews, the following Dahirs or Viziriel [sic] Decrees have been issued: (1) The Dahir of August 19, 1941 (Bulletin Officiel No. 1504), prohibiting Moroccan Jews from living in the European municipal quarters of the city, (2) the Viziriel Decree of September 16, 1941, relating to prohibited occupations, (3) a Viziriel Decree of August 18, 1941 (Bulletin Officiel No. 1509), regulating the exercise by Jews of the profession of lawyer.

Article 1 or [sic] the above Dahir (*of Aug. 19, 1941*) [the date is a handwritten addition] ordered all Jews who were Moroccan subjects, occupying under any title whatsoever dwelling quarters in the European quarters of the municipality since September 1, 1939, to vacate these premises within one month from the date of the publication of this Dahir in the Bulletin Officiel (August 22, 1941). Article 4 imposes on all Jews who are Moroccan subjects living in such quarters before September 1, 1939 the obligation to vacate these premises within a delay to be fixed by Viziriel Decree.

This Dahir was brought to your attention by my letter of August 25, 1941, because of its discriminatory and abusive character, especially taking into account the acute scarcity of lodgings in all Moroccan cities.

However, this Dahir has thus far received no execution, although its terms are mandatory and no Viziriel Decree as listed under Article 4 has thus far been published. The Jews concerned under these drastic measures called on the competent local authorities to inquire where they could move to in view of the notorious scarcity of lodgings and even the material impossibility of finding lodgings anywhere. It is understood that in general the competent local authorities received the Jews courteously and after some discussion had to recognize that the Dahir cannot be executed, and that steps are being taken to clear up the situation. As a matter of fact several solutions have been envisaged.

One of these solutions is the return of the Jews to the Mellah. Although the text of the Dahir does not mention Mellah, everyone anticipated that the Dahir meant that the Jews should return to live in that quarter, although in almost all cities it is very crowded. In the city of Casablanca, for instance, the size of the Mellah has been appreciably reduced for municipal improvements and by the invasion of the quarters by the Medina itself. The authorities then contemplated the enlargement of the Mellah, by the addition thereto of various adjoining streets. But this project was found impracticable. The proposed enlargement would have included the street on which the Consulate is located. Several other solutions were put forward, but found so absurd that they are not worthy of mention. Now that the stream of emigrants has more or less stopped, and since the movement of families arriving from Syria and the Lebanon was not of any consequence, the matter has died out and appears to be in the process of being forgotten.

It may perhaps be of interest to report the substance of a conversation between a member of the Staff of this office and a functionary at Rabat on this matter. Speaking of the Dahir of August 19, 1941, the member of the Staff asked whether the Residency was in earnest when it published this Dahir and whether it had the intention of enforcing it, as the Dahir was after all a Moorish law. The functionary in question protested and affirmed that it was a French law, or at least the Dahir was regularly drawn up by the Protectorate, signed and sealed by the Sultan and promulgated by the Resident General and that it would be strictly enforced like all other laws concerning the Jews.

The member of the Staff stated that all the laws drawn up by the Protectorate concerning the Jews were based on similar French legislation, except the Dahir of August 19, 1941, which was certainly based on a Moorish tradition or custom, which out of mockery called on the Jews to go to the Mellah each time they were involved in any important internal or external matter; that the said law could not be humanely executed; and that he could not believe that the law in question was a French law because the French are self-respecting and incapable of putting into force such an abusive piece of legislation. The functionary blushed and readily acknowledged that the Residency General had been certainly compelled to have this Dahir published. In reply to another question, the same functionary acknowledged that in spite of all the laws and agitation, the situation of Moroccan Jews in practice has undergone very little change, and that the Jews continue, as in the past, to hold practically all the trade of the country; and that the Jews under the present system of restriction are entrusted with the distribution of about 80% of the supplies and provisions.

The Viziriel Decree of August 18, 1941, is apparently a reproduction of the French law which in France has not as yet been fully executed. It is now whispered about that a further Viziriel Decree will be published, extending the delay for its execution to March 31, 1942.

The Viziriel Decree of September 16, 1941, relating to prohibited occupations is certainly a reproduction of the French legislation. A notice appeared in the local press of November 16, 1941, substantially stating that the next Bulletin Officiel would contain two Viziriel Decrees of November 14, 1941, extending until December 31, 1941, the date at which the Jews should have vacated the prohibited occupations. As a matter of fact, the Bulletin Officiel No. 1517 of November 21, 1941, published the two Viziriel Decrees referred to concerning Moroccan and alien Jews.

Thus far none of the executions, under the various Dahirs and Viziriel Decrees concerning the native Jews, except in the matter of filing declarations, have taken place, and it may be said that many native Jews have already adjusted their positions to the requirements of the different laws above mentioned, specially [sic] in the matters of prohibited occupations. It is evident that all these laws are rather ambiguous and lend themselves to different interpretations and constructions. It is believed that they were accompanied by confidential circular instructions to those entrusted with their execution, giving them discretionary power as to the application of the law.

It should be added that the most disagreeable feature concerning these laws does not result from the legislation itself, but from the atmosphere created around them and the different abuses which the Jews are daily meeting and suffering at the hands of irresponsible persons and from the harshness of the administrations. It is further believed that the publication in France and the news received from there and from Algeria on the subject of the treatment of Jews have been most depressing and have caused the native Jews here to expect harsh and abusive treatment at least equal to, it not worse, than their co-religionists have met with at the hands of the Germans. A few examples may throw some light on the matter.

The "Petit Marocain" of October 13, 1941, published on its front page, under the following heading: "Des textes nouveaux vont bientôt reglementer [sic] l'accès des Juifs aux professions agricoles; le commerce des céréales, des bestiaux et des chevaux leur serait interdit" ["New laws will soon regulate Jews' access to agricultural professions; they will be banned from the grain, livestock, and horse trades"]. It is very difficult indeed to describe the anxiety and depression produced on the Jews by this publication. It caused them to understand that they would be subjected to an organized system of spoliation. Their trust and hopes in agriculture vanished. Agriculture had thus far not been mentioned in any of the laws concerning them and, although the dispositions announced by the local press were not made a Moorish law, the Jews ceased to purchase real estate properties and put on sale, though discreetly, all their properties, which produced a notable effect on the market, causing the boom in the sale of all properties to come to a standstill.

The Jews thereafter endeavored to send abroad their capital. Apparently informed of the important exodus of capital across the Spanish Zone to Tangier and Melilla, as previously reported by this Consulate, the Residency General devised means to restore some confidence and trust on the part of the Jews. What measures were taken is not absolutely known, but it is believed that some strictly confidential assurances were given to certain leading Jews, especially some religious chiefs.

On the other hand, the Contrôleur Civil de la Région de Casablanca, called the Jewish Community to his office and substantially told them that his Majesty the Sultan had graciously been pleased to dispense with the declarations by Jews of their personal property, jewelry and banking accounts and that he desired to notify the Community that an inquiry had been opened with relation to the exodus of Jewish capital, and that if the Jews were charged and convicted of exportation of capital, their cases would be dealt with with the utmost severity and even collective sanctions taken. This was reported in the above dispatch of the Legation.

There is no agreement as to whether the Jews are dispensed from the necessity of declaring their banking account or only the money in cash. It would appear that the term used by the Contrôleur Civil was that money in cash "espèce ou argent liquide" should not be declared, whereas "créances" should be declared. The word "créance" implied bank accounts. At any rate this is purely academical, as those who have not make their declaration on October 21, withdrew their banking accounts and did not include them in their declarations.

This communication from the Contrôleur Civil at first badly impressed the Jewish Community, especially on account of the collective responsibility threat and because most of the declarations had already been filed. Shortly after the above notification, it became known that the Department of the Treasury had opened an inquiry concerning the use made of large sums drawn by the Jews from the banks since July 15, or of money collected by them as the price of crops or form sales of properties and stocks. There have also been incidents calculated to increase anti-Jewish feeling, if not actually to excite mob spirit against them.

It is reported that certain cinemas here have reproduced views of the anti-Jewish exhibitions which took place in Paris, showing the Jews Blum, Mandel, etc., followed by a statement to the effect that these were the traitors who sold France and are responsible for her defeat. There have also been noisy demonstrations, both private and public, carried on by the legionaries and radio transmissions from Rabat, mostly delivered by legionaries.

Nevertheless, it has become evident that the attitude taken by the authorities with respect to Jews was forced on them and that this attitude had principally for its object to lead the Jews to comply by themselves with the requirements of the various laws, especially those concerning prohibited occupations. It now appears that the Residency General has realized that the measures it has adopted have gone much beyond the limits it desired to attain, and as a result for the past few weeks, there has been a noticeable change in its standing and in the standing of the whole matter. It may now be safely stated that the Jewish question is dormant, or that it is at least no more a matter of actuality.

This change in the attitude of the Residency appears to be due to various causes of different nature. The full application of all laws against Moroccan Jews would mean in practice the complete eviction of Jews and the complete ruin of their trade, industry, etc., and the taking of their assets.

The assets of the native Jews are very important. They amount to 55% or 60% of the total in the country and are included in the French assets, estimated at 75% to 80%, including the Jewish assets. For obvious reasons, the French do not deem the moment opportune to diminish the statements of their total assets. The ruin of the trade of the Jews would practically mean the ruin of the whole trade of the country. The Arabs are not organized, they have no practice or sufficient knowledge of foreign languages and methods and they do not dispose of the necessary capital. The situation is beyond the capacity of French and foreign settlers who, in a large majority, do not understand the business methods of the country.

It was thought In high quarters that the Jews might be forced, under the circumstances, to entrust their assets to the French, or at least to sell them to the French. However, it resulted that in view of the prevailing difficulties, and above all the present financial disorganization, that the Jews found only foreign purchasers, especially Italians and Spaniards, which was of course most displeasing to the French who are endeavoring to prevent any assets, especially industry and real estate properties, from falling into the hands of such foreigners. It should be recalled that the Residency General, with this object in view, had caused to be published the Dahir of November 29, 1940.

There are many political considerations prompting the actions of the French Government, especially those connected with the after war policy and the standing under review will therefore be limited to local matters.

It is well known fact that Spain is looking forward to increasing her influence in the French Zone of Morocco and possibly to enlarging substantially her zone in both northern and southern Morocco, and that the Spanish Government has sought and enlisted the support of native Jews. It should be recalled that the Government of Franco, soon after the termination of the civil war, followed a benevolent policy towards Jews which enabled them to settle all their difficulties with Spain. After the Armistice and the publication of the law concerning them in France and in Morocco, the Jews have become warm supporters of the Spanish policy in Morocco, although they are putting all their reliance and trust in the United States and Great Britain. It is known that the Jews are carrying on a discreet, but in a certain way efficacious, propaganda in favor of Spain and that this probably has contributed largely to change the trend of public opinion in favor of Spain.

On its part the Spanish Government has already declared that the laws against Jews, natives or foreigners, are not applicable to Spanish citizens and former Spanish protégé Jews. It has likewise taken up position against the application to Spaniards or former Spanish protégés of the supplementary patente [sic] tax, which it declares to be a "war levy." It would seem that the French Government, cognizant of these facts, has been attempting to react somewhat, but the form under which the reaction has taken place is not yet known to this office, though the two following instances may serve to throw some light on the subject.

The Consulate is authoritatively informed that the Jewish owner of a canning fish factory at Fedala was negotiating its sale to a Spaniard. A representative of the Residency General called on the Jew and asked him why he was selling his factory. The latter replied that it was in compliance with the laws concerning the prohibited occupations. The representative of the Residency then urged him to keep on with the factory, guaranteeing to him that he would not be molested in any way, shape or manner.

It is also affirmed—as pointed out in the Legation's despatch by you—that his Majesty the Sultan received the Jewish Deputation which waited on him subsequent to the sacrifice made at Fez and other places, without the presence of any French official, and that his Majesty told the Deputation that the Dahir published was not the Dahir he had seen, signed and sealed and authorized the publication, and that he would not permit the value of even one small piece of silver to be taken from the assets of the Jews. It is affirmed, in well informed circles, that his Majesty made this statement with the previous knowledge of the Resident General.

In conclusion it is the belief of the Consulate that the Jews have been since time immemorial the pillars of trade and the principal intermediaries between Morocco and the outer world and that they will continue to hold this position for many years to come, although their present situation appears to have been somewhat shaken.

Very respectfully yours,
H. Earle Russell
American Consul General

H. Earle Russell, American Consul General, Casablanca, to J. Rives Childs, Chargé d'Affaires, American Legation, Tangier, Morocco, December 13, 1941, RG 84, Records of the Foreign Service Posts of the Department of State, 1788–ca. 1991, US Legation, Tangier (1940–1954), Box 79, National Archives Record Administration, National Archives at College Park, MD.

19. A JEWISH MERCHANT STRATEGICALLY RECALLS HIS FAMILY'S FOUNDATIONAL SUPPORT FOR FRENCH COLONIALISM [1941]

With the introduction and application of the Vichy regime's anti-Semitic laws of 1940 and 1941, Jews in cities such as Casablanca and Fez were prohibited from working in the public and private sectors, and many were expelled from public administration. The Vichy regime's General Commission for Jewish Affairs then initiated the so-called Aryanization of the economy, pushing Jews out of property ownership and restricting them from many professions. Jewish women and men sought, in various ways, to limit the harmful impact of these anti-Jewish policies. Raymond Bensimhon was one such individual. Born in 1905 in Fez, Bensimhon worked as a real estate agent until he received an official letter from the Vichy administration in October 1941 notifying him that he could no longer work in his chosen profession. Here, Bensimhon argues his case to the local authorities. He describes how, decades earlier (in the summer of 1883), his grandfather, Juda Bensimhon, a leader of the Jewish community, hosted the cavalry officer Charles de Foucauld during Foucauld's trip to southern Morocco. Foucauld conducted foundational research that would culminate in the publication of Reconnaissance au Maroc, *setting the stage for the French colonization of Morocco and earning the explorer a reputation as a geographer of note. By dwelling on the story of his grandfather, Bensimhon displays that he is descended from a historical family that contributed to the expansion of French power in Morocco. His letter also highlights that his family donated historical materials to the Library of the Protectorate, including Foucauld's original notebooks; the donation led the colonial administrators to honor the Bensimhon house with a commemorative plaque, which was installed in December 1933 during a showy, official event. Citing the family's "service" to the French empire, Bensimhon's petition was met with favor by Vichy administrators. In February 1943, he was granted the right to work again as a real estate agent. Most Jewish petitioners were not so lucky.*

October 17, 1941
To the Commissioner Resident General of France in Morocco, Rabat

Dear Sir,
  As an established real estate agent in Fez since 1926, I am affected by the

Statute of Moroccan Jews, subject of the Dahir of 5 August 1941, and completed last month by the Vizerial Order of 16 September.

However, according to the stipulations in Article 10 of the aforementioned Dahir, which allows exemptions to be claimed in favor of Jews who have provided exceptional services to Morocco, I have the honor of requesting that you kindly allow me to benefit from this article's stipulations and grant me the authorization to continue practicing my profession.

I am requesting this exceptional favor because I believe that the services provided by my family to France and Morocco, in a time well prior to the establishment of the Protectorate, are—to my family and me—the best proof of our selfless devotion and attachment to France.

These services—which dire necessity has forced me to flaunt today, even though my family has never before wanted to report or take advantage of them whatsoever—are as follows:

In 1883, when Father Charles de Foucauld came to Fez to do the research that became of the subject of his book *Reconnaissance au Maroc*, he took refuge at the home of my grandfather, Mr. Juda Bensimhon.

Dear Sir,

My family has never tried to benefit from or gain recognition for the help my grandfather gave to this illustrious traveler;

During the establishment of the Protectorate, we could have brought this up and asked for positions or posts: we did nothing of the sort.

We could have tried to take advantage of the logbooks that Father de Foucauld left at my grandfather's home by selling them to amateurs who would have paid a lot for them; we preferred to donate them free of charge to the Protectorate Library;

During the inauguration of the commemorative plaque placed on our house in December 1933, we could have responded to General Caillaut's and Consul Ismaire's request with one of our own, but we preferred to refrain from doing so. Our greatest and only reward was having provided a service to France.

If today we find ourselves forced to request recognition from France, it is only and absolutely because events have forced us to do so.

My father is currently the head of this family, which has entered into Moroccan history. It is this seventy-year-old head of family, father of six children, who appeals to you today!

His personal means are extremely limited. My older brother has been without steady work for several months.

Only I have succeeded in making an honest living and in giving my family and my father a bit of material comfort.

Today, since my role of family breadwinner has been threatened, I have been forced to knock on the door of the great and glorious France, a country who acknowledges and recognizes those who have served her, to remind her—much in spite of myself—of her debt to my family.

I dare to hope that you will favorably welcome my request for an exemption and remain sincerely yours,

Raymond D. Bensimhon
Cabinet Raymond
121 Bd Pocymireau
Fez V.N.

Attached I have taken the liberty of sending you a folder composed of the following in support of my request:

INFORMATION FORM
ON MR. RAYMOND BENSIMHON WHO IS REQUESTING TO BENEFIT FROM THE EXEMPTIONS OF ARTICLE 10 ON THE STATUTE OF MOROCCAN JEWS

SURNAME & FIRST NAME: RAYMOND D. BENSIMHON
LINEAGE: son of DAVID BENSIMHON—grandson of JUDA BENSIMH[ON]
DATE & PLACE OF BIRTH: born in Fez on 10 May 1905
NATIONALITY: Moroccan
PROFESSION: Real estate agent and property manager
CRIMINAL RECORD: never been convicted
ADDRESS: 121 Boulevard Poeymirau in Fez, Ville-Nouvelle
REGISTERED ADDRESS: CABINET RAYMOND, 121 Bd Pocymirau in Fez
MISCELLANEOUS INFORMATION:
Settled in Fez as a business agent since 1926
Authorized cotrustee by the Lower Court of Fez
Appointed building manager by authority of law
Office open in the new [part of the] city since 1 October 1935
Business register 4493 FEZ
Son of a family with six children
Certified as accurate

Fez, October 16, 1941
Fez, November 14, 1941

Political Affairs Division, Fes Region, General Secretariat to the Director of Political Affairs, Political Section

Request dated 13 November, presented by Mr. Raymond Bensimhon, real estate agent, in order to benefit from the exemption provided for in Art. 10 of the Statute of Moroccan Jews.
Petition dated 17 October.

I issue *a very favorable opinion* to this request.
As a matter of fact, Mr. Bensimhon is the descendant of a very honorable Jewish family from Fez, who provided the following services to the French cause prior to the establishment of our Protectorate.
The hospitality given to Father Foucault [sic], in 1883, and the selfless devotion of the petitioner's grandfather cannot be disputed. Furthermore, this family has received no honorary position, medal, or distinction, and it would be just that, as a measure of kindness, the French Government recognize the services provided to our cause in a difficult time. Dismissing this request would have a lamentable political effect on the Jewish and Muslim populations of Fez.
Attached is a copy of Mr. Raymond Bensimhon's police record.

Raymond Bensimhon to French Bureau of Political Affairs, Fez, October 17, 1941, RG 81.001M, Reel 1, Selected Records from the National Library of Morocco, 1864–1999 (bulk 1925–1945), United States Holocaust Memorial Museum Archives, Washington, DC. Courtesy of the Archives du Maroc. Translated from French by Rebecca Glasberg.

20. MUSLIM ALGERIAN DOCTORS CALL FOR THE REINSTATEMENT OF THEIR JEWISH COLLEAGUES [1941]

In 1941, the very same year that the Vichy regime imposed a 2 percent quota (numerus clausus) on the number of Jews serving in the medical profession, a typhus epidemic surged in Algeria and Tunisia. Jews were well represented in the

medical professional in French North Africa: with the adoption of the quotas in Algeria, only 150 of 938 Jewish doctors were permitted to practice their profession. As the medical profession was crippled by Vichy restrictions, an explosion of typhoid racked poor Muslim and Jewish communities, which had neither medical resources nor vaccination protocols. In response to this calamity, Marcel Lūfranī, an Algerian Jewish doctor, and the Muslim doctors Saʿadān and Būmalī, gathered to discuss solutions. Lūfranī drafted a petition calling for Muslim support of the reintroduction of Jewish doctors into the medical sector, precisely to serve the large population of Muslim patients at risk of typhoid. The document was signed by other Muslim doctors, including Drs. Ghudbān, Bensmāyya, Saʿadān and Būmalī, who also promised Lūfranī the support of the then-upcoming politician (and pharmacist) Ferhat ʿAbbas, future first president of the National Assembly of Algeria, and Dr. Mohammed Saleh Benjellūl, a deputy to the French National Assembly. This French colonial government document gives details of the meeting of the doctors, the petition they produced, and a list of licensed Jewish doctors prone to the quota.

Algiers
    Intelligence
    Re: Jewish doctors and the Muslim population
    An informant reports the following conversation that he supposedly had with Dr. Loufrani.

"At lunch a few days ago," Dr. Loufrani declared, "I received—in addition to a few Jewish notables including Mr. Elie Gozlan—Dr. Saadane and Dr. Boumali from Aïn Beïda (the latter of whom is a member of the Board of Physicians). Mr. Ghodbane, Municipal Councilor, was also present.

"During the course of the meal, the main topic of conversation was the dismissal of Jewish doctors under the new regulations concerning Jewish occupations.

"Everyone lamented this measure, which will, especially under the current circumstances, deprive the Muslim population of [medical] care delivered with absolute dedication and a complete understanding of Muslim traditions. Indeed, the majority of the Jewish doctors speak Arabic and go out at all hours of the day and night to care for Muslim people, including the most unfortunate. Do you believe that our Catholic colleagues are capable of maintaining the same attitude, and above all, do you believe them inclined to show good will and complete concern towards Muslims deprived of [financial] resources?"

Still according to Dr. Loufrani, a petition has been written to bring the attention of the Public Authorities to the unpleasant consequences of these dismissals. This petition has reportedly been signed by Mr. Ghodbane, Mr. Bensmaya, Dr. Saadane, and Dr. Boumali, who promised the support of Ferhat Abbas and Dr. Bendjelloul.

Dr. Loufrani wished to obtain Cheikh El Okbi's signature. He was dissuaded from doing so, as petitions of this genre can harm the "Circle of Progress," due to the flurry of opinions they can provoke. Therefore, he [Cheikh El Okbi] was counseled to go and see Mr. Boukerdenna and Mr. Ibnou Zerki.

Furthermore, according to the latest intelligence gathered by the informant, Dr. Loufrani has reported already circulated this petition in the Casbah and has reportedly received several additional signatures. Contrary to what Dr. Loufrani said, it is reported that only Mr. Ghodbane and Mr. Bensmaya have signed this petition, as Dr. Saadane and Dr. Boumali refrained.

Below, according to Dr. Loufrani, is the list of Jewish doctors whose dismissals are pending:

Algiers

Dr. Zerathe, 18 rue Marengo

Dr. Mechiche, Place Cardinal Lavigerie

Medecins juifs et de la population musulmane, RG 11.001M.60, Fond 99, Opis 2, Comité exécutif international du rassemblement mondial contra le racisme et anti-sémitisme, Paris (Fond 99) (1935–1940), United States Holocaust Memorial Museum Archives, Washington, DC. Translated from French by Rebecca Glasberg.

21. A PHOTOGRAPHER'S LENS ON THE CAMPS [1941]

Walter Reuter (1906–2005) began his career as a photographic reporter in his hometown, Berlin, where he contributed to local and foreign newspapers and art magazines. In 1933, he emigrated to Spain, where during the Civil War he oversaw the production of cultural films for the Republican resistance and photographically documented the conflict for foreign papers. Reuter's art was represented by Black Star, a photography agency founded in New York City by refugees from Germany. Black Star introduced photojournalists like Reuter to Henry Luce—the publisher of a novel illustrated magazine, Life. At the outbreak of the Second World War, Reuter, in France at the time, was arrested and interned in Vichy-run camps throughout North Africa along with so many other foreign nationals who had volunteered for the Republican cause in Spain. Reuter spent time as an internee in Morocco and Algeria, in Sidi El Ayachi, a camp located near Azemmour (from which he wrote this appeal for help in 1941), and Colomb-Béchar, where he was forced to labor on the pre–Second World War colonial pipe dream of the Trans-Saharan Railway. While in Colomb-Béchar, Reuter was able to swap wine for a French officer's camera, taking sixty rare, artistic pictures of life in the camp: today, these negative are held in a family-run archive in Mexico, which has kindly allowed for their reproduction in this book. In 1942, Reuter managed to escape internment and flee with his family to Mexico, which was (like many other Latin American countries) at the time eager to grant visas to Europeans who would "whiten" its population. In Mexico, Reuter would continue his career as a photojournalist, rising to fame for his artistic documentation of the indigenous people of Mexico until nearly one hundred years of age, continuing to take photographs until his death. Here we read a range of documents pertaining to Reuter's attempt to leave North Africa—one by Reuter, two by volunteers assessing his case—drawn from his case file at the American Friends Service Committee, the Quaker organization that sought to deliver humanitarian relief to refugees and displaced persons in wartime North Africa.

Sidi-El-Ayachi, April 11, 1941
American Friends Service Committee,
    Gentlemen:
    For the past five months I have been in a concentration camp in Morocco, and would like to ask your help to emigrate to the USA. I tkink [sic] my past fulfills all the requirements of your committee. A brief outline of my life follows.

Walter Reuter—born Jan. 4, 1906, Berlin, Charlottenburg.
    Protestant, public school education. Until 1930 I worked in color photography in a large printing office. I was connected with all kinds of lithographic organizations. Later I became photographic reporter for Berlin papers and

The World News. Later I worked on many other European newspapers, also for the American Agency, Black Star, 420 Lexington Ave., N.Y., Graybar Building. In 1933 I emigrated to Spain. During the Spanish War I worked in the republican office of the Sec. of State with Alvarez del Vayo. I took care [sic] of cultural films and assisted the Norwegian Committee and the Swedish Committee (Nini Haslund and Lisa Lindbaek).
  References;
  Lisa Lindbaek, Lisboa
  Martin Gleissner
  Charles Schokken
  Ernst Mayer, BlackStar, N.Y. (Gruppe Neubeginner)
  Proofs;
  Press-Cards from Arbeiterbladet, Oslo
  Black Star, N.Y.
  My picture in the Zurich paper as worker.
  Morocco travelers permit
  Staatszugehorde Apatride
  Physical condition, —entirely normal.
  I have no money and no visum [visas].
  My American friend, Ernest Mayer, would like to help me, but cannot give an affidavit, because of financial difficulties. Hoping for a positive answer to my request,
  Respectfully yours
  Walter Reuter

[Undated typed American Friends Service Committee internal communique]
  Walter Reuter was born in Charlottenberg [sic] near Berlin on January 4, 1906. He went to grammar school and was then apprenticed for 4 years to printing plants where he became a reproduction technician. He worked in several plants from 1924–25 (names may [be] gotten from Walter). During his apprenticeship and later on he was active in the youth organization of his trade union. During 1928–29 he was retrained for newspaper-photography, worked for democratic papers and art magazines. Continued this work until 1933, during this time volunteer work for the Youth org. of the Social Democratic Party in the field of Social Work of young people. 1933 emigration to Spain where he worked as a newspaper photographer, Contributed to

IMAGE 7. During the Spanish Civil War (1936–1939), tens of thousands of volunteers served in the Republican Army's International Brigade, fighting on behalf of the fledgling Spanish Republic against the nationalist, conservative allies of General Francisco Franco. When Spain fell to Franco, and later, France to Germany, these émigré, volunteer soldiers found themselves vulnerable as political enemies of (or foreigners in) the ascendent Francoist dictatorship and Vichy regimes. Many International Brigade members fled to France, only to be deported to Vichy prison, internment, and labor camps in North Africa. The men pictured here, likely erstwhile Brigade volunteers who had become forced laborers, were photographed by fellow prisoner Walter Reuter in the Vichy camp of Sidi El Ayachi. Walter Reuter, "Palas," Archivo Fotográfico Walter Reuter, Cuernavaca, Mexico.

[M]anchest[er] Guardian and other liberal papers during the Spanish Civil War. Went to France in 1939, to cure a wound, worked as a Prestataire at the beginning of the war, was demobilised at the time of the armistice, went to Casablanca, send to Camp Sidi el Ayachi, Maroc. then demobilised. Sent to Algiers to work on the Transsahara railroad, Now Groupe S, Groupement B. Colomb-Bechar, Algiers.

Dear K. O.

Please take care of Walter it is more important than doing something for us now, or he will perish. You can also mention that he did the first big reportages.

Walter Reuter, Sidi El Ayachi, to American Friends Service Committee, April 11, 1941, Accession Number: 2002.296, American Friends Service Committee Refugee Assistance Case Files, File of Walter Reuter, United States Holocaust Memorial Museum Archives, Washington, DC. Courtesy of the American Friends Service Committee.

22. SHOES, CIGARETTES, AND THE NEEDS OF THE INTERNED [1941]

What toll did internment take on the mind and body? Here, we encounter a source that speaks of its impact on that most instrumental of body parts, the feet. The Vichy labor camp at Oued Akreuch, Morocco, was of modest scale, with approximately 100 prisoners laboring in 1942 within its walls and an additional 120 assigned to work on projects outside its perimeter. The camp, which mostly housed foreign workers, was overseen by the Directorate of Industrial Production in nearby Rabat. The facilities at Oued Akreuch were rudimentary, as was the case at most Vichy camps throughout North Africa. Internees slept on the floor on straw and branches: they were given a single outfit of shirt, pants, jacket, and shoes, and their diet was strictly limited, though more generous than internees in other Moroccan camps experienced. In this letter, three men interned in Oued Akreuch appeal to the Red Cross—in particular its representative in North Africa, the prominent Moroccan Jewish human rights lawyer and wartime activist Hélène Cazes Benatar—for the funds to obtain proper shoes and cigarettes, the better to face the hard labor to which they were sentenced. From their names, the four supplicants were likely German Jewish refugees.

Oued Akreuch
November 9, 1941

Sir,

You must know that we have been in a camp here in Morocco for the past year. As long as we have been here we have had the most minimal material resources, whether we earned them here at camp through hard labor, or [had them] as a leftover from better times, [but] we refrained from asking anyone for assistance. Today, our situation has become critical: being considered unfit [for work], we are no longer earning any money. It is no longer possible for us to obtain anything whatsoever—not even cigarettes or soap, let alone necessary clothing. We urge you to come to our assistance because you are the only ones who can help us. There are four of us who are in the most acute need. Here are our names: Mozes Baum, Jacob Geller, Sam Westreich, and Jacob Kagalny. We hope that our request will not be made in vain.

Most sincerely yours,
M. Baum
P.S. Our address: M. Baum
G. T. 10 Oued Akreuch
by way of Rabat

Oued Akreuch
Mr. M. Baum
Sir,
We have received your letter dated Nov. 9, which we read with our undivided attention.

At present, we are not authorized to serve Camp Oued Akreuch.

The undersigned [woman] has already taken steps to obtain the necessary authorization. This request is currently under review.

We are keenly interested in your situation. Please be aware that the reason you have not yet received any help from us is by no means due to oversight or disinterest.

We ask for your continued patience, as we hope to soon be able to help you efficiently.

Best regards to you and your comrades.

Oued Akreuch
November 30, 1941
Mrs. Benatar,
We have received your response to our first letter and we are very grateful that you are still thinking of us. We fully understand that the authorization to help us does not rest only on you. However, three weeks have since gone by; if you are unable to send us any financial support, we urge you to do what

you can to send us some items of clothing which we have a pressing need for, given the season. I would also like to bring to your attention that, in addition to the four men whom I previously mentioned, there is now a fifth, who has just left the hospital where he had a leg amputated. He needs a size 42 shoe for his left foot.

I look forward to hearing from you soon.
Sincerely,
M. Baum

M. Baum, Oued Akreuch, to Hélène Cazes Benatar, Casablanca, November 9, 1941, RG 68.115M, Reel 5, Folder 40, Private Collection Hélène Benatar (1936–1953), United States Holocaust Memorial Museum Archives, Washington, DC. Courtesy of Central Archives for the History of the Jewish People. Translated from French by Rebecca Glasberg.

23. AN INTERNED MOTHER APPEALS FOR FOOD [1941]

In August 1942, a Red Cross representative toured the internment camp of Sidi El Ayachi, located on the western coast of Morocco, and noted the presence of ninety-nine interned women, fifty-one interned children, and five interned infants. The author of this appeal for philanthropy, written in 1943 to Red Cross representative (Moroccan Jewish lawyer and human rights activist) Hélène Cazes Benatar, is one such internee: Chil Bekerman, mother of an interned child. As Bekerman describes in the rough French of a nonnative speaker (represented here via creative translation), she did not have enough funds to acquire adequate food for herself or her child, having spent all she had en route to the camp and on shoes for her child. In keeping with Vichy practice, the Bekerman family was divided in the course of the war. Her husband was interned in the labor camp at Bou Arfa, a thousand kilometers to the east. Although Bekerman's letter does not specify the circumstances that brought her to Sidi El Ayachi, it is likely she and her family were refugees from Germany or Austria, arrested by the Vichy authorities by dint of their foreign status. Among the other internees in Sidi El Ayachi were Jewish and non-Jewish foreigners, as well as Belgian and Norwegian sailors. A repurposed military camp that was previously a reception center for French Foreign Legion volunteers, Sidi El Ayachi was not a site of forced labor, and conditions there were considered relatively reasonable: its Jewish internees were even allowed to attend religious services in the adjacent town of Azemmour.

Sidi El Aichi, October 28, 1941
  Dear Mrs. Benhatar,
In the begining I got 250fr from the committee and I thank you with all my hart for it. Now I don't even have a penny. Because the sootcases that I bringed back with me cost me 170fr here I paid the workers 20fr to bring them from Azemour. And for the children I buyed 2 pares of shoe. I can not feed them every thing because he do not wanting to, and me I can not eat every thing. So if you got some money you can some times some things buy in Azemour for to eat. For my husbind in Bou Arfa I had to sended something for to eat, and I hav to buy a pare of shoe for him because he don't have. So it useless to tell to you the situation I am in because I can not do all that, because no money. I beg you dear Mrs. Benhatar to being kind and give some finanshall aid thru the Aliance Committee and I wood be so gratfull. I wood like also to let you know that since 3 week since I arrive at Sidi El Aichi I don't hav any news of my husbind in Bou Arfa. I allready telegraph many time, but I am still with out response, I going to ask you an advice what shood I do in this situation? Because I am very worry on this subject. I count on your goodwill and thank you in advance with respect.
  Sincerely,
  M. Bekerman

M. Bekerman, Sidi El Ayachi, to Hélène Cazes Benatar, Casablanca, October 28, 1941, RG 68.115M, Reel 5, Private Collection Hélène Benatar (1936–1953), United States Holocaust Memorial Museum Archives, Washington, DC. Courtesy of Central Archives for the History of the Jewish People. Translated from French by Rebecca Glasberg.

24. IS A FRENCH CHRISTIAN DIVA AN ALGERIAN JEW? (1941)

Students of history can learn a great deal from rumors and falsified news, even if unfounded. The intrigue that circulated around the diva of stage and screen Gaby Morlay (1894–1964) offers one such example. A global sensation in her day, Morlay (born Blanche Fumoleau) performed in more than seventy films and forty plays, and she was celebrated as an icon of French cinema and theater. During the war, Morlay had an affair with, and subsequently married, Max Bonnafous, a French sociologist who was appointed by the Vichy government to serve first as cabinet secretary to the minister of the interior, then as prefect, and finally as minister of agriculture and supplies. For this service, Bonnafous would be tarred as a collaborator after the war, although ultimately he was pardoned for his work with the Vichy regime. Because of Morlay's high-profile status and romantic intrigues, her private life and hobbies (including the fact that she was the first woman ever to be licensed to pilot a dirigible) elicited public scrutiny in the Francophone world. This coverage could verge into the political, as when the right-wing newspaper Dépêche Algerienne *claimed that Morlay was Jewish and from Algeria; in fact she was Christian and a native of Angers, France. In this clipping from the Tunisian monthly women's magazine* Leïla, *the facts are emphatically denied, ostensibly by Morlay herself: the diva retorts (with a possible touch of racist haughtiness) that she was neither "Jew nor Arab." The article identifies* Dépêche Algerienne *as the source of the rumors, hinting that the myths about Morlay might have been spread intentionally, perhaps to encourage an association of Jewishness, the stage, and female independence. Strikingly, biographies and online discussion of Morlay continue to recycle mythological stories of her Algerian and/or Jewish past, suggesting that some of the misogynistic and racist mythmaking that circulated in the Vichy era continues to find resonance today.*

Shooting Star . . .

The vibrant movie star Gaby Morlay, who has been accused of being Jewish, is energetically protested this assertion and even sent a scathing refutation [of it] to the *Dépêche Algérienne*, which she was keen to inform of her place of birth and religion. She says she was born in Angers and is of the Christian religion.

Thus, until further information comes to light, [we are meant to understand that] Gaby Morlay is not Jewish.

However, below her own signature in the magazine *Algéria*, you can read, "I was born in Biskra. When I came into the world, the melodies of an Arab flute permeated the air beneath my mother's windows."

The proof is irrefutable. We can no longer doubt the place where [this woman] who was destined to be a movie star was born.

A shooting star, if ever there were one.

Like the philosophers, Gaby Morlay has no motherland. She was born everywhere. She is indivisible. The refutation that she sent to the *Dépêche Algérienne* cannot be proven.

"Étoile filante . . ." *Leïla: Hebdomadaire tunisien indépendant*, April 16, 1941. Translated from French by Rebecca Glasberg.

25. A PHARMACIST'S DESPERATE APPEAL [1941]

Maurice/Moïse Guedj, a native of Batna, Algeria, received training as a pharmacist at the University of Marseille, subsequently settling in Brussels with his wife, a Catholic woman native to that city. According to French law, intermarriage between a Jewish and North African man and a French, Christian woman did not guarantee the man French citizenship or protection. Conscripted into the French army in 1939, Guedj served the military as a pharmacist stationed in Algiers, only to be pushed out of service by the Vichy regime's notorious Statut des Juifs (Jewish Statute). These laws defined Jews as a racial group and excluded them from public function, including service in the armed forces and civil administration. Four days later, Algerian Jews were denied the naturalization they had been granted by France some seventy years earlier, by the Crémieux Decree of 1870. The regime went on to "Aryanize" the Algerian economy, barring Jews from engaging in myriad financial occupations and imposing quotas on Jews in the legal and medical professions. Desperate to continue working, Guedj appealed to the Vichy authorities to be transferred to what the French colonial government called the Southern Territories of Algeria, the largest of the French administrative departments in what is today Algeria. With this request, Guedj banked on the fact that, given the modest number of Jews dwelling in the Algerian Sahara, and that the Crémieux Decree had never applied there, a move to the region might allow him to evade the Vichy regime's anti-Jewish quotas and laws. Guedj was not alone in looking to southern Algeria as a potential site of wartime refuge. Other Algerian Jewish medical professionals, including dentists, doctors, midwives, and homeopaths, anticipated that in southern Algeria, Jews were unlikely to fill, let alone exceed, the regime's racial quotas. This was a canny bet but, alas, a losing one. Guedj's request was denied, and he lost his cherished professional post.

Algiers, October 18, 1941
The Governor-General of Algeria, Algiers
Dear Sir,

It is with the most respectful deference that I come to request a moment of your time to present the following for your esteemed consideration. Please allow me to outline for you the purpose of my letter.

Lieutenant-Pharmacist in the Reserves, upon mobilization I left my home and my wife in Belgium without waiting for orders in order to reach Paris and request assignment. For the duration of the war I was assigned to medical train number 103, which undertook evacuations in the Vosges [and] Alsace-Lorraine. Then finally the withdrawal that preceded the Armistice [arrived]. Faced with the impossibility of rejoining my wife (from whom I have not received any news in what will soon be two years), Dr. Colonel Montel, Head Doctor of the Gard Département assigned me to the Nîmes Military Hospital (Center for Dermatology and Venerology) as Head Pharmacist and Laboratory Manager.

[As a] consequence of certain orders, I had to leave the army in April '41, meaning I was demobilized just a few months ago. Since then, despite all of my efforts and requests, I have remained without employment . . . without work.

Having exhausted my resources, I sent you a letter begging you to *please allow me to create a pharmacy in Ghardaïa*. First, I was asked to put together a dossier with my service record, which I did right away. On 25 August, 1941 I received a second letter from the Governor-General, Head of the Southern Territories N9493 South/S informing me that, "My request can only be investigated once the legislative measures limiting the number of Jews in the liberal professions have been implemented."

It is for this reason that I [seek] your kind attention.

One or two months before the date of my demobilization, all university graduates were permitted to submit requests regarding their [professional] designation and appointment. All were granted.

Yet through no fault of my own, Sir Governor General, I had to remain in the Army until the month of April 1941. Furthermore, I worked in Biskra, Algeria for seven years previously and *I am neither a newcomer nor a foreigner*. In the event that the *numerus clausus* intervene, I would certainly be one of the beneficiaries. Finally, I'll add this: [I am a] member of a large and loyal family [that is] proud to have always served France. My elderly father, today seventy-six years old, served in the Zouaves [infantry regiment]. We were four brothers: the eldest was killed in France fighting the enemy ([19]14–18). Awarded the Croix de Guerre—Military Medal. The youngest one was wounded in combat and is a war pensioner ([19]14–18). *Glorieuse blessure* [wounded in glory]. The latter served in France for three years ([19]37–40) with the Alpine Hunters. Finally, as for myself, I have done my duty as a French Officer.

Given all this, I have come to beg you, Sir Governor-General, to please take my request into consideration. Allow me, a forty-year-old refugee, and in addition, a victim without any resources at all, to yet again beg you to grand me the authorization to create a dispensary and to use my degree for work. Moreover, Sir Governor-General, in Ghardaïa, *where no pharmacist has ever had the idea to settle down*, I would not hinder or overshadow anyone. In addition, wouldn't I be doing something useful, and above all, wouldn't I contribute a bit to advancing the Benefits of Science and French Civilization? Have I not described a unique situation, hopeless but worthy of interest? Be that as it may, I trust your unbiased and benevolent ruling and your fair assessment.

Sincerely,
Guedj Maurice: Pharmacist
56 Rue de Constantine. Hussein Dey. (Algiers)

General Governor of Algeria, Algiers
Dear Sir,
I have the honor of sending you the items of the dossier that you asked me to compile for you on 1 July 1941 in order to examine my request.

The goal: to request of your high benevolence the authorization to create a pharmacy in Ghardaïa.

Attached:
A certified copy of my pharmacist's diploma.
My birth certificate and those of my father and mother.
My service record with mention of war campaigns.

Sir Governor, please permit me to bring your kind attention to this last item, which I have just barely received after [having previously] requested it in vain at the head office for Health Services in Constantine, Tunis and Royat. Thus you can see for yourself that it is incomplete, unfinished, and contains a significant gap. In fact, the Paris archives—the Region in which I received my posting—may have been misplaced or may be being reconfigured. In any event, here is what has been omitted:

1. That I remained in the war zone from the first to the last day of the war. (Only benefitted from 10 days of leave in a year and a half of mobilization.) ...

4. That until March 1941 I was [illegible] Nîmes Center for Dermato. Venerology as Lieutenant, Head of Department and Laboratory Manager: (Laboratory that I designed myself.)

5. That I was a volunteer for the T.O.E. [*Théâtres d'opérations extérieurs*]

6. That I was demobilized on 13 April 1941.

In my first letter, I also pointed out that my older brother, who received the Croix de Guerre and the Military Medal, died fighting the enemy ('14–'18).

That my youngest brother is disabled. War Pensioner ('14–'18)

Permit me to remind you once again, Sir, that I had settled in Belgium (Brussels) before the war and because of this war, I've got nothing left. Nothing left except the hope that I will be able to use my degree and work. As for that, I have complete faith in your utter fairness as well as in your kind understanding.

Sincerely,
Guedj Maurice, Moïse, Pharmacist
C/O Mr. Guedj Pharmacist
56 Rue de Constantine
Hussein Dey (Algiers)

Maurice [Möise] Guedj to General Governor of Algeria, July 19, 1941, Les Archives nationales d'outre-mer, Aix-en-Provence, 24H/256, "Service de Santé, autorisations d'exercer la médecine," letters by Maurice [Möise] Guedj to the Governor-General of Algeria, 19 June 1941, the second with date obscured and the third dated 18 October 1941. Translated from French by Rebecca Glasberg.

26. RACIST LAWS IN ACTION—A FRENCH OFFICER'S BOON IS A JEWISH MERCHANT'S BUST [1941]

Mere weeks after Morocco came under Vichy rule, in early October 1940, the ascendant regime issued a series of anti-Jewish decrees excluding Jews from civil service and the military and restricting their numbers in liberal professions. These policies applied to metropolitan France and Algeria: in Morocco, they were issued by the Makhzan (government). Eight months later, more stringent economic regulations were signed by Sharifian decree. These new quotas demanded the accounting of Jewish property and ultimately facilitated the confiscation of this property. The regulations of June 1941 all but eliminated Jews from Morocco's economic life. How were these dramatic transitions experienced by individual Jewish merchants in Morocco? Victor Harrosh (Ḥarrūsh), whom we meet here, was among the many who found his economic stability upended by Vichy quotas. The shipping agent was forced to sell his business to a French officer, likely for less than its worth.

I, the undersigned, *Harrosh* Victor, forwarding agent living in Casablanca at 6 rue Oudjari, born in Casablanca on 17 March 1908, of Moroccan nationality and Jewish, have the honor of informing you that I manage a transit business at 6 rue Oudjari, which I registered with the commercial register in Casablanca under the N° 13816.

As it is now forbidden for me to practice the profession of forwarding agent due to the 5 August 1941 Dahir and the merging of the professions of forwarding agent and purchasing agent, I have decided to cash out on my investment, which the 16 September vizerial order permits me to do.

I decided to sell this business to Mr. André FOUQUE, born 26 February 1903 in Amiens (Somme), of French nationality, Reserve Marine Officer, acting as the sole manager of the limited liability company "Adrien Martin & Cie (Africa," which is currently being established with 200,000 Frs. as capital, and whose headquarters will be established in Casablanca at 6 rue Oudjari.

The sale of my business will concern intangible assets and leaseholder rights, assessed at 45,000 Francs, and equipment and furnishings, appraised for 10,000 Francs.

The total price of the sale will therefore be 55,000 Francs. . . . This cost will be payable in cash.

I will have a copy of my police record, which must be included with my request, sent to you in the next mailing.

I would be much obliged if you would kindly grant me the necessary authorization to undertake the sale of my business in the above-mentioned conditions to the person indicated.

Casablanca, November 29, 1941

Victor Harrosh, Casablanca, to Grand Vizir, Rabat, November 29, 1941, RG 81.001M, Reel 25, Selected Records from the National Library of Morocco, 1864–1999 (bulk 1925–1945), United States Holocaust Memorial Museum Archives, Washington, DC. Courtesy of the Archives du Maroc. Translated from French by Rebecca Glasberg.

27. A MOTHER'S STRUGGLES UNDER INTERNMENT [1942]

The experiences of children interned by the Vichy, Nazi, and fascist Italian regimes in North Africa are among the hardest to reconstruct, as children left behind scant documentary evidence. We are particularly lucky, then, to have relatively extensive accounts from Abraham and Chana Drezdner and their children, ages three and eight, over the course of their internment in the Vichy camp of Sidi El Ayachi, which lasted at least six months. Sidi El Ayachi, located near Azemmour and roughly seventy-six kilometers southwest of Casablanca, was originally a reception center for representatives of the French Foreign Legion during the course of the war, but it was repurposed in October 1941 as an internment camp. Sailors from allied and other nations were its first prisoners, but soon it was used by the Vichy regime to house women and families like the Drezdners, most of whom were refugees from Europe. The camp was surrounded by a tall wall, but within its boundaries, families were housed together and given freedom of movement. Conditions were relatively comfortable in Sidi El Ayachi, and interned physicians were even allowed to treat their sick, fellow internees. Chana Drezdner was among those who required medical care during her internment: she was diagnosed both with conjunctivitis and postpartum depression in the course of her stay. This medical emergency, paired with a shortage of food and necessary supplies, drove Chana and Abraham to write a series of appeals to an American Jewish Joint Distribution Committee (The Joint) representative in Casablanca. Here, we offer two such letters by Chana Drezdner; both shed light on the dramas unfolding for her family during a time of war and under occupation.

Safi, May 13, 1942

Esteemed Mrs. Benjo,

As you know, I have already been at the Camp for seven months and I am sick all the time. The Camp has already sent me to the hospital three times. It is very difficult to cure this illness, so I always have a lot of expenses—hundreds

IMAGE 8. Esti Freud (née Drucker) and her daughter Sophie, daughter-in-law and granddaughter of Sigmund Freud, the founder of psychoanalysis, were among thousands of European Jewish refugees to seek sanctuary in North Africa during the Second World War. The pair stayed in Casablanca for six months while securing visas to Portugal. Most refugees were not so lucky and faced internment in Vichy camps. "Esti and Sophie Freud visit an outdoor pottery market in Morocco while awaiting their immigration papers to the United States," Photograph No. 54623, United States Holocaust Memorial Museum, Washington, DC. Courtesy of Sophie Freud.

of francs—each week for the doctor and my medications. The best proof is the attached doctor's note, indicating that I must have regular treatment, which is certified by the Head Doctor of the Safi Hospital. We do not eat what they give out at the Camp, but instead cook for ourselves, because we are religious and, above all, ill. I am taking the liberty to remind you that you used to pay me 150 [francs] each month for my sick son.

I thank you with all of my heart for the six hundred francs that you send us, but I regret to inform you that this is not even enough for the Doctor, the medications, and the travel.

As a result, I beg that you please take the preceding information into consideration and send me a supplement each month so that I can manage the expenses of my illness.

I hope that my request will be met favorably, and thank you in advance.
Sincerely,
Mrs. Drezdner
P.S. my address: Mrs. Drezdner, in Sidi el Ayachi Camp, via Azemmour
Mrs. Drezdner Chana

Sidi El Ayachi Camp
To Mrs. Benjo,
Esteemed Mrs. Benjo,
I thank you greatly for last month's supplement of 150 [francs] that you surely gave for my sick little boy, who is still sick and in need of this money, and which you always paid when I was living in Casablanca.

I am taking the liberty to inform you that I have noticed from your letter that you haven't taken *me* into consideration.

In my last letter, I enclosed a note from the Head Doctor of Safi Hospital that explains my illness and concludes by saying that I must be treated regularly, with medications and diets that cost a lot of money.

We do not eat the Camp food, because sick people cannot eat what others eat, so my family and I must cook for ourselves. We receive a lot less than a family that cooks for themselves, which is why I have requested money for my illness and diet, as well as for the cost of traveling to the hospitals in Casablanca, Mazagan, and Safi. Especially now that my children have whooping cough.

I kindly request that you take the preceding information into consideration and please give me, in addition to my son's supplement, a supplement for myself so that I can keep myself among the living.

Sincerely,
Drezdner
July 2, 1942

Mrs. Drezdner, Sidi El Ayachi, to Mrs. Benjo, May 13 and July 2, 1942, RG 68.115M, Reel 5, Private Collection Hélène Benatar (1936–1953), United States Holocaust Memorial Museum Archives, Washington, DC. Courtesy of Central Archives for the History of the Jewish People. Translated from French by Rebecca Glasberg.

28. AN INFLUENTIAL PSYCHIATRIST DECLARES HIMSELF NOT JEWISH [1942]

Born in southwestern France, Robert Poitrot (1908–1975) grew up in Morocco and pursued medical training in Algeria and France, ultimately receiving his medical degree, in 1937, from the University of Marseille. Poitrot returned to Morocco to work as a psychiatrist in the small town of Berrechid, at a new hospital founded by the public health department of the French Protectorate. There, he was part of a young and vibrant (and problematic) field of colonial psychiatry that had been shaped in the first decade of the twentieth century. Poitrot's work continued under Vichy rule, but only after he testified (in the document reproduced here) that he was not Jewish and was therefore exempt from the anti-Jewish quotas that the French administration used to squeeze Jews out of professions in public administration, civil service, teaching, and medical as well as legal fields. With the conclusion of Vichy rule in Morocco, Poitrot served as a French military physician in a battalion of goumiers *(indigenous Moroccan conscripted soldiers) who fought against the Third Reich. After the war's end, he was put in charge of the supervision of public health in French-occupied Germany. During this period, Poitrot produced what is referred to as the "Poitrot Report" (the full title:* Rapport sur la destinée de l'assistance psychiatrique en Allemagne du Sud-Ouest pendant le régime National-Socialiste*), the first public account of Nazi practices of euthanasia, which totaled 190 pages, detailing the murder of psychiatric patients by staff and providing a plan to reestablish psychiatry in Germany, free of euthanasia. The report also included documentary evidence and testimonies from high-ranking medical and administrative staff that Poitrot himself conducted. Poitrot's denunciation of the complicity of the German medical establishment with the crimes of Nazism was among the bolder such reports of the time. Poitrot returned to Morocco in 1946 to direct the hospital at Berrechid.*

June 18, 1942

Dear Sir,

I have the honor of asking you which steps I must take, which information I must furnish in order to have a certificate confirming that *I am not of the Jewish race* delivered to me. I have been asked to attach this document to a "name correction" petition that I filed in 1939 with the Minister of Justice.

A civil servant, I have already officially declared that I have no ancestors of the Jewish race.

Sincerely yours,

Dr. R. Poitroit Head Ward Physician at the Ber Rachid Psychiatric Hospital

August 31, 1942

Re: certificate of non-belonging to the Jewish race

Dear Sir,

In your letter dated 18 June 1942, you kindly requested that I send you a certificate of non-belonging to the Jewish race.

I have the honor of informing you that the General Commissioner for Jewish Affairs has just informed me that he is personally in charge of evaluating requests of this sort. As a result, you will have to send your petition, accompanied by all the supporting documents—notably the civil-status and baptism records of your forbearers, if applicable—directly to Vichy.

Sincerely,

Roland Cadet

Dr. R. Poitrot, Berrechid, to General Secretary, June 18, 1942, RG 81.001M, Reel 12, Selected Records from the National Library of Morocco, 1864–1999 (bulk 1925–1945), United States Holocaust Memorial Museum Archives, Washington, DC. Courtesy of the Archives du Maroc. Translated from French by Rebecca Glasberg.

29. VICHY LAW FORCES OUT A JEWISH SHIPPING AGENT [1942]

Born in Casablanca in 1907, Ya'qub Al-Qrishī (referred to in French documents as ElGrichi) worked as clerk for the French Ministry of Post, Telegraph, and Telephone before he established himself as a shipping agent in early 1930, serving mostly small businesses. In August 1941, following the introduction of the Vichy regime's second round of anti-Jewish laws, which excluded Jews from trade and business, Al-Qrishī was forced to withdraw from his business. He sold his firm, Comptoir Marocain de Transit, to Jeanne Ferreau, a European Christian (settler) businesswoman. In this document, a letter to the French resident-general in Morocco, we encounter Al-Qrishī's oath to authorities that he has followed the mandate of the General Commission on Jewish Questions, the Vichy office that oversaw the "Aryanization" of French North Africa. Al-Qrishī's experience was mirrored by that of many North African

Jewish businessmen and women, who were driven from the business and finance sectors (among others), and compelled to sell their property and businesses at reduced value, for fear of it being stolen from them with no compensation at all.

[July 8, 1942]
To: The Resident-General of France in Morocco.

I, the undersigned: Jacob ElGrichi, trucking agent, residing in Casablanca at 65 Avenue du Général Drude, born in Casablanca on 18 September 1907, of Moroccan nationality and Jewish, married and the father of three children, have the honor of disclosing to you that at the above-mentioned address in Casablanca, I operate a transit business that I licensed with the commercial register in Casablanca, under the number 20.876 and under the name "Moroccan Transit Bureau."

For all practical purposes, I have worked as a trucking agent since 1932.

As of now, I have been banned from working in the trucking industry in accordance with the Dahir of 5 August 1941 and the merging of the freight forwarding profession and that of broker, by a memo from the Ministry of Commerce and Trade on July 8, 1942[.] I decided to keep drawing a paycheck, in accordance with the right granted to me by vizierial order on 16 September 1941 and the above-mentioned note from the Head of Trade and Provisions.

I decided to sell my business assets to Mrs. Jeanne Ferreau, wife of Mr. François Lamidey, with whom she resides in Casablanca at 34 rue de Condorcet[.] [Mrs. Ferreau was] born in Bouy (Marne, France) on December 22, 1912, [and is] of French nationality.

Jacob ElGrichi to the Resident-General of France in Morocco, July 8, 1942 RG 81.001M, Reel 1, Selected Records from the National Library of Morocco, 1864–1999 (bulk 1925–1945), United States Holocaust Memorial Museum Archives, Washington, DC. Courtesy of the Archives du Maroc. Translated from French by Amber Sackett.

30. A JEWISH CINEMA OWNER SEEKS RESTITUTION OF HIS BUSINESS [1943]

Prior to the Second World War, Elie Bendayan (also referred to as Bendahan) ran a successful cinema in the heart of Casablanca. Then the anti-Jewish laws implemented by the Vichy regime in France and Algeria beginning in October

1940 imposed a racial definition of Jews and stripped them of their citizenship: the Statut des Juifs (Jewish laws), which followed in 1941, prohibited Jewish women and men from working in any public capacity, whether in the military, public administration, civil service, teaching or medical professions, or the media. Like so many Jewish owners of movie theaters, Bendayan was forced to sell to a new owner of European origin. With anti-Jewish laws lifted in 1943, Bendayan felt that the restitution of his property was in order. To reclaim the business, he initiated a legal claim, a portion of which we reproduce here. In his appeal, Bendayan outlines his claim to the cinema and calls on the new French leadership to take a broad look at Moroccan cinemas like his own, which had been forcibly passed from Jewish to Italian hands.

June 17, 1943

Dear Sir,

I have the honor of respectfully bringing to your kind attention the situation in which I find myself as a result of the application of racial laws:

I used to operate a movie theater in Kasba-Tadla (Morocco). In his letter of 16 January 1941, the Protectorate Secretary General notified me that I could no longer manage the theater, even indirectly, and that as a result, I had to yield the company to a third person, according to the terms of Article 6 of the 31 October 1940 Dahir. (Attachment N° 1)

Therefore, subjected to administrative injunction, I had to turn over my cinema unwillingly to Mr. Jouret, who currently manages it and whose address is Hôtel Rialto in Casablanca.

Yet according to the 22 April 1943 presidential decree (Protectorate Official Bulletin N° 1591 from 23 April 1943), those who by dint of their Jewishness had been excluded from the professions and activities listed in the 5 August 1941 Dahirs, may return to their professions and activities without delay.

Article 4 of the 5 August 1941 Dahir pertaining to the Status of Moroccan Jews included movie theater director in the [list of] prohibited professions.

As this prohibition has been lifted, it seemed possible that I may be permitted to take back my cinema in Kasba-Tadla.

This does not seem to be the opinion of the Protectorate Secretary-General.

However, the Legislative Committee established by the General Government of Algeria had presented proposals to the Governor-General—which he officially approved in an order dated 5 April 1943—that state (in the last part) the procedure to follow for the return of furniture and business assets that were deeded as gifts [as dictated by law].

The Resident-General of Morocco did not make similar arrangements for this order.

It is therefore legitimate, legal and fair that I be restored ownership of my movie theater, as is my right and in keeping with broader developments.

I must inform you that the spirit that motivated the application of racial laws in Morocco was such that all my requests for authorization to take on a new occupation (after my eviction from the cinema) were systematically refused. Due to the willful obstinacy of the Moroccan administration, I have been forced into unemployment and inactivity since 1941.

It does not seem that any objection or obstacle should get in the way of the restitution of my cinema to myself, just as if a civil servant were restored to his duties.

However, if this proves impossible, and against all odds, and this solution creates some sort of difficulty for you, I would be much obliged if you would consider the following solution:

Cinemas that were run by Italians in Morocco were sequestered. I would ask that one of these cinemas be given to Mr. Jouret first, after returning my cinema to me.

It would be equally possible to envision the direct transfer of one of the aforementioned cinemas to me.

Here is a list of cinemas owned by Italians in Morocco:

Casablanca: Monte Carlo, Appolo, Mondial, Chaouia, Paris

Fez: Bijou, Apollo, Star

Marrakesh: Eden, Regent

Please note that I have been involved in the film industry for over ten years.

I am married and the father of two children. All I ask is to work so I can manage my responsibilities. The Moroccan administration has so far not allowed me to secure my family's livelihood.

I dare hope that, through the application of democratic laws, you will restore my rights.

With uttermost gratitude, I remain, sincerely yours,

Bendayan

Elie Biendayant

12, Rue Mouret
Casablanca

On 2 October 1943 and according to A.E. N° 8240, you were kind enough to forward me a letter from Mr. Elie Bendayan in which he asks to be restored his property rights to a cinema that he sold in accordance with Article 6 of the Dahir of 5 August 1941 pertaining to the status of Moroccan Jews.

As the Commissioner of the Interior's response clearly explains to the concerned party, about whom you have so kindly informed me, Mr. Elie Bendayan's cinema was not, at any moment, subject to administrative sequestration and therefore is not subject to the exemptions of the General Governor of Algeria's 3 April 1942 order concerning the restitution of goods placed under provisional administration—which besides, is not applicable in Morocco.

Mr. Elie Bendayan sold his cinema to Mr. Jouret under the provisions of common law following the prohibition on working in the profession of cinema manager, which affected him as a result of Article 6 of the Dahir of 5 August 1941 on the status of Jews, and not due to administrative order. This prohibition was lifted by the order of 14 March 1943, which was made applicable in Morocco by the 31 March 1943 Dahir. [The latter Dahir] reestablished the legislative and regulatory measures put in place after 22 June 1941, which include discriminatory measures based on Jewishness that pertained to the accessing and exercising of professions.

As the administration did not interfere with the sales contract between Mr. Bendayan and Mr. Jouret, there is only one way for the former to have it annulled, and that is to petition in the court of common law, if he deems this appropriate.

Dear Sir,

I have the honor of acknowledging receipt of your September 3 letter, in which you explain that so far, it has not possible for you to take back the movie theater that you were managing in Kasbah-Tadla and that, in accordance with the orders of the administration, you had to sell to Mr. Jouret.

The 14 March 1943 ruling and the Governor General's 3 April order only provide for the restitution of goods placed under temporary administration and only determine the conditions in which a person, whose goods were sold without his consent, can bring a nullity suit. Despite the silence of these texts on the matter of the sale of property by Jews during the time when the existing legislation could have made them fear [forced] seizure or sale, it is nonetheless possible for any interested parties to file a nullity suit under common law, as the mental coercion to which they were subjected can indeed be grounds for the voidability of contracts.

As a result, it is up to you to file a nullity proceeding concerning the sale to which you agreed with Mr. Jouret in the appropriate court.

Please note, moreover, that I am forwarding your request to the Commissioner of Foreign Affairs, who is in charge of following up with this issue, and that I am informing him of the remarks that I have conveyed to you.

Sincerely,
Mr. Bendayan, Elie
12, rue Mouret
Casablanca

Elie Biendayant/Bendayan, Casablanca, to Minister of the Interior, Algiers, June 17, 1943, RG 81.001M, Reel 1, Selected Records from the National Library of Morocco, 1864–1999 (bulk 1925–1945), United States Holocaust Memorial Museum Archives, Washington, DC. Courtesy of the Archives du Maroc. Translated from French by Rebecca Glasberg.

31. A WRY ACCOUNT OF OCCUPATION {1942–1943}

Few biographical details are known about Eugène Boretz, including whether his name is a pseudonym and whether he was Jewish and Tunisian. Published in Algiers in 1944, during the war, his French-language chronicle about the two-year Italian and German occupation of Tunis reads like a diary, giving vivid details about how the war was felt on the ground. For example, his account describes the scarcity of foodstuffs, spoliation, the transformation of Tunis's cityscape through the introduction of new signs, sounds, and regulations on the use of public space, and the particular vulnerability of Jewish women and girls to sexual violence at the hands of the occupiers. Boretz's wry, even ironic tone makes his account particularly relatable.

Two days later, a complete change of scenery. Emerging from who knows where, they swarm everywhere. Countless groups of soldiers roam the streets. They inundate all the restaurants, all the stores, purchasing with rapacity and carelessly removing wads of large bills from their pockets to pay. They spend abundantly and have easy money. Everything interests them, particularly wine. They have bottles under their arms, in their hands, they fill trucks and cars with them. The Bank of France's money waltzes with joy!

But it is above all the garages that become the centers of feverish activity. They are all busy with the invaders who take over all the private cars that have been parked for years due to lack of gasoline. [It is the] first attack on private property even before any decree initiates the right to requisition.

The Germans are busy, the cars are repaired in haste and swarms of vehicles crisscross the avenues like race cars, mingling with the first foreign military trucks.

Tunis, deprived of automobiles for two years, rediscovers the intense traffic of before the war, and its appearance is changed. A few days later the first street signs with German inscriptions appear at the most splendid intersections, insulting the beauty of Paris,[1] and completing the modification of the city's appearance.

... They are everywhere. The most sumptuous hotels, Tunisia-Palace and the Majestic, are requisitioned, first in part, and then the civilians are [totally] driven out. In the entrance hall to the Tunisia Palace, signs in three languages inform interested parties that "Jews are unwanted." Second-class hotels do not escape their control. The *Dépêche Tunisienne* office building is theirs. That of Standard Oil houses the [German] general staff. The Casino's café, the biggest and most comfortable café, transforms into the Wehrmacht-Kaffee (entry verboten) and is equipped with an orchestra, [while] the Palmarium mutates into the Soldaten-Kino (one must think of the morale of the troops). The schools are now barracks (so much for public education), the garages remain theirs. The new Belvedere neighborhood has become a colony of Germans. First the Jewish villas are requisitioned, but soon the others are as well. In fact, it is rare for a building not to be either totally or partially occupied. The Germans camp in the superb Belvedere Park, the pride of Tunis. Entry there is forbidden....

It should be noted that, on the intervention of the Italian authorities, Italian Jews were not taken as hostages. On this subject, there arose a conflict between the Italian and German commands, and, in a rare twist, the Italians prevailed after Rome had been alerted. Italy intended to protect its Jews as best it could. It proved this on many occasions, despite its submission to its powerful and irritable ally....

1. The urban plan of modern Tunis was modeled on that of Paris.

Let us note here that the fate of the Jewish laborers consigned to the surveillance of the Italians was infinitely more kind. Humane working conditions, lack of bullying. In their conversations with the Jewish officials, the Italians like to declare that they were participating in political racism, but they vehemently protested when we pointed out that this policy could lead to cruelty: you are not dead, Machiavelli![1] . . .

We easily appreciate that the spirit emerging from these official acts could only have the effect of unleashing the army rabble's basest instincts and opening the gates to violence and arbitrariness. Without doubt, we will never be able to know the extent of all the excesses with which the occupation troops defiled themselves in the darkness of the Tunisian nights. But those who lived in Tunis during these months of shame know of isolated, controlled, undeniable events. They know that, revolver in hand, Germans entered Jewish homes and took their linens, clothes, and valuables, and threw the men out into the street in order to be one-on-one with the women. . . .

Such was the influence of the occupation on the appearance of Tunis, on its charm. Caring about complete accuracy, let us stick to the facts. Suppose that you want to spend an evening with friends somewhere in or around Tunis. Where will you go?

To Carthage or Sidi Bou Saïd? Impossible; the commuter train that used to leave every half-hour from downtown has been eliminated. And the journey is fifteen to twenty kilometers. Furthermore, the restaurants in the suburbs are closed. Military necessities. Troops everywhere.

Will you go to Belvedere Park? Don't bother thinking about it. The Axis troops are camping there and entry is forbidden.

Will you opt for the movies? Alas! They are all closed, except the Deutsches Soldaten-Kino. But this is not for you.

The theater? Give it up. Besides a few shows for the German army, the theater is only used for propaganda shows organized by the infamous COSI or collaborating companies, with official representatives of the occupation army, national revolutionaries, high-ranking collaborationists, etc. A bit uncomfortable.

1. Here, Boretz mocks the Italians for recognizing that their policies are anti-Semitic while remaining oblivious to the inhumanity of the same policies. To do so, he references the philosophy most often associated with the Italian Renaissance diplomat and writer Niccolò Machiavelli; that is, politics are rife with deception, cruelty, and unscrupulous actions.

IMAGE 9. The presence of countless Axis and Allied troops in North Africa left girls and women prone to sexual violence and exploitation, both during the Second World War and after the Anglo-American landing. As this young woman is serenaded at close range by German Air Force soldiers and Italian soldiers, the vulnerability on her face is palpable. "Nordafrika, Tunesien / Libyen.-Luftwaffensoldat mit Akkordeon, italienische Soldaten und junge Frau; KBK Lw 6, c. 1942–1943," Bild 101I-421-2065-16, Das Bundesarchiv, Berlin.

So, you think you will go to one of these intimate restaurants where they usually serve copious and succulent, if not always lawful, meals. And you are already on your way. You open the door and, in the overcrowded room, you see officers from the occupation army at almost all the tables. But, weary and famished, you resign yourself and your friends to wait for a free table. You have accepted the idea of... "protecting" neighbors.

But while you wait, a hand places itself familiarly on your shoulder and a friend leads you all into the street under some pretext. "You are free to dine at this restaurant," says the friendly voice, "but at the very least, know the risks of such an undertaking. A German officer could very well ask your names and addresses and invite you all to spend the next day at the Kommandantur. There, they will ask for proof that you are Aryan and, as he who is suspected to be Jewish is also suspected to have false papers, they will ask you to submit to an exam of your head, from the front, side, and three-quarters angle, according to phrenology's most modern methods." You laugh heartily, but the friend continues: "This is exactly what happened yesterday to a young woman from high society, and pure Aryan, to boot. Believe me, it is better to follow the wise counsel of Colonel Heym, vice president of the Municipality, who, in a recent notice, asked his people to remain in their homes as much as possible. So, return to your homes, and the sooner the better, since you are with a woman. Ever since the 'tourists' have been here, a woman who looks young, even if she is accompanied, risks a lot being in the street after sundown."

So much for fun times!

Boretz, Eugène. *Tunis sous la croix gammée*. Algiers: Office français d'édition, 1944. Selection from pages 11–12, 17–18, 34, 36, 39, 51–52. Translated from French by Rebecca Glasberg.

32. SIX MONTHS UNDER THE "NAZI BOOT" (1943)

The first known Holocaust chronicle to be written by a North African Jew and published in North Africa was the personal diary of Paul Ghez (1898–1971), published in Tunis in 1943, immediately after the liberation of Tunisia. Ghez's voice was formidable. Born in Sousse, Ghez volunteered for the French military during World War I, studied law in France, and worked as a lawyer in Tunis. There, Ghez associated himself with the progressive, assimilationist Tunisian Jewish newspaper Justice, *which promoted the granting of French citizenship to the Jews of Tunisia by the French Protectorate. Notably, throughout French-colonized North Africa, although Jews were at times able to obtain French citizenship without disavowing their religious identity (particularly in Algeria), Muslim communities were not afforded the same privilege. When the Nazis occupied Tunisia in 1942, Ghez became chair of the Recruitment Committee for Jewish Labor, responsible for forcing Jewish men to work for the paramilitary organization the Schutzstaffel, or SS. In this selection from Ghez's wartime chronicle, he describes the quotidian affronts of occupation, including harassment, physical violence, internment, arrest, and spoliation. He also outlines the logistical and ethical challenges he confronted while serving as an intermediary between the SS and Tunis's Jewish community. "My task is so out of the ordinary, so crushing," wrote Ghez, "that my conscience has often been obsessed with doubt."*

On Paris Avenue, we see SS officers circulating, wearing machine guns around their necks.

What is my plan? I admit that I have no clue.

For the moment, I have only one goal. Stiffen up in order to not put on the "trembling Jew" show.

The colonel is not at the Kommandantur. He is probably at the synagogue.

We head there promptly, accompanied by Dr. Beretvas, volunteer interpreter.

What a lamentable sight.

The armed SS are making all the Temple's occupants exit with unheard of brutality. The rabbi, the officiant, the beadle, the faithful.

In the nearby streets, they round up all the Jews who are passing by.

They are there, numb in the rain: old men with venerable beards, the ill, children. I locate several of my friends in the group, stuck in the mousetrap.

We approach immediately and the explosion happens.

Colonel Rauff, foaming with rage, brandishes a cane that he waves under our noses and vomits a stream of insults: "Swine, dogs, worthless men" (and other kind words.)

"I consider your behavior in regards to the Resident as an act of sabotage towards the German army. In consequence, you will be shot in one hour with the rabbi, whom I have sent for. You will see just how well the SS can subdue Jews."

The brave Dr. Beretvas did not dare translate. He tried to cushion the blow. But I insisted, it is better to know everything.

I give M. Borgel a reassuring look. I do not feel very comfortable, but I act tough.

While the head of the SS yells, I take mental stock of the situation.

We are really quite small in front of a raging, colossal force.

I look to my right at the pitiable group of gloomy and quiet prisoners. I make out the white beard of the officiant, I see a child shivering with fear.

What will become of them?

Our work is cut out for us. We must save them at any price.

I take advantage of a lull in activity to ask for a word.

"Who is this man?" asks the colonel.

I introduce myself right away, responding dryly and formally. As a former officer, I am ready to try and gather the requested men, on the condition that they give me the necessary time to do so. This is all that I have to say.

I steady myself and, with all my strength, look directly at the zealot.

He ends with, "You can leave. You will report to me at noon."

Phew! Already something. But a three-hour extension is quite short.

We return to the community.

The germ of an idea for a recruitment committee immediately starts to form in my mind.

My childhood friend, Dr. Moatti, a man with a big heart and limitless dedication, is going to join me in this endeavor.

Georges Krief will see to the organization of the barracks at the Alliance Israélite school.

This courageous boy inspires the most acute sympathy in me.

In 1939, he enrolled, despite being cleared from any obligation. He was admitted to an excellent rank in the infantry officers' school. Unfortunately, the armistice interrupted his career, but the gesture speaks for itself.

He is a dynamic, impulsive, and selfless boy.

A real pure blood.

We make our way to a printer.

Quickly, we have published and posted a notice summoning forthwith all Jews of all nationalities, born between 1915 and 1924.

Then, we walk to the police. We ask for significant police presence to urgently direct the young people targeted by our call towards the barracks.

Fortunately, we find understanding civil servants who realize the gravity of the moment and promise us their full support.

I decide therefore to head toward the Alliance Israélite to participate in the recruitment developments.

The Krauts have done like they did at the synagogue.

The two exits are blocked by armed soldiers.

Inside, I make out schoolteachers in charge of handling recruitment, as well as numerous men of all ages, forced to the sides of the courtyard and kept under control by machine guns.

Women and young girls have been imprisoned in a classroom.

In the middle of the courtyard, two officers check identity cards.

Men younger than fifty are held off to the left. They will go to work.

The old men will be taken to prison, as hostages.

I try to negotiate with one of the officers who can speak French, and whose cheek is embellished with a fantastic scar. He dismisses me dryly and orders me to join the group of workers.

After a moment, I reenter the fray. I have taken on weighty responsibilities. I need to have freedom of action.

This time, I am brutally rebuffed.

There is nothing left for me to do but accept the situation. After all, life outdoors and manual labor do not scare me. And my fate will be without a doubt less grueling than the galley on which I have embarked.

But what will become of these poor young people? How will they be housed, fed, cared for? I anxiously ask myself these questions, enraged by my forced inaction.

During this time, I see new contingents of people rounded up by the Germans and the first recruits responding to the summons.

Brave young people. It is they who will save us.

Around midday a soldier arrives and hands a letter to the lieutenant.

"Is Mr. Paul Ghez here?" I immediately step forward.

I receive the order to go to the Community straight away, which I do in a rush.

There, a new mouse trap. The Council members are in police custody.

I find myself in the presence of Colonel Rauff, still just as worked up. It's decision time.

My colleagues inform me that the colonel had arrived an hour ago accompanied by some SS and had taken all the assistants who were not part of the Council as hostages. He had then asked what had been done since the morning and where the tall man in charge of recruitment was. (He was talking about me.)

They tried to explain to him that in all likelihood I was at the Alliance School organizing the recruitment service. The colonel did not want to hear it and announced that he would shoot the entire Council if I did not present myself within ten minutes.

It was a dreadful wait.

To keep himself occupied, the colonel visited the offices and helped himself to a dozen typewriters, gathered together to draft the recruitment lists, and a collection of rugs belonging to the president.

Finally, at the insistence of the Council members, he agreed to have me sent for at the Alliance.

This new conversation is less violent than the first.

I summarize the assembly of the ten classes and the preliminary results we've obtained.

A Gestapo agent confirms the relayed information.

"You can continue. I am going to arrest one hundred hostages and I will have them and you shot if you do not carry out my orders and if I notice the most minor attempt at obstruction."

The colonel withdraws, without forgetting the typewriters and the rugs, his glorious trophies.

An hour later, the one hundred hostages are imprisoned.

We have stopped the German round-ups, but we have taken on a frightening responsibility.

There is no time to think now. We must organize, safeguard our young people, limit suffering, avoid pogroms.

I am engaged in a ferocious combat: at stake is the existence of the Jewish population.

The adversary seems to have all the advantages.

Even so, we will fight by all means.

Because despite everything, we still have one great hope: liberation! . . .

Things go from bad to worse.

Alger Street is jammed with crowds made up of laborers' families, especially those in Bizerte.

The women dominate now, and they are all the more formidable because they yell a lot louder and you can neither rebuff nor confront them.

They shout, they demand, they insult.

Everything is a pretext for complaints.

Why is the son of So-and-So still in Tunis?

Why did such and such a laborer come home, while my son is still over there?

Why didn't my package arrive?

Why did someone steal my husband's blanket?

We must respond to everything, put up with the most injurious insinuations, the most vulgar insults.

The "yelling place" [*gueuloir*] has been pillaged, the archives ransacked.

I arrive in the middle of this frenzy and I am immediately surrounded.

I do my best to explain calmly that I am only there to help the population through a tragic time, that I will do all I can to improve the fate of the laborers and have as many as possible brought home.

I affirm that I never granted any favors or facilitated any cushy jobs [*planques*].

A lot of people calm down and put their trust in me. The women who insulted me lower their hands.

The scene is moving and ridiculous.

But the mad women [*forcenées*] resume the offensive and the mayhem recommences.

I extricate myself with great difficulty and go to the barracks with Bismut and Krief.

There, a new concert, but with a different melody.

The relatives and friends of the summoned youth are laying siege to the school door and we must clear a path for ourselves in the middle of all the loud protests.

Inside, recruits wait for us to explain their situations.

Each one shows us a document: a medical note, proof of employment, declaration of exemption signed by some individual with no authority.

I try to explain things to these young people.

I set out the terrible threats that weigh on the population, I speak to them about the ill, the fathers who are waiting for their replacements. I call upon their good sense, their spirit of solidarity.

Wasted time. Each one holds out his document.

"Send off whomever you want, but not me."

"Your doctors are imbeciles."

"I am going to complain to the Kommandantur."

Discouraged, I have the service personnel empty the office, not without difficulty.

Then it's the parade of the well-to-do bourgeoisie, friends, relations, parents.

Each one of them whispers in my ear that it is quite understood that his son or brother would never be implicated in such a story, and that I can do one simple thing to clear them.

I refuse calmly and clearly.

And the gentlemen leave, threatening fire and brimstone.

Bismut and Krief deal with the same thing, put up with the same assaults.

An image obsesses my spirit. That of the shooting gallery dummies you see in festival stands.

We are a lot like these dummies; the difference being, however, that we have a heart and nerves.

After the last visitor leaves, I break down.

I am completed discouraged, deflated.

The task is beyond me.

I cannot continue. I give up.

Come what may.

My very depressed lieutenants, they too declare that they're joining me, despite my protests.

Faldini, the director of the medical service, who is also present, joins us.

We head immediately to the Community headquarters to announce our decision.

M. Borgel and his learned assembly protest, affirm that we are exaggerating, and that we are too worked up.

This judgment makes me explode.

I unleash my fury against these wise senators, who are perhaps too wise, and who pontificate in their office while we struggle in a hellish atmosphere.

I express my resentment with harsh, aggressive words.

I will regret them later, but I have lost control of my nerves.

We leave the room, slamming the doors.

I head home, determined to stop thinking about everything, and to regain my balance playing with my children.

On the way, a shopkeeper calls out to me, informing me that a woman has just thrown something at my back.

I remove my overcoat. It is full of lice.

The woman yells. Her son was rounded up and has just been taken to Zaghouan.

Enough! Enough! . . .

We are discussing the situation when someone announces that several people, very emotional, are asking urgently to be seen.

We have them enter. Their emotions are very reasonable.

These are the inhabitants of the resettled building in the *hara*, an enormous cement cube in which all the inhabitants of the slums that were demolished while implementing the city's urban development plans are being housed.

German soldiers brutally entered, opened all the doors, and took all the mattresses, blankets, and a large portion of the furniture.

They went after the poorest Jews and stripped them of what was most necessary.

Dozens of families are going to suffer from the cold.

The committee is taking necessary measures.

Blankets will be distributed.

Reports of protest will be submitted to the French and German authorities.

These events must not be repeated.

February 7

Alger Street is still in turmoil.

Escapees from Bizerte arrived at sun up and spread word of a violent bombing that took place overnight.

There are two dead and many injured.

Immediately, the women from the Jewish neighborhoods enter the streets and protest with violence.

Informed at home, I decide to leave and head directly to the Community.

En route, I am approached by numerous protestors hurling the usual curses and threats at me.

Sfez is traveling, in Bizerte, to be exact, and I cannot use his car.

I call the transportation service, which provides me with a soda merchant's truck.

Dr. Moatti asks to come with me.

We leave together to go get ready, but a monstrous protest is waiting for us at the exit.

We are immediately surrounded by a crowd of several hundred women who are all yelling together.

They demand to know the names of the dead and injured, right that moment.

They want a shift change, and for the pen-pushers to be arrested.

I try to get out. Impossible. A veritable human knot has stuck itself to me.

I want to speak. The shouts drown out my voice.

My clothes are pulled, the buttons ripped off.

A few meters away, Moatti is immobilized, too.

At one point, I feel a liquid running down my neck.

A protestor has poured the contents of a bottle of alcohol on my overcoat.

She is trying to light a match, but the stirs of the crows prevent her from doing so.

The situation has become serious.

I try again to extricate myself without violence, but I do not succeed.

Finally, two policemen, alerted by phone, come to the rescue.

The prestige of full uniform. The crowd calms down and I can finally join Moatti in his office.

After we leave, Krief will suffer the same attack.

I understand the anxiety of these poor souls.

I excuse their insults, their violence.

They lash out at us. It isn't fair, but it's human and it's better this way.

Imagine for a moment a protest like this in front of the Kommandantur.

But can I keep this up for a long time? I feel so weary.

Here we are on the road.

The soda merchant's truck, two platforms without rails, is broken down.

It is poorly adapted to alcohol.

We find an expedient. The conveyor lays on the mud-flap and, with his hand, partially seals the air inlet.

Indifferent to the glacial wind and the rain, he wisely measures out the mixture, adapting to the road profile.

This human carburetor functions without fail until our arrival.

Midway, we pass Sfez's gray car; he is returning with men on leave.

He has the list.

The wounded, numbering thirteen, have been taken to the hospital in Ferryville.

The bodies of the two dead have been dispatched to Tunis on the provisions truck.

We go to the hospital first, where we visit the wounded.

Two of them are serious: severed leg, penetrating lung wound.

I give these poor souls the money and sweets that I brought: tobacco, jam, biscuits.

In the same room, there are wounded Arab laborers, who watch with an envious eye.

No one is thinking of them.

I give them everything I have left. They thank me emotionally....

I have been at Bizerte since yesterday.

Max Berdah, head of the clothing service, who was rounded up in Cheylus, accompanied me.

He came to distribute the complete outfits that we managed to fashion to all the camp laborers.

The outfits consist of one pair of work boots with wooden soles (for want of leather), overalls, a shirt, a pair of socks, and a sweater.

It took miracles of perseverance and ingenuity to get ahold of the materials, leather, and wool.

We had to harass the administration, solicit merchants, requisition workshops.

All the camps were equipped. There will be no more down-and-out Jewish laborers.

Distribution, which began yesterday afternoon, continues this morning.

The men are satisfied. . . .

March 23

The call for work for all Arabs aged seventeen to fifty has been officially decided.

In fact, this recruitment existed already, but on a smaller scale.

A vaguely worded official message inserted into the papers exhorts Tunisians to obey the occupying powers.

The census is instituted in all municipalities.

But this time, the government is shouldering its responsibilities. It is the administrative services that are undertaking these operations.

There are neither hostages nor threats of reprisal, and the Muslim notables are not involved.

It is true that they are not Jewish.

As they did for the military service, the Krauts have maintained exemptions for inhabitants of major cities and the well educated.

As the newspapers have not mentioned nothing about this issue, the question has not caused a commotion in Tunis.

I saw the Arab workers who were previously recruited suffer from the invader's switch, I saw them in the throes of death at the hospital, I witnessed the horrible carnage in Alouina and Bizerte.

There are pages to write on the martyrdom of these *meskines*, our brothers in oppression. . . .

April 3

My neighbors invited me over to listen to Radio London.

We huddle together around the radio with the volume turned down low and all the windows shut.

We hear comforting news about the war. Liberation is near.

One piece of information, however, troubles us profoundly.

Several thousand Jews were massacred in Poland. Hundreds of hostages were shot, children torn away from their mothers.

The procedures employed by the Krauts are more horrifying than you could ever imagine. They used machine guns, gas asphyxiation.

I have a retrospective shiver thinking about the first days of our oppression. Colonel Rauff's bragging was not an empty threat.

A speaker then gives instructions to the silent warriors, those in the occupied territories.

"Sabotage, slow the German war machine as much as you can."

"Avoid all acts of open rebellion [*rebellion spectaculaire*]."

"Take no unnecessary risks."

I hear these lines with an intense satisfaction.

Without knowing it, and based solely on my intuition, I have followed these logical and objective instructions down to the letter.

My task is so out of the ordinary, so crushing, that my conscience has often been obsessed with doubt.

Fighting France has ruled in my favor.

Ghez, Paul. *Six mois sous la botte*. Paris: Éditions le manuscrit/Fondation pour la mémoire de la Shoah (FMS), Collection Témoignages de la Shoah, 2009. Selection from pages 59–65, 162–65, 202–5, 224, 257, 276–77. Translated from French by Rebecca Glasberg.

33. SONG OF THE OPPRESSED—LYRICAL RECOLLECTIONS OF AN ADOLESCENT BOY IN TUNISIA [c. 1943]

Alush Trabelssy of Tunis was only twelve years old at the height of the Second World War when he composed the extraordinary Judeo-Arabic poem "Gnayet Madloumin" (Song of the Oppressed). A supplication to God, the poem was meant to be sung to the melody of the popular Tunisian Arabic song "Al-qasm ʿalā

Āllah mina al-Karīta" (Swear by God on the Cart), which speaks, in a playful tone, about the difficulty of agricultural labor. At the time of the song's composition, Trabelssy was a student of Asher Shimon Mizrahi, the renowned, Jerusalem-born Jewish tenor, composer, and musician who, after spending many years as an adult in Tunis, became one of the great Arab singers of the era. Trabelssy had his eight-page poem printed by Tunis's Uzan Press and personally took charge of the pamphlet's distribution—but with time, all but one copy were lost or destroyed. Because the sole known, surviving copy was incomplete, the scholar Michal Saraf decades later reconstructed the poem through composite memories, relying especially on the help of one person, Pinchas Buchris. We share the results here. "Gnayet Madloumin" details the suffering of Tunisia's Jews in four-line, rhyming stanzas, offering a haunting view of Tunisia's occupation by the SS from the eyes of a talented young musician.

There were [families] whose houses were confiscated
and they were thrown into the streets
Sleeping on the floor, old and young
their belongings on the street, discarded
Pity us, my God
Their belongings were thrown out
from every county they came crying
They escaped on their own, wandering
oh God, they fainted, poor souls
Pity us, my God
Oppressed, pity us, my God. Oppressed, pity us, my God.
Barefoot and ripped clothes, pity us, my God.
We were ambushed
and made to stand row by row
We were surrounded by soldiers and the commander
My God, what will happen?
My God, how is this
the soldiers took us by force
They continuously told me: "Hey, Jew
follow us immediately!"
The lodging was in the dark
Every night passed in reflection
How will I get up early tomorrow for work

we resembled prisoners
Pity us, my God.
I resembled a prisoner
I think, how will this unfold
They transported us to Ksar at-Tir
[There] we remained, fasting for four days
Pity us, my God.
They started to disperse us
in Zaghouan and Djebebina
Except for the wounded in el-Aouina
They continued and took us to Megrine
Pity us, my God.
They continued, taking us to Mateur
and tears flowed from my eyes
From Bizerte, many people have fled
because of the bombs that fell like rain
Pity us, my God.
From the bombs, my mind became confused
and I didn't know what to do
Lice distressed me
my hands were wounded from shovel work
Pity us, my God.
My hands dried up
oh mother, go and see the lists
Your son is cast to the mountains
at least you will know where he is
Pity us, my God.
At least you will know how he is
This cry, this perturbation, why?
Be patient like me and like the others
And Incha'-Allah [hopefully], we will return happy
Pity us, my God.
Hopefully, we will return healthy
and my brother will return from Ferryville
And my friends will return from Enfidaville
and we will be reclining around the table

RACE LAWS, INTERNMENT, AND SPOLIATION 143

Pity us, my God.
We will be reclining [around] the table and grief will cease
How much they abused us in Sidi Ahmed!
He [God] will reward everyone as his reward
and God will sentence all the wicked.
Pity us, my God.
God will sentence them
and "Khamous" will prevail over them
And they will throw their weapons from their hands
and they will become prisoners for him
Pity us, my God.
They will be imprisoned by him
and the Jews will get their holiday and Shabbat
God forgive us wrongdoing
Say "Amen," all of you are present!
Pity us, my God.
Say "Amen," hopefully Khamous will come to us
and remove the shovel and the ax
God will destroy the government of slugs[1] which we fear
Pity us, my God.
Because of the [Italian government], ration cards were created
After a little delay, there will be no more bread [for you].
How many trucks loaded up [with loot],
and we were left hungry
Pity us, my God.
And we were left struggling on the black market
How will you make do, oh, father of children?
Even if you work night and day
Still your sons will be lacking
Pity us, my God.
You and mother [your wife] will always struggle and
you will find neither fish nor meat
Nor potatoes, nor vegetables nor eggs
also [the stores of] the donut sellers are locked.
Pity us, my God.
Also, the rich were arrested

1. "Slug" was a popular nickname for Italians.

and when they gathered,
they [the Germans] ordered them
"Protect our soldiers.
If one dies, we will kill fifty of you."
Pity us, my God.
If one dies, we will take revenge on you
and we will send the army upon you
Soldiers will enter houses and torture
they will surprise you while you are
sleeping.
Pity us, my God.
They will scare you all with the shell fire
and they will continuously sound alerts
When will they see planes
While you are still trusting God!
Pity us, my God.
We will continue to complain in the face of the Merciful,
who is present everywhere
How many fell from sheer cliffs!
and so many died, torn in pieces.
Pity us, my God.
There were those who died in puddles
There were those who died in trenches
There were those who died in shelters,
There were those who died in fear
Pity us, my God.
There were [families] whose houses were confiscated
And they were thrown onto the street
Sleeping on the floor, old and young
their belongings on the street, discarded
Pity us, my God.
Their belongings were robbed
From every city they came crying
They escaped on their own, running
Oh God, they deserve compassion, the poor souls
Pity us, my God.

Alush Trabelssy, "Gnayat al-madloumin" (Song of the Oppressed), cited in Michal Saraf, *The Hitler Scroll of North Africa, Moroccan and Tunisian Jewish Literature on the Fall of the Nazis.* Lod, Israel: Habermann Institute for Literary Research, 1988. Translated by Jessie Stoolman and Joseph Chetrit.

34. CONTROVERSIAL INTERCESSION—A JEWISH COMMUNITY LEADER'S WARTIME MEMOIR {1942–1943}

Born in 1909, Robert Borgel grew up in one of the most privileged families of Tunis. Descended from a long line of rabbis, Borgel's father Moïse served as the president of the Tunisian Jewish Council, which represented the community, and Borgel himself, trained as a lawyer, served as adviser to his father. Borgel completed his legal studies in Paris, specializing in maritime law. Upon his return to Tunisia, Borgel married into another prominent Tunisian Jewish family, the Bessis. In the fall of 1940, the Vichy Statut des Juifs, anti-Semitic and racist laws, barred Jews from the legal profession; at this time, Robert joined his father's insurance agency, which he would continue to run after the war. Borgel's wartime memoir, published recently by the Foundation for the Memory of the Shoah (France), offers an unusually vivid, day-to-day account of the suffering of Tunisian Jews during six months of German occupation (November 1942–May 1943), when they were interned, recruited into forced labor, pillaged of their property, businesses, and belonging, and (in small numbers) deported to concentration camps in Europe. During this period, Borgel and his father mediated between the Jewish Council and the Nazi occupiers, seeking to free interned Jews and negotiate for the release of Jewish hostages. In the postwar era, the ethics of the Borgel's actions would be questioned in a wide number of testimonies. In the decades after the war, Borgel oversaw an organization devoted to researching and documenting the history of Tunisian Jewry during the Second World War and served as vice president of the Commission for the Management of the Tunisian Jewish Community. He relocated to France in 1963.

Oh happy day, November 8, 1942! This day has restored to us the dignity of our human condition, breathing staunch faith back into our long-distraught hearts!

Finally, our luck was turning around; would the god of armies, who for so long had seemed to protect and favor the endeavors of the forces of Evil, finally situate himself on the side of the Good, the Just, the Decent?

Sunday, Monday . . . We wait, impatient and restless. Contradicting rumors, news that surpasses our wildest dreams:

Alger, Oran, Casablanca, and Bône are possibly in the hands of the Allies and the French resistance fighters, tomorrow Tunis will be as well, without doubt.

Will we finally see the dissipation of the oppressive atmosphere that has gripped our hearts? Will the chains be broken, is this the onset of liberation? Is it the beginning of the end?

For our poor Tunisia, it is—alas!—just the end of the beginning.

Tuesday, November 10, planes marked with swastikas are flying over Tunis. In the afternoon, the Aouina, already sullied by elements of the Luftwaffe, is bombed by allied planes.

The prologue is over. The drama begins!

Overwhelmed, roused by revolt and indignation, the people learn that we will not welcome our liberators with a gesture of immense gratitude. The Enemy, as indicated by everything from the tears of mothers to the dreary dawns of the firing squads, the enemy that grips an enslaved Europe in its claws, this same enemy is going to be presented to us as a defender coming to help us combat "cowardly Anglo-Saxon aggression." The German will be the brother in arms to whom we must open our airfields, our barracks; he is coming to help Tunisia "combat the traitors who would divert her from the path of honor."

Saturday [November] 14, the first squads in *feldgrau* appear in the streets of Tunis. A tense silence welcomes them, a nervous shiver rattles us now and again.

They continue to settle in methodically.

In the Community, despair abounds: everywhere, we know what the arrival of the Germans means; given their persistent concern, without a doubt they will take an interest in the Jews.

Some are less worried: the Allies are so close, London announces their arrival at a forced march in Tunis and Bizerte; the Germans will not have time to crack the whip.

Yet they continue to arrive, day after day; around eleven thirty, on Jules Ferry Avenue, we regularly see a carrousel of armored tanks around which group together proud *ballili* [Italian youth fascists, as from the youth organization Opera Nazionale Balila]; at the same time, transport planes pass by again and again, roaring overhead.

Even the optimists are worried.

Depressing news circulates: the Germans are going to attend to the Jews; people talk about lists of public figures being drawn up, of concentration camps to be organized.

Hostages, concentration camps, realities that seem so distant on our Tunisian soil! Our hearts have bled upon hearing of the suffering endured in the occupied countries by all the righteous men who would not renounce their views, the unhappy men who displeased despotic rulers, the Jews who committed the expiable crimes of being born and living. To be sure, we have often recognized, in the long lists of deportees, familiar, kindred names, but we never realized that this could reach us here, in our flesh and blood. The Jew has suffered horrifically throughout the centuries, but he retains, at the bottom of his heart, a hope that enables him to make it through the worse ordeals; until the end, man holds within him the thought that evil will spare him yet again.

A steady anxiety brings together, the afternoon of Saturday, November 21, two members of the Community: uncle and nephew, one, acting president, the other, he who held the position for four years: both of them had the same thought, a memory that oppresses them, that of their dear cousin, almost a brother, arrested by the Gestapo while he was trying to flee the occupied zone, brought to the Drancy internment camp, and from there to Poland, after which . . .

The Germans are settling in; we must assume the worst, expect to suffer ourselves, to pay with our persons for the reviled community that we represent. Make provisions, put your house in order. And wait!

Some advised us to flee.

That would be easy, temporary shelters would abound, surely, hospitality would be reliable. But of this, there is hardly any question; duties, even those that one does not solicit, impose certain obligations.

In truth, we do not entertain any illusion about the protection that a seventy-one-year-old man would be worth in the eyes of a disciple of Heydrich of Stülpnagel.

No matter, we must remain at our posts: representative or delegate of a group or of a population, we must be there to endure the first blows that will rain down upon them.

A Community president is not a military chief who can judge it necessary to leave and pursue the fight from the outside, or a militant who disguises himself to carry out a necessary task more efficiently. He is a pastor who, in the face of danger, gathers his flock around him to shelter it from the storm. If he were to flee himself, who would be left to gather the flock and lead it to shelter with minimum damage? Noblesse oblige! . . .

They left in a herd, taking bread and a can of food, a shovel or pick at the shoulder, poorly equipped against the cold, losing their shoes in the mud and the clay of waterlogged trails.

Led by hostile and contemptuous soldiers, like beasts to the slaughter, they walked for a long time, under a torrential rain, finally stopping after thirty kilometers, locked in for the night by the hundreds in barns and stables.

Just to move on at sunrise, always tormented when they were weary and worn out: "*Los, los!*"

Memory dims these torments, this misery; other events, other more serious misfortunes endured elsewhere, hold our attention and beckon our horrified pity. But, in the moment, what horrible sadness, what anxiety must embrace these men, at the mercy of an implacable enemy!

What an ordeal for the mothers! How much can one live, suddenly very old, slumped, and trembling, anxious to collect news, later distraught at the announcement of bombings that may have reached the labor camps!

Around 3,700 left in the first few days:
300 around Massicault and Ksar-Tyr
435 at Cheylus
250 at la Mornaghia
including a very significant proportion of those who had been rounded up and were among the first evacuated
nearly 1000 in the Italian sector (97 men in La Goulette, 256 at Enfidaville, 250 in Sainte-Marie-du-Zit, 26 in La Mohammedia, 345 in Zaghouan)
1,050 around Mateur and Bizerte; finally,
500 were moved to Aouina airfield, and 150 to the port of Tunis.

IMAGE 10. Jewish forced laborers in Tunisia wearing the obligatory Star of David, with German officer in foreground. "Nordafrika, Tunesien.-jüdische Männer mit provisorischem Judenstern bei Zwangsarbeit. Fegen eines Gehsteigs; PK XI.Fliegerkorps, c. 1942–1943," Bild 101I-556-0937-36, Das Bundesarchiv, Berlin.

As time went on, these numbers fluctuated many times.

The number will increase . . . until mid-January, then it will decrease, dwindling continually.

The men from Massicault and Ksar-Tyr, the first from Cheylus, returned before the end of the year.

Only some are left, less than thirty, they were going to make up the camp of Bir-M'Cherga, moved then to Boucha and to Goubellat.

They were among the most miserable. Infested with lice, covered in scabies, they were shut in hovels throughout the day, because of the proximity of the front and the intensity of the artillery fire. At 8 o'clock, in the evening lull, they were taken out and forced to work all night, just to be imprisoned again in the morning.

With no water, save a brownish and contaminated liquid, and isolated every night at work, even when ill, they lived the existence of convicts called on to die of misery. [This went on] until the day that furloughs were granted—which the men, of their own volition, extended indefinitely.

The youth of the Italian sector were going to become numerous in Zaghouan, then they began to travel around in various directions, tailing off little by little as they scattered about.

Those of Mateur were going to follow the same waning movement. Those of Sidi-Ahmed, owing to so-called Passover leave, were evacuated in the middle of April, thanks to a daring play by their boss, Alex Bonan.

But Bizerte remained, the last canker that we could not get rid of.

In Tunis, at the port of Aouina, men went back home in the evening, regaining the warm and welcoming atmosphere of their homes.

The same was true of the groups forming a ring around Tunis: Ariana, Mrira, Gamarth, djebel Djelloud or le Bac.

Their number was far from constant. It decreased quite perceptibly, until the moment a German inspection cracked the whip, demanding an improvement in discipline. To decrease once again a few days after.

And all that lasted for five months with various outcomes! . . .

Mateur

Of those who left during the first week, more than six hundred stopped in the region of Mateur. They set off again starting December 13 for a certain number of worksites about fifteen or twenty kilometers from the center, poorly connected by flooded and mountainous paths; it took us five hours to get there by horse-drawn buggy. . . .

Two hundred at Saf-Saf, 120 in Jefna, 50 in Rossignol, 70 in Katach-Baya, 40 in Michaud, 40 at Dumergue farm, 40 in Maa-Abiod and 60 in Aïn-Zammit.

We were lucky enough to find extremely valuable support in Mateur. Assisted by a team of friends and another Mateurois, Moïse Chemla, pharmacist Maurice Taïeb devoted himself immediately to all these men, working tirelessly, desperately attempting to better their living conditions, to protect them, to pave their way to freedom.

As intelligent as realistic, excited for each task, commanding, audacious and knowing how to dare, his success marked a real triumph of mind over matter.

In this fight against the enemy, whose prey we had to wrest away, he knew how to take advantage of the most minor, temporary asset, playing tricks and keeping an eye out for a moment of calm in order to pull out all the stops.

In Jefna ... a labor camp where men were condemned to work eighteen hours a day transporting munitions to the front lines, climbing rails on the hills, hardly sleeping a wink in the mud and the water, far from everything, receiving only, from time to time, a visit from a provisions truck from Mateur, these unhappy, weakened, sick, exhausted men foundered in dreadful despair.

To avoid sleeping in the mud, some deemed it appropriate to place a few old boards they had found by chance in an empty pond, to stretch out upon. In the night, they often woke up floating; sometimes the boards flipped over and they plunged into the glacial rainwater that had filled up the reservoir.

Among these slaves was a young painter, the future artist Edgard Naccache.

The evacuation of fifty-one sick men was permitted as of December 26. The first fruit of our labors, but there were seventy men still there who were suffering horrifically.

On the occasion of a visit by Henry Sfez, Taïeb leaves for Jefna with him; by car, then on foot, crossing the tunnel, running, crawling, taking shelter, they succeed, in the middle of artillery fire, in arriving at the camp.

After a conversation with the German officer, they finally reach an agreement for the men to have a three-day break in Mateur; they must return immediately after.

We had absolutely no intention of holding up this end of the bargain.

These seventy-six poor souls arrive in Mateur.

They relax at the hammam, are shaved, washed, and fed abundantly.

On the day foreseen for the return, Taïeb, bluffing, obtained the return of thirty-six men to Tunis from the Kommandantur of Mateur; as for the others, instead of returning to Jefna, they are sent to Saf-Saf, where our friend affirms that workers would be needed....

Bizerte

From the beginning, this camp has been plagued by ill fate. Bizerte, war port, essential location of the Axis defense system, crushed, bombed, evacuated of its civilians, seemed a cursed place, and those who left for it were destined for a terrible end, a descent into hell, from which you never climb out.

The first convoy for Bizerte left Tunis on December 11, 1942; it was made up of 496 laborers who, after numerous incidents, arrived at their destination and were lodged in the Philibert barrack.

Living conditions soon revealed themselves to be precarious. Lice, scabies, and other parasites were becoming the laborers' faithful companions, as they slept on straw mattresses that were never replaced. Their civilian clothing, hardly appropriate, had turned to rags, leaving them exposed to the damp cold and shivering in the rain. Sometimes, they were even barefoot.

Outside of the city, their work consisted of transporting ammunitions and burying them under trees. Others had to unload coal or cement from ships. Everywhere, they revealed themselves as second-rate workers, sabotaging the work as best they could.

Sabotaging the work: there was no need for a watchword for these boys; the inhuman torture of millions of their brothers had forced them to learn to hate.

In Bizerte, but also elsewhere—in Tunis, Mateur, and Zaghouan—they tried hard to win minutes that, multiplied throughout the day by the number of workers at the site, represented hundreds of hours stolen from the enemy.

They learned to take advantage of a guard's momentary lapse of attention, dropping part of their load into the sea. How many shovelfuls of coal, bags of cement, gas leaks, and cases of ammunition met the swells of the sea?

This was not without risk.

At Big Mountain [*djebel Kebir*], a young rabbi was stripped naked, still sweating profusely from the long march on the difficult slope he had just climbed, and exposed to the cold and rain for one hour, for having stopped a moment to wipe the sweat running down his brow.

Caught in the act, someone else almost lost his life for dropping a bag in the water.

Around the same time in Tunis, it took urgent intervention, a happy coincidence, and courageous action for two workers to avoid the same fate.

Incidents of sabotage soon made themselves known: workers hid in the mornings during roll call. Once they were discovered, they were whipped raw by a sadistic torturer, Soldier Rough, a former legionnaire, the damned soul of Elfess, the lieutenant in charge of the camp.

Some strong-headed men imposed their authority onto their comrades and made themselves into the men's representatives to the Germans.

When on December 22 a new contingent of 250 laborers—which included a certain number of volunteers—arrived at the barracks, they found themselves in the midst of a covert revolt.

Two days later, Jacques Krief was brought to the Community to give a most somber report: morale is at its lowest, with dangerous consequences. People are already talking about replacements. The word is going to make a killing [*le mot va faire fortune*]. Men are ill dressed and are often barefoot; the tins of provisions leave much to be desired.

Other equally worrisome letters arrive at the Community.

Henry Sfez is a delegate on inspection at Bizerte.

He has received authorization to have thirty sick men evacuated. This is his first attempt at emptying the camps. In the end, sixty men leave, with whom slipped several of excellent health. . . .

The Italian Sector

Zaghouan—The first days were very miserable, crammed into cramped warehouses without roofs, exposed to the cold and the rain, condemned to rot in a fetid environment, without being able to wash up at the nearby fountains and streams, since the guards were so fearful of evasions. Moving forward, these workers would suffer less, thanks to the activity of our delegates in the field.

The Community had designated Robert Bellaïche, a young teacher who had been dismissed from his teaching position by the Vichy government, as the representative at Zaghouan. Passionate, and fervently devoted to the tasks entrusted to him, he shared in the existence of all these boys, on whom he had a profound influence. He sometimes took initiatives for which others reproached him, but they were marked by his desire to better everyone's well-being. Thus in a position of authority, he shared among all the workers the packages that had been sent to certain individuals.

Starting December 20, the situation got distinctly better: provisions were organized and clothing distributed. The Italian authorities displayed their humanity.

Bellaïche was sending less worrisome reports to the Community, when, on December 30, they transferred the Zaghouan camp to Djebibina and, on January 12, the Saouaf camp to Djouggar. Two days later, one hundred men from Djebibina made their way toward Sbikha, near Kairouan. Others stopped in Djelloula.

The migrations began just as we were managing, with great difficulty, to establish connections. Everything had to be redone entirely. Work sites were further away from the center of Zaghouan. Distances of fifty kilometers would be separating the various groups, poorly connected to one another by impassible routes.

The Community delegate begged for transportation; it was impossible for us to satisfy him completely, as we ourselves had trouble maintaining contact for provisions. We succeeded, however, in sending him two arabas.

He would write, come to Tunis, insist that we satisfy a multitude of requests—which were often impractical—lose his temper, and then cave. He was not always aware of the obstacles we were struggling to overcome.

He did excellent work; besides the created organization, he obtained rest days for our workers from the Italian authorities, as well as the evacuation of sick men, who were never replaced.

Impulsive, sentimental, and even a bit mystical, he inspired sympathy through the sincerity of his passion.

In mid-January, there were around:

200 men in Djouggar
100 men in Sbikha
235 men in Djebibina
20 men in Saouaf

One of our young men, André Assuied, was dying in Djebibina. The health service, alerted by rumors of an epidemic—typhus, they were saying—immediately appointed head doctor Dr. Moatti to the field, and Dr. Maurice Uzan for general inspection.

The wretched Assuied had gotten septicemia. The rumors were unfounded.

Furthermore, the material conditions were rather generous: not everywhere was like Saouaf, where you bought a two-kilogram chicken for forty francs and exchanged a sheep for a few packets of cigarettes, but the provisions in general were far from precarious.

Morale, however, was lacking: filth; isolation, occasionally in the middle of a battlefield; obsession, the obsessive fear of rotting away in these internment camps.

We had asked numerous times for another shift to take over for at least ten days; finally, after a favorable report by the Italian military doctors, we were able to get an on-site three-week break for Djebebina's laborers.

The Italians, we must admit, behaved humanely with our families and friends. With them, we could talk things over, and eventually get them to admit that certain of our points were legitimate. . . .

We settled in a little while ago on Alger Street; the coming Christmas is creating many stressful tasks for us, which we are forced to execute: the Germans want to celebrate this holiday, of which they are most unworthy, the birthday of the Righteous One who came to Earth and told men to "love one another."

In reality, they want to organize huge feasts and drinking sprees, and, always under duress, they demand that we furnish them with all that will be necessary for their orgy at the Wehrmacht-Kaffee and at 168 Paris Avenue. Upon noticing their interest in all the details of the preparations, we feel a bitter deception; they settle in comfortably and without worry, whereas we will not yet have seen our friends at Christmas.

They ask for paintings, rugs, cloth placemats, candelabras and candles with fasteners for the Christmas tree.

Intendant Smeets, a horrible SS officer, brutal and vulgar, also asked for a pretty sleigh harnessed to a thoroughbred, harnesses, a pair of riding breeches, boots and . . . a Hanover hound that can swim and hunt. Loba, the young *Oberstleutnant*, will come to retrieve these items.

Fortunately, for several days Émile Hagège and the interpreter Rousseau have relieved us of these unpleasant and fastidious tasks.

One morning, in the midst of preparing for a holiday that is not ours, we receive a visit from a national police force [*gendarmerie*] corporal and a police inspector.

Discreetly, they inform the president of a discovery made on the city's outskirts by Melassine: the dead body of a Jew, a young, eighteen-year-old man, on whom they found papers in the name of Victor Nataf. He had a wound by his heart and had been thrown on the road. He was without a doubt shot by the Germans. His death seems to set us back a day or two. We need to find the body immediately and give him a proper burial.

An awful sorrow grips us. Mazouz, slaughtered in Cheylus on December 9, and now Nataf. Already two murders, with very little time between them! We think about this young, unknown man, who was slaughtered and abandoned like a dog on this somber and rainy day. They would have treated an animal better... he might have a mother and a father who are anxious, and who will have to hide themselves to mourn and bury their son, as if he were a criminal!

We received information: Victor Nataf is a young rabbinical student from Ariana, a simple and pious soul who was the victim of a revolting denunciation. Several days beforehand, he was arrested by the Germans after being denounced by stupidly mean and cruel people: he was accused of having made signals to the Allied planes during the night. What a hateful, crass lie!

Victor Nataf is Jewish. Lacking entertainment, the German soldiers don't look any further than that. They arrest him, completely surprised and too poorly armed in his simplicity to defend himself. They made him endure all sorts of tortures to make him confess that which couldn't possibly be.

Judged, condemned, shot!

We hadn't known anything of this. He has family, but in the confusion of this horrible December week, his loved ones didn't realize the danger he was in; or rather, they were afraid to have us intervene, seeing as we ourselves were in a bad way.

Furthermore, would we have been able to avoid this crime? Our relations with the Nazis were so tense!

Tunis-Journal, Guilbaud's gazette, will publish the following communiqué on December 21:

> The German authorities inform the population that, on December 19, 1942, the Jew Victor Nataf, domiciled in Ariana, was condemned to death for having compromised the security of the German troops by transmitting light signals during the course of an airborne attack on Ariana during the night of December 13, 1942.
>
> The sentence was executed.

The murder was carried out legally. "Germans are decent."...

The grand rabbi and a delegation from the rabbinical corps pay us a visit; Passover is coming. The people, most of whom are religious and especially attached to certain thousand-year-old traditions, are worried about manufacturing matzah. The factory on Arago Street has been requisitioned to meet the needs of the Italian Supply Offices. We have already made every effort to try and find a solution, but it is very difficult to reconcile the obligations stemming from the Occupation with ritual necessities.

We don't give up, however, and the grand rabbi leaves with our promise that we will not ease our efforts....

Led astray by nefarious propaganda, Arab workers increase their quarrels with their Jewish brothers, instead of feeling closer to them. We fear untoward accidents. The Community president will visit Cheikh el-Medina in order to have the neighborhood leaders offset these pernicious influences. Muslim notables, with whom the Jews have always had excellent relations, are also working towards this goal.

The morning of January 27, in the wake of an incident provoked by Arabs and Italians, Mr. Victor Valensi, a coreligionist, is arrested at the Tunis-Nord train station and brought to Manoubia. We are made aware of the affair. We speak to the commander, who is already up to speed: Valensi stands accused of espionage; according to an Arab worker, he tried to obtain information concerning the German arsenal in Aouina. Ghez announces that he knows Valensi, a former soldier and artillery officer, personally. Zaewecke rejoices immediately: "You see that the accusation is founded," he says. "Only an artillery officer would be interested in weapons."

Finally, we simplify the affair to its actual proportions and Valensi is released....

A large number of Italians, refugees from Tripoli, arrive every day. Most of them are skilled masons or pavers; what is more, nationals from Axis countries, they are more concerned with the work than us. We proposed to hire them on our dime as workers, replacing those of our men who have already partaken in the suffering.

Refusal....

Fines are raining down on the Sousse and Sfax Communities following one of Zaewecke's inspection tours. Our coreligionists are very unhappy about this, notably in Sousse, where the legionnaires, heads of the civilian command, were in charge of the labor service for quite some time. Men, women, and children wear the yellow star; they are subjected to all kinds of humiliations and receive very insufficient provisions.

Pariahs!

The students want to surpass the teachers; they could almost, by dint of cowardice and belligerence, make one prefer German beatings to subjugation to the legionnaires.

Here, in spite of Von Arnim's orders, we have so far avoided the yellow star. We do not consider this new badge a mark of disgrace; it will pass like the old one. However, wearing it would risk making it easier for our persecutors to single out their victims. The population fears it. . . .

A friend, a leading Muslim figure, recommends very discreetly to the [Community] president that he disappear as soon as he learns of the breach at the Enfidaville front. He is in a position to know that the Germans have drawn up a list of the latest men to deport; M. Borgel will be on it. To prevent such a painful end to his career, this friend nobly offers the president a secluded dwelling in the Arab town, a temporary sanctuary where he will find everything he needs.

Borgel, Robert. *Étoile jaune et croix gammée: Les juifs de Tunisie face aux nazis*. Paris: Éditions le manuscrit/Fondation pour la mémoire de la Shoah, Collection Témoignages de la Shoah, 2007. Selection from pages 75–79, 227–32, 234–37, 243–46, 261–63, 322, 326–27, 334, 343, 362. Translated from French by Rebecca Glasberg.

35. FLIGHT, INTERNMENT, ANNIHILATION, DEFIANCE—THE MANY WARTIME PATHS OF A JEWISH FAMILY FROM TUNIS {1943}

Frédéric Gasquet (b. 1941) was born in Tunis as Frédéric Scemla (sometimes spelled Chemla) to an elite family with close ties to the political elite of the Tunisian Protectorate. The family's connection to power was long-standing: Gasquet's maternal great-grandfather, who came from Djerba, even served in the bey's court in Tunis. Gasquet was only a toddler when the Nazis occupied Tunisia. As Gasquet's recently published memoir reveals, his father, grandfather, and uncle fled the German zone, hoping to join the Free French troops of General Philippe François Marie Leclerc. The men's exit was planned with a Muslim friend of Gasquet's grandfather, Hassan Ferjani, who subsequently betrayed the family by acquiring their assets. Ultimately, the Gasquets' flight brought neither safety nor opportunity for military engagement. The German authorities apprehended young Frédéric's father, uncle, and grandfather, deporting them to the Dachau concentration camp and eventually annihilating them. Back in Tunis, the women of the Gasquet family sought desperately to learn of the men's fate, engaging in their own forms of resistance and struggling with despair.

Working under German orders repulses my father, who had fought courageously at the Somme, and my uncle, raised with patriotic sentiments like his brother. They both want to cross the German lines that are fifty kilometers from Tunis and enlist in General Leclerc's Second Armored Division. They put their trust in their father's "friend," Hassen Ferjani. He proposes lodging them in his house in Hammamet while they wait for the right moment to cross enemy lines to join the Allied Forces. My grandfather decides to stay with them in Ferjani's house. Consequently, my mother and my grandmother stay in a neighboring villa, rented for the occasion. Four months go by. Hassen Fernaji, who, through his daily visits, had gained the complete trust of my grandfather, my father, and my uncle, proposes to the two sons that he help them leave. He offers to purchase my grandfather's stock of goods, which he will pay for little by little, he promises, because he doesn't have money. My grandfather accepts. And that is how he sealed their downfall, all three of them! Indeed, on the pretext that the moment is right, that the neighbors are starting to talk and are threatening to report them to the Kommandantur, Ferjani energetically advises my father and uncle to cross the German barricades in the region near Zaghouan in a cart: they will have the help of a smuggler he knows, a cart driver from Bouarada, in exchange for twenty thousand francs. My grandfather gives his agreement, giving the money to Ferjani and deciding to follow a few hundred meters behind his sons until the German barricades at the town of Zaghouan, in order to make sure that they make it across. The scene is set.

March 10, 1943. My father and my uncle, dressed as natives, driven by their makeshift smuggler, have not even gone three kilometers when they are arrested with their father by German soldiers who were waiting for them. First my grandfather, then his sons. The smuggler disappears. We find Hassen Ferjani at my grandmother's house a few hours later. He warns her of her husband's and children's arrests and advises her to give him her money and valuables, so as to prevent their likely confiscation at the hands of the Germans. Which, in her panic and trust, she resolves to do. He succeeds in his operation. He got in good with the German authorities and got rich off my grandfather's merchandise and my grandmother's possessions. . . .

My grandmother makes use of her network of relations in the French and Tunisian communities, which includes a friend, Aziz Djellouli, minister of the Bey of Tunis. In vain. No one can do anything. The orders come from the highest level of the German power structure. From SS Colonel Rauf himself, they say. Despite everything, mother doesn't hesitate to confront the German authorities on several occasions. To mask her Jewish origins and pull the wool over their eyes, she visits the village church every day, with me in the stroller, passing by the Kommandantur on her way. She stops there on several occasions. She demands news of her family, without any success, of course. The lack of knowledge about what is really happening in France, but probably also a bit of recklessness, prevent her from understanding the pointlessness of her actions and just how dangerous they are. She tells me that one of the German officers at the Kommandantur who would see her told her one day, "Madame, I am sorry, but you should not have married a Jew!" She tells me also that he made advances towards her and that she threatened to tell his boss. The effect, she tells me, was immediate. He stopped bothering her. In the German army, you were well-mannered and disciplined. My mother must have had exceptional courage and an unshakable faith in her right to hold the Germans accountable in these troubled times to threaten them for inappropriate behavior towards a woman—married to a Jew, moreover!

Weeks pass, and still nothing: no news from the three Scemlas! My mother and my grandmother imagine the worst. And yet, hope is not far away. Rommel retreated in Libya under the joint assault of General Montgomery's Eighth British army and a French army corps. They are winning ground and are closing in on Tunis. They finish by surrounding the German troops, who surrender on May 12, 1943. But the three Scemlas are no longer in Tunisia.

As for Admiral Esteva, he left Tunisia for Paris by plane with the Germans on May 7, 1943. He reaches Vichy, where Pétain congratulates him for work done in enforcing Vichy law and in collaborating with the Italians and the Germans. Ribbentrop himself sent him a note of thanks for having helped the Axis Forces in Tunisia, whereas in Alger a War Council presided over by General Giraud sentenced Esteva to death on May 15, 1943. Arrested in Paris on September 22, 1944, the former admiral would have the right to a new trial. On March 15, 1945, he would be found guilty of treason. Stripped of his military status by the High Court of Justice, he was sentenced to life in prison. Ill, he would be pardoned on August 11, 1950, and would die a few months later.

It was from a Red Cross document dated August 18, 1943, which was sent from Paris by Jean-Tony Jenn, a former student at the École polytechnique and classmate of my father's, that my grandmother and mother learn that the three men were deported to Germany, to a camp whose name they discover: Dachau. Jenn's message is very short. It states: "Gilbert n° 46 881 Geb. 14.2.18 Dachau 3K Bloc 22/1 is well, as are father and brother. May receive unlimited packages and money." How does Jean-Tony Jenn, whom my mother knows, know that the Scemlas are in Dachau? Might he have more information? But during these times of war, she did not succeed in finding it. News from Europe reaches Tunisia little by little. My mother and my grandmother are both full of anxiety. They try to find out more about Dachau, this camp where, they now know, the three Scemlas are locked up. What people say is frightening. But people say so many things during this time. Who to believe? Who to ask for information? The local French authorities that they ask, who know nothing about what is happening there? "We are sorry, we can tell you nothing, we don't know. Be patient. As soon as we know more, we will contact you." The Red Cross, through which they try in vain to send packages? Not there either, they know nothing about the fate of the three Scemlas. For how long must they stand this unbearable wait? A thousand questions come to their minds. First about what happened between the three men's arrest in Hammamet and Dachau. But no one in their circle knows; being deported from Tunisia to Germany for crossing enemy lines seems implausible, impossible to everyone. And dramatic, of course. Considering the current state of the world, the only possible means of transportation between Africa and Europe is via airplane. Furthermore, if they did go by plane, where did they land? In France, in Germany? Why did the Germans, who have quite a few other concerns, send these three prisoners under such exceptional conditions? Are they considered that dangerous? What could be the serious charges being held against them? Is it for having wanted to join up with the "enemy"? Jews arrested in Tunisia are for the most part sent to labor camps or put in prison in Tunis or its environs. So why were they deported? Why them? Nothing but uncertainties! Patience, patience, people tell them, the Allies are winning the war. My mother and my grandmother are not out of the woods yet; nor are the three Scemlas, who cannot imagine the infernal cycle in which they are stuck....

For Claire, life stopped with the death of her son and her two children. She was then forty-six years old. Everything afterward was nothing but a second-rate simulacrum of life for her. Several days after she found out the terrible news, broken down, hopeless and inaccessible, she lost her mind. She had to be hospitalized for a few weeks in a psychiatric establishment located in the near suburbs of Tunis. Upon her release, she spent six months bathed in affection in the home of one of my grandfather's brothers, Raoul Scemla, who lived in Morocco. Upon returning to Tunis, and despite serious depressive episodes, she made the decision to work in order to avoid being crushed by the ever-present memory of her loved ones. She took exams and found a position in the administrative service of the Social Security System. A serious disagreement with a member of my father's family made her cut off ties with the Scemlas who lived in Tunisia and had not clearly picked her side. Interpersonal problems with my mother who had "stolen" her son, and which dated from their life together during the few months when my father was still at X, were not resolved after the arrest. The events exacerbated their sensitivities. Shut away in their pain, they distanced themselves even more from one another.

Gasquet, Frédéric. *La lettre de mon père: Une famille de Tunis dans l'enfer nazi*. Collection Résistance, Liberté-Mémoire. Paris: Félin, 2006. Selection from pages 39–40, 42–43, 46, 71–72. Translated from French by Rebecca Glasberg.

36. "SWEPT UP IN A MONSTROUS WHIRLWIND": THE WARTIME DIARY OF ALBERT MEMMI {1942–1943}

Born in Tunis, Albert Memmi (1920–2020) grew up on the border of the ḥāra (Jewish neighborhood) and neighboring Muslim quarter, raised by parents of Livornese Jewish/Sephardic and Berber Jewish descent. Like most indigenous Jews, Memmi's family spoke a mixture of European and Arabic languages at home, a reflection of Tunisia's multifaceted cultural milieu. While attending the local school of the Alliance Israélite Universelle, Memmi was exposed to the economic and cultural resources of the Tunisian Jewish elite and became conscious of his own economic precarity and that of many other local Jews. Memmi was consumed by the subject of his own social development as a Jew in colonial French Tunisia, where he witnessed at an early age vast economic disparity and social conflicts between its diverse religious and ethnic communities. Memmi recognized that his acceptance by privileged French society hinged on his rejection of his Jewish, Berber, African, and Arab self. He sought refuge in books and schooling, and in time, his voracious thirst for learning carried him to the University of Algiers, where he studied philosophy. During the Nazi occupation of Tunis, Memmi was sent to a forced labor camp, from which he managed to escape, but not before coming to terms with his own Judaism. In Memmi's view, the social stratification that he witnessed before the war continued even within the Nazi labor camps—where he refused to join the ranks of those Jews spared from forced labor because of their elite status. Perhaps most known for his prolific anticolonial (and later colonial apologist) writing, both fiction and nonfiction, this diary of his life in the camps, published in 2019, provides a glimpse into this formative period in Memmi's life, before his rise to fame.

Fundamentally, the Germans had won. Always the same method: put the defeated populations into situations that pit them against one another. It is impossible to convince young people to leave for a labor camp. That would be serving the Germans, they'd tell you. It is impossible to defend having a cushy job to those who are in the camps. They ask to be relieved, as that is justice. The majority haven't been relieved since the creation of the camps. The ill and the heads of families are the only ones who have a chance to return home.

"Two months ago," Valensi continued, "I tried to get myself evacuated for illness. I smoked five cigarettes soaked in oil, on an empty stomach. I had a fever and I was deathly pale. The doctor was distraught. He didn't understand it at all. He was even paler than me. Then I chickened out. The doctor and the head of the camp spoke personally. It seems that I was doing very poorly and that he was unable to tend to me. Moreover, I felt really ill. My head was spinning at top speed and I couldn't lift a finger. I thought that I was going to die, so I confessed everything. The doctor said nothing, he seemed relieved. He tended to me in silence, and then gently said to me, 'Get out of here, asshole!' But I regret it now. If I had stayed the course, he might have evacuated me."

"As for me, I swallowed an entire can of snuff. I started to vomit and I was as yellow as a lemon. And the nitwit nurse thought I had appendicitis! I must admit that it was me who suggested this to him. There was no doctor at camp. The sweat was pouring down my forehead . . . oh, how uncomfortable it was! But they got me even so, the bastards! I think that they had decided to send me 'to die' in Tunis when the provisions truck brought my young brother, whom they had just rounded up. The asshole really thought it was a good thing to ask to be brought to the same camp as me. I called him all the names in the book, but I couldn't leave him there. I told the head of the camp that I didn't want to go home. Imagine the surprise on his face! It was the first time that a sick man had refused to be evacuated.

"As you wish," he said to me, "but if you die, it's on you."

"I won't die. I know what I have and I also know that it'll be over in two days."

He looked at me curiously and added, without any indignation:

"Yet another one who acts like a dumbass."

I didn't answer, but we understood one another. You know, the heads, they don't always understand these stories and they don't hold them against us."

"And your brother?"

"Oh, he's no longer here. I managed to get him to leave."

The man winked with a knowing look.

The other day, Georges Krief saw a laborer who should have been much further away.

"What are you doing here?"

"Me? I'm in order."

"What? That's not possible! How did you do it?"

"You really want to know?"

Krief insisted.

"OK, well, here you go: a German offered me his a** and freedom. I accepted. Which means," he added, "that I got two things: both the German, and my freedom." . . .

Above all, there is the requisition. All those who have a profession that is susceptible to being used by the Germans are hurrying to offer their services to the German commissariat, which accepts rather easily. On this subject, the desire of the commissariat matters very little. Only the SS, meaning the Nazi party, has the right to decide. A requisition is only valid if it is stamped by the SS.

Some were able to get into an officer's good graces, occasionally through incredible means. I once heard the story of a requisition including the mention "supplies for Captain X." These supplies consisted in the procurement of one woman a week. It's not a pretty picture. Some requisitions are purely imaginary, thus on the list of workers requisitioned from a shoe factory are

IMAGE 11. The Vichy and Nazi occupiers compelled North African Muslims and Jews, as well as European refugees and prisoners, to engage in forced labor in camps and on infrastructural projects. As these forced laborers look on, a German soldier extends a cigarette and light to a local man who was either passing by or employed as an overseer. The soldier's backward-pointing rifle serves as a reminder that during wartime, all such encounters took shape under threat of violence. "Nordafrika, Tunesien.-Soldat gibt Einheimischem eine Zigaretteund Feuer, im Hintergrund Männer beim Graben; KBK Lw 6, c. 1942–1943," Bild 101I-418-1831-33, Das Bundesarchiv, Berlin.

the names of two lawyers and several workers of different professions. There is the medical corps and the medical auxiliary. Whoever had even the slightest understanding of medicine or pharmacy was bombarded with "Doctor" or "Pharmacist," or "Nurse," to say the least. It is also amusing to see these young students in their first year who dignifiedly wear their armband with a red cross—that, incidentally, the older doctors don't wear—called "Doctor."

. . .

Friday, April 9—The provisions truck arrived empty. There is not yet another shift to replace us. The men will continue to wait. There are some who have gotten used to this, who no longer raise questioning looks.

Boublil is the epitome of these psychologically exhausted men. I have not yet been able to understand how he functions. He never changes clothes.

Maybe he doesn't have another set of clothing, maybe he no longer has anybody. He never speaks. Adding to his moral isolation is a pitiful physical solitude. Lice cover his clothing. He inspires disgust. People forget him, even when joking. You can make fun of a small misfortune, but you forget the irremediable. During the hours when men attend to their business in the camp, freed from their shovels and picks, they exist for themselves. He disappears. I think that he must be sleeping. He would never dream of asking for more, of requesting a bit more soup, of insulting the cook or of slacking off. He has given up. Boublil represents the camps' ugliness and misfortune in the most acute way.

But apart from this, there are all sorts of miseries. Scabies infections that men no longer hope to cure. Defeated by the lice that invade the entire body, our clothing and blankets, even the tent canvas, which we no longer try to fight. The invasive filth that grows back after an hour of work. Oh, to think I thought it was a question of unwillingness!

"The men are dirty," people said to me.

"Well, they should clean themselves!"

When people responded that they didn't have the time, I shrugged my shoulders. You always have the time to wash up. But no! You don't have the time, you don't even have the desire to wash yourself, to take care of yourself. Life itself becomes monotony, emptiness. Sometimes, we ask ourselves if living is worth the pain. When you wake up at dawn and stop working at sundown, you only wish for one thing: to throw yourself on a tarpaulin on the ground and to sleep without suffering too much from the dampness. . . .

I have since asked myself, why were we so distraught? After all, soldiers spend many a day on the much more challenging front lines! The thing is, though, we were not soldiers, we were fugitives. We had the terrifying sensation of being tracked by men and by fire. In addition to the Italians who were chasing us, all the Germans were our enemies; we are in the middle of the enemy front. As for the machine guns, we didn't behave like those who can defend themselves, or at least entertain the thought that they can do so. We had neither the leaders nor the instructions in which soldiers blindly put their trust, to which they entrust their entire identity, particularly when in danger. We were running away. That was the only directive, the only goal. Bomber attacks recommenced their terrifying relays. The hills that surrounded us were literally doused. Enormous billows of smoke and dust rose up and remained in the air for a long time, as if in slow-motion. The bombings always widened their target areas. One load of bombs fell two hundred meters from us. I can still smell that awful odor of explosives, particular to aerial bombs, that for weeks permeated our street in Tunis, as well as our furniture, the air that we breathed and even our food....

The next morning, I pack my bag, hug my parents, and leave to join them. I had prepared my bag for an open-ended trip. Like all the others, I don't have the slightest idea of what the next day will bring. I only have the impression that I am sinking into a bottomless abyss.

In the street, on the edge of the square, the police are preventing a crowd of women from overrunning the school, which still contains those who were rounded up the night before. The inside is swarming with people. Several Nazi giants guard the doors with their beautiful, glistening machine guns in hand. Men, already tired from a sleepless night, are wearing that broken and distraught look that I have since seen so often on the faces of many young people. Even so, a lot of them had tried to sleep directly on the ground, under the December sky. A small group had found space in the classrooms; already, the lack of privacy that leaves no room for feelings of individuality has taken hold. I think this might even be the overwhelming impression: the feeling of no longer existing as a distinct personality, of no longer having any hold over what happens. We are swept up in a monstrous whirlwind that is carrying us away at an extraordinary speed. You have to bring your arms and legs as close to your body as possible if you want to avoid being torn limb from limb. This impression will never completely disappear during what happens after.

And I dream with anguish about the psychology of the youth who have felt like this for years, and who still do. Men continue to arrive. They take names. We are urged to sign up. A curious haste of the lamb to the slaughter. But we must finish! Around eleven o'clock in the morning, the school courtyard looks like an immense metro car in rush hour. We can hardly move. The Nazi officer is arresting anyone who enters. He yells something in German, and of course no one understands. Suddenly, he puts up his fists and punches his way through the crowds. We are somewhat surprised, but we have already been introduced to this method. The first group of slaves is equipped with shoves and pickaxes, traverses the narrow passage, and disappears through the door. The work camps begin....

One day, faced with the round-ups' lack of success, the Germans ordered the recruitment committee to arrest parents in place of their uncooperative children. Complete turmoil among the leaders. How could the Jews themselves consent to using such abhorrent German methods? It was requested that the French police take care of it. The police also refused, and asked for confirmation from the Germans, who gave them a formal order. But this order only eased minds. They still had to see to it that this new aggravation wasn't too odious. It turned into a pleasant walk in the park. Several mothers were arrested. They settled into the Alliance school courtyard with their kitchen utensils. They chatted and played cards for two or three days, even with the jailer's wife. After which they were released, once the German officer began to forget the matter.

Memmi, Albert. *Journal de guerre 1939–1943: Suivi de, journal d'un travailleur forcé; et autres textes de circonstance.* Edited by Guy Dugas. Biblis 205. Paris: CNRS éditions, 2019. Selection from pages 132–34, 144–45, 155–56, 200–201, 239–40, 295–96. Translated from French by Rebecca Glasberg.

37. SEXUAL VIOLENCE IN THE ḤĀRA {1942–1943}

We have already encountered the voice of Robert Borgel in this volume. Child of a privileged Jewish family from Tunis, Borgel's father served as the president of the Tunisian Jewish Council, which represented the Jewish community, and Borgel himself, a lawyer, as adviser to his father. In the fall of 1940, Vichy anti-Jewish laws, the Statut des Juifs, barred Jews from the legal profession. Borgel's wartime memoir, from which this source is drawn, offers an unusually vivid account of the suffering Tunisian Jews during six months of German occupation (November 1942–May 1943), through the rising tide of anti-Semitism, internment, forced labor, and the spoliation of property and belongings. Here, Borgel reflects on a distressing trend—the propensity of German soldiers to enter the Jewish quarter (ḥāra) of Tunis, beating men and raping women. These actions terrified Tunis's Jewish community, but they also disturbed Nazi order, especially since they violated the Nazi racist taboo on sexual relations between so-called Aryans and Jews. In Borgel's account, various people brainstorm solutions to the crisis: Maximilien Trenner, a Jewish Austrian émigré compelled by the Nazis to serve as a translator for the SS in Tunis, proposes the ingenious use of dyes to mark the aggressors. Leaders of the Jewish community propose community policing and the diversion of German troops to another neighborhood outside the ḥāra, likely populated by poor Muslims. Combined, these proposals reflect creative, though at times morally questionable, attempts by Jewish women and men to maneuver within the constraints of a violent and harrowing occupation.

At the presidential residence, we are obsessed with a new worry.

Grave abuses were committed in the Hara, our ghetto. Drunk German soldiers, led by lowlife natives, entered Jewish homes during the night. The soldiers attacked the men, rendering them powerless, and sexually assaulted the women.

Some of these doleful women did not dare to come complain, preferring to hide their shame. Others came to Algiers Street with frightened looks, believing they might reencounter this horrible scene.[1] What consolations could we provide them? Assistance, moral comfort. Above all, we must prevent the return of this disgraceful mob of unruly soldiers.

When Zaewecke arrived, the president expressed his feelings of indignation. His interlocuter demanded a report and promised an enquiry, but it will be really difficult to find these criminals. He will speak to his boss about it.

We discuss the following, thoroughly: what is the point of enduring contact with the Germans, if not to spare our loved ones unbearable abuses?

Trenner has an idea: requisition all the stocks of paint and red ink and distribute them to the Hara's inhabitants. All victims of a sexual assault could smear this mixture on the face and clothes of the soldier who would force himself upon her. The guilty will thus be identifiable.

However, Trenner is concerned about the poor quality of the dyes, which are not permanent.

Each day brings more complaints.

Visiting the Hara seems to be a mandatory attraction for off-duty soldiers.

Following their informers, people from the area, they force their way in, demand a drink, extort money, jewelry, and then satisfy their animal instincts. Threatened with guns, kept at bay, families witness the events, horrified and powerless.

1. The original, which says that women visited Algiers Street "croyant revoir toujours l'affreuse scène," leaves ambiguous whether they feared other, future acts of sexual violence or whether such a visit might trigger traumatic memories of the past.

The police? Where can you find police at ten o'clock pm, or in the middle of the night? Furthermore, they never intervene against the German army. Mustn't cause trouble!

We increase the number of reports and requests for assistance from Zaewecke.

He objects that, when certain victims were interrogated at the *Feldgendarmerie*, where we had taken them to lodge their complaints, they had taken everything back. Faced with the German political machinery, they became afraid. This does not facilitate our task.

Placing ourselves on a more human level, we insist on the serious disadvantages—from the disciplinary point of view—that these nocturnal expeditions can bring about. The German army claims to have strong discipline; these actions are hardly in character.

We add that we cannot send or keep workers in camps if the security of the families in Tunis is not guaranteed.

We also suggest that the commander have military police patrol the streets to arrest drunk soldiers who might venture into these neighborhoods.

Zaewecke does not lose sight of the issue.

One must admit, the proposed measures are radical; experience tells us they are efficient: prohibit the entry of Axis army soldiers into the Jewish neighborhoods, *Feldgendarmerie* patrols at night, contact with the local authorities and French police. Finally, posters citing the prohibition will be hung at the entry of each street leading to the Jewish quarter.

We are tasked with establishing a circular plan delimiting the forbidden area. For good measure, we even include certain neighborhoods that could potentially offer German soldiers multiple pleasures.

We are rather proud of this achievement.

In Tunis, you won't hear—as you so often do in certain cities in German countries or occupied areas—this official sentence, full of meaning: "There is unrest in the Jewish quarter."

May we prevent pogroms, all the way!

Borgel, Robert, *Étoile jaune et croix gammée: Les juifs de Tunisie face aux nazis*. Paris: Éditions le manuscrit/Fondation pour la mémoire de la Shoah (FMS), Collection Témoignages de la Shoah, 2007. Selection from pages 281–84. Translated from French by Rebecca Glasberg.

38. "WHO IS MORE OF A DOG?" A RADICAL POET'S VIEW OF INTERNMENT [1942]

Max Aub Mohrenwitz, known by his middle name, Aub (1903–1972), child of a French Jewish mother and German Christian father, spent most of his life in Spain, where he fought on the left-leaning Republican side of the Spanish Civil War against the conservative Nationalists, led by General Francisco Franco. After Franco's triumphant entry into Barcelona in January 1939, which marked his near consolidation of power, Aub fled to Paris. There, Aub was denounced as a communist and imprisoned in the Vichy penal camp Le Vernet d'Ariège. Later, he was deported by the Vichy authorities to Djelfa, in southern French Algeria—one of the forced labor camps erected in North Africa by the Vichy regime to house Spanish Republicans, French communists, and others perceived as political rivals. Aub was one of the few prisoners to record his memories of the camp in a lyrical, poetic personal diary, totaling forty-seven poems. In the collection's introduction, Aub describes reading aloud from his poems to other inmates at night, by oil lamp, hidden in their tents, "hungry and livid." In 1942, Aub escaped from Djelfa and hid in a Jewish maternity hospital in Casablanca with the help of the Hebrew Immigration Committee (HICEM), an organization formed to facilitate Jewish emigration from Europe, as well as Jewish refugees. That fall, he was granted Mexican protection, including a visa, and fled North Africa for Mexico City, where he eventually became a well-known literary critic, playwright, and experimental novelist. Because of his political experiences and lasting commitment to the Spanish Republican cause, he was barred for most of his life from returning to either France or Spain. Here, we present three poems drawn from his Diary of Djelfa (1947). With their complex literary imagery and figurative style, the poems emphasize the harsh treatment that French military authorities imposed on prisoners, sometimes through the use of so-called goumiers, *colonial Moroccan soldiers, at times forced by their precarious circumstances to serve in the French army. Aub's poetry touches, too, on his relationship with the local indigenous population (particularly local women) in a poem informed by the orientalist imagination.*

God, So Many Dogs!

The commander and his dog,
The assistant and his dog,
The sergeant with his dog

God, so many dogs!
There goes the commander
With the horn-handled whip
How well the light red color
Complements the man's brown skin!
There goes the assistant
Up to his neck in wine,
[The two are] holding onto one other
And behind goes the sergeant
God, so many dogs!
Tell me: Who is more of a dog,
The drunk or the teetotaler?
Where milk is enough,
The other is missing wine's dryness;
One strikes through the liver
And the other through the wineskin.
Tell me, between gentlemen,
The strike breaker or the master,
Who is more of a dog?
The one that hits or the one that licks boots,
Blind with fear?
Who is more of a dog
The master or the servant?
The commander and his dog,
The assistant and his dog,
The sergeant with his dog
God, so many dogs!
The dog trembles
Licking the stick that is there to kill him.
Who is more of a dog,
The dog or the head honcho?
Jump, lie down, lick!
Who is more of a dog,
The dog or the commander?
Who is more of a dog,
The one with the whip or the spiked collar?

RACE LAWS, INTERNMENT, AND SPOLIATION   173

IMAGE 12. Commander Julius Caesar Caboche stands with German shepherd in front the Djelfa internment camp. The camp housed political enemies of the Vichy regime, who were forced to labor on a trans-Saharan railroad building project. Behind Caboche stands the "marabout tents," each of which housed between twelve and twenty prisoners. "Camp de Djelfa," "Les Camps et Centres d'internement du Territoire, de Septembre 1939 à Juillet 1943," Report by André Jean-Faure, May 16, 1942, Archives Nationale, 100W127, vol. 4, Departmental Archives of Meurthe-et-Moselle, Nancy, France.

Who is more of a dog,
The one who obeys or the one who commands?
The greyhound or the hound?
[The difference, a splitting of hairs]
Everyone wears a collar,
Everyone wears a muzzle,
Some on the neck,
Others on the chest
And everyone wears a cross.
Who is more of a dog
A stray or a lapdog?
Sons of parents

Getting drunk:
Who is more of a dog
The bull mastiff or the foxhound?
The commander or the foreigner?
One is long, the other short-tailed.
God, so many dogs!
They call the bootlickers
"Frenchmen,"
Those for whom the ass
Is as good as the face.
Oh, my French fuckers[1] of a thousand dogs!
Oh, my fancy Frenchmen!
Oh, my French fuckers with a silver tongue!
Those of you who have dogs instead of children:
If it weren't for the town,
Where would you go with so many dogs?
The commander and his dog,
The assistant and his dog,
The sergeant with his dog
God, so many dogs!

   3-15-1942

Aub, Max. *Diario de Djelfa*. Guaymas, Mexico: Joaquín Mortiz, 1970. Translated from Spanish by Jessie Stoolman.

39. AN ALGERIAN MUSLIM'S MEMORIES OF INTERNMENT {1940–1943}

Scholars have uncovered only one firsthand account by a Muslim who experienced the camps of North Africa: the diary of Mohammed Arezki Berkani. Before the Second World War, Arezki Berkani was an active member of the North African Star, a political party whose leader, Messali Hadji, called for Algerians to rise up against French colonial rule in the 1920s and late 1930s. After the party's dissolution in 1937, Arezki Berkani joined the new nationalist Algerian People's Party (Parti

   1. Original word is *gabachos*, a pejorative Spanish term to refer to foreigners, here French people.

du peuple algérien, or *PPA*) *and became involved in political resistance against the French colonial authorities in metropolitan France and its Algerian colony. His work with this organization, which began prior to the creation of the Vichy regime, extended into its reign. In 1941, Vichy authorities imprisoned Berkani in the labor camp (and erstwhile detention facility) of Djenien Bou Rezg, located near Aïn Sefra, in the Algerian Sahara. Others deemed politically objectionable by the Vichy authorities were also sent to the camp, including prominent PPA member Maamar ben Bernou and communists such as Mohamed Badsi, Larbi Bouhali, and Ali Rabia (who were all Muslims). Upon his release from this camp, Berkani documented in a memoir the daily lives and experiences of the Muslims and Jews imprisoned in Djenien Bou Rezg. The account offers a precious perspective on the experiences of Muslim internees in the Vichy Saharan camps of Algeria and Morocco, including, in this selection, their marking of ṣalāt, the Muslim daily prayers, and of ʿĪd al-Aḍḥā, one of the most important feast days in the Muslim calendar. Noticeably, Arezki Berkani's memoir features not only his own voice but also the testimony of other Muslims and of Jews imprisoned alongside him.*

The departure of European prisoners and Moroccan Muslims took place during this period of time. There were approximately sixty of them, including a captain who used to be in the same regiment as Major Richard, back when both of them were doing their military service. According to certain intelligence, this captain whose name I have forgotten was arrested on the charge of actively supporting Allal El-Fassi, the leader of the Moroccan nationalist movement. As for the departure of the Moroccans, they say that during this period the Algerian government did not want to bear the financial burden of Morocco's political prisoners, so they directed them towards Morocco.

Each week there were new arrivals. Among the liberated, there were members of the PPF and SOL, freed immediately by official telegram. The PPF is Doriot's party (ex-communist). The SOL is a French right-wing party.

There were also some Europeans and indigenous Muslims freed. Muslims and Europeans were represented among the liberated, and were represented in all the political parties and organizations.

Let us list the names of the parties, organizations, groups, etc. who were detained in this camp. Among the groups, organizations, and Algerian political parties, there was the Association of Algerian Ulamas (AUA), the Algerian Communist Party (PCA), the Algerian People's Party (PPA), the Union of

Friends of the Algerian Manifesto and Liberty (ULEMA), members of federations from Constantine, Alger, and Oran, union activists, independent representatives, Hadjs, Imams, etc....

Among the Europeans: SFIO Socialists, the French Communist Party (PCF), union members, Left Republicans (RG), PPF and SOL as stated above.

In addition to the Moroccans mentioned above [who came to the camp] around 1940, there were Tunisian patriots that joined us in 1943, before the liberation and dissolution of Djenien-Bou-Rezg camp....

I think highly of Zanettaxi due to his integrity as a communist. I remember that, in order to hear a report approved by Major Richard, they gathered together all the Muslim and European inmates. It was at the beginning of the month of Ramadan. A Muslim delegation had gone to see the camp's commanding officer to ask him to improve the menu during the month of fasting and to eliminate half a day of work.

In this report, Major Richard said he could not satisfy the Muslims' request to stop working on account of the presence of European inmates: he could not make the Europeans work while the Muslims rested. Zanettaxi responded that he himself agreed to make the Europeans work and let the Muslims fast. Finally, the commanding officer agreed to improve the menu, but I do not remember very well if the afternoon rest was granted to us or not during the month of Ramadan....

Let us now examine the interior of the camp's sections. It is not for me to describe what happened in the European section. Furthermore, I did not live there in the beginning, and a wall separated us [Muslims and Europeans]. From our arrival in the first section, there were those that had arrived a few weeks beforehand, namely the first contingent from Oran and the first contingent from Alger. We had come with the first contingent of Constantine even though we formed the second contingent from Alger. Our brothers from the PPA, the Oulamas and other independents, informed us that our indigenous communist comrades were not happy on account of our early morning prayers. In addition, before our arrival, each of the Muslim brothers prayed alone, even though they should have done their prayers together, as Islam recommends. Boukhroufa, the representative of the indigenous Algerian communists, came to see me on several occasions. I apologized to him for the bother, and I intended to contact the practicing Muslims first.

Boukhroufa did not stop coming to see me after this. He knew my name, he had heard about me at the exercise area at a clandestine meeting in Alger. He said to me:

"I know that you are P.P.A. Introduce me to your friends so that they are respected." This was the sort of [political] distinction that I understood to be desired. I therefore responded:

"Dear comrade, do you know the communists?"

He responded, "Yes."

I continued, "So, all the rest are nationalists."

Those are the only words that I said to the communist representative. This exchange was publicized among the non-communist internees. They were all very happy, above all the independents. The same day, Bradaï Si Abderrahmane PPA started to call all the faithful at prayer times. All the practicing Muslims would get together at each prayer time during the day. There were only a few communists who did not pray. But harmony prevailed among them, since we had directed the practicing men to do them favors in order to encourage them to begin practicing like us.

Classes were given not only in Arabic, but in French as well. Teachers were provided for us for these classes. There were several: elementary classes to teach the alphabet, secondary classes, even advanced classes. They took place not only on Sunday and Thursday afternoons, our days off, but also during the other days after lunch and in the evening. Four teachers shared the evening course duties, either interpretation of the Coran or explanation of the Hadith. There were even frequent conferences.

We must thank these teachers, the majority of whom had studied in Zaitouna, others with the Cheikh Benbadis, may God fill him with blessings and peace. There was even one who had studied at El-Azghar, and another substitute teacher. We bought notebooks, chalk, etc. via the post officer, who went to Beni-Ounif for the postal service and served as our intermediary. Others obtained the supplies they needed in packages from their parents or friends. For more than four months, the practicing believers proselytized the non-practicing Muslims, especially the thirteen communists, and the few who belonged to other organizations. Two communists ended up joining us for prayers.

During the period of Ramadan, a change sprung up between the communists and the practicing Muslims. The communists were moved from the first section and put into the second section. According to certain intelligence, they stopped observing Ramadan. The camp commander decided that, from that day on, all Muslims who arrived at the camp who did not practice religion would be directed to the second section. He had authorized, with a sort of free pass, those who wanted to take classes to visit the first section either during the day or even in the evening. I also remember that there were a few *indigènes* who had been authorized to take classes in French in the second section. The first section was full, and the camp commander was obligated to put the new arrivals, both Europeans and Muslims, in the second section....

The camp began to fill up. There were more people arriving than leaving. There were also some black-market traders who arrived and were integrated with the political prisoners, but the number was not large. Among the black-market delinquents, there were both Muslims and Europeans. There were also political prisoners who arrived from the camps in France. Among these internees, the largest number were communists. The majority of them could not walk, let alone climb stairs, due to hunger-induced weakness.

According to the stories they told us, there was no longer any food in the French camps. They would put salt on a piece of newspaper that they would swallow in order to alleviate the demands of their stomachs.

They were therefore very happy to arrive in the Djenien-Bou-Rezg camp after having spent a few weeks in Morocco. According to them, life in the camps in France was unbearable, and they had buried several of their colleagues who had died of starvation.

Camp life began to change. As for food, we had green vegetables, carrots or cabbage, also often lentils or split peas, and meat twice a week, Thursday and Sunday. Packages became more and more rare. Fabre had assigned two internees from the North as cooks, as he and the second commander Louis were both originally from this region. Work also became very grueling and more and more severe. They restarted propaganda in support of Marshal Pétain. Directly or indirectly, they spread collaborationist propaganda in the camps. They talked about the soldier from Verdun who won the war in 1914 and who had just saved France for a second time. Each liberated prisoner was made to sign the oath of obedience to the Marshal.

One fine day brought the release of several union members from Akbou who were working in a mine. I don't remember how many there were. In any event, they didn't know how to read or write in French any more than in Arabic. When they were called to the office to sign the promise of loyalism to Marshal Pétain, one of them refused to do so. The release of this man was delayed several weeks because of his refusal, but he was liberated anyway. Frames and photos of Marshal Pétain arrived at the camp, and all the internees had to buy them. They promised release to each buyer, adding that those who did not purchase anything would not only not be released, but would be considered bad Frenchmen.

The camp commanders and their subordinates had dangled freedom in front of the internees so much that some of them ended up gluing the framed photo of Marshal Pétain above their beds. But the vast majority made common cause with De Gaulle, who was in England—except for the Muslims, for us it was always *kif-kif*. We would often have visits from camp inspectors and the colonel from Colomb-Bechar. One day, they assembled all the internees to make them work the [sharp and tough] esparto grass. The refusal was unanimous among the Muslims as well as the Europeans. Because of this refusal, the colonel himself came and ordered us to do this work. The refusal persisted. The colonel promised to pay us one franc per hour, but not one internee accepted this work, not even the poorest among us.

In a report several days later, the commander asked us if there was someone among us who wanted to salute the flag each Sunday. In the beginning, following this report, there were five or six Europeans and the same number of Muslims who would go salute the flag. They began refusing to do this task, as there were several hundred other Europeans and Muslims who did not do it. The commander opposed some of the most well-known internees on the pretext that they had spread propaganda in order to dissuade their comrades from saluting the flag. The commander believed that the internees would come in larger and larger numbers to salute the flag, but this is the opposite of what happened.

The Muslim section sent a delegation to the commander in order to obtain a compensation of figs or dates to replace the quarter liter of wine that was given to the Europeans, because Muslims do not drink wine; or at least one cup of coffee more than the Europeans. The first days, even the first weeks, they gave us a cup of coffee instead of wine. Then this was phased out, despite our protests and demonstrations asking that the General Government service send a sum of money proportional to the number of internees to distribute equally. The commander refused to satisfaction our demands. He was happy to give us a quarter liter of wine, but no compensation for those who would not drink it. In the beginning, there were a few Muslims who would go get their ration of wine and offer it to European friends. Later, when the commander learned this news, he refused to give the quarter liter of wine to the Muslims. During the tenure of this commander, almost every week there was some new offense directed at the internees....

During the festival of Eid-Seghu [Eid-Sghir], at the end of the first Ramadan at Djenien-Bou-Rezg, the commander authorized the Muslim internees to go outside of the camp to pray. However, it stung bitterly that he had the *goumiers*, our guards, form a circle around us. They were armed with their rifles. It is unfortunate to pray under the surveillance of armed soldiers on a religious holiday after the month of Ramadan. That day, after the imam's *khotba* (sermon), there were some speeches delivered when all the Muslim internees visited the cemetery next to the camp.

There were fathers among us Muslim internees. There were also several leading figures of distinction, such as Cheikhs Azoug Tahar, 84 years old, Ach El-Hammam from the interfaith town [*commune mixte*] of Sidi-Aïch; the Cheikh Chetout Ahmed, 75 years old and from the town of Lafayette, interfaith from Guergour, Hadj Kheli Ahmed, 70 years old from Mascara, El-Haous, 70 years old, originally from Saint Arnaud, Sétif Cheikh El-Kebati from Nemours, 65 years old, Rersat Rabah, 60 years old, from Mechras, town of Tizi-Ouzou. Rebaï Mohamed, called Ben Hemena, 60 years old from Saint Arnaud Sétif etc.... I also remember that there was a change in the menu and each internee received a quarter of couscous. What was remarkable was that there was a big conference in the evening given by Sheikh El-Hadj Hocine and Cheikh Saïd Salhi. It is the latter who composed a poem about Aïd-Seghir. It was not bad, this soirée. Furthermore, the camp commander had authorized the organization of this event all while sending the police service off to spy.

In order to receive authorization for this Eid Seghir soirée and [for the opportunity] to go pray outside of the camp, we had to appeal to the commander. I remember that the Muslim section had delegated the imam in charge of prayer, Hadj El-Hocine, and myself. We had promised to take on all the responsibility for this appeal. It was with great difficulty that we succeeded, especially in regards to the authorization to stay up until midnight. I still remember that there were two commanders, Fabre and Louis. Both had

IMAGE 13. The Vichy regime assigned indigenous Moroccan infantry (the so-called *goumiers*) as guards in forced labor camps in the Sahara. These soldiers, some of whom had served the French military during colonial military campaigns or the First World War, were in most cases forcibly recruited and scarcely more than prisoners themselves. This guard, seated in front of a forced laborer, is pictured in Sidi El Ayachi. Walter Reuter, "Guardia," Archivo Fotográfico Walter Reuter, Cuernavaca, Mexico.

the same rank, of officer cadet. The first, who was in charge, was a bit more humane than the second. The second, who was in charge of the *goumiers*, would incite them to provoke the internees, European and Muslim. He was both anti-Muslim and anticommunist. He was a German language teacher. I can safely say that he was 100 percent fascist. It was quite rare to see him speak to an internee. He was quiet, but he did considerable harm in the camp. We will see later that not only was he sentenced to four years in prison during the trial of the Djenien-Bou-Rezg camp torturers, but also that Fabre, who was the head of the camp, was subsequently placed under his command. Sergeant Mohamed, head of the *goumiers*, also bullied the internees. He was severe, often he hit them several times, both Europeans and Muslims. This sergeant came to the camp at the same time as the *goumiers*. He was in the habit of hitting the *goumiers*, just as he hit the internees. A lot of internees lamented not seeing this sergeant on trial next to Deriko, Louis, the Adjutant Grangel and Deriko's secretary....

Sometimes, small squabbles would break out among the internees. The section's secret office resolved these disagreements. But Deriko tried to foment trouble. From our arrival in Djenien-Bou-Rezg, the Muslims in the first section prayed together at the times prescribed by our religion. The muezzin, one of us internees, would recite the call to prayer for the faithful. Singing the call out loud provided the added bonus of informing the detainees in the second section of the time for prayer.

One day Deriko arrived at Maghrib (evening prayers). He told us that from that day forth, it was forbidden to sing the call to prayer. He said:

"I forbid your prayers: you are anti-French and you pray against France."

He called the *goumiers*, yelling:

"To arms, to arms!"

We Muslims did not respond, preferring to first finish the prayer that we were in the middle of, in compliance with the opinion of Imam Hadj El-Hocine Slimani.

He declared:

"We die praying, like those who died before us." We were thus in the process of praying when the *goumiers* arrived, in a rush, rifles and bayonets in hand. They entered the first section. We were doing our prayers in pious silence right at the entrance.

I think that the *goumiers* must have thought to themselves, "Commander Deriko is crazy." Be that as it may, he and the *goumiers* waited for us outside the section. Deriko told them to bring the person who had recited the call to prayer to his office. As for us, we unanimously decided that the Muezzin El-Ghazi, who recited the call, must be accompanied. Furthermore, he was a blind internee. The imam asked the believers:

"Who wants to accompany El-Ghazi?"

He was afraid, as he was father of three children. I told El-Ghazi that he mustn't be afraid in these circumstances, which did not concern just him, but which were everyone's business. After a short moment of silence, Djaker Ali, an internee, spoke up to say that he was ready to accompany him. It was a gesture of noble courage, but Djaker was young and would perhaps not know how to answer questions. So, it was I who accompanied him. Indeed, I took El-Ghazi by the arm, and the practicing Muslim internees encouraged us, saying that they were all behind us and that no one would abandon prayers. We entered Deriko's office. He repeated his order:

"You must not sing prayers."

Deriko is neither intelligent nor educated. He knows only the switch, the whip, torture, etc. I offered him explanations, informing him that we do not sing prayers, we only sing the call to prayer, the call for the faithful to pray together; that we have been there for over fifteen months and no commander had prevented us from praying. Deriko called his secretary and questioned him about Muslim prayers. The secretary responded poorly, and I found myself obliged to add a few words. Finally, a big disagreement sprang up and the commander still wanted us to stop praying. We were not hit, but we were on the point of being locked up. I avoided a lot of problems, but according to the commander, we could no longer sing the call to prayer.

We left his office without obtaining anything. I summarized the interview for the Muslim brothers of our section, who decided to continue with religious observance as had been done in the past. The next day at dawn, a new man sang the call, instead of the one who usually did so.

Before eight o'clock in the morning, Deriko showed up. If I remember correctly, it was a Sunday. The internees did not work. Immediately, he called the head of the section to find out who had made the call to prayer. He put both the section head and the man who had actually sang the call for prayer in cells. But commander Deriko was supremely mistaken this time. He believed that, by putting faithful internees in cells, he would succeed in dissuading us from practicing our religion and our duty to pray. But the entire Muslim section is like one single man and we decided once and for all to prefer death to abandoning our religion.

Each faithful took his turn calling for prayer and was brought to a cell. The cells were full, and at each prayer time, there was always a good-willed internee who did his duty, meaning that we continued singing the call to prayer. For about two weeks this repression continued. Finally, it was not the Muslims who gave up, but Deriko who abandoned his policy and released the militants. The Muslims won as they had decided never to abandon the call to prayer.

The commander had written to the General Government Service about this subject. For its part, the Muslim section wrote four letters in the Arabic language, addressed to the three prefects of Alger, Oran and Constantine, as well as a fourth authority, whom I do not remember. Ibnou Zekri was a national advisor to the general governor at this time. These letters carried the signatures of every one of the practicing Muslim internees, including those in the second section. With the help of a native sergeant, we were able to secretly mail these letters.

What happened? Us Muslims, we continued, as we had done in the past, to fulfill our religious duties. As for the commander, he probably received instructions. One thing is certain. Deriko knew the names of all those who had signed the letters. The governor general probably sent him a copy of the letter with the signatures.

A lot of us suffered as a result of this. Several were called to the commander's office numerous times, where he tried to intimidate them.

This was not all. He was always searching for new ways to create problems between internees. He demolished a wall that separated the first section from the second section and added four or five rooms to the first section. These rooms had belonged in the past to the second section.

There, he assembled the camp's Jews, who had previously been mixed in with the Europeans, and separated them from the French, or rather, from the Europeans. This wretched Deriko was responsible for yet more provocations. The Europeans to one side, the Arabs to one side, same for the Jews. The latter again share the first section. The same courtyard serves both Muslims and Jews. There was no doubt: Deriko did this with the intention of seeing Jews slaughtered by Muslims, since there were not many Jews. But, the Jews understood his scheme. So did the Arabs. Commander Deriko wanted Arabs and Jews to stab one another, but the opposite occurred. A friendly understanding spread between the two communities. Never would you have believed that the Arabs and the Jews in the camp's first section would become real friends, even brothers. Indeed, whether they wanted it or not, they were brothers in hunger, suffering, misery, sorrow, etc. in Deriko's camp. I do not hesitate to say that the worst thing that happened in the camp was Deriko being in command. Nevertheless, we must not forget his second in command, Louis. I do not believe that this opinion is unique to me, it is that of all the internees without exception or distinction. Under Deriko's orders, commander Louis did more harm than any other commander, especially those who wanted to observe their religious rites.

Since the trap set for the Jews and Arabs did not result in anything, one fine day commander Louis divided the courtyard between Jews and Arabs with a piece of chalk—a demarcation of the border—and informed everyone that each person had to stay within his bounds.

I would like to conclude simply by paying homage not only to the Muslim militants, and in particular to the organizers, but also to the Jews who knew how to thwart all of Deriko's and his deputy's petty attempts to provoke incidents among Arabs and Jews....

Deriko has dates gathered from the gardens. The internees are formally prohibited from eating even one. Several internees were punished with twenty days of lockup for having supposedly picked dates that were still green. They had not picked them; they had fallen. The internees are starving. There are some who eat grass from the garden, others swallow peels, etc. Upon our arrival in the camp, there were several cats. They started to disappear. According to certain intelligence, the internees were eating them. One day, I happened to see a rock resembling a piece of bread. What a disappointment. Hunger makes you believe that a stone is bread. I have no doubt that what happened to me has happened to other internees. When you cut bread with a knife, there are tiny crumbs that fall. Yet this ant food benefits the unfortunate victims of famine. For more than a year, the internees ate carrots morning and night. Certain ones declared that they preferred to have their portion raw rather than cooked because then there are no longer any vitamins. All the internees' stomachs suffer.

What do we do with the dates from the garden? The commander sells them to the internees at an exorbitant price instead of distributing them for free like he said he did in a report sent to the colonel saying that all that the internees grow in the garden belongs to them as a supplement. Furthermore, all the produce from the garden is at the commander's and his subordinates'—the *goumiers'*—disposition. As for the internees who grow it, they get nothing but the refuse, since it is twenty days in lockup for swallowing one green date that fell to the ground....

I already had the opportunity to speak about the climate around Djenien-Bou-Rezg. It is a healthy place, with clean air.

I have also mentioned the suffering of the internees, especially under

Deriko's command. There are so many events to mention that you cannot describe them all. I ask for forgiveness, because I am writing my memoir after a long period of time. I will not repeat the fact that the internees were deprived of water for several months. Before, the restrooms worked well. Then when the motor broke, water became rare in the camp. Let's add to this fact that for several months, we did not receive any soap. Let's not forget the famine either. Under these conditions, the spread of typhus was inevitable. This is not all. Us internees, we had our underground networks, we knew that there was typhus in the Barberousse prison in Alger. However, several detainees were transferred directly from Barberousse to our camp, Djenien-Bou-Rezg. Instead of housing these newcomers in an isolated area, separating them from other internees and taking indispensable preventative measures to prevent the spread of typhus, they did just the opposite. They put the new arrivals from Barberousse in among the other internees. Neither Deriko, commander and director, nor the medical service did anything to prevent the propagation of this contagious illness. As a result, nothing prevented one from thinking that the Barberousse typhus made its way to Djenien-Bou-Rezg camp. If the measures taken after the fact had been taken before, we could have avoided the epidemic. It's always *kif-kif* (the same thing) with the French Algerian administrative agents: they don't notice things until it's too late, and then enormous sums of money are spent to repair the damage done. Do I need to add who suffers the consequences of these useless expenditures? It is always the people, meaning us, who pay the taxes. Likewise, there was also a case of dysentery at our camp. Instead of immediately sending the internee affected by this contagious illness to the hospital, they waited until there were thirty suffering from it. There was the case of Hasani Ramdane, an internee coming from Bossuet camp, a man of very strong constitution. I remember that the internee doctor Lelouche drew his blood with a plunger, which made him lose a great deal of his strength. He remained stretched out on his straw mattress for nearly two months in the camp and he was about to die. How many others suffered in the same way, all those whose names I have unfortunately forgotten? . . .

Let's talk about the celebration of the third and last prayer for Eid El-Kebir. I have already more or less explained the difficulties that we faced with the notorious Deriko in regards to prayer. The Muslim internees won the case, since the G.G. ordered the zealous commander Deriko not to prevent the Muslims from doing their prayers. During each Eid El-Kebir festival, they authorized us to go outside of the camp in order to perform the big prayer, in memory of the sacrifice made by the prophet Abraham, peace be with him. We did this for the first time in 1941. Our guards, armed with their rifles, came to keep an eye on us. In fact, the armed *goumiers* surrounded us while we prayed together.

During the festival during our second year in the camp, the *goumiers* declared to their bosses:

"We are happy to monitor these praying Muslims, but we do not want to do it armed."

The administration acquiesced, and it was a done deal.

The third Eid El-Kebir festival in Djenien-Bou-Rezg was the last, since they subsequently released us. On this occasion the vast majority of the *goumiers* refused to monitor us with arms: in addition, they even joined us for prayers. They understood that the names that the French Algerian administration gave to us, namely: enemies of France, internees, herds, deportees, prisoners, etc., and even public enemies, counted for nothing, and that designating us public enemies was a sign of bad faith.

When the commander learned that the *goumiers* (our guards) had done the Eid El-Kebir prayers in our company, he became furious and overexcited, not knowing what to do. I believe that he even tried to lock up some of the *goumiers*, but he did not succeed, given the spirit of solidarity that reigned among them. Let us not forget either that our behavior and our sincerity for the Islamic faith touched almost all of these Muslim *goumiers*, despite their lack of knowledge.

Berkani, Mohammed Arezki. *Trois années de camp: Un an de camp de concentration, deux ans de centre disciplinaire, Djenien-Bou-Rezg, Sud Oranais (1940 à 1943 Régime Vichy)*. Koudia-Sétif, Algeria, 1965. Selection from pages 21–24, 27–31, 41–43, 52–53, 55–56, 59–60. Translated from French by Rebecca Glasberg.

40. DAILY LIFE IN DJELFA {1940–1945}

Communist in his political leanings, Paul Caillaud was arrested by Vichy authorities in the spring of 1940 for serving as the head of the Committee against Fascism and War in Surgères, France, where he lived and worked as a teacher. A series of internments in France followed, until Caillaud was brought to North Africa and imprisoned for five years in the labor prison camp of Djelfa, at the northern edge of the Algerian Sahara. Like other Vichy-run camps in the Sahara, Djelfa was meant to support the construction of a trans-Saharan railroad that would connect North Africa's Mediterranean ports with West African and sub-Saharan mines and regions, thereby abetting French extraction of African minerals and other coveted goods. The camp population at Djelfa was made up mostly of perceived political enemies like Caillaud, including men and women who were communists, antifascists, or had fought in the Spanish Civil War as members of the International Brigade. Caillaud suggests in his introduction to his French-language memoir that the Communist Party subsequently expelled him for refusing to become mayor of Surgères after the war, as well as for his ostensible bad behavior in the camp during the war. In this selection of Caillaud's French-language memoir, written under the pseudonym Paul d'Hérama (under which Caillaud published a number of books), the author illustrates the daily hardship of life in Djelfa, its power structures, and interactions between those inside and outside the camp.

To help with their agricultural labor, and to repair their homes and machines, the colonists in Bossuet had asked the lieutenant for the help of camp comrades, who were all admittedly happy to work outside of camp walls, like regular citizens. Soon, farmers, pavers, electricians, and mechanics were hired.

In addition, after reaching an understanding with the municipal authorities, three big task forces were organized for cemetery upkeep, landscaping the public square, and building a stadium on the site of the livestock market, a vacant lot separating La Redoute from the village.

Finally, so as to furnish firewood for the whole camp—kitchens and canteens—a team of forty lumberjacks went out into the forest, six kilometers from La Redoute, and camped in makeshift tents under the surveillance of a non-commissioned officer.

The lieutenant and his entire cadre of officers and non-commissioned officers treated the five hundred men in their charge in a dignified manner, as men dealing with other men.

Bossuet, a hamlet fifteen kilometers from its commune's capital, Le Télagh, was managed by a special assistant, a delegate to the Municipal Council.

The population of this small center of approximately two hundred inhabitants, made up almost exclusively of colonists and storekeepers, cared very little for politics. But, the majority espoused the opinions of the government in power, whatever it was. Thus, at that time, the people of Bossuet stood behind the Marshall of Vichy. A section of legionnaires had formed there, with a section of young women.

This did not prevent this population from showing their sympathy towards the camp's deportees, sympathy that was especially due to the fact that they were exiled.

How many comrades, while being paid by the colonists who employed them, also ate at their homes, treated like family with friendly consideration!
...

Celebrations and quarrels

In the first courtyard of La Redoute was the camp commander's office and quarters, the stores, the officers' quarters, the canteen, the troop barracks, the kitchens, the infirmary, and various workshops for woodworking, shoemaking, smithery, etc.

In the second courtyard—that of the internees—were located the dormitory buildings and the co-op [*la coopé*].

To tell the truth, after the hell that was Djelfa, the move to Bossuet was like a rebirth for the political prisoners. At least as regards the food and the semi-freedom that they gave us; as for sleeping arrangements, no improvements could be made, with the exception of an allotment of straw mattresses.

The health and general spirit—exceptions made for the core of the Tordus—having improved, the need for amusement began to be felt, concurrently with the resumption of scholastic courses, which had ceased to take place since the departure from France.

We created a Celebration Organizing Committee, with a theater section and a music section. A chorale in four-part harmony was assembled, as well as a small orchestra. Musicians were not lacking among the deportees, but instruments were. People asked me to direct these two programs.

Two concerts were given in the infantrymen's mess hall, assembled ad hoc; concerts comprised of rounds of singing, choral music, and skits written by comrades.

The lieutenant had sent invitations to the town's population. Many inhabitants came, not angry at all at having a bit of fun. These two concerts were a great success. . . .

At my post as infirmary secretary, I had immediately gained the trust of my boss, the auxiliary doctor.

It is true that I put myself to work right away, since we had to create everything, and I organized the service, with appropriate record keeping, an accounting department, physical facilities . . . since we knew the sick would be on a restricted diet.

Shortly, seriously sick men were able to be evacuated to hospitals, especially at Sidi-Bel-Abbès. At times, I even had to answer the camp telephone on the doctor's behalf, and with his complete approval, stubbornly express my opinion to the hospital directors. The hospital patients, seriously ill men, were grateful to me. Others, who were nothing but slackers, hated me . . .

Likewise, through the steps that I took under the guise of the head doctor, and on his order concerning bedding, the camp got sixty straw mattresses! For five hundred men! So many calculations to establish a just distribution!

We did it. The infirm, chronically ill, and comrades over fifty-five were all given a straw mattress. But . . . what complaints, what spiteful attacks of all sorts did this bring me!

There was worse. The infirmary medications, already few in number, existed in measured quantities, and were extremely difficult to replace despite our repeated requests, since they all came from France. However, quite a lot of ill men required multiple treatments. So, the head doctor used drugs and ointments sparingly . . .

Yet, the two internee-doctors, who secretly went to the village to care for certain civilians, took medications from the infirmary. The threat was grave for the internees. Deprived of the essential, what would become of them in the event of an epidemic? The head doctor, alarmed, had the medicine chest locked and ordered me to guard the key, since the health of the camp was at risk.

What a cause for irritation between me and the internee-doctors!

In addition, these comrades—due undeniably to their humanitarian spirit—would permit native civilians with the most dangerous and repulsive illnesses to enter the infirmary, despite the formal prohibition of the head doctor, in order to care for them on the operating table. (Note that these sick people had the right to free medical care, provided by colonial doctors, under the condition that they take the necessary steps at the town hall.)

Here again, the head doctor stood in the way of such undertakings. The camp commander could not tolerate this either, since entry to La Redoute was forbidden to civilians! I received many orders from them concerning this issue... yet, a group of adversaries formed against me!

Finally, posted regulations clarified that the work of nurses (care, cupping, massages, etc.) would take place from nine o'clock to noon and from two o'clock to five o'clock p.m. But certain ill men would arrive well after twelve o'clock, when the nurses had begun to eat. These comrades therefore had to put their own hands into the plasters and pomades used for the more or less appetizing rubdowns.

As department head, I had to protest! Much later I would learn that several men are quick to hold grudges... and keep them!

No matter! What mattered was the proper functioning of the infirmary. In any event, such was the opinion of the head doctor and the commander, who understood that, through my perseverance, more than fifty internees had been hospitalized, infirm men had been able to replace their orthopedic braces, and medications had arrived to augment the infirmary's supply.

This was also the opinion of the colonial medical inspector, a coarse character sent on a mission to the camps in the beginning of the month of September. He oversaw my work, my accounts, my organization, my results... and congratulated me.

After his departure, the head doctor and the commander summoned me and confirmed: "The inspector was pleased by your work at the infirmary. He assured us that he is going to put you forward for release."

But I did not become excited upon hearing the word "release," which I had heard already so often... And I continued to draw upon my work for the most certain encouragement to persevere.

d'Hérama, Paul [Paul Caillaud]. *Tournant dangereux: Mémoires d'un déporté politique en Afrique du Nord (1940–1945)*. La Rochelle, France: Imprimerie Jean Foucher & Cie, 1957. Selection from pages 139–41, 150–53. Translated from French by Rebecca Glasberg.

41. A YIDDISH ACCOUNT OF A JEWISH BURIAL IN THE SAHARA {1940–1943}

Benjamin Lubelski's Oyf Gots Barot *is rare among memoirs of internment in North Africa, one of few such accounts to be written in Yiddish. A proud communist, the Polish Jewish Lubelski volunteered to serve the Republican Army in the Spanish Civil War. Specifically, he served in the Dambrowski Brigade, composed primarily of Polish volunteers, including many Polish Jews. So heavy was Jewish representation in the Dambrowski Brigade that its members inaugurated a distinct Jewish, sub-battalion known as the Naftali Brigade; Lubelski did not join this unit, fearing (as did many of his peers) it a propagandistic stunt to lure Jewish volunteers to the cause. When the Spanish Civil War tilted in favor of General Francisco Franco and his allies, Lubelski fled to France, only to face arrest by the Vichy regime and deportation to Djelfa, a Vichy-run labor camp in the Algerian Sahara. Djelfa held large numbers of Spanish Republican Army volunteers: in August 1942, 899 prisoners were counted at the camp, 189 of whom were Jewish. In the selection presented here, Lubelski describes a burial of a camp inmate in the Jewish cemetery in the town of Djelfa, on the outskirts of which the camp by the same name was located. His description documents a rare encounter between the Jewish internees and Saharan Jews whose homes neighbored Vichy sites of internment. While Vichy anti-Jewish laws applied to the Algerian Sahara, Jews in this region faced a different sort of occupation than did Jews of the north. In keeping with Europe's continual redefinition of race to suit colonial needs, Saharan Jews in French-controlled Algeria were racialized as inferior just like their Muslim neighbors. Thus, unlike Jews in the rest of Algeria, Saharan communities were not granted French citizenship in 1870, so could not have it taken away by the Vichy regime. After surviving his internment, Lubelski moved to Jerusalem, where, in time, he became chief librarian in the Russian and East European Center of Library of the Hebrew University.*

We use to go on various jobs. This time, we—a group of Jewish inmates—were summoned for a special job outside the camp: to bury Shpilgarn, a deceased inmate, in a Jewish cemetery...

Shpilgarn did not like us. To him, we weren't refined, we were wild—Polish Jews. But Shpilgarn, he was a German Jew. He looked down on us with a world of complaints. By God, it was not our fault that he ended up with us in the same camp.

In Germany, Shpilgarn was an admirable bourgeois man. In Kassel, he had a large photography business, and he lived and worked at ease. With little brown whiskers, neatly combed, with a thick signet ring on his little finger, a gold watch, a bone-handled walking stick—all signs of respectability—Shpilgarn roamed around the streets of Kassel proud and confident.

All of this ended in one stroke: when Hitler came to power.

Shpilgarn left for Paris. Did he leave behind in Germany a wife or children? I don't know. I never asked. But he managed to take enough along with him so that in Paris he was also able to quickly open a photography business. From his perspective, life had to march on as it had in Germany. And why not? But something meanwhile changed, something that Shpilgarn did not foresee: Hitler began the second World War.

Like other foreigners, Shpilgarn was obligated to report to the Marching Regiments. As a former German citizen, he ended up in the Foreign Legion. There, everyone was good.

"You came to die!" Marshal Lyautey once announced passionately to the assembled legionnaires.

But Shpilgarn, apparently, was not pleased there either. In 1940, he ended up in the Berrouaghia concentration camp, in North Africa, in Algeria. From there, he came with a small group to us in the Djelfa concentration camp. In our camp, there were Spanish Republicans, ourselves—a considerable group from the International Brigade—Poles, Czechs, Germans, Hungarians, Romanians, and, of course, Jews. At the end of 1941, the French did not know what everyone else could sense and transported them over to North Africa.

The most disparate figures rotated through here—some in a military coat, some in a jacket, buckled with a belt or a cord, some in a beret, some in a hat or something else, neither beret nor hat. Anything to protect from sand and sun.

Shpilgarn lived in one of two brick barracks that stood in the uppermost part of the camp, the so-called Jewish barrack, "Brenner's" barrack. Brenner was a lawyer from Vienna. He stressed everywhere his quintessential Jewish spark. Shpilgarn did not like this and he kept away from him. He was a bit closer, but far from chummy, with Surkis and Goldkraut, with whom he served in the Foreign Legion.

A difficult person, but Surkis and Shildkraut shrugged it off. He was constantly out of sorts, stressed. On top of the stress, the woman with whom he was involved in Paris took his photography business, all of its wealth, without leaving word and not wanting to hear from him.

There are times and places where one cannot be alone, where one mustn't be alone. Together, people can help one another and it is easier to bear through difficulties. A large number of the internees in the camp endured only thanks to solidarity. Shpilgarn didn't know, or didn't want to know, of it and for that paid a high price. He fell ill with jaundice. A group of us went through the same disease. Friends helped as much as they could. At first, they brought the sick to the infirmary, a sort of provisional hospital. We didn't eat roasted pigeon there but we could stay in bed without having to get up to report at seven in the morning to go work. They brought our meager food to the bed, not having to wait in line with canteen in hand. Friends came to sit and chat. No German camp was like this! When you used to spend a few days lying all wrung out, friends used to bring warm tea a few times a day. It was tea from burnt and crushed date pits. With a little sugar, it was drinkable.

Shpilgarn was also placed in the infirmary. On one side of his bed was Godel, a small Yid from Paris's Belleville, from the Pletzl. Godel, it seemed, had done everything in his life: He was a tailor, a cook, a merchant, and other things about which he didn't speak. He was a finagler, a jack-of-all-trades, a lively fellow, and didn't like any "honest" business—a plain pot of noodles. Politics did not concern him. But we, a Jewish group from the International Brigades, we were "my boys" to him. With Shpilgarn too he tried to chat (he was not a man of few words!), but chatting requires two people, and the second, Shpilgarn, was clearly not up to the task.

On Shpilgarn's other side lay "Iron-King" Berman, a Lithuanian Jew, a strong Jew with the torso of an orangutan. On the Paris boulevards he used to show off: bending iron beams, ripping chains, and at the same time, to the amazed onlookers, speaking a sort of Lithuanian French, which only a true *litvak* could understand . . .

Between Berman and Shpilgarn there was no respect at all. Berman held that Shpilgarn stank of arrogance, and Shpilgarn held that Berman stank in general.

Some doctors from our group came to Shpilgarn to try to help and give him some advice. But it was difficult to get him to agree to anything. As for his diet, he showed very little discipline. Once he spent all his money to cook a gigantic pot of food that was totally unsuitable for his health, gorging himself on it. Before he was even done eating, he became ill. He didn't want to give the food away, but he couldn't stop eating it either. The disease progressed rapidly.

And quite astonishingly, unexpectedly for a disease that had until now claimed no deaths, Shpilgarn was transported to the small-town hospital due to his catastrophic condition and, in a few days, word came around to us of his death.

In the camp, as I mentioned, there were various jobs. And there were also jobs outside the camp, which we were glad to go to. Far from the camp, an Arab man would often sneak up near us and, for a pair of pants or a shirt, as long as they were in good shape, we used to get bread, rice, oil, or meat. We could eat our fill and still take some back to our friends in the camp. Truthfully, upon returning, the guard used to inspect us again, just as when we left, but it was no problem. The guard did not think to look under the knee, or under the tights...

On the west side of the camp, on a hill, lay the Muslim cemetery. We looked at it every day because it was close enough to see and you couldn't miss it. Only later did we learn it was a cemetery. Who could have known? A big hill with a bunch of rugged stones lying around in no particular order is not a rarity in the sandy, stony Sahara. There weren't any funerals at the time, or because of their particular character we simply didn't notice them. Small groups of people that appeared from time to time, appeared as small as mites on the side of the mountain. Later it became clear to us that the smaller and bigger stones lying around were tombstones.

Now, a group of ten men, arranged in rows of two, guarded by a *goum* [indigenous Moroccan soldier serving in the French army] marched to the Jewish—or, as they call it here, "Israélite"—cemetery.

The cemetery, surrounded by a wall, was located halfway between town and our camp. The entrance was through a little door, just like the entrance to the old cemetery in my hometown. Immediately, its air of familiarity made me really sad. The slender poplar trees reminded me of the birch trees that "quietly murmur a prayer," and the Hebrew letters on the tombstones brought a stir from my old, faraway home, of the little flame in the hearth, of the Rebbe with the little children ... this cemetery in the faraway Sahara was not foreign to me.

It appeared that Shpilgarn was already buried. It was a question of filling the grave and, under the supervision of a local rabbi, going through the proper ceremony. While in the camp, we did random work, but this time we specifically had to accomplish the work of a *khevra kadisha* [Jewish burial society].

The rabbi was not yet there; we separated and walked around the cemetery to catch a glimpse. At first glance, they were the same headstones as ours. However, they had their own accents. On all of them was engraved the "Here is buried . . ." On some of them, it was written below, "A friend of the *khevra*," meaning the *khevra kadisha*, which here plays a significant social importance. Not all of them are members of the *khevra*, but the ones who are considered praiseworthy.

Not far from us a young girl, dressed in the European style, like a French girl, put some graves in order. I approached and tried to start a conversation.

"Your family's graves?"

"No, I'm a member of the *khevra*."

"Is there a women's section too?" Take me to the devil that I should make a joke! Luckily, she didn't understand. We continued chatting. Soon enough, she became my guide.

"These are children's graves."

"Where are the headstones?"

"Children's graves don't have headstones."

"Why?"

"It's a *segula*."

"A *segula* for what?"

"That other children shouldn't die."

We passed a headstone beside which there were no little burning candles but *ner tamids* [eternal lights], tin boxes with oil-soaked wicks, [next to which] matches, oil stains appeared on the ground.

"This is the Rebbe's grave."

The Rebbe's grave is a place for special prayers at a moment of distress. As its surroundings attest, he is visited often.

Slowly, various figures slid in through the little door. They approached us, trying to start a conversation. To the left of the gate stood a tall, skinny, energetic man gesturing with his hands. He wore a long, thin, dark robe, a kind of burnoose, like the Algerian peasants. His hat was a round, brown mantle and, in the middle, a circle of maroon. He had no beard but a healthy, Muslim mustache [*mahomet-vontzes*]. He stood there, surrounded by our group, and at first appeared completely deaf and mute. But not for long, for he had enough words for ten speeches. He gestured with his hands the whole time, letting no one get a word in. He clarified everything with his hands. It's

January 1943—he is preparing for Hitler: He put his hands on his neck, stuck out his tongue and—finished it off. We knew quickly where he stands with him. With the fascists too—he shook his fist from left to right, from right to left—*kaput*! He was a strong supporter of de Gaulle. Why wasn't he wearing de Gaulle insignia, now, when the Allies were already in North Africa? Here came a clarification by way of a fist to the chest: de Gaulle's sign is a Cross of Lorraine, but no! We, Jews, cannot wear a cross. We—a *mogen-dovid* [Star of David] . . . one and two, and he revealed the symbol in the air.

It's possible we wouldn't understand everything from his gestures, but near us stood the fourteen-year-old Nancy and his mother, a widow with eight children. They explained everything to us right away in French. Nancy, dressed like a French boy with a beret, didn't appear Jewish in any way. So he hinted to us by boasting that at home he had a big picture of the Western Wall . . .

He lost his father not long ago. "Poisoned by Jews," came the explanation from the woman. This shows the conflict that goes on in this small Jewish community, secluded somewhere on the edge of the Sahara. After his mother's explanation, Nancy raised his eyes to heavens and swore to take revenge . . . On the face of it they seemed fellow Jews, but with customs from another world . . .

At once, the group sprang to life. A strong Jew, a type of *Nalewker* [tough] Jew, dressed in a white, Arab burnoose, his head wrapped like Maimonides in the pictures, moved cheerfully towards us.

The rabbi came.

His face smiled. He asked that they send us [a minyan, or prayer quorum] to mourn the dead. The rabbis aroused respect among those present. Even our guard at the gate stepped aside, to a corner. The rabbi approached us, delivered a warm "*salaam-aleykum*," extending to each one of us his hand.

A rabbi or not, for us he was a vision of a free Jew. For us this was a feeling of satisfaction, revenge, and hope. The Palestinians among us turned to him with a few Hebrew words. The rabbi was moved, filled with happiness: one he stroked on the head, another he touched with his hand, with a caress.

He made clear what we were to do: dig up a small shovelful of soil to smooth out the grave. We did it quickly, and then after?

It wasn't easy to understand his Hebrew, but we understood this: He wanted us to make an "*El maleh rakhamim*." We knew what this is, but who knew the actual words of such things?

"I will say it," said Tzentner, the former medic of the Dabrowski Battalion. He started—it's forbidden if I understand until this today—and recited an *"El maleh rakhamim,"* and by heart even, without stuttering. We stood there with our mouths gaping.

"Tzentner, say *kaddish*!" Yankele Rauch called out.

"What, you think I can't?"

Tzentner was not intimated and recited *kaddish*, which years of revolutionary struggle in Spain and imprisonment in the camps did not seem to have erased from his mind.

The rabbi and the other Djelfa Jews stood in a close circle around us and almost without pause said, *"Amin, amin* [Amen, amen]," not like usual just after the prayer. They said *"Amitn-amin,"* when it's required to say and when not, as soon as they would want to confirm that the prayer was and would be true, or even express their appreciation that these young people, many of whom have fair hair and blue eyes, are in fact Jews . . .

The rabbi then passed everyone his siddur, each read a verse and once again heard the continuous "Omen, omen" [in Ashkenazi Yiddish pronunciation: *Amen, amen*]. The Djelfa Jews wiped their eyes, casting us looks of love and pride.

After the Allies' landing in North Africa, the camp regime had become milder. We even obtained permission to go into town and became frequent guests of the Djelfa Jews.

We eventually parted ways, some to France and some onward.

Shpilgarn remained in the Djelfa cemetery, in the Sahara desert. Fate had carried him far away.

Lubelski, Benjamin. *Oyf Gots Barot*. Tel Aviv: H. Leiwik Publishing House, 1996. Selection from pages 31–39. Translated from Yiddish by Ben Ratskoff.

42. AN INTERNEE SEEKS EMERGENCY DENTAL CARE [1942]

Some sources speak to the existential pain of forced labor and internment: others speak to the physical pain associated with forced internment, exposure to extreme weather, and lack of proper hygiene, shelter, clothing, or medical care. Here, we encounter an internee suffering from an extreme dental emergency. The internee in question, Beidruh Schopf, was in Sidi El Ayachi, a Vichy internment camp southwest of Casablanca that was used to intern families. Thanks to the intercession of an official, Schopf managed to obtain an appointment with a dentist in the adjacent town of Azemmour, but the dentist demanded a fee he was unable to pay. In this letter, he appeals for philanthropic support to diagnose and treat his condition. In addition to drawing attention to the varied agonies associated with internment, this source points to the porous nature of certain Vichy camps in North Africa. Internees in Sidi El Ayachi were allowed to visit Azemmour for certain approved reasons, including attending religious services in that town's synagogue.

July 4, 1942

Dear Madam,

Last year, I asked the Azemmour Civilian Command for dentures, which I desperately need. Unbeknownst to me, the Commander spoke with you about this issue. According to your letter dated 26/2/1941—a copy of which was sent to me—you gave the Commander your consent and asked him to grant me leave for this purpose.

Having obtained leave, I went straight away to the Committee where Mrs. Fuchs gave me a letter for a dentist asking how much my dentures would cost. Eight days later, Mrs. Fuchs gave me another letter that I brought to M. Lévy, who agreed to the price and asked the dentist to make the dentures for me. But before doing so, the dentist asked for a down payment, which I then asked for from Mrs. Fuchs. Mrs. Fuchs promised me she would take care of it. However, the down payment was not given to the dentist, my leave ended, and I had to return to the camp without having gotten my dentures. As the dentist had already pulled several teeth in preparation for fitting the dentures, you can imagine how much pain I was, and still am, in. I have become sick to my stomach.

I kindly request that you consider my difficult situation. I cannot even eat and I feel terribly ill.

Sincerely,

(Beidruh Schopf)

Beidruh Schopf, Sidi El Ayachi, to Hélène Cazes Benatar, Casablanca, RG 68.115M, Reel 5, Private Collection Hélène Benatar (1936–1953), United States Holocaust Memorial Museum Archives, Washington, DC. Courtesy of Central Archives for the History of the Jewish People. Translated from French by Rebecca Glasberg.

43. A RABBI IN AZEMMOUR [1941–1942]

Some historical sources raise more questions than they answer, as does this fascinating letter by Rabbi Pinkas Josef Thumim, addressed to the American Jewish Joint Distribution Council's representative in Casablanca, the indefatigable Hélène Cazes Benatar. Thumim writes from the Vichy internment camp of Sidi El Ayachi, Morocco, one of few North African camps to which the French wartime regime deported entire families, as a unit. In Sidi El Ayachi, Thumim's child contracted a persistent, aggressive fever (quite possibly a symptom of typhus, which ran rampant in the camps), forcing the rabbi and his wife to take him to a hospital in an adjacent town. Were the parents compelled to leave their child there, in the hands of medical professionals? Or were they obliged to return to internment, leaving their child to face an arduous recovery on his own? Equally vexing is the family's backstory. The Thumims might have been North African, but they could also have been European Jewish refugees. Regardless, one can sense from Rabbi Thumim's letter the anguish of a parent doing his best to protect a sick child in punishing conditions, all the while forced to choose between respecting the Jewish laws of kashrut and contending with the meager, non-kosher food made available to prisoners in Sidi El Ayachi and camps like it.

January 8, 1942

Dear Mrs. Thumim Pinkas,

We have the benefit of sending you the enclosed money order of 300 francs, which represents the allotment that we set aside for you for the month of January.

The current state of our finances has forced us to reduce the monthly amount that we were hoping to be able to secure for you.

As this step was taken due to very serious reasons, please understand that it will be impossible for us to respond favorably to any complaints and, as a result, no letters about this matter will be taken into consideration.

We will take it upon ourselves to improve your situation as soon as our means provide us the opportunity to do so.

We remain sincerely yours.

Attached: 1 money order

January 19, 1942

Dear Mrs. Benatar,

I am happy to inform you that I was transferred to Oued Zem, where I am together with my wife and child. I am in possession of your kind letter from the 8 of this month, well as the money order of 300 francs. I believe that there has been a mistake if for three people you sent us 300 francs for an entire month, unless you are of the mind that the least [support] should be given to those who are in the most acute need.

Furthermore, for religious reasons we do not eat the camp food. Moreover, our child—who suffers from liver and intestinal issues—is certainly unable to eat the camp food.

In a request that I sent to you four months ago, which was confirmed by Dr. Roubleff, about an [allowance] increase for my ill child, you agreed at the time to allocate him an extra 50 francs per week for six weeks. As we had to leave for the camp in the meantime, we only received this increase for two weeks; the rest was forgotten and has not yet been paid.

Therefore, Madame Benatar, I beg you to please take into consideration all the aforementioned reasons and to please [reconsider] your unilateral decision by considering our need and our sick child. I have included in this letter a note from the doctor explaining that [my child] needs detailed care.

I much anticipate your response.

Sincerely,

N.B.—Attached is the note from Dr. Roubleff [sic]. I humbly request that you also obtain further information from Dr. Roubleff about the status of our son's health.

Doctor Sophie Roublev   Casablanca, September 29, 1941

I certify that the three-year-old child Alfred Thumim suffers from fever and severe gastroenteritis and needs to follow a special diet.

Dr. Roublev

Sidi-El-Ayachi, May 20, 1942

Madame Nelly Hélène [Cazes] Benatar, Casablanca Refugee Committee

Dear Mrs. Benatar,

I have the benefit of informing you that my wife, my child and I have returned to the El-Ayachi camp and I kindly request that you please send us our monthly installment here.

I would like to take this opportunity to remind you of my letter from the 13 October, in which I asked for an illness supplement, confirmed by Doctor Rublev [sic], as I am still sick and so is my child, who currently has whooping cough.

With my best wishes and most friendly salutations,

Rabbi Josef Thumim Pinkas

Selected correspondence between Mrs. Thumim Pinkas, Sidi El Ayachi, and Hélène Cazes Benatar, Casablanca, January 1942, RG 68.115M, Reel 5, Private Collection Hélène Benatar (1936–1953), United States Holocaust Memorial Museum Archives, Washington, DC. Courtesy of Central Archives for the History of the Jewish People. Translated from French by Rebecca Glasberg.

44. MARKING THE DAYS OF AWE IN SIDI AZIZ {1942}

As Italian troops pushed the British military out of eastern Libya in 1942, Benito Mussolini ordered Libyan Jews in this region of Barqah (Cyrenaica) deported to labor camps, theoretically to remove them from the war zone. The roughly 2,600 Jews deported from Cyrenaica were interned in the crude camps of Giado, Buqbuq, Gharyan, Jeren, Tigrinna, and Sidi Aziz, all sites of forced labor. In his recollections of internment in the Sidi Aziz camp, Amishadai Guetta describes a hostile environment pocked by snakes and scorpions, scorching heat, and cruel overseers. In this selection of a book edited by Guetta on the fate of interned Libyan Jews, Guetta focuses on the experience of marking the Days of Awe—the ten most holy days of the Jewish calendar, which include the holidays of Rosh Hashanah and Yom Kippur—in Sidi Aziz. In Guetta's conjuring, the experience brought back to the imprisoned the smells, sounds, and social and spiritual worlds they had been forced to leave behind. Guetta ends his recollections by referencing the Zionist dreams that some imprisoned Libyan Jews may have been cultivating even while in internment—a conclusion that affirms the stated purpose of his edited volume, to commemorate and celebrate Libyan settlement in Israel after the war.

Women pleaded in vain, crowding around the government offices to [demand] release [of] their husbands giving any excuse whatsoever, but their wailing cries yielded nothing. The police brutally pushed them and did not even allow them to come close to the office doors.

Many families revolted overnight without a source of livelihood [and] in the absence of their husbands and compassionate mothers also were consumed with anxiety and grief.

The month of Elul, the month of preparation for the (High) Holidays, became a month of preparation for travel and bitter exile. The enlisted [forced laborers] scattered to the city's markets, looking for straw, down, suitcase, shorts, straw hat, sunglasses, and so on.

About ten days before Rosh Hashana, the first enlisted people were sent. . . . On rickety trucks, without inspection, without organization and in no order, everyone crowded and standing, hundreds of boys and heads of families were sent, mercilessly cut off from their relatives, and abandoned in a place within the Libyan desert sands—Sidi Aziz.

They lived in tents, destitute, and most of them lay on the ground], snakes and scorpions ran [all] around them, and annoying mosquitoes disturbed their moments of sleep. Their food was only bread and murky water, sparingly, which was pumped mercifully from the Bedouin wells, quelling their thirst somewhat. From early morning until dusk, the exiles were engaged in all kinds of grunt work, laying the Libya-Egypt railroad under the scorching sun and at the hands of cruel taskmasters.

The awful days had come: instead of the elegant and glorious synagogue, a small, meager, low-rise tent was erected. Instead of seven ornate Torah scroll decorated with flowers, only one Torah scroll was used. Instead of freshly ironed clothes, the worshipers wore dirty, torn clothing. Instead of the smell of perfume, the smell of sweat and grime (the severe water shortage prevented the worshipers from bathing and washing their clothes). Of course, prayers on the night of Rosh Hashana and Yom Kippur were held in the dark because of the prohibition against turning on lights during the war.

Rosh Hashana and Yom Kippur, the days of awe for which fathers and sons filled the synagogues en masse until no room remained, to pour out, whispering, in [the] glory of holiness and melancholy melodies, turned into days of sadness, grief and sorrow. The rumors of the Nazi extermination camps caused endless worry and anxiety both in the hearts of detainees and in hearts of their relatives, [all worried] about their own fates.

From the Sidi Aziz camp, the detainees were then sent to Bakbuk ("Bottle

Camp"), very close to the front lines, and there as well they lived in inhumane conditions and were employed in hard labor. Two instances of deaths recorded among the residents of the camps signaled the beginning of a fascist trend and their treatment of the Jews who were left in their hands signaled the beginning of the fascist trend and their relations toward the Jews who had been forfeited to them: one twenty-four-year-old named Camus Zanko, who used the camp commander's book, was shot and killed by a fascist soldier without any wrongdoing. And the death of Jacob Laguai, a husband and father of small children, killed in a car being driven by exiles, [which] rolled over—May god avenge their blood.

The sorrow of separation from their families was especially felt by the prisoners at the closing prayer that Yom Kippur. At this time, in which all Tripolitan Jews used to bring their children, including the babies, to the synagogues for the "priestly blessing," there was a shared and strong feeling. The question of "will I return and see my children?" nibbling at their hearts. And with tears on their faces and a broken, gloomy heart, they uttered the most sublime and special prayers of the year. There is no doubt that the tears of these depressed people rose to the heavens and the next day, the memory of fascism was erased and its end hastened.

Not many days passed and all the detainees received good news that they could return to their homes. And from the distant "Bottle Camp" (Bakbuk) two thousand [kilometers] from Tripoli to the Gorgi camp near the city, all the exiles returned home happy and good-hearted.

There was a wonderful saying commonly used by the exiled community: "May we use these railroad tracks we laid down to make aliyah to our holy land," and, indeed, many achieved this hope some months later.

Guetta, A. *Va'ad kehilot Luv be-Yisra'el, Yahadut Luv: Ma'amarim u-reshimot 'al haye ha-Yehudim be-luv: yotse le-'or le-regel melot 'eser shanim la-'aliyat Yehude luv*. Tel Aviv: Va'ad kehilot Luv be-Yisra'el, 1960. Translated from Hebrew by Jessie Stoolman.

45. CELEBRATING PURIM IN THE BIZERTE CAMP {1942–1943}

For six months of the Second World War (November 1942–May 1943), German Nazi representatives directly occupied Tunisia, bringing with them the threat that

Tunisia's Jewish community would fall prey to deportation and annihilation. By this time, the eighty-five thousand Jews of Tunisia had already experienced deprivation of their civil rights as well as an assault on their property and professions by the Vichy regime. Nazi rule intensified this assault. The arrest and public humiliation of Jews became commonplace, as did the sentencing of Jewish men to forced labor and the introduction of punishing taxes on the community as a whole. Some Tunisian Jews were even deported to camps in Europe at this time. Although he was the son of a prominent rabbi in Tunis, Jacob André Guez, twenty-four years old at the time, could not escape the newly installed Nazi regime. In December 1942, Guez was sent into forced labor at a camp near the city of Bizerte. Guez began recording near daily notes about his experience on loose pieces of paper: after the war, he gathered these reflections into a single diary that he published in 2001. Guez's brutal, bald account sheds light on Bizerte's punishing conditions. The internees' work regimen was punishing, and conditions at the camp filthy. German guards used unrestrained violence against the prisoners, ruthlessly suppressing escapes and acts of resistance. One of Guez's fellow inmates describes Bizerte simply as hell. Notwithstanding these conditions, Guez's diary touches on moments of relief within the context of internment—a beautiful day, a stunning moon, the occasional bit of decent food, companionship, even (as in this selection) merrymaking in honor of the Jewish holiday of Purim. It also hints at the complex and sometimes strained relations among Bizerte's Jewish, Muslim, and Christian prisoners, including those whom Guez calls "free Arab laborers," who were in fact interned colonial subjects compelled to forced labor by their Nazi overseers.

I now have a solid pair of military-grade boots that my cousin Roger Adda, who serves as camp mule driver, was able to get for me yesterday evening. . . .

Each Friday evening, the camp's religious Jews gather discreetly in a barracks room in order to observe Shabbat services, despite the Krauts' ban on doing so. Some men stand guard at the door and keep an eye out for the arrival of any Germans. Young Rabbi Assuied and his two brothers officiate: their faith is powerful, and they apply themselves completely, through their short sermons, to give us hope in our unique and all-powerful support: God. . . .

They sleep like sardines, squashed one against another, on straw that has not been changed since their arrival. They cannot even take their clothing off at night, due as much to the bombings as to the need to stay warm in these vast, bare rooms whose windowpanes are broken and whose doors have been blown out by explosions, and also so that they are not robbed. Because the penury is such that people commonly steal clothes and food.

They are all covered in vermin: you can hardly think of seriously cleaning yourself when you know that there are only three sinks for the camp's 1,400 men, and when you have no more than one hour between waking up and departing for work.

"But you are lucky to have arrived now," my comrade says to me. "The camp leaders are seeing to everything; already some of the showers are starting to work."

You can access them . . . when they work. Unfortunately, those who leave for work return too late, when there is no longer any water, so they rush over to the camp's only barber, or towards the postal office, or they prowl around the kitchen to try and scrounge up an extra helping, because the food is wretched.

There is never any rest, unless you are seriously ill: an infirmary with two Jewish doctors and some nurses has been organized.

The Jewish leaders are in permanent contact with the *Feldwebel*, who has his office at the camp. This man takes orders from a lieutenant who comes each morning during assembly.

Finally, there are some soldiers in charge of camp surveillance: there are Fritz and Roukh who speak French; the latter is reputed to be taciturn and a total brute who only knows how to argue with his fists.

But now, our *polizei* keep them at a distance and take care of reprimanding us rather noisily in order to alleviate their resentment: riding-crop whippings are rarer now. . . .

Close by, a building is completely flattened by a large caliber bomb. All that remains is an enormous hole, about six to seven meters deep, and a dozen or so meters wide. Next to it, there is a wooden hut full of bars of white soap.

The Germans came with trucks to take possession of it. From time to time, an Italian marine comes to ask timidly for a bit of soap, but he is brutally mocked, and in general, his request is denied. You would hardly think them to be allies. How they hate one another! What nasty looks they give each other!

A bit further, at the dock, there is a large Italian cargo ship that is being actively unloaded. Closer by, there is a French submarine, the *Nautilus*. People say all its engines have been sabotaged. Furthermore, the superstructures of numerous small, abandoned French buildings surface near the docks.

Silvera got the group some bars of soap; we share them. There is a half-bar for each of us, and there are still several left over.

In the afternoon, I succeed in entering the hut under pretext of helping the Krauts load the soap, and I leave with two bars in my pockets; for that matter, several other workers do the same.

There is an alert at four o'clock pm. The Italian marines run like madmen, and are already far in front of us.

The truck comes to get us shortly thereafter. We are stationed for a moment in Ferryville; it is Sunday: the large population are taking walks in the streets, people are sitting at cafés, others are going out to the movies: the face of peace that we had forgotten. We distribute some bars of soap to Jewish women who come up to our truck....

Tuesday, February 9, 1943

We have an order for ten graves at the cemetery. Like each morning, the donkey-riding Arab milkman comes to resupply our milk; he knows us all now; he knows that we receive our pay every ten days, and often agrees to let us pay on credit....

Thursday, February 11, 1943

In Tunis, they have summoned the men born in 1911 for work. The result is rather pitiful: today, the nine laborers who responded to the summons arrived at camp. Charles Riahi is there: he escaped two weeks ago, but they put his wife in prison and he was forced to return.

He brought with him, to our barracks room, an "old guy" from this group, a gullible man from Casablanca, a chubby father and family man, Élie Cohen. Riahi also changed the straw in our barracks during the day and, at the same time, lost my helmet.

Terrible weather all night long....

Monday, March 15, 1943

Cloudy weather with intermittent sun.

The cemetery is flooded with a liquid mud in which we sink up to our ankles.

Several incidents have caused fights between Jewish and Arab workers, who are about to come to blows using their picks and shovels. We don't know how the quarrel began, but the implicated Jewish worker has absolutely no intention of letting himself be pushed around. He meets insult with insult, and all the Jews have come together in solidarity by his side. Mathias energetically intervenes when the situation threatens to turn into an outright brawl. To the Arabs' great surprise, he takes our side completely:

We vaguely understand that he shouts at them: "Aren't you ashamed at making it worse for prisoners who have it bad enough already? Get back to work! You are very well paid for this, since you get eighty francs a day, whereas they only get twenty and are malnourished! Even so, and even though they are forced laborers, their end product is better than yours!"

Mathias's intervention completely astounded us. Who would have thought that he would do such a thing, that he would show himself to be in such total solidarity with our group? We knew that he looked upon the Arabs with contempt, that he considered them all to be looters, thieves and hypocrites. But we also knew that he didn't like Jews, at least on Nazi principle.

He himself was not a Nazi. He was a laborer, a factory worker from the Ruhr where he had left his wife and his young son, and who considered the war detestable, a universal catastrophe.

He often told us this often, and we know that he did so willingly and that, beneath his teasing and sardonically bad-tempered exterior, he really liked us. He became attached to our group, and he cared for his workers. He knows each one's flaws and sorrows, and he is rarely fooled when, working, we laugh and sing in order to forget. He laughs too, and he teases us and scolds us, to forget as well.

This incident taught us more about his feelings for us; and he must have read a comforting thank-you in our expressions. As for us, we were touched and felt less alone.

The Arabs got the message and returned to their work, grumbling. Their furious "corporal" insulted us again from afar, damning the Jews who "succeeded in bewitching even the Krauts." Mathias made him be quiet.

Old Youna, who continues to make the trip back and forth between Tunis and Bizerte, brought a package and a letter to me at the camp.

Tuesday, March 16, 1943

The weather is beautiful again.

In the wake of yesterday's incident, we are being picky about the division of labor between forced Jewish laborers and free Arab workers.

And now, the task of going and unearthing long-dead cadavers from the old cemetery and transporting them to the new one falls uniquely to them.

At 3:00 p.m., a funeral arrives. We are going to rest during the ceremony and the gun salute....

We are actively preparing for the Purim holiday. It seems that we will have beignets made with honey, *makroud*, chicken, eggs, etc., and that they will give us a half day off, like last Sunday....

Purim is tomorrow, and the festivities will begin this evening. Young Rabbi Assuied, in a barracks room, reads us the megillah, the story of Esther, Mordechai and Ahasuerus.

As the night falls, echoes of the celebration ring out. A guy comes out with a drum that he nicked from some barracks. He wanders about the camp, striking it like a deaf man: a crowd of laborers follow him, shouting out and dancing. They yell: "Purim, Purim! [*Quel Djaja bekhemstach!*]" or else they sing, "[*Aror Amane! Quel Lila Liltou! Oughadougha dfintou!*]" They even sing together, "[*Yom chemha, Yom chemha, Yom chemha leisraël!*]" (day of joy for Israel).

One Jew rushes over with a *darbouka*, taken from who knows where. Others tap on bowls with spoons, adding to the cacophony and the confusion.

In the night, one group, a bit further away, yells, "Yom chemha ..." while carrying a German on their shoulders: it's Ernst Schwartz, called "casserole" because, to keep the Jews on their toes at work, he always repeats "Que ça roule!," which he pronounces as "Kassaroule."

Once again on the ground, and in the middle of the ovations, he wishes us a happy holiday; he speaks French: "My children, my friends, celebrate! Have fun! And I hope that you will celebrate Passover with your families!"

Thank God that not all the Krauts are brutes.

Then we get into a big circle around the drums and the *darbouka*. The players, crouched in the middle, beat out a savage negro rhythm. Some Jews contort themselves in the middle, shrieking, like the *aïssaouia*. Then, carrying sticks, they dance negro dances, simulating combat and galloping on their broomsticks. The Krauts must really take us for savages. Arab-style *youyous*, and yells of "Purim!" break out everywhere.

One Jew imitates a snake charmer and, with some assistants, begins to waffle on rapidly and without end in a comical Moroccan accent. The rhythm of the drums punctuates his jokes, and laughs burst forth from everywhere. Frenzied line dances in the moonlight, frenetic dances, all the resentment and bitterness are pushed away, far, far into the bottom of our hearts. Hope, the immense strength of the Jews, fills our chests.

In the midst of captivity, cries of joy rise up towards heaven in memory of our liberation, centuries ago, in memory of the fall of evil men.

Even with nothing, the Jews will celebrate Purim!

But no! It will not be with nothing. Here is Roukh who is returning with his truck: he is bringing nine sheep! The camps' well-to-do paid for six and the Krauts, three.

Roukh rebuffs the sentry who tries to quiet everyone on account of the late hour; Roukh the savage, Roukh the brute, will he have been softened by this contact with sheep? We have the right to celebrate! The sheep are on shoulders, carried to the wild rhythm of the drums. We cross the barracks, singing Hebrew hymns, shaking the few who are still down in the dumps. Everyone must have a good time, we must have a feast!

We return and lay down, having lost our voices. Rain starts to fall. We won't even miss the traditional Purim firecrackers.

The DCA [Défense contre les aéronefs, or air defense] replaces them: airplanes attack the large, broken down cargo ships that arrived today near La Pêcherie. It's rare, a bombing in the middle of a diluvian rainstorm.

Sunday, March 21, 1943

This morning, it's beautiful out. The barracks gleam in the sunlight. The cooks worked a large portion of the night to prepare for the Purim feast.

Now, a rabbi is cutting the sheep's throats. We also send for large bottles of kosher wine and, this afternoon, the workers will have time off.

All the barracks' services are busy.

In the vast courtyard, people have made a vast circle out of big stones. In the middle, they have set up a spit and a hearth. The cooks come and go busily.

I am going to see my cousin Dédé: the entire infirmary is giddy with curiosity and overwhelms me with questions about the festival preparations.

Two more calves have been brought. Behind the kitchen, they are butchering the sheep; it is beautiful out, and the sun is shining for Purim.

Noon! The workers start to return. Squatting around the circle, we witness the *méchoui*: one after another, the sheep are put on a spit and roasted whole while a cook lightly bastes them with fat.

The drum team from yesterday begins playing noisily again. The German soldiers observe us, amused: they must think that, due to our customs, we are very close to the African savages. They give us free rein, in order to allow the festivities to retain their true character [*afin de rien faire perdre à la fête de son cachet*]. There are also officers who have come as tourists, and even a commander who takes photos.

For lunch, we have fava bean soup, a slice of honey bread and a sweet lemon. The meat will be for this evening, because it is not yet well cooked.

Once the courtyard has been cleared, a soccer match is organized between two teams. Tutor is the referee.

Since this morning, a truck has been bringing furniture raided from the city's evacuated houses to the camp. They have just brought a piano and a lot of chairs and armchairs: they put them in one of the rooms in the buildings at the end of the camp that used to serve as a jail for English prisoners. The Germans have given us permission to use them for this afternoon. Ok, let's go!

It's a good piano, and we have a laborer, Fernand Slama (a math teacher in the civil sector) who plays really well. Another laborer regales us with Arab music. I have a lovely afternoon. The walls of the rooms display inscriptions in English. The prisoners all wrote their names: for the most part, they come from the Hampshire Regiment.

Outside, the rabid soccer players continue their game.

In the conservatory, on the first floor of the infirmary, the rabbis and very religious men sit around a long table and sing "Bar Yohaï." I go up there around 6:00 p.m.: Émile Debache, who is there, invites me to share their meal: three slices of bread, a delicious dish of chicken and eggs with potatoes, another potato dish, and a salad. Then, a slice of honey bread for each. I must say, the infirmary's cook outdid himself.

Insatiable, I rush down the stairs so as not to miss supper: yet again, I gulp down an entire bowl of rice and a plate of mutton with potatoes and gravy. They have also given us a ration of wine.

This time, I must admit that I am full.

In their mess hall, the camp's leaders stuff themselves as well.

The sky is pure. The full moon is as bright as daylight. A long way away, the silhouette of several warships completes the picture. . . .

Friday, March 26, 1943

Roll call this morning to note the names of escapees. News of German round-ups in Tunis is confirmed. They say that two hundred Jews will arrive at Bizerte tomorrow.

At noon, they brought the cadaver of an unfortunate Jewish laborer from Sidi Hamed: it's Lellouche, from the clothing service. The truck that brought him is full of blood and bits of brain. Half his head is gone.

The official reason for his execution is an attempted escape. But off the books, people talk about the miserable tragedy he lived through. He's an "old guy" (about forty), denounced as a communist by his wife who was involved with a Kraut officer.

Living in Mateur, he was sent to Bizerte where, due to his age, the camp leaders got him a job at the clothing service, to prevent him from doing any hard labor.

I knew him well following a dispute that sprung up between us: one day, while checking his records, he concluded—as a result of some mistake unknown to me—that I had received two sets of clothing, one in Tunis and one in Bizerte.

Through an excess of zeal, he posted a notice to his office summoning me, and when I arrived, he dragged me to Gilbert Taïeb, the camp leader, calling me a profiteer and accusing me of being one of those who disrupt the already extremely difficult allocation process.

Of course, I protested, demanded evidence, but, due to the camp's expedited justice processes, I was facing ten days in prison if it were not for the unexpected intervention of Tutor, who had the records verified.

Lellouche had to admit that he was mistaken and had gotten confused, and he was so pitiful in his apologies that I sincerely forgave him.

And now his disfigured cadaver is right here on the truck. His wife must have really wanted to get rid of him, because, following a second denunciation that could only have come from her, it dawned on the Krauts that the regime to which he had been subjected was much too pleasant for a communist.

That is how his execution was decided. Only, they wanted to set it up so it wouldn't look like a murder. So, they sent him to do forced labor in order to find a pretext for an escape attempt.

Since the day before yesterday, the sentry of the group where he had been placed had received the order to take him out. But this sentry, who was not a brute, was unable to make himself do it, and Lellouche had returned alive.

Even yesterday, despite his boss's threat of sanctions, the Kraut did not have the courage to execute his mission. Accused of treason by his officers, he had ended by promising to obey today: this morning, upon leaving, he was frightening, completely drunk, and he spent all morning mistreating the workers and yelling at them for no reason.

It seems that Lellouche knew what was coming, and this morning, he bade goodbye to his friends, who called him crazy.

In his fury and intoxication, the Kraut had missed his first shot, and hit him in the leg. Desperate, Lellouche started running like a crazy person to get away. He was shot down while running, and the sentry, who had become a raving lunatic, emptied the entire belt feed of his machine gun into Lellouche's head until it was pulp. He then went to bed, sobered up and hopeless, far away from the distraught laborers.

Riahi, who was at the same work site as Lellouche was today, is no longer strutting around: he has been deathly pale and silent since the horrific scene played out before his eyes, and we can only wrest details from him a bit at a time.

Guez, Jacob André. *Au camp de Bizerte: Journal d'un juif tunisien interné sous l'Occupation allemande, 1942–1943.* Collection Mémoires du XXe siècle. Paris: L'Harmattan, 2001. Selection from pages 26–27, 69, 72–73, 76–78, 106, 112–13, 114, 115–19, 122–23. Translated from French by Rebecca Glasberg.

46. KEEPING KOSHER AND CELEBRATING SHAVUOT DURING THE WAR [1942–1943]

The following letters follow the wartime travails of a single, Polish Jewish family through war and peace. Moses and Macha Pack and their fourteen-year-old son Samuel were interned in the camp of Sidi El Ayachi at least as of September 1941, perhaps because Moses had volunteered for the French Foreign Legion earlier in the war, only to become a political enemy of the ascendant Vichy regime. Macha Pack was the first to reach out to Hélène Cazes Benatar, representative of the American Jewish Joint Distribution Committee (JDC) in Casablanca; the poor interned woman had a dental emergency and was desperate for the funds to address it. Macha's appeal was answered by the JDC, and over the course of the subsequent year and a half, she and her husband wrote intermittent follow-up appeals outlining their ongoing challenges. A number of these concern how hard it was for the Pack family to abide by the laws of kashrut through internment, when kosher food was simply unobtainable. After Operation Torch, the Packs found their religiosity circumscribed by a new set of challenges. Moses worked the graveyard shift for the American military in Casablanca. When it came time to celebrate the holiday of Shavuot (marking the giving of the Torah on Mount Sinai), which some Jews celebrate by studying Jewish texts all night long, Moses would lose out on a day's worth of wages, putting the family in an untenable financial position. The Pack family's numerous appeals to the JDC (only a portion of which are reproduced here) point to the unique challenges of being an observant Jew under occupation and internment; they may also signal that some internees had the ability to be more persistent or even canny in appealing for philanthropic support than others.

March 10, 1942

Dear Mrs. Benathar [sic],

Today I received the money order for 500f for the month of March, for which I thank you greatly. At the same time, I thank you for February's money order—please excuse me for not responding right away because my wife was sick.

I request that you send me a bit more, because my entire family does not eat in the kitchen because it isn't kosher. So, I must purchase everything myself that we need to eat, and everything gets more expensive day after day.

I hope for a larger allowance for the month of April, and remain sincerely yours,

Mr. Pack and family

July 28, 1942

Dear Mrs. Benathar [sic],

Thank you so much for the 200f increase these past two months, but I beg you to continue sending me this same sum each month, because with 400f per month I cannot get by. Here, everything is very expensive: 1 liter of milk costs 8f and I need it daily for my health. 1 kg of coal costs me 6f (black market), etc.

I beg that you take pity on me and do your best to send me the sum of 600f each month. You know very well that we eat nothing from the kitchen except the bread.

I thank you, Mrs. Benjo and Mrs. Fuchs in advance.
Sincerely,
Mrs. Pack

June 8, 1943
Dear Mrs. Benathar [sic]!
Four months ago, I started to work for the Americans. I am in a section that works from 8:00 p.m. [to] 5:00 a.m. Each week, I must miss the joy of [celebrating] Friday and Saturday evening's [religious] festivities. Now, we are celebrating the holiday of Shavuot, and I will lose [miss] Tuesday, Wednesday, Thursday, Friday and Saturday evening['s work], and the rations [that accompany them] because I am very religious.

I beg of you, dear Mrs. Benathar [sic], to take heed of this and to sort out this loss.

I went to inquire about a day-time position, but it is impossible. I would really like to take one day off per week, and for you to pay me for a second. Otherwise, I cannot exist. Please give your answer to Mrs. Benjo.[1]

Thank you in advance for all that you are doing for us.
Sincerely,
Mr. Pack

Pack family, Sidi El Ayachi, to Hélène Cazes Benatar, Casablanca, June 8, 1943, July 28, 1942, and March 10, 1942, RG 68.115M, Reel 5, Private Collection Hélène Benatar (1936–1953), United States Holocaust Memorial Museum Archives, Washington, DC. Courtesy of Central Archives for the History of the Jewish People. Translated from French by Rebecca Glasberg.

1. The Packs spell this name differently in the two different letters. For the sake of clarity and consistency with other sources, we have chosen to use the spelling *Benjo* for both.

47. AFTER LIBERATION, TORTURE {1943}

A German Jew who had volunteered for the French army in 1939, Peter Winckler was among tens of thousands of non-French, Jewish men who offered their services to the French Army in the autumn of 1939 (as engagés volontaires à la Légion étrangère pour la durée de la guerre, or volunteers for the French Foreign Legion for the duration of the war), as France mobilized for war against Nazi Germany. Some of these volunteers joined foreign volunteer infantry battalions, while others became associated with the Foreign Legion. Once anti-Jewish laws took effect in France, many of these men were deported to Vichy camps in North Africa. Winkler was first interned in the camp at Oued Akreuch before being moved to a camp near Casablanca. Despairing that his release would be infinitely delayed, Winkler attempted escape and was subjected to a punishment known as the tombeau *(grave), a unique feature of the Vichy camps of North Africa. The tombeau compelled a given victim to dig his own grave and lie in it for a period of time, sometimes as long as twenty-five days, exposed to intense sun and frigid cold, deprived of nourishment, and sometimes beaten for making a movement. According to one survivor's account, those who managed to survive the* tombeau *emerged stiff as skeletons, obliged to go directly to the hospital for amputation of frozen extremities. In her letter to French colonial authorities, Moroccan Jewish lawyer and human rights activist Hélène Cazes Benatar investigates Winkler's fate, writing on behalf of the American Jewish Joint Distribution Committee, an organization she tirelessly represented in North Africa during and immediately after the Second World War. Horrifically, Winkler's punishment was meted out in March 1943, several months after the armistice following Operation Torch, when many Vichy camps remained in place, their structure, leadership, and practices still intact.*

February 7, 1943

Sir,

We have the honor of respectfully bringing your kind attention to the case of:

WINCKLER, former Engagé Volontaire

stateless ex-German

of the Protestant religion

who is currently found in the SOCICA [Society pour la construction de la cite des industriels de Casablanca] holding camp (Roches Noires) in Casablanca.

Winckler spent the 1st of February before the Holding Commission but has not yet been released. On Thursday, he, as well as several other internees, went down to town in the morning.

Upon his return, he was invited by his camp leader to dig a "*tombeau*" and to stay in it for seven days, we have been told ... According to the intelligence that we have gathered from his camp companions, Winckler has been in the *tombeau* for four days, malnourished, with little cover—and this, in the vicinity of Casablanca.

We will not permit ourselves to discuss whether or not Winckler deserved a punishment; we have come to you respectfully in order to vigorously protest the treatment that he has been given, if the facts that have been told to us are correct.

It seems unusual that this truly inhumane punishment is in use in a holding camp.

We understand that, following the intervention of Doctor Wyss-Dunan, the Red Cross Delegate from Geneva who kindly interviewed the undersigned, penal camps for laborers were eliminated, as well as punishments such as the *tombeau*.

We beg of you, Sir, to please abide by the findings of this investigation, which you will deem necessary, and, in the event that Winckler is still in the *tombeau*, to authorize him to go to the camp infirmary in order to receive the treatment that he must need after these four days of suffering in the damp ground.

We hope that you will act favorably upon our request and remain sincerely yours.

Hélène Cazes Benatar, Casablanca, to Director of Public Safety, Rabat, February 7, 194[?], RG 68.115M, Reel 5, Folder 40, Private Collection Hélène Benatar (1936–1953), United States Holocaust Memorial Museum Archives, Washington, DC. Courtesy of Central Archives for the History of the Jewish People. Translated from French by Rebecca Glasberg.

48. SURVIVING THE "TOMBEAU" [c. 1943]

The scars of internment were many and long-lasting. For Ernest Sello, they were also unavoidably visible. Sello had dedicated himself to the French Foreign Legion (as an engagé volontaire à la Légion étrangère pour la durée de la guerre) early in the war: with the Nazi conquest of northern France and creation of the Vichy government, he was deported to the forced labor camp of Bou Arfa, Morocco, which, with its subcamps and satellite camps (including Aïn al-Ouraq, Foum-Deflah, and Tamlelt), was the largest of the regime's camps in North Africa. In September 1941, Sello attempted to escape Bou Arfa. Following his capture, he was sent to the subcamp of Aïn al-Ouraq, where he was sentenced to spend eight days in the "tombeau," which entailed laying still in a grave-shaped trench, unable to move or rise. Sello's time in the tombeau coincided with a winter freeze, during which he suffered severe frostbite on both feet. Sello was returned to Bou Arfa after his corporal punishment was complete, only to discover that Commandant Janin and Captain Avelin, who oversaw the camp, hoped to deport him to Germany. Thanks to the intervention of the Bou Arfa doctor, Sello was instead sent to a hospital in Oujda, where both his feet were amputated. When his case came before employees at the Hebrew Immigrant Aid Society/Jewish Colonization Association, philanthropic organizations that collaborated in North Africa during the war, one philanthropist ruefully called Sello "the person who most embodies contemporary history." The organizations arranged for Sello to have artificial limbs fitted to his body, but at the time they were corresponding with the unfortunate man (in December 1943), he had no way to pay for the medical devices. Here, we encounter Sello's wartime testimony, as was shared with the American Friends Service Committee.

I, the undersigned, Ernest SELLO, engagé volontaire for the duration of the war and appointed to the Foreign Legion, was placed in Bou-Arfa labor camp after the armistice.

After escaping from the camp at the end of September 1941, I tried to cross the border into Spanish Morocco, where I was arrested and taken back to French Morocco.

At the end of the month of November, I was sent to the Ain-el-ourak penal camp. There, I was punished with eight days in the *"tombeau,"* having only my tattered clothing and one light blanket to cover myself with. The only food I received was one round loaf of bread every twenty-four hours. This was the end of the month of December, and it was very cold. At the end of my punishment, I was taken out of the *"tombeau"* with two frozen feet and sent to the Bou-Arfa infirmary.

During my punishment, I asked for help and care several times, but had no success whatsoever.

When I found myself in the Bou-Arfa infirmary, Captain Avelin and Commander Janin made efforts to have me repatriated to Germany. Only the intervention of the Bou-Arfa doctor prevented my departure.

In January 1942, I was sent to the hospital in Oujda where I had both of my feet amputated.

For the past twenty months, I have been in different hospitals without having ever received help from the Industrial Production,[1] which didn't even judge it necessary to clarify my situation with regards to my becoming unfit for service and my pension.

Undated testimony of Ernest Sello, c. 1943, American Friends Service Committee Refugee Assistance Case Files, Accession No. 2002.296, File of Ernest Sello, United States Holocaust Memorial Museum Archives, Washington, DC. Courtesy of American Friends Service Committee. Translated from French by Rebecca Glasberg.

49. A CORRESPONDENT'S WARTIME TRAVAILS [1943]

Hans Dammert experienced a dizzying wartime itinerary that was not atypical of the European refugees who found themselves in North Africa in the course of the Second World War. Using the alias "Georges Gordon," Dammert first fled Germany for Spain in 1933 due to his leftist political leanings, which rendered him a political opponent in the eyes of the ascendant Nazi regime. A year later, his request for a renewal of his German passport was denied, leaving him legally stateless. By 1936, Gordon was working in Civil War–torn Spain as a journalist. Fluent in German, Spanish, English, and French, and speaking some Italian, Gordon was an exceptionally dexterous wartime correspondent: his writings, though, as well as his political leanings, made him vulnerable to the right-wing, nationalist dictatorship of General Francisco Franco. Gordon fled once again, in 1938, for France, where he volunteered for the French army for the better part of a year. When German troops conquered and seized control over that country's north and west, Gordon, along with so many other engagés volontaires étrangers *(foreign volunteers) in*

1. Industrial Production (Direction de la production industrielle) was the Vichy administrative body under whose jurisdiction camps and camp prisoners operated in North Africa.

the French army, was demobilized and sent to the Algerian internment camp of Crampel (including the site of Boghar and Saïda, where Gordon was located), just south of Oran. Five months later, Gordon was transferred again, this time to the forced labor camp of Béchar (Colomb-Béchar), where as a result of strenuous labor, his leg was injured, infected, and eventually amputated. While in Saida for recovery, the Allies landed in North Africa. Falsely assuming his own liberation was at hand, Gordon abandoned the camp for Oran, where he offered his services as a switchboard operator for the Continental Hotel, working for US military officers. Alas, Gordon's troubles were not over. In December 1942, he was arrested by Vichy authorities for having overstayed his leave in Oran and condemned to a month's imprisonment. In prison he contracted typhus and was relocated to the internment camp of Mecheria, where he was interned alongside many European internees (including Norwegian, Danish, Belgian, and British sailors), as well as some North Africa civilians. Gordon wrote the following report on the Mecheria camp while recovering from typhus there. The report offers an unusual amount of intimate details about the camp's inmates and their skills, which Gordon believed could be marshaled by the Allies. Subsequent to writing the report, Allied representatives facilitated Gordon's release, prepared for him a letter of commendation, and managed to acquire an artificial limb for him. Gordon was then offered a position as a writer-composer for the Municipal Theatre of Oran. Whether Gordon subsequently returned to Europe or remained in Algeria is not known.

A. Observations

Méchéria camp is by far not the worst I have been in during the last three years. But I think it is rather important.

Except from a special camp for "black market" and similar people with whom no one could be concerned, there are four camps which might, to some extent, interest your office. Camp (B) is the "oldest" institution: rather uncontroled but mostly non-fascist Italians of North-African extraction, mingled with a dozen definite and controled Italian anti-fascist local leaders (from Oran, Bône, etc.) are living there since over ten months. Something like 220 people on the whole.

Camp C is reserved to the Italian civilian "war prisoners" mainly engaged in transport work and only quite recently shipped over from Sicily. (120–130 men.)

IMAGE 14. During the Second World War, Edward Bawden served the British army as a War Office artist in France, Africa, and the Middle East. Upon recall to London from Iraq in 1942, Bawden's boat was torpedoed and he was rescued by a French ship. Vichy authorities imprisoned the artist in the Mediouna internment camp, near Casablanca, along with a range of other British subjects who counted among the immensely diverse prisoner population of the Vichy regime. Edward Bawden, "Mediouna Internment Camp, Casablanca: British Subjects Rescued at Sea and Detained by Vichy Government—Sailors, Soldiers, Airmen and Merchant Seamen," watercolor on paper, Art. IWM ART LD 2887, Imperial War Museum, London.

Camp D englobes mostly newly arrested Italians from Tunisia (Nearly 200.)

Camp A, finally, comprises almost without exception French political internees who might have held jobs of certain prominence during the Vichy period. (Some 80–100.)

I don't count the natives in this list. I think that the most interesting cases are to be found in the Camp B, and sometimes C.

Among these people, there are men aged up to 72, some others ill or disabled, and, I should say, about 60 percent perfectly harmless individuals, some interesting on account of their . . . potentialities, many others doubtlessly inclined now (according to the Italian national character, for what this is worth)—to show this goodwill towards the Allies. In this way, according to the general policy of the United Nations, they might be helped to a certain extent.

Especially interesting seems to me the case of twelve people still retained in Méchéria, whose prolonged internment while being sure anti-fascists and mostly members of the Italian Democratic Union is, quite frankly, a scandal, since almost all of them have helped the landing of the Allied forces and have, for *this reason* precisely, been arrested in December 24 by the Darlan authorities. Here goes the list of the most essential of these people.

B. List of Controlable Italian Antifascists (to be checked with M. Favero)

(1) Berini, Giovanni—aged 40—father of 3 children—Oran secretary of the Italian Democratic Union—was interned since 10 months because of having helped the disembarkement with his local trade union associates in Oran port during the November days, 1942.

(2) Berini, Guglielmo—aged 38—3 children—prominent Oran innkeeper who handed over his restaurant "Le vert frogis" to the American Red Cross in November—would go volunteer for any F20 work [brigade] concerning his country; very cultured, good radio voice, etc.

(3) Borsi, Umberto—40—3 children—skilled mechanic of Milano region—one of first members of Democratic Union in [*rest of sentence cut off*]

(4) Zennaro, Mario—48—2 children—plumber and skilled metal worker of Algiers—actually secretary of antifascist prisoners section in Méchéria camp.

(5) Cagge, Giulio—43—at this moment deputy spokesman of Méchéria prisoners—railway trade-unionist, Algiers, arrested after disembarkement on account of pro-Allied sympathies, very able organizer.

(6) Vincenzo Azzarello—aged 70—Sicilian member of Italian Socialist Party—gravely ill.

(7) Lorenzo Lecchini—aged 54—pipe and briar wood manufacturer from Bône—gravely ill. (30 years in France)

(8) Pietro Menotti—aged 52—member of Italian Socialist Party—health badly shaken. (20 years in France.)

(9) Andrea Carli—aged 57—former secretary of Italian mason trade union—health badly shaken. (16 years in France.)

(10) The twin brothers Arturo and Guido Sanna, both aged 51—members of Italian Democratic Party—Bône specialists for mining construction—health badly shaken.

(11) Iguazio Razetti—aged 54—organizer of the antifascist resistance in Parma in 1921—Garibaldian fighter during World War No. 1, over 20 years in Algiers—member of Italian Republican party—health very badly shaken.

On special request, this list could easily be enlarged by at least half a dozen other names of old or sick people whose cases, interesting and urgent, would require immediate help.

C. Final Propositions

Of course I am quite aware that it is not always possible for the Allied forces to claim liberty for people in which they are but very mildly interested.
Nevertheless, a point could maybe be reached, where

(1) the aged and the sick could be granted WITHOUT DELAY what the French call a "résidence forcée" in comparative, if controled [sic] freedom, as far as they have their own means of living—and if they haven't, that they could be assisted by means of food, medicine, clothing etc. in that very camp;—

(2) the competent Italian Democratic organizations could be enabled, through M. Favero, and impelled to intensify their interest for their suffering fellow countrymen (the 97 percent of the Méchéria camp inmates)—sending delegates for propaganda and social relief down there, and trying to get the maximum of honest Italian citizen[s] out of the claws of Axis prejudices and the ensuing misery.

Algiers, September 12, 1943.
George Gordon

Handwritten report by George Gordon, Algiers, to American Friends Service Committee, September 12, 1943, RG 67.008M, Box 3, George Gordon "Observations," Algiers, September 12, 1943, American Friends Service Committee Records Relating to Humanitarian Work in North Africa, 1942–1945, United States Holocaust Memorial Museum Archives, Washington, DC. Courtesy of American Friends Service Committee.

50. A GERMAN PHYSICIAN INTERNED [1942–1944]

American Friends Service Committee (AFSC) representatives in North Africa maintained extensive files on the refugees who appealed to them for aid, sometimes amassing letters from individuals over months, if not years, even after their successful emigration. Dr. Erwin Müller caught the attention of AFSC representatives not only because of the inherent pathos his story commands, but because of his personal, heartfelt, and elegant appeals to the organization: surely this is why one AFSC representative stationed in Casablanca wrote her colleague in New York City that Müller "is particularly highly recommended because of his human quality." Before the outbreak of the Second World War, Dr. Müller, a German, Christian physician, was interned for five years in a series of Nazi prison and internment camps, presumably deemed politically suspect by the regime. The details of his wartime story remain vague, but at some point (likely 1938) he fled Germany for France, perhaps to serve the French army as a foreign volunteer. When the Third Reich occupied northern and western France, and the Vichy regime established in its south, Müller was deported to North Africa, where he was interned in a series of prisons and labor camps, including Djelfa, Saïda (El Kheiter), Crampel, Bedeau, and Boghar. At times, he volunteered his skills as a physician to minister to other internees. Müller was in Crampel, in northwestern Algeria, when the Allies landed in North Africa. For evincing support of the Allied cause, he was threatened with hanging, sent to a prison in Bedeau, and then to the labor camp of Boghar, where he remained under the oversight of the same overseers who had represented the Vichy regime. As Müller describes here, while Jewish internees in North Africa had parties advocating for their postwar release, no institution was prepared to come to the defense of those Christian German and Austrian internees who languished in the Vichy camps after the Allied victory in North Africa. While Müller is correct that these European, non-Jewish internees lacked organizational support, they were at least able to apply for refuge in other countries (as did Walter Reuter, who eventually moved to Mexico). Such mobility was not available to North African political internees, who remained under European colonial control well after the Second World War.

November 26, 1944

    Dear Mister Heath:

    I was very pleased of your letter of Oct. 16th and I thank you for your congratulations to my advancement. Your visit at that time in Africa, and the kind interest you took in our little affairs, are well stored in my mind. I am glad to hear that you are safely back in the States continuing your high profession of being helpful without reward.

    Yes, Mister Heath, a big change in the that time miserably living refugees has taken place, since they are in the Army. It was the end of hunger, filth and mental torture for them. Many, as we doctors for instance, are even working as specialists in their profession; others have found a job in the Psych. Warfare Branch, where their lingual knowledge and their experience of special problems are used. All this has been done against the resistance of narrow-minded people, by men like you and Major Brister, who looked further than to somebody's nationality restoring thus his original value as a human being. It is this fact which makes me answer your kind letter, though we are certainly very different in our political opinions, and still more perhaps in our interpretation of the sense of this world. Because I do feel that, in the non-socialist sector of the present political conceptions, you people are like a vaccine against stupid prejudice, dishonestly and self-interest. I should could it an honour for me to be of any use for you, whenever you request it. The chance for this is small, now. But it might be different later. Please do let me know, if I can do something for you.

    I don't know Major Brister's present address. But you could find out by writing to the "Postal Tracing Section, 2nd Echelon, C.M.F." I understand he is again doing some refugee relief work, this time for people who had a chance to escape the enemy's power during the war.

    Shortly before I left Africa, your address proved very useful in the case of a colleague of mine, Dr. Haase, an eye specialist whom the Vichy French had succeeded in treating as an enemy Alien, even in spring '44, though he is a clear anti-Hitler refugee. You had already left Africa then. But my letter to you was delivered to a gentleman who, in a surprisingly short time, managed to find a protection from the French authorities and a job for that poor fellow.

Without your address things would probably have developed very differently, i.e. Dr. Haase would have been cent [sp.] to a concentration camp, again, together with his Aryan enemies who, in 1934, had driven him from his country. With kindest regards, Yours very truly,
 Erwin Muller

February 28, 1943
 Dear H.:
 No news of yours have reached me, since August 1942 when you let me know the prospects of the immigration-visa-affair.

Fortunately, there is no need of it any longer. A fortnight after I wrote to you that nothing had changed for me, my and many comrade's situation changed entirely by the possibility to join the British army. Since December 16 we are British soldiers trying to do some useful job for the general cause—not in the front, it is true.

You imagine how glad we are for having escaped, in a decent way, from these French camps, where curious Vichy-people kept prisoners, those who had been in their army [since] 1940. The French—the same persons who collaborated with the Germans before the debarkment [sic]—even dared ask us, whether we would join once more their bl. . . . Foreign Legion or a substitute for it. Icy silence of course. It's very strange to see that: until 1940 they called us "boches," from 1940–1942 they hated us for being anglophile, now they call us "deserters"—but never they were able to distinguish between Nazis and Refugees.

I suppose you—as an ancient camp-fellow—to be still a bit interested in what is happening with us, as a whole. That's the reason why I should like to let you know that, though the camps of Boghar and of Saida have been emptied (except the Spaniards), nothing had been done yet for Djelfa, "camp des internes politiques."

It's a shame, but in this camp of Djelfa, 320 km from the coast, are still held a good deal of ancient Antifascists (Spanish civil war fighters, political refugees, etc.) who struggled against Hitler or his vassals at a time already, when their guards still kissed Herr Hitler's boots.

The Djelfa camp is moreover extremely badly supplied in food, clothes, medical attendance (1941/42 more than 50 men died of Typhus there) and has to suffer from the arbitrary direction of a 100% Vichy-man who is still on duty there.

In the South, nothing has changed after the November events. The same men, the same sympathies with the Nazis, the same critic of democratic state-systems, the same bad treatment of (supposed) political adversaries. A commission composed of both an American and a British officer was at Djelfa on January 23, 1943 promising much. But the difficulties caused by the French authorities are too many, so one should help them a bit...

November 25, 1942

What a change in the political and military situation! What a decisive step toward the end of this war! Now everything seems easy which, even yesterday, seemed barred with obstacles. One sees victory itself, until now hidden within the clouds. And that this miracle was carried out quite close to us, on our African soil, that is an ulterior justification of the choice we made in 1940. Imagine the desolate situation of our comrades in France! One had almost let oneself be influenced, for I too, for example, and asked for my transfer to France. Fortunately the paths of the Administration were long...

When speaking of proves friendship, I am thinking especially of you the fact that you have not forgotten us. That's rare, my old friend. Of all my friends, comrades, etc. who have gone to America hardly one-quarter tries to maintain a correspondence with me. Fate has even favored me a good real in this respect, for here are some men who have not had any news at all from their friends after their departure. For the second time, at Crampel, I had received money from you, 645.-fr, through a mediation of the "Quakers" of Marseille. I had acknowledged them the two receipts[sic] of money from you: the first in the summer of 1942 (860.-fr), the second in the fall of 1942 (645.-fr). The last letter which I wrote you, dates from about the month of August; the last received from you was in the spring of 1942. I cannot give the exact dates because I do not have my little address book with me—for we are on our way.

Well! It is this journey and everything that has happened to us that I would like to talk to you about now. On hearing this word you probably believe that we are en route for mobilization etc. But no, my dear! We are only returning from Crampel—our abode in the demi-desert south of Oran—to Boghar. Since there is such a lack of trains, we have to wait here, at Oran, for the day when the transport can be continued. I wee the question on your lips: But your situation must have changed, fundamentally... Well then, nothing, nothing at all has changed, until present. On the contrary: The day on which the Americans arrived in Algeria was for us a day of unheard-of persecutions. With us, at Crampel, for example, it was dramatic. We had—and still have—the misfortune of being placed under the command of two Frenchmen, 100% Vichy-men, declared and convinced adherents of the politics of collaboration with Hitler-Germany. I cannot explain to you here all the sufferings which we had to undergo at Crampel: the work of ten hours per day in the heat of the semi-desert, where nothing grows except these miserable herbes [sic] called "alfa"; the completely insufficient soup (for example, cooked beets as [the] only dish without anything, neither oil, nor even vinegar; as-small fried cucumber; onions cooked in water, etc.)—these afore-mentioned dishes are meals! Besides the cooked onions, for example, there was nothing else!—so that most of the comrades have had to sell their last personal effects, shirts, sweaters etc. which will be felt when winter comes; and the bad treatment ... Is it necessary that I tell you about it? You know all that. And then the Americans arrived. That was on the 8th of November, a Sunday. We had heard something rumored, but nothing precise; we didn't even know whether it was the Germans or the Americans who were in Oran. There was no news to be had from our two Vichy-men (M. Roger Auger, Chef, and M. Vincelet, Surveillant). Imagine our unrest! The Chief of the Factories of Alfa, M. Ollier, had formally forbidden the civil workers to give us news. The members of the "Legion des Combattants" (Vichy guard) were mobilized, and we were told that anyone who left the house, took the risk of being shot. Monday morning, Nov. 9. I finally succeeded in having some news, especially the certainty that is wasn't the Germans who were at Oran. I transmitted this news to my comrades, for which I was reproached later as "having assembled my comrades in order to incite them." Monday afternoon, relying upon my exceptional position as physician of the detachment known by the Government, I talked to our chef, M. Auger to ask him for the following (am giving below the text of the conversation between him and myself):

> Muller: In case new Franco-American authorities should arrive at Crampel, I beg you, Monsieur, to ask their authorization for me to talk to them, in your presence, in order to better explain to them our special situation as foreign refugees.
>
> Auger: But that's conspiring with the enemy!

Muller: With the enemy?

Auger: Yes because the Government has ordered resistance. What you want to do is contrary to its orders.

Muller: But the Americans are not our enemies. They are the friends of France, and the friends of our Spanish and German refugees, too.

Auger: We shall see about that...

The following night (Nov. 9/10, 1942), I was pulled out of my sleep by armed soldiers of the "Foreign Legion" of Bedeau (9 km from Crampel), commanded by Sergeant-Chef Fischer, a German brute. One didn't even give me time to get dressed, [they] dragged me across the yard, and threw me on a truck, always giving me kicks with feet and bayonets. On the truck, I was mistreated again, and threatened, with a cord being presented, with being hung on the nearest tree. Comrad Levy, Jesf, a German biologist who had emigrated to France was treated a little less brutally, for having expressed toward the Surveilland Vincelet his joy about the arrival of the Americans. We two were transported to the prison of the Foreign Legion of Bedeau where, under miserable conditions, we had to stay until the 17th of Nov. One certainly would not have let us free even then if the Government had not ordered departure for Boghar. (On the side: that evening my watch was stolen; the comrades were threatened in all possible ways and received almost nothing to eat; in Saida, also south of Oran, all Traveilleurs Etrangers (Foreign Workers) were imprisoned for three days, without being mistreated, it is true). On our arrival at Oran, we were received by an armed detachment of native soldiers, surrounded, led to an old camp, locked up in a barrack (all 34) and insulted in a humiliating manner, called undesirables, etc. On the way from the station to the camp, three Spaniards (Caja, Palma, Luvas) received blows from the Surveillant Chef of our present camp "Port Gambetta," because, by reason of age or health, they could not march as fast as the others. But for this also the really responsible man is M. Auger, having furnished the camp personnel with false explanations ("undesirables") regarding our qualifications.

My dear . . . , please excuse my having written all this with the details which, perhaps, don't interest you. But we are in distress and I think that with this letter you might, if possible, interest some democratic friends in order to remind them that, until now, nothing has changed here as far as the interior situation of the country is concerned. The status of the Jews still exists, too.

And a thousand other things that are a disgrace for a country which wants to fight against Nazi tyranny.

I hope that, even though little by little, the weight of the great democracy overseas will modify the state of things. For ourselves, however, I remain pessimistic. Everybody, the Polish, the Czech, the Belgians etc. have their governments; even the Spaniards have their deputies. We others, German and Austrian refugees who, as the first ones, have fought against Hitler, we have nobody, are left to the mercy, often of types like this M. Auger.

If possible, transmit this letter to our friend . . . . whose exact address I don't know at the moment (I have it in my address book with my baggage). Or have I told you his address in my last letter of the month of August 1942? You would do me another great favor, furthermore, by forwarding the enclosed letter to . . . ., with the original or a copy of yours which I am addressing to you.

This letter is being sent to you through the help of the *American Commission* (Civil Affairs), S Boul. Gallieni, Oran—an organization to which one can address (perhaps) propositions or demands in our favor. If you want to write to me, take the address of Boghar-Sussoni, that's safer.

I hope to have news from you and from . . . . soon, being also very much interested in your present life down there, of which you will certainly give me some new details.

Again sending you all my sympathy, dear . . . . . . , I cordially shake hands with you

Yours

Case #7589
August 27, 1942

My dear Friend:

Your letter of 6.6 arrived yesterday unleashing a vague hope. Your realistic manner of analyzing the situation of the possibilities still existing of a visa is worth more than all the promises. It is really a thin thread which attaches [*sic*] 30 persons to liberty and to actual life, and a possibility that this small thread will be transformed into a solid cord one day and even here, the dangers which increase, they also, for those who are from European culture.

I have already spoken of it in a letter addressed to Nobel, an old comrade from here, who is now actually in the US By the hope of the Quakers he has sent me $20. In thanking him, I told him of our new situation here and I asked him to send you this letter, because of some information herein. I therefore repeat:

1) As I told you in my letter of April, after a relative calm of 1 ¾ years, the transfer of the former internees. (?) to the South has commenced, middle of April, the sending of about 55 to Kenadra (centre minier near de Colomb-Bechar (?)).

Toward the end of May, 51 others, myself among them, were sent here, 200 km to the south of Oran, half desert country, to work there with dry and rigid grasses of which they actually make lots of "ersatz" things. Our grasses are piled in packs of 5 kg and afterward pressed into bales of 180 kg. and then baked in electric ovens. This is normally the work of natives. But these nomads (there are no others), having come once in the dry season, take refuge in the coastal regions to feed their cattle and help in the work of harvesting. That is why the society of the alfas [sic] are forced to make use of a different kind of hand labor and it is we who have drawn this fate. The salaries, cut to the needs of the natives, obviously do not cover those of the European, even though the latter do the same amount of work as the nomads—which unfortunately is not always the case. In this situation, the government has generously decided to pay us a premium for food. But the difficulties of getting food here in the desert have increased enormously. In addition to that which I earn in 5 hours of work, I need 300 frs a month in order to buy enough food so that I don't lose weight. Happily, by the sum which you left me, I can get along somehow—otherwise . . .

I am affected here in my profession quality, but I work ½ a day all the same, be it for economic or disciplinary reasons, opposite my comrades who are able to stand this life better than I. I will not speak to you of this desolate country here, of this life empty and deprived of all meaning; at least there is hope for the future.

Rumors cannot be silenced about that which concerns a repatriation, more or less forced of all those interested. A bill has been posted inviting all to be repatriated voluntarily up to July 31, in the known conditions of the racial order and "in his own interest." Since the spring, a new rumor—except for the change of the regime in France—the most important factor is perhaps the new "general inspection for work distribution," Sauckel. In that case, I will make my application (as before the war) for French naturalization because of hugenotte [sic] origin, but I am afraid that it is not worth much. The wife of a friend living in Paris, Aryan, has been asked to return to Germany. News is not very exact on that which concerns the evacuation of pro-invasion elements in France to the East, probably Poland. Almost all our comrades (Jewish) about July 20th have lost contact with their families in the occupied Zone. Letters are returned with "left without leaving an address"; one letter speaks of "journeying toward the East." For several days the same measures may have been taken in the non-occupied zone, but that is not confirmed. However, I am surprised, that for some time I have had no news from my friends in Marseille with whom I was in regular correspondence. Chance?

You see, there are very somber thoughts. One does not loose courage, but . . . Only one hopes again for other possibilities of life—and then your letter arrived, a letter from the kind of friend who does not forget others. A thousand thanks, Henry and thanks to Jerem, Minna, etc. Depending for the moment entirely on the success of your efforts, I can do nothing but wait. It is a joy, believe me, to be able to have confidence in some men, and in their capacities and their perseverance.

I have not been able to get in touch with Diamant. Do you know his address? Before having received your letter and the advice it contained, I had tried once more to cable to Bab. For a visa. But it was useless, due to the situation explained in your letter, and I could have saved the money. I have received no letter from Jerem. Neither in '41 or '42 But I am sure of his willingness to assist. I am in contact with the Unitarians in Lisbon. The last time they were very kind.

Marvelous that you find all the money necessary for the president. You are really resourceful. And the passage already assured . . .

You see that with all these things personal, I have not one line for you, yourself. But you know that I wish you everything good in this imperfect world. I hope soon to be able to greet you soon as collaborator of research in the Institute of Social Research and Minna will certainly take change of some large establishment for feeding her professor.

A clasp of hand from your E.

Selected correspondence between Erwin Muller and Leslie Heath, 1942–1944, American Friends Service Committee Refugee Assistance Case Files, Accession No. 2002.296, File of Erwin Mueller, United States Holocaust Memorial Museum Archives, Washington, DC. Courtesy of American Friends Service Committee.

51. A PIANIST'S INJURED HAND, AND A QUEST FOR A VISA [1943]

What must it be like to be an interned pianist, crippled by sciatica, interned in a labor camp, with an injured hand that no amount of treatment can help? This source speaks of the agonies of thirty-two-year-old Karl Stössler, a privileged Austrian Jew—and hobby musician—who volunteered to serve the French army (as an engagé volontaire à la Légion étrangère pour la durée de la guerre) *during the Second World War, after a short internment in the Dachau concentration camp. After France fell to Germany, Stössler fled to North Africa, ending up (along with so many other volunteers for the French Foreign Legion) in a series of Vichy internment facilities in France and North Africa, including Oued Akreuch, Sidi Bel Abbès, Saïda, and Colomb-Béchar (Béchar). All the while, Stössler experienced a great deal of physical agony, both from his paralyzed hand and from acute sciatica. When Stössler prepared this letter to Moroccan Jewish lawyer and philanthropist Hélène Cazes Benatar of the Hebrew Immigration/Jewish Colonization Association (HICEM) in 1943, he sought the aid of that organization in obtaining a visa and financial support for his exit from Morocco, and his possible reunification with family in England, Canada, or France. What he apparently did not know at the time of this writing was that his family in Strasbourg, France, had likely already fled or been evicted from their homes, their property and assets seized.*

March 8, 1943

In accordance with the recommendation made by Mrs. Benatar during a conversation at the GTE [*groupes de travailleurs français et étrangers,* or forced labor battalion] 14, I have taken the liberty of writing you this letter.

I urgently request that you help me to obtain my liberation, paid employment, and eventually, [permanent] lodging.

My case is quite different from the others.

I, Karl Stössler, ex-Austrian Jew, was born on 2 September 1910 in Mödling, near Vienna (now Vienna's 24th district). I am a pianist, [formerly] employed in the wine trade. I was an Engagé Volontaire [*engagé volontaire à la Légion étrangère pour la durée de la guerre,* or volunteer of the French Foreign Legion engaged for the duration of the war] in the Mle 89054 Legion for the duration of the war. I have all my papers and documents, and I have my military service records and a certificate of good behavior from September 1940. I have witnessed in detail the pogroms in Austria since Hitler's arrival on 11 March 1938, and I was even forced to help burn down temples. Following the

Grynszpan Affair on Nov. 6 in Paris, I was sent for four and a half months to the worst of Germany's concentration camps, Dachau, situated three kilometers from Munich, because of my religion and my origins.[1] I saw men murdered. I saw them die and be killed. Through the help of my mother and my dear French relatives I was able to leave Dachau with my papers in order at the end of March 1939. Thank God, on 25 July 1939 I left Vienna, Austria, that is, German territory, with my papers in order, after having been subjected to numerous delay tactics. Likewise, I arrived in Strasbourg, France with my papers in order, equipped with a passport and special visa. After my residency permit expired, I left for Paris, stayed there for four days, and then left for Martigny-les-Bains (Vosges) to the Rot[h]schild vocational retraining camp by means of the Committee [Comité d'assistance aux réfugiés]. I had to wait there two or three months to assemble the documents necessary for entry into England and authorizing me to engage in agricultural labor.

My sister has lived near London since 2 January 1939. Her last address was: Miss Alice Stössler, "Fairlawn" Riverwoods Drive, Marlow, Bucks England. But then on 3 September 1939 the war broke out. Like most, I enrolled right away in the Legion for the duration of the war at Martigny-les-Bains; I was only able to sign on 17 November 1939 in Sionne near Neufchâteau. On 11 December 1939 I disembarked in Oran.

During my service, I broke the joint in my right wrist due to strenuous labor. It is true that I had already broken this wrist, but it had been fixed and healed as it should have. I was able to continue playing piano at the highest level and even worked as an ironmonger in one of my relative's factories, where I wasn't bothered [by my wrist]. After having verified everything, including my right wrist, the doctor at Bel Abbès declared me apt in mid-December 1939. After, they started making things difficult for me: they wanted to declare me unfit in Saïda but not pay [me]. Needless to say, I was not happy about this. I went to hospital in Saïda, where they put a cast on my broken wrist. This was 24 January 1940. For six weeks I was in hospital in Saïda. As my hand was paralyzed, they sent me to Mascara for X-rays. Two days prior,

---

1. On November 7, 1938, Herschel Feibel Grynszpan, a Germany-born Jew of Polish heritage, assassinated the German diplomat Ernst von Rath in Paris. The Nazis used the event as a pretext to initiate Kristallnacht (November 9–10, 1938), the so-called Night of Broken Glass, during which paramilitary troops and civilians ransacked German Jewish homes, hospitals, synagogues, and schools.

before being sent to the Bandens Hospital in Oran for electro-therapeutic treatment, I suddenly developed horrible lower-back pain. This was 19 March 1940, and it is the origin of the pain that I am now so dreadfully suffering from: sciatica. It continues to get worse, despite the fact that I've already had it for three years. I was in the hospital in Oran for a month. After, I had a reduced workload at the PDO for two months. (This is a small Legion warehouse in Oran.) On 19 June 1940 I returned to Saïda, not healed in the least. I was given a torture treatment against sciatica (the treatment was probably [illegible] but it was more of a punishment). Discharged on 10 October 1940 I left with my group for [the forced labor camp of] Kersas, four hundred kilometers to the south of Colomb-Béchar in the desert, where we had to stay for half a year. After, I spent fifteen months in [the forced labor camp of] Kenadsa. On 29 August 1942 I was marked out for the Moroccan group by Commander Viciot due to my illness and dismissed. On 1 September 1942 I arrived at Bou Arfa. I was in the hospital until 30 September 1942, released the same day, and sent to Oued-Akreuch, where I was posted for two and a half months. On 21 December 1942 Commander Kieler assigned me to the GTE 14 in Casablanca. On 26 December I had to go to Colombani civil hospital, where I had three electrotherapy sessions. Released on 25 January 1943, I received a summons from Chief Doctor Speeder at the end of March 1943.

Over the course of these three years, I underwent numerous point of fire [likely acupuncture] treatments, I took enormous quantities of medication, but nothing really helps. I have permanent pains (attacks) that are often so strong that I want to cry out for help. I fear for my future health. In Austria I was always healthy. I only had childhood illnesses. I never got mixed up in politics and I was only a simple member of the National Front ("Vaterländishe Front") who regularly paid the membership fees. (Besides, all the Jews in Austria were part of this "Vaterländishe Front.") In this respect, my blood as well as that of my parents and grandparents is without fault, and I do not have any hereditary illnesses. My father, who died in 1935 in Mödling, Vienna, was born in Bisentz in Moravia in 1882, and was a Czech citizen. He fought in the 1914–1918 war, was taken prisoner by the Italians in 1918, and returned in 1919. Under the influence of certain pressures, but also due to commercial considerations, he opted for Austrian nationality. We have two buildings in Mödling, a brewpub and a thriving wine store. For years, my father was vice president and treasurer of the Israelite Consistory in Mödling and a lot of poor and sick Jews were helped by us. Unfortunately, my father died as a result of an illness he had contracted on the front. So here I am, in this terrible situation.

For a year and a half, I have been without news of my sister. The last letter I wrote to her was sent on 23 October 1942 via airmail from Oued-Akreuch, but I have yet to receive a response. And of my poor, dear mother I have had no news since the beginning of the war, that is, since 3 September 1939. I fear that she may have been transferred to Poland and may no longer be alive.

As for a demobilization allowance, I received a total amount of 200 francs on 20 November 1940. For the remaining 935 francs I sent a request to the bureau of the GTE 10 in Oued-Akreuch. I have not yet received a response. (I was an *engagé volontaire* for the duration of the war, Gunner No. 89.054, Infantry Regiment, Bel-Abbès-Saïda.)

I have no possessions, as I had to leave all my belongings—two large trunks—in Martigny-les-Bains. I still have my receipt from Director M. Bouley, but this territory has been occupied since the very beginning of the war.

At the GTE 14 I make 5.25 francs per day and, since I was posted to Casablanca, that is, since December 42, I receive 50 francs a week from the Committee on 93 rue Coli. I have no other income.

I have saved nothing but my documents—I have them all. I can establish who I was and who I am, that I have always been honest, proper, and loyal, and I can give references. A man of many talents, I adapt easily to all kinds of work. I have a strong sense for business, and I know how to drive. I worked at the Austrian Automobile Club in the publicity and marketing section and I was the exclusive representative in Vienna of "Erfa-fabrication" (S. Erben and Sons, automotive accessory factories). The automobiles of Emperor XXX Joseph I were equipped by this company, which, for that matter, was the only one that manufactured Austrian spark plugs (Silverrex brand) and which had the general representation of the English company Ferodo (clutches and brakes for airplanes, cars, and motorcycles.) Alas, Hitler came. He took Austria by force, destroyed the situation of the Jews by pressuring them to emigrate or kill themselves. As for suicide, he was vigorously aided by the SS ([*Schutzstaffel*,] the elite guard of the National Socialist Party) and the Gestapo (government's secret police).

My relatives in Strasbourg who had a good reputation in France also had to abandon all of their belongings, but as far as I know, they were able to make it to Canada. I am just unsure of which city. They lost everything in France:

an immense tinplate packaging factory and several magnificent properties in Strasbourg, several buildings in Saint-Briac (Ille-et-Vilaine), a tremendous, brand-new factory in Boulogne-sur-Mer, obliterated by the bombings. Just before the occupation of the Free Zone by the German troops, I received in Bou Arfa a letter from the brother of my uncle in Juan-les-Pins (Alpes-Maritimes).

I kindly urge you to define the situation of the following families in Canada:

Léopold and Ella Hirschfeld
Charles "
Oscar "
? Isidore and Marthe "
Dr. Oscar and Käthe Roos (née Hirschfeld)

all of whom lived previously in Strasbourg, France at 52 allé de la Robertsau 52 and after in St. Briac (Ille-et-Vilaine) France.

The Hirschfelds were manufacturers and, in addition, my uncle Léopold II had a large, well-known goose-liver shop.

Please accept my gratitude in advance for all of your help, and excuse me for using a pencil. I was unable to procure any ink in my haste to write.

Devotedly yours,
Karl Stössler

Casablanca, March 8, 1943
Karl Stössler, Ex-Austrian, Israél.
Legal refugee due to racism, [former] employee in the wine trade and pianist, man of good conduct, former legionnaire
Engagé volontaire for the duration of the war, Mle 89.054 assigned to GTE 14 Casablanca
I do not drink and I smoke little.
539 Médéa Street
Without financial means, suffering, thirty-two years old, I have all my documents and beg your assistance.
1st Freedom and the possibility to regain my health.
2nd Work in the private sector.
3rd Determine the situation of the Alice Stössler sisters, last address in "Fairlawn" England

Riverwoods Drive   Marlow Bucks
4th Determine the address of Léopold and Ella Hirschfeld and of Doctor Oscar and Käthe Roos in Canada
still residing in Strasbourg at 52 allée de la Robertsau
after having lived some time in St. Briac (Ille-et-Vilaine), France
5th The rest of my demobilization severance?

Karl Israel Stössler, Casablanca, to HIAS-ICA-Emigration Association (HICEM), March 8, 1943, RG 68.115M, Reel 5, Private Collection Hélène Benatar (1936–1953), United States Holocaust Memorial Museum Archives, Washington, DC. Courtesy of Central Archives for the History of the Jewish People. Translated from French by Rebecca Glasberg.

52. A DOCTOR IN THE BOU AZZER MINES [1943–1944]

Fifty-three-year old Julius Ullmann, a Jewish doctor from Strasbourg, was sent by the post-Vichy French authorities (led by Admiral François Darlan, commander of French forces) to the labor camp of Bou Azzer in early 1943, ostensibly to minister to the health of interned children. Under Vichy rule, and after that regime's collapse, Bou Azzer was a deplorable camp, located next to cobalt ore mines, where its internees were forced to labor in the same horrific working conditions that local indigenous (Arab and Berber) forced laborers experienced before, during, and after the war. The interned suffered from extreme heat and inadequate shelter, clothing, and shoes. When Ullmann reached his post, he found no children at the sparse camp, and thus no outlet for his expertise. When German engineers visited the mine—a site the Vichy regime had touted as a marker of its technological prowess—Ullmann was subject to their anti-Semitic vitriol. The doctor's health deteriorated quickly. In a series of letters, Ullmann narrated his tragic lot while asking for counsel from Hélène Cazes Benatar, the Moroccan Jewish lawyer who represented the American Jewish Joint Distribution Committee in Casablanca. Ullmann was desperate to be moved elsewhere and sought philanthropic support for his immediate physical needs. His requests for relocation were denied by authorities, and he languished in Bou Azzer until 1945, two years after his appointment began.

October 8, 1944

Dear Esteemed Mrs. Bénatar,

As it happens, I meant to tell you about the following topics which both concern and interest me. Someone demanded a census of the refugees. I am not sure which category I belong to, and I was anticipating that this recount would surely be done by your refugee services.

Was I wrong?

I returned to the mine on September 13 and my facial paralysis hasn't substantially improved. Things have happened here that offend me, and I am not paid well enough. I don't know if this is the moment to change positions, but I would really like to know my chances of finding another placement if I am denied a raise. I would like to remind you that I am a specialist in childhood diseases and sports hygiene.

I won't do anything for the time being, I direct this matter to you and ask for your opinion.

Sincerely,
Dr. Ullmann

October 8, 1943

Dear Mrs. Bénatar,

It has been six months since I asked Monsieur Kuhn, who left us in May, to pass on my gratitude and best wishes in his letter. Meanwhile, things were moving along a little here and I was rather satisfied. Recently I found myself facing a conspiracy hatched by three or four of the most heinous men employed at the mine, whose principle motive is hate (*anti-semitism!*) and envy.

Although Management gave me their assurances, for me—who wants above all to rest easy—it is very unpleasant to be exposed to and always be on the lookout for these conspiracies.

It's been two weeks since I reported this matter to Mr. Herschel, the appointed administrator of the Society in Casablanca. Even today, I had to deal with one of these people, whose every word is a lie, and I told him that his rumors won't hold up. Therefore, he called me a Jew Nazi and he has already done everything in his power to make me leave. Leaving Bou-Azzer to do something else—if I could get an equivalent if not better post—wouldn't be the worst punishment for me, especially since I find myself doing very poorly in terms of health. The only thing I still fear—[and] if I didn't, I would have

IMAGE 15. Located fifty-nine miles southwest of Casablanca, Morocco, the Im Fout forced labor camp was located near a dam construction project on which its prisoners—most of whom were classified as "foreign workers"—were compelled to carry out backbreaking work by the Vichy Department of Industrial Production. "Two prisoners [Sami Dorra and Rosenthal] Stand by the River and Smoke Pipes at the Im Fout Labor Camp in Morocco," 1941–1942, Photograph No. 50724, United States Holocaust Memorial Museum, Washington, DC.

already taken the necessary steps [to seek reassignment]—is that I will find the same thing [dynamic] but with different faces. Please, Mrs. Bénatar, take my letter seriously and consider carefully if there is anything that can be done for me.

Dr. Ullmann, Bou Azzer, to Hélène Cazes Benatar, Casablanca, October 8, 1944, and October 8, 1943, RG 68.115M, Reel 5, Private Collection Hélène Benatar (1936–1953), United States Holocaust Memorial Museum Archives, Washington, DC. Courtesy of Central Archives for the History of the Jewish People. Translated from French by Amber Sackett.

53. SHORN OF HER CURLS—INTERNMENT IN GIADO THROUGH A YOUNG GIRL'S EYES {1942}

In the winter of 1941–1942, British troops temporarily captured the eastern coast of Libya, Barqah (Cyrenaica), once ruled by the Italians. When the Italians recaptured Cyrenaica in February 1942, Benito Mussolini ordered the Jews of the region moved out of the war zone—ostensibly to prevent them from aiding the British. The persecution of Jews in Libya has deep roots in Italian fascist rule. Violence against the Jews in the region began soon after Italian fascist rule took hold in Libya (at the end of October 1922), with attacks on local Jews by Italian soldiers and local supporters of fascism. Anti-Jewish legislation took shape in 1935, against the backdrop of Italy's war against Abyssinia. At this time, Italy developed racist policies in Italian East Africa (encompassing Abyssinia, Eritrea, and Italian Somaliland) that dictated the segregation of local Black populations and Italian settler colonialists and state representatives. These policies in turned catalyzed the implementation, as of 1938, of anti-Jewish legislation (the Leggi per la Difesa della Razza) in Libya. Thousands of Jews were deported as a result of Mussolini's February 1942 orders, with the property of many being confiscated. Italian officials sent the bulk of displaced Jewish families to the labor and internment camp of Giado, site of a former military post located 150 miles south of Tripoli. Other Libyan Jewish (and some Muslim) women, men, and children were deported to the camps of Buqbuq, Sidi Azaz, Gharyan (Garian), Jeren, and Tigrinna, all of which were also sites of forced labor. Among these camps, Giado was the most notorious. It is estimated that five hundred of the imprisoned died in Giado from starvation, disease, hunger, or from the hardships of forced labor. In this selection of her personal testimony, Shoshana Arviv recounts her family's expulsion from their native Tripoli, their journey to Giado, and the day-to-day experience of internment in this miserable environment. Of note is her attention to gendered experiences of captivity and her sharp memories of the material objects that members of her family carried, relied on, lost, missed, or dreamed of during their imprisonment: for example, her grandmother's treasured sewing machine, somehow ferried all the way to Giado, and Arviv's own curls, shorn by her captors ostensibly to prevent lice but perhaps to compound the child's humiliation. Arviv was a nine-year-old girl when the family was deported to Giado, and her somewhat-fractured oral testimony also offers a rare, child's perspective on the devastating events unfolding in Libya.

Ronit Wilder-Steiner (Interviewer): *When they came, did you think at all about running away or hiding or resisting?*

Shoshana Arviv: My father prepared our things and the next day the trucks came to our house and they started moving things.

What I understand is that you prepared wood, food—

And the sewing machine, we took wheat, rice, dry goods, maybe sandwiches, maybe something for the childr— . . . we didn't know how long it would be, they didn't say how long it would be. We got on the trucks, or first we loaded all of these things, they got to the crate and it weighed a ton and they couldn't lift it and my father said he wouldn't leave without it. It was war with the drivers—maybe they were Italians, I don't know, the Sicilians were also there—anyway, in the end they lifted the crate. It took maybe twenty people. They loaded all the parents and children and families and the children stood on the feet of the parents like animals. There was no space. It was our family, my grandmother and grandfather, our neighbors, the whole neighborhood . . . and we were crying, there was no room to stand, tired . . . and we drove and we drove and we drove, a huge distance. I think we drove for four or five days in the desert. Sometimes we would get out for a bit in the Sahara, go to the bathroom, and they'd put as back on the trucks like sheep. We ate dust—if there was something to eat, they gave it to us, but if not [waves hand] and continue driving and driving. The trucks were enclosed, open at the back. It was hot, crowded, the children on top of the parents, calming this one and that one, and the girls are together and fighting and the boys are fighting and we don't know where we're going.

Did you have time to say goodbye to your Arab girlfriends before leaving?

No, no, we were embarrassed, we hid ourselves. Maybe those who were older, but children, no, we didn't see them. It seems like maybe their hearts hurt. It could be, it could be.

You didn't know where you were going, right? You didn't know the name Giado?

No, we were children, we didn't know. Wherever the parents went, we went and that's how it continued and continued and continued until the trucks stopped. What was there? There was a camp, long, long, long, with two sides. We put up blankets to divide the cabins. We organized our things, brought everything in. The crate my father left outside. My grandmother brought in her millstones with the bags. My mother also brought the sewing machine. We brought in a crate you could sit on. There was no furniture, nothing, with difficulty we had just taken a few things, blankets . . .

IMAGE 16. Some months after the Italians recaptured the eastern coast of Libya, Barqah (Cyrenaica) in late 1941, Prime Minister Benito Mussolini ordered the region's Jews moved and their property confiscated. Most of these Libyan Jews were sent to the notorious labor and internment camp of Giado. Hundreds of the imprisoned died of starvation, disease, hunger, or the hardship of forced labor—among them Haim Habib, just sixteen years of age. Photograph of Haim Haviv/Habib (b. Benghazi, 1927; d. Giado camp, 1943), Item ID 14156354, Yad Vashem, the World Holocaust Remembrance Center, Jerusalem.

Did your father ask the neighbors to watch your things? Or did you keep things with them?

No, no they didn't even lock the house. Everything remained, things, clothes, it all remained. We didn't take anything except for the millstones, some pots, wheat, rice, this and that, and we left. We arrived there and put them in. My grandmother made from clay and sand and made a hole—

An oven?

A hole, we put three rocks. My father always opened it and took it, and cooked.

I don't understand. You mean you built a kind of oven from local clay?

Yes, we made a hole in the ground this size and put clay here, red sand with water. First, we put sand, then wood, which I think my father brought, maybe he also brought kerosene, I don't know. And they put three pieces of clay on top and then the pot so that there would be air underneath and you'd put [on] the pot, you need the air.

So you had an oven and even wood and pots, but what did you have to cook in the pots?

We had what we took—

And how much was that? How long did it last?

It didn't last. We were living there in great fear. The Germans used to enter with their big boots, holding flashlights and whips. Sometimes all the children would all sit in one room, children sitting together and telling stories. And we would hear the German enter, cursing, with the Jewish *Kapo*. Did he have a choice? He brought him with. "Dirty, with lice, who needs you, your end has come," and he'd start to say all kinds of things. And we lay one on top of another, *shhhh*, so he wouldn't hear us and lift it up and see.

I assume that luckily at least you didn't understand what he was saying. If he was speaking in German then surely not . . .

Yes, but those who translated understood lice—there were lice.

That was a major problem, right? Because immediately there was lice and then with lice came typhus. And we said there were big cabins that were only divided by blankets and the disease was infectious—

The disease was infectious. I also got sick with typhus. With the lice, one day they came to shave everyone, and I had hair that was really something. Beautiful curls to here [points to her lower back]. They shaved us and we ran away and we hid and—

The Jews themselves did it? To prevent the lice within the camp?

They shaved everyone. They would take the men to work outside, they'd pick up stones from here and place them there. They had the whip, their yelling and cursing, "Do you understand or not!"

Most of the time those you were interacting with were Italians, right? The guards and such were Italian?

They were Italian.

And how did they relate?

We didn't relate well.

Everyone?

Everyone. And me with my uncle, who I told you was almost blind—my mother's brother—they would push him and as a girl, I would feel for him, and would take him and would help him. Me and him moving stones from here to there. They were always pushing him, knocking him over, insulting him, spitting on him. They weren't nice at all, not nice at all.

Usually the Italians are held up as nice and OK and ready to help and so on. But here, it sounds like the Italian head of the camp, because he was anti-Semitic, he influenced everyone.

After they shaved everyone, another girl and I ran away and hid and they didn't find us. I remember today that one old man in the camp they shaved him. They took off all his clothes—what can I say to you, my god—the lice that burned the clothes [makes an eating sound]—the lice are as big as rice. Rice! The poor guy they ate his entire body. They left him naked until someone gave him something to wear below [e.g., on his lower body]. That's how it was.

So in the end did they shave your head?

Yes, they caught me. My elderly grandmother, she said, "Why? Why? I'm old, I'm old, why do you need to shave my hair?" You didn't see anyone with hair. Everyone, men, women, children.

And they did it so there would be less lice?

I didn't see lice on me. I only saw them on that young man.

But you were all living in close quarters. But the shaving you remember.

I remember.

Did you cry?

I cried! What hair! Now I see my granddaughter, like hers.

But it grew back again.

It grew back, slowly. So we stayed there, I don't know, a year and a half or more in Giado.

You were a girl, nine and a half. There was no school, so what did you do all day?

We played all day. During the day, no. At night, the whole camp was empty. No guards, everyone went to sleep. So we used to go out of the camp and there we big rocks everywhere and we used to hide behind them.

There were other children that you knew from before, from the neighborhood, and also there were children you didn't know.

Yes, yes, there were many I knew. Many died. Only one I know is left. I don't know if he died, I haven't heard. Yes, we played as children but when a guard came, we ran into a corner, threw ourselves down onto each other, until he left. My aunt, I told you about her. She was pregnant. She married at an older age and she didn't know, she went to the shower area. I don't know if she walked behind this officer or in front of him, but he pushed her and she fell. She lost her baby. And she was older. She was fortunate that there was a midwife in our section of the camp who helped her. And until she died, she wasn't able to have children. And when people were receiving money from Giado, she didn't say anything and she didn't receive anything! . . . the poor woman died and she never received any money. We suffered a lot there. We really suffered. He came to Giado—

Who?

Farjun. He brought us two blankets . . .

His family was also there? He had relatives there?

No, no, no one. And I remember he brought two bags. It seems like he was friends with the Italians there. He brought one bag of wheat and one of rice.

So at least your grandmother's millstones were put to use.

Yes, yes, the millstones. I remember that too. The blankets we took back with us to Benghazi and then to Israel. Afterward, they said that the war had ended—

Wait, before that. It seems like outside the camp on the hill there was a machine gun? Do you remember anything like that?

I don't know, I never saw it.

Did anyone ever leave the camp outside the fence?

Yes, me too, me too. There was one young man who became friendly with the guards. He would dig a bit under the fence and pass over to an Arab village on the other side. But they didn't speak our Arabic. It was impossible to understand them. They would say, "Kudai." He would buy all kinds of things. So he said to my dad, my dad said, "Great, I've found a solution. My wife will sew these shirts and we'll take them." The Arabs were naked, they wore clothing like this [indicates tied across the chest]. My dad told my mom to sew, took all that she had sewn, and went to them. But they don't speak the same Arabic. You can't understand them. I didn't understand them. The children saw the clothing and what happiness! They put them on. You'd see the girls with just a piece of clothing here [indicates her chest] and here [indicates her waist]. Men just with a piece on their waists. And in the end, they caught him.

Wait, but how did they pay? Rice or what?

Rice, flour, things like that. It was important for us. You can't make bread with nothing. Without flour, you can't live. My father told me and I snuck out after him and went to see. In coming back, they caught my father. They put him in jail and he stayed there for one or two days. It was a cabin, a room with iron. And the young man, who had become friends with the guards, asked them and my grandmother sat next to the jail and didn't leave there. "I'm not going, I won't eat anything until my son comes out." And in the end he was in jail for a day or two, hungry. I also sat with her and we cried and in the end it saved him. And after that he didn't leave the camp anymore. Me neither. I didn't go out alone. I was my father's tail.

Did someone else—

The boy, who'd made friends, maybe he'd steal things and gave to the poor, maybe helped, I don't know.

Since you were in a large cabin, let's assume that you received some shirts, let's assume a bag of wheat, you made food. And there were those next to you who didn't have anything.

We divided it up.

It wasn't every person for themselves?

It was every person for themselves.

Everyone had to watch out for their own children.

Of course, we gave to the children. Especially my mother. We couldn't made it on our own. We'd give.

Did they give to others in the cabin or every family was for itself?

It wasn't a cabin. It was a barrack from here to the other room, everyone worried for themselves. But they gave food to us every day, bringing three or four bags of bread, like a roll. Bread, the size of a pita. Each one was split between two people.

Everyone could live only on this?

Yes, but they died from typhus. They died from lice. They died from hunger.

And your family?

We became sick.

But everyone stayed alive.

We all stayed alive. I got sick with typhus. My mother got sick with typhus. My uncle had typhus. And my grandmother, when she saw that her son was sick, she was infected as though she were sick, but she wasn't. But when the war ended and the British arrived, and they saved everyone who was left and they gave everyone biscuits. I remember the rolls that are like those they give out in theaters today, there was nothing like it, it was really something. We started to eat, my mother and father didn't eat theirs, they saved it for my sister. My sister Sarah was little. She maybe ate something small, I don't know.

Wait, when you were there your sister was already walking? Or she was still a baby?

She didn't walk. She was a baby. And there was an American or a Brit, I don't know, and he went crazy. He took her and held her in his arms and said, "She's like my daughter. I have a daughter at home." He took her and he'd bring us more biscuits and more things and would take things from the storeroom and bring them so that she'd gain weight.

Were there also Arabs who came to the fence of the camp and would sell things?

No one, no one was allowed. We were destined to be killed. What I heard was that if not, it would be enough to be gathered for trains.

So you didn't know these things.

No, we didn't know.

There was no connection to the outside?

Maybe they knew. Maybe Farjun knew and told my dad, but I didn't know. They said that the train had to come here and then took all the Jews to this train. And then the Americans or British came and saved us.

But tell me a little about how, before we get to the British, a little about life in the camp. Were there things you needed to do, like everyone standing in a field so they could count you, things like that?

The men. The men were lined up in a roll call like that, but the women I never saw. There was one woman though who had a child out of wedlock and she threw it out and they started to look and check [to see who had done it]. My (female) cousin said, "They'll also check me," but we said, "You're a girl, they're not checking you" [laughs]. So this woman threw out her child. It seemed like she gave birth alone, the poor girl. And it died, and she threw it out, and they discovered it. And they started to look for all the girls to check who had done this. Incidentally, the mother of the girl also had a baby, but the baby lived. So she said one lived and one died. I remember this. I liked to see things.

So even in the camp you would go around with your eyes and ears open?

Yes, with the dirty, square dress that was never changed, hard fabric with asbestos.

Arviv, Shoshana, interviewed by Ronit Wilder-Steiner, October 12, 2021. "Edut." Shoat Luv, Merkaz Moreshet Yahadut Luv, shoatluv.org.il/תויודע/. Translated from Hebrew by Rachel Smith.

54. LIBYAN JEWISH HOLDERS OF BRITISH PASSPORTS LANGUISH IN ITALIAN CAMPS {1943–1945}

Before the outbreak of the Second World War, the Jewish population of Libya included more than 30,000 Libyan Jews that the Italian colonial government characterized as "indigenous" because they did not hold any European passports, and nearly 2,500 Jews that the administration labeled "foreign" for holding the citizenship of a European power. In many cases, these "foreigners" were members of long-standing Libyan Jewish families who had managed to acquire foreign papers through work or inheritance. During the war, Libya was a key battleground, its territory passing back and forth between Italian and British hands: in 1942, German forces, specifically Hitler's Afrika Korps, would also aid the fledgling Italian colonial government in Libya. In February 1942, Italy's Prime Minister Benito Mussolini ordered the Jews of Cyrenaica (Barqah) moved out of the war zone. Approximately half of the six thousand deported as a result of Mussolini's orders were sent to the labor camp of Giado, a former military post located 150 miles south of Tripoli. Other Libyan Jews were deported to the labor camps of Buqbuq and Sidi Aziz, or to internment camps in Tunisia. A distinct fate awaited Libya's "foreign" residents, Jewish and non-Jewish. In the early months of 1942, Libyan Jews and

Muslims with French citizenship (including those under Tunisian protection) were sent to waystations (including La Marsa, a suburb of Tunis that was bombed, killing more than fifty of the deported) and ultimately to Vichy-run camps in Tunisia and Algeria. The 870 Libyan Jews with British citizenship were deported to Italy, with at least half ending up in camps. A portion of those in Italy would be deported once again when Italy capitulated to Germany in September 1943, when 370 of the interned Libyan Jews with British citizenship were sent either to Bergen-Belsen or to a German internment camp in Vittel, France. The following testimony by Sion Burbea—a Libyan Jewish holder of British papers—recounts her internment in Civitella del Tronto, in the central-eastern Italian town of Camerino, and her subsequent deportation to Bergen-Belsen. What is striking in Burbea's account is the variety of people she interacts with in the course of her internment: other Libyan British Jews, "European" Jews (as she calls them), German representatives, local Italian civilians, Jewish survivors of Auschwitz, representatives of the Red Cross, Swiss officials, and more.

We arrived all of 107 of us, in Civitella del Tronto on the 17th, [and] we were accommodated for two [or] three months at Casa Migliorata at 109 Corso Mazzini and later in the Hospital Filippo Alessandrini. Here we celebrated the Passover with wine and our foods. Alfredo Labi and Abraham Reginiano, having sick family members, [were lodged] in private apartments with ministerial permission.

The people in the town helped us every way they could, as it was the middle of winter and we did not have anything. We had lost much of the baggage in the transfer from the port of arrival to the train station of Teramo. Dr. Rosati came from the Ministry of the Interior and sent me and three others to look for our belongings, first at the camps in Fraschette of Alatri and then in Carpi. The outcome was negative.

In Civitella, Rivo Migliorati was the first person who helped us. He was the owner of a general store whose wife Giovannina, among other things, supplied the oil for the ceremonial lamps. The parish priest, Don Fioravante D'Ascanio, indicated the dates on which we could celebrate our anniversaries at a room at the Ospedaletto, which we used as Oratory. There is still is the prayer book that bears on the red cover this writing in Hebrew: "Oratory of Civitella del Tronto." The pharmacist Ariberto Minutes gave us oil with which, in the early days, we cooked the food. The cook was Herbert

Jacobson, a German Jew, helped by one of our women, the mother of Shalom Reginiano. I will talk about her again later. The tobacconist gave us, upon his arrival, the magazine *International Relations*.

We also had a close relationship with Eugenio Tucci, who was distributing, from a small table placed in front of the hospital, benefit money to every head of family. Initially the benefits came from the Italian Government directly. Subsequently, the money orders also came from the Legation of Switzerland on behalf of the British Government, as we were all British citizens. The two security agents Paolo Di Genova and Giuseppe D'Andrea, who delivered the money to us, have to be remembered for their great humanity. Some of the "European" Jews only received a small subsidy from Delasem from time to time. Among them was Richard Stein, whose son Orestes often came to visit us at the Ospedaletto. Oreste belonged to a band that often played in the camp. Alfredo Wachsberger, a professional violinist from Vienna, was the conductor.

The security agents mentioned before, and also Quaglia as well as the military police officer led by the commanding officer Bernardini, were generally kind to us. In the evening, as there was a curfew, Eugenio Tucci came to play cards with us in the Ospedaletto. Equally kind were the officials that came from Teramo. Drs. Ermanno Malaspina and Manlio Scesi were the appointed official medics in the camp. However they often allowed qualified inmates to undertake their medical tasks in exchange for goods.

The directors appointed by the Ministry behaved less well and often when goods parcels came from the Swiss Legation, they would hold back some items. Alfredo Labi, an inmate, sent a complaint [about this] to the Legation. After a week two Swiss officials came and later Dr. Rosati did, too: there was an investigation and the director was replaced by Dr. Taranto, the brother of Nino.

The International Red Cross supplied a small pharmacy, which was managed by Dr. Bersciadskj Semil, a friend of Dr. Aribert Minuti and of Fulvia his daughter, whom he used to visit often in their pharmacy. Semil was killed in Auschwitz on the day after he arrived; the same happened to Zieg Samuele, a fabric trader we met in Tripoli, and Eskenazi Joseph, a teacher at the Berlitz School in Trieste—who gave me English lessons too.

During my period at Civitella seven children were born, two of whom were boys. The elderly Dr. Ascarelli came from Rome to perform the circumcisions. The vast majority of "European" inmates, however, were male. I remember that there was a couple, Ignaz Haina, a Jew, and his wife, [who was] not Jewish. Hain: could be have been the magistrate that I recall being present in Civitella when there was a final deportation in early May 1944? His wife wanted to follow her husband, but a German soldier pointed his gun, shouting that he would shoot right away, if she insisted.

The situation worsened after September 8, 1943, corresponding with the arrival of the Germans. The military police left the country and only Paolo Di Genova and Giuseppe D'Andrea remained in plain clothes. Somebody gave me a falsified ID card certifying I was resident in Civitella and said to show it only when necessary. On 25 September of the same year, on Saturday, between 11 and 11:30, Germanic soldiers arrived on a couple of trucks. Two inmates at Convento S. Maria dei Lumi panicked and fled down the road leading to the village of Borrano. They were machinegunned: the first died instantly—he was a Maltese named Aquilina, perhaps his first name was Antonio. Immediately he was stripped by a military representative of all personal belongings and I remember his body lying by the friars by a door and left in the porch of the cloister, on the right hand site of the entrance. After the war, when I returned to Tripoli, I met Frederick Aquilina who was looking for his brother and I gave him the sad news. I know that Federico wanted his brother's remains to be returned from the new cemetery of Civitella where he had been meanwhile buried. The second [man shot] was Herbert Jacobson, who was wounded in the shoulder. However he was spared because I met him [later,] in the displacement camp of Como, on my return from Germany in 1945.

On the afternoon of the 25th, the Luftwaffe aviators arrived and confiscated all the food and parcels of the Canadian red Cross in our accommodation at the Ospedaletto.

Two Tripolitania Jews were buried in the new Civitella cemetery. They had died of natural causes: one is Hlafo Habib, uncle Haim Shalom "Mino" Habib, always a spokesman for our group, and the other is Jacob Reginiano.

The following October 26 the drunken Lithuanian soldiers arrived (I remember one had a circle booby bag on his head), who shouted "Komm Cieti"—"Come to Chieti"—they forced only males Tripolinian and European inmates to climb on their four trucks, kicking and punching them. Nemni David was the only one who escaped, as he had no family ties whereas the rest of us had families and many also had several children. (In 2004 a nephew of David Nemni married my niece, Scilla Di Segni). Our destination was the defensive line "Gustav."

They took us away to a brick factory, in Crocetta on [the river] Sangro, near Castelfrentano, and we worked all day digging holes for mines and antitank. They gave us very little food and the soldiers said: "Organizziren" [organize yourselves]. Put simply about ten of us went around to procure (even steal) food. Almost every day the owner of the factory, Mr. Frontoni, came to check on a gig with his son, until the soldiers hid his horse and the next day they gave it to us to eat.

My feet were swollen with chilblains and I could not walk, but a German soldier forced me to continue working, pointing his gun to my chest. When he saw my tears of pain he asked me how old I was. We were the same age, he said, and in the evening, to make amends for his brutality, he brought me a mess tin full of food and meat.

Another day we saw the German senior officers scour the area thoroughly with binoculars. Josif, a Romanian enlisted in the Wehrmacht who occasionally gave me cigarettes, shouted [at me] to hoe without looking up. Then, slowly, he told me that closer to us was General Albert Kesselring. Fifty meters away was General Erwin Rommel.

We stayed there about a month and after a heavy bombardment, the Germans abandoned the line and even forced us to retreat, but this time on foot. On that occasion the Maltese John Spiteri, among others, fled without being caught. We arrived in Ortona in the dark. They locked us in a disused school and prevented one of us, a certain Mr. Labi to get out to urinate: he urinated inside and then drank it. This was the father of Lulli Alba, who now lives in Israel. At Chieti Scalo we suffered a strafing by Canadian planes.

We were a ragged caravan, weak and emaciated to the point that, when we reached Pianella, the parish priest and the mayor sounded the alarm. An auctioneer informed the population that they could bring food to us to prevent us from dying on the street. The mayor, before we left, made some of us sign an account telling how he had helped us.

Subsequently, the trucks came and they were loaded, but for me, Jacob Reginiano and four others there was no room. The Germans, not knowing where to put us safely, locked us for two nights in Penne jail. On December 5, we returned to Civitella: it was the day of Chanukah [and in] the evening we were able to kindle the lights of the "festival of miracles."

The final deportation took place on May 4, 1944. There were soldiers, not SS, and they loaded us into trucks with trailers (six, seven vehicles in all). Near Fano, the convoy was gunned down and my father, trying to hide himself, fractured a leg. In the Fossoli di Carpi camp, a European Jew, Samuele Hacker, managed thanks to his entrepreneurship to become an assistant to the German commander. I had met him in 1938 in Tripoli, where he sold some cuts of fabric together with Zieg Samuele, and I found them both in Civitella.

Once in Verona, the German police on 15 May compiled the list of those at the station. They were loaded onto railway wagons intended for Bergen-Belsen and I own a copy of that list.

These were terribly terrifying moments. Among the jerks and screams, well it happened that the clerk did not register the members of the Habib family as such, but under their mother's surname, Haschi.

Once we arrived in the camp at Bergen-Belsen, our British passports were confiscated and we [received] different treatment from the other "European" Jews. The Germans did not communicate to anybody that those nationals [citizens] from allied countries were merchandise for negotiations and in fact, this happened very soon, with an exchange of prisoners.

Also some women coming from Auschwitz arrived at the camp.

Our group remained compact with neither divisions nor selections. However, in another group one of our inmates from the camp, Shalom Reginiano, was tortured and left to die of gangrene in the cabin, as a warning for having stood up to a guard. In Civitella his mother was the assistant cook.

When, Mino Habib, head of the group, forwarded a letter to the Red Cross, under whose auspices we were, the office of censorship handed it to the head of the camp, who came in person to the cabin and, after having gathered us, ripped [the letter] in pieces, screaming that never again should he dare such a gesture.

Soon after, we were put to work with young women and other men. Except my father, who had a broken leg. The food we knew too well, a black brew that drove us to rummage through waste bins near the kitchens of the SS.

We realized that something was changing, and for the better, the day we were each given a levelled teaspoon of jam. We tried for hours to savor it slowly. On November 16, 1944 we were dispatched to Biberach in Bavaria, in an area that would not be controlled by the Soviets. On the 23 April 1945 the French freed us; then, we were sent to Jordanbad, a beautiful spot where we were looked after by nuns. After a short stay in Italy, we returned to Libya on September 12, 1945.

Terracina, Giordana. "Hidden Responsibilities: The Deportation of Libyan Jews in the Concentration Camp of Civitella del Tronto and the Confinement Town of Camerino." *Trauma and Memory* 4, no. 3 (2016): 9–31. Selection from pages 22–24, with additional translation and editing by Sarah Abrevaya Stein.

55. REFUGEE FORCED LABOR IN CASABLANCA [1943]

Rick's Café, from Michael Curtiz's 1942 film Casablanca, *is an iconic space in modern cinema. Who were its fictional patrons? Caricatured refugees from Europe; Jews from Germany, Poland, Greece, France, and beyond; women and men who fled the Third Reich for the seeming safety of Morocco. Had it been real, Rick's Café would have been able to offer only temporary shelter. In all likelihood, its patrons would have been deported to labor and prison camps by the collaborationist Vichy regime that controlled France's colonies in North Africa: the fate of thousands of North African Jews and Muslims, and thousands of European Christian and Jewish "Reds" in flight from Franco's Spain. This internal memorandum, sent from a field officer in Casablanca to an administrator in the United States, reveals how the Public Welfare and Relief Division of the North African Economic Board (the North African agency of the United States Office of Foreign Relief and Rehabilitation Operations) assessed the persistent refugee crisis in Casablanca in the late winter of 1943. Nearly a year after the defeat of the Vichy regime in Morocco, thousands of refugees remained in and around Casablanca, fearing forced labor, dreaming of exit, and uncertain as to what home they could to return to, since so many of their communities were destroyed or rendered unrecognizable by war and genocide.*

October 1, 1943

Referring to Major M. L. Furcolow's and my conversation with you on the morning of September 30, 1943, I respectfully submit the following information about refugees in the Casablanca area in whom this office is interested and who constitute a present and potential labor supply for the US Army.

There are at present about 2,100 refugees in and around Casablanca. About 1,700 of these are Spanish, and the rest are principally Germans, Austrians, ex-Germans, ex-Austrians, Poles, Italians, and others from Central Europe. These refugees are all almost fanatically anti-fascist and pro-Ally, as their histories will show very clearly.

Most of the Spaniards who are fled from Spain after the defeat of the Loyalist armies early in 1939. Some came direct to North Africa, and a large number first went to France proper and then were transferred here later by the Vichy government. Since the Spanish war, these refugees have spent most of their time in concentration camps, where they were put, first by necessity by the French before the war because there was nothing else to be done with them, and later as a Nazi-inspired Vichy measure. Excepting this office, these Spaniards have no consulate or other organization to represent them or to protect their interests.

The other nationalities fall mostly into two classes. The first consists of men who fought with the Loyalists in Spain during the civil war as members of the International Brigade and suffered the same fate as the Loyalist Spaniards. The second class consists of foreigners who found themselves in French territory in 1939–1940 and volunteered for the French army for the duration of the war. These "engages volontaires" were demobilized after the defeat and put into concentration camps.

When the Allied armies arrived in North African on November 5, 1942, they found about 7,000 anti-fascist refugees in concentration camps and forced labor companies. Among the first efforts made to liberate these people were those of the American Friends Service Committee (Quakers), which had had a delegate in Casablanca since September, 1942. After November, the refugees in camps, knowing that the Allies had arrived, took matters into their own hands very often and escaped from the camps, coming to the Quaker office in Casablanca. From that office they were sent to various hiring organizations of the US Army for employment. The Army at that time was in very urgent need of labor. The French practice in most cases was not to molest escapees who were working with the US Army.

In January, as an answer to a loud public protest in England and America against a situation which found concentration camps almost in the shadow of the American flag, the British and American governments formed an Interallied Commission to arrange for the liberation of anti-fascists still held in camps. After much negotiation, General Giraud decreed the dissolution of the concentration camps and foreign work companies on April 27, 1943. The bulk of liberations actually took place in May, June and July. In Morocco the liberation of refugees was conditional upon their joining one of the Allied Armies, the French Army, or signing a civil work contract with the American Army of with a private French concern. On this basis all of the men in camps have now been freed.

Since February, the work of the American Friends Service Committee in providing emergency relief for refugees displaced in this area, has been taken over by the Office of Foreign Relief and Rehabilitation Operations (Governor Lehman's organization), and this Office has procured Lend-Lease clothing which it has distributed to refugees working with the US Army, as these men were released from camps. It is the hope of OFRRO [Office of Foreign Relief and Rehabilitation Operations] to do whatever is necessary to make life possible for refugees in North Africa, and to prevent the necessity of their being put back into camps or forced work companies by the French authorities.

Naturally, the scope of this task will depend largely upon whether the refugees here are able to continue to support themselves. If there is no work for a foreigner in French territory, then, under the present laws, he is illegally here and must either return to his own country, which is impossible for these refugees, or be put into a camp or work company. In recent weeks, with the contraction of US Army activities in Casablanca, our principal task has been to redirect refugees to other divisions of the Army, as common labor usually, and at a lower rate of pay, or to French concerns. In addition, many of the refugees have made the transition from temporary army employment to relatively permanent French civilian employment without our aid.

Of the 2,100 refugees at present in Casablanca, 1,723 have been sent by the Refugee Section, between January 1 and September 29, to various US Army organizations. 108 have been redirected from the Army to French concerns.

It is almost impossible to state how many refugees are now working with the Army, since after a refugee once leaves this office we have no further contact with him unless he comes back for reemployment. Many refugees, once

IMAGE 17. Located southwest of Tunis, the Vichy internment camp at Le Kef housed British officers and sailors, German and Austrian refugees, French political opponents of the Vichy regime (including communists and syndicalists), and Tunisian nationalists. Here, imprisoned men walk within the barbed-wire-enclosed camp and through a courtyard adjacent to the barracks under the watchful eye of a Vichy guard. "Le Kef," "Les Camps et Centres d'internement du Territoire, de Septembre 1939 à Juillet 1943," Report by André Jean-Faure, May 16, 1942, Archives Nationale, 100W127, vol. 4, Departmental archives of Meurthe-et-Moselle, Nancy, France.

sent by this office to the Army, have since obtained permission to resign or have been discharged without prejudice—and have obtained jobs with the French or have moved out of the area. It is impossible to inquire for figures directly from the Army organizations because they naturally do not have any separate lists of refugee and non-refugee workers.

However, our best present estimate is that there are now about 1,000 refugees working for the Army in this area. Of these, about 350 are at the airport, about 320 with the QM Dump #1, and 330 scattered about among smaller organizations such as the 66th General Hospital, the port, motor pools, assembly plant, filling stations, etc.

Every day our office received from eight to fifteen refugees who are looking for work. So far we have been able to place every one, although it has not always been easy. It would be reassuring to know that the US Army was not only going to continue to employ the thousand they have at present, but that they could in some way use the men who are each day losing their jobs. It would be impossible for this office to state that we had a group of, say, 200 men who could be formed into a battalion, but on the other hand such a group could gradually be collected over a period of two to three weeks, provided they could be employed almost at once after they came to this office. It would not be possible to ask them to wait until there was a group of 200 ready for presentation, since they have no money saved up and would be a relief problem during the waiting period.

This information is presented in the hope that the US Army will, as long as it remains here, see fit to employ experienced refugee labor, and this office is at all times ready to do anything in its power to procure such labor.

Eric W. Johnson
Refugee Section

Memorandum by Eric W. Johnson, October 1, 1943, RG 67.008M, Box 1, Folder 15, Eric W. Johnson, Refugee Section to Col. Ratay, Commanding Officer, October 1, 1943, American Friends Service Committee Records Relating to Humanitarian Work in North Africa, 1942–1945, United States Holocaust Memorial Museum Archives, Washington, DC. Courtesy of American Friends Service Committee.

56. MUSLIMS PROTECTING JEWISH NEIGHBORS IN A POOR LIBYAN TOWN {1943}

This poem of praise honors a Muslim, Ḥamīda al-Sayyid, for protecting the property and person of neighbors Bibi Shapir, head of the Jewish community of Msallata, Libya, and his daughter during the Allied bombing of Tripoli in early 1943. According to Jewish survivor Joseph Luzon, who recorded this poem for posterity, Muslim residents of Msallata also protected Jewish women from sexual violence during an outbreak of anti-Jewish violence in 1939, when Hajj ʿAbdul-ʿAẓīm, Faraj Gan Pasha, Mukhtār El-Daʾūdī, and the head of the Msallata police hid the vulnerable women in their homes and "defended them from the excited and incited mob." The poem carries forward a regional tradition of using poetry to give thanks, but is unique in that it was written collectively by the Jewish community of Msallata as a token of its members' appreciation and to pass shared memories to the next generation. All told, these dynamics point to a sense of mutual alliance and kinship harbored by Jews and Muslims in Msallata, reminding us of the extent to which diverse subjects of colonialism and wartime occupation had shared experiences of racialized violence.

1.

Hamida el-Sayid did a good deed defending the property of Bibi Shakir.
 Bibi and his daughters, at the moment that the mob arrived to loot their property, he (Hamida el-Sayid) rebuked them saying, "Get lost, you swine!"

2.

Oh! A nice of disgrace of the world, they placed Bibi Shakir and his cousins, Kalifa and Salma, in the protection of the police. The officer of the station rebuked the rioters saying, "Get lost! You swine!"

3.

Hamida el-Sayid, may his days be blessed and those of his mother, protect his father, inshallah, that he may receive the rank of senior officer.

Yousef Luzon, poem-song written by the community of Msallata, Libya, regarding the rescue of the community's leader by an Arab and the experiences of the father of Yosef Luzon during air raids on Tripoli, October 12, 2011, Item ID 10533659, RG 0.76—Songs and Poems Collection, Sub-RG 0.76.2—Songs/Poems Collection, File 288, Yad Vashem Documents Archive, Jerusalem. Translated from Hebrew and Judeo-Arabic by Jessie Stoolman and Rachel Smith.

57. INTERNMENT IN DRANCY—A YOUNG ALGERIAN JEW'S ACCOUNT {1943}

Gabriel Bénichou's wartime experiences traversed dramatic historical and regional boundaries. A native of Tlemcen, Algeria, Bénichou was expelled from school in 1941 due to Vichy anti-Jewish laws. His sister, who lived in Marseille, France, took Bénichou in, allowing the young man to enroll in a local high school. Bénichou's identity papers declared him a "French subject, Algerian Jewish native"—a colonial legal formulation that left him prone to a wartime regime that identified the Jewish foreign born (and many French-born children of the foreign born) for deportation. In the spring of 1943, Bénichou and his sibling were arrested during a family dinner by the Gestapo and sent to the Drancy internment camp on the outskirts of Paris. The sixteen-year-old spent three months in Drancy (as represented in the following selection of his memoir), before being deported to the Nazi death camp of Auschwitz-Birkenau. Because of his age, Bénichou was selected for forced labor. In October 1943, racked with typhus, Bénichou was identified by the SS to assist in the dismantling of the Warsaw ghetto, which German troops had recently razed in the course of the Warsaw ghetto uprising. Ten months later, SS officials compelled Bénichou to take part in an agonizing death march to Kutno, from which he was transferred to the concentration camp of Dachau, where he survived for three horrific days before that camp's liberation by American troops. Bénichou's wartime journey crisscrossed North Africa and Europe, showing in intimate terms the inextricability of these theaters of war.

One day in Saint Pierre, the door opens and the watchmen call out names, around twenty, [and] we must take our stuff and leave. This isn't the first time that SS men have come to take prisoners, we know that we are [going to be] transferred, where and why is what we don't know. We arrive at Saint Charles train station escorted by the SS, we are kept at the far end of the platform, separated from the other travelers who we see moving through the crowd, not too far away. I tell my brother-in-law that, if there were a diversion, some of us could escape and blend into the crowd. He dissuades me with the fear of retaliation for those who remain.

We board a third-class [train] compartment still escorted by the SS, and make the trip to Paris. At the Gare de Lyon, we are taken into custody by the French police and driven in "paddy wagons" to the Santé prison. The paddy wagons are open vans with wire-mesh tops, meaning that we are completely confined, yet in the open air. These vehicles are generally used to take prostitutes to the police stations during raids. I was becoming acquainted with Paris through mesh wires, between the Gare de Lyon and Santé prison, surrounded by French police. At the Santé prison, the cells house five or six people, and at night you lower the beds that are folded up during the daytime.

We only stayed one day in this prison and the following day we were transferred to Drancy in mobile cell units. The mobile cell units are busses with a central aisle and small locked cells on either side. These cells are about forty of fifty centimeters wide, with a small bench, but we were two to a cell, meaning that we couldn't even move. They are normally used for the transportation of very dangerous criminals. Once at Drancy, we had to hand over our papers and valuable objects, but we had already done this at Marseilles. We are assigned a place to sleep; for us, it's staircase 4 on the third floor. The women are kept separate and I don't remember the number of my sister's staircase.

Drancy, the *cité de la muette*, is a rent-controlled housing project under construction, meaning that only the structural work was completed. The partitions between apartments, let alone bedrooms, have not yet been erected; the only separations are between staircases. The dormitories are big, immense rooms, with outlines and corners, all filled with beds, which are bunked most of the time. To the right of the entrance: sinks, where at least a dozen faucets are lined up, their water flowing into a common tray. It is around April 23, 1943; my sister's birthday, her twenty-eighth birthday (June 3), passed by without it even occurring to us to talk about it.

The life conditions in Drancy are similar to those in the prisons. Apart from the lack of freedom, there are no particular obligations, nor is there any compulsory work. However, the space is bigger, which makes it possible to move about within the camp. We have nothing to do during the day. We spend our days as we can. We are guarded by French policemen whom we rarely see. We are allowed to receive packages and mail. Personally, having no acquaintances in Paris or even in France, this didn't change anything for us. And yet, once or maybe twice, I received a package from the Jewish Scouts of France who, in order to do complete their BA [*Branche aînée*, or scouting] badge, sent packages for the prisoners which, naturally, didn't contain anything fancy. They included herring and a bit of food, but as the Brassens song says, "It was nothing but a bit of bread, but it warmed my heart like a big feast." It must be mentioned that the packages that arrived were impressive: sausages, jams, cakes, and all kinds of foods that many received. Precisely upon receiving this package I caught a glimpse of this culinary orgy. The policemen inspected to ensure that there were no weapons or prohibited items, and looked the other way on the rest in exchange for a few sausages or other bonus.

At night, men are separated from women, but we visit each other, not during the morning, which is reserved for washing up, but in the afternoon, which we spend with one another. We found the Blums, who were arrested in Marseille the same night as us. We usually spent the afternoon with them.

They were all together as a family, the parents were much older than us and their son was around my sister's age. We would sit on beds since there were no chairs....

From the window of the women's room where Mrs. Blum was staying, we had a view—through barbed wires—of Drancy, one street and some shops and, in particular, of one shop sign that Mr. Blum repeated over and over, and that I think I'll never forget: "André Gilote, charcoal." Life was organized at Drancy. Some time later, people who were with us at Saint Pierre arrived at our sleeping quarters. Of them, several come to mind.

Mr. Nathan, whose son would swim across the old port on Christmas day. He drags me to the showers every morning at 7:00 a.m. Even though it's the month of May, it is nice out—but the morning-time freezing shower while half asleep is hard for me. However, I care about him [Mr. Nathan] enough to let him take me. This is an experience that I never had again. Mr. Nathan died in Auschwitz; like all those who were over fifty, he was gassed upon arrival.

Robert Azoulay, a crooner of Tunisian origin who was beginning to become known, and whose career in France seemed very promising, founded a singers' agency after the war.

I used to play chess for whole days with Arluc, a White Russian, [who was] about fifty years old, short, and already graying. Since he was a very good player, he required worthy opponents. He showed sympathy towards me, given my young age; he would warn me when I was making a mistake and would let me go again, and he gave me a handicap: he would play with one piece fewer (a rook or the queen). He would always beat me, but I got progressively better, and the day where I [finally] won a match, he threw a fit. He was taken during a selection and was gassed in Birkenau.

Rosenberg, or perhaps a like sounding name, was that of a rather old man who spoke seven or eight languages fluently. In the camp we talk a lot about Young Peres [sic], the world champion of boxing from Constantine. His Jewishness outweighed his fame; he suffered the same fate as his brothers and never came back from Auschwitz.[1]

A group of athletes would do gymnastics every morning on a platform not

1. Tunisia-born Victor "Young" Perez, a French Jewish boxing star and in 1931 the youngest flyweight campion in boxing history, was deported by the Nazis and annihilated in Auschwitz.

far from the barbed wire.... In the afternoon, many [prisoners] would go up to the barbed wires to see the people who came to visit them, [who were] on the other side. They were able to communicate by yelling or making signs. They often sent each other letters with more or less complicity from the guards.

One day I got sick. I had a strong fever. I can still see myself in a bed next to the entrance, with my brother-in-law and my sister leaning over me. I was crying and asking them to go see my parents after the war and tell them what happened. Some prisoners aimed to distract the others by organizing evening or afternoon gatherings where storytellers, singers, and other comedians did shows. Even today, when I hear certain songs, like "Plaine, Ô ma plaine" and "Mon legionnaire," I find myself back in Drancy, and my mind gets stuck there for a few moments. We met someone from Tlemcen named Eugène Ayache, who had been in love with my sister and whom I think had even proposed to her. He left in the convoy of June 23. After the war, he became a lawyer in Paris. I didn't see him again; I tried to contact him but he was not too keen to see me. Should I have insisted?

I brought back a recipe from Drancy: pasta cake. It is like semolina cake, but with pasta. I never cooked this recipe after I was freed. The pasta cooking takes place in the barracks, the hearth is composed of a can with a rather big hole on the side, running from end to end, in which we burn paper that we must replace continuously.

One day at the courtyard sinks, I met an Algerian woman who was much older than me and who was speaking Arabic. So, we chitchatted in Arabic and, during the conversation, she reproached me for some terms and words that, she said, were not correct. I was surprised; I thought about it a lot and ended up realizing that we used to speak as she did at home. I had taken Arabic classes during high school in Marseille. It was only much later, after I thought about it again [that] I finally understood that [she was speaking] Judeo-Arabic, while I was using pure Arabic expressions. I realized then that Jews everywhere had the same behavior vis-à-vis the countries where they lived. They would take the country's language (as they did with the dress) and modify it slightly, making a dialect. Yiddish was Judeo-German, Djidio [Ladino] was Judeo-Spanish, and there was the Judeo-Arabic, and even in France in the Middle Age, there was the Judeo-Comtadin [Judeo-Provençal, or Shuadit/Chouadit]. And everywhere, these idioms were written phonetically with Hebrew characters.

I don't know if it was at the end of May or the beginning of June 1943 that the Germans occupied Drancy, meaning that the SS took over managing the camp from the French. The change was felt immediately.

Elimination of packages. This ban was instituted right away; all packages that were on their way or arrived before the senders were notified were requisitioned. In theory, they were put towards the common good, and were supposed to improve the banal [foodstuffs] in the kitchens. In fact, we saw no change whatsoever in this respect.

Putting all the prisoners to work, no matter the task. That is how we, along with my brother-in-law, became painters. We had a big bucket of paint and were tasked with painting staircase number 22. Our pajamas served as our work clothes. We used to put as much paint on the floors and on ourselves as on the walls.

Census of all the prisoners in preparation for deportation. Up until that point, the SS would demand a specific number of people for a precise date and the French police would make sure to fulfill the request. Once the SS took over, all the detainees were listed: each one was put on record with all their characteristics and, after a long interrogation, classified according to certain criteria. I don't remember very well the numbers of the different classes, but there were those who were supposed to be deported in the next convoy, those who had to stay and [were] therefore non-deportable, at least not immediately; all in all, five or six categories. My sister, my brother-in-law and I, we were in the fourth group, which was the one made up of families not fully accounted for [*en attente de famille*]. During interrogation we were asked whether we had family and their address in order to round them up. We didn't hesitate to give the address of our family in Algeria, thinking that if they wanted to look for them, we would have some time before they noticed the deception.

Indeed, the deportations started right away. We left in the second convoy, the one in July. It was only in Drancy that I wore the yellow star. We didn't wear it in Marseille, even after the occupation of the free zone in April 1943 when I was arrested. For me, it was quite paradoxical to wear the yellow star in Drancy where there were only Jews, since I thought that the yellow star was used to differentiate them from the others.

Bénichou, Gabriel. *L'adolescence d'un juif d'Algérie: Récit autobiographique*. Collection Graveurs de mémoire. Paris: L'Harmattan, 2004. Selection from pages 33–40. Translated from French by Rebecca Glasberg and Jessie Stoolman.

58. A "TOTAL VIOLATION OF HUMAN DIGNITY"—GIRLHOOD INTERRUPTED IN AUSCHWITZ {1944}

Simone Lagrange (née Simy Kadosche) was born in Saint-Fons, France, one of five children of immigrant parents from Essaouira, Morocco, and part of an increasingly large and dynamic population of French Jews and Muslims of North African origin. During the German occupation of France, Lagrange's father, Simon, helped the resistance amass weapons and facilitate the evacuation of refugees. His daughter Simy, thirteen years old, assisted her father by distributing resistance literature. On a tip from a family acquaintance, the Gestapo arrested and imprisoned Simon, his wife, Rachel, and two of their daughters, including Simy, in June 1944. In Gestapo hands, the young girl was interrogated and tortured by none other than Nikolaus "Klaus" Barbie, the sadistic Nazi official known as "the Butcher of Lyon" for having personally tortured Jews and members of the French Resistance (Christian and Jewish) while he was posted there. After nearly three weeks of imprisonment, the SS transferred Lagrange and her mother to the Drancy internment camp outside Paris; from there they (and later Lagrange's father and cousins) were deported to the Auschwitz camp complex, where her mother and cousins were murdered in the gas chambers. In this vivid and wrenching selection from her memoir, Lagrange speaks of her horrific deportation to and confinement in Auschwitz. After the war, Lagrange returned to France and was reunited with two siblings who survived in hiding. In the decades that followed, she testified and frequently spoke about her wartime experiences, yet rarely is Lagrange or her family recognized as among the Holocaust's Jewish victims of North African origin. (A second selection of Lagrange's testimony appears as the last source in this volume.)

The low building we arrive in front of houses the showers. Around us, everything is sad and dirty, and yet we are so tired that we wait for restorative water to recover from the long, exhausting trip. We then regain a bit of hope. Oh, how little we need to regain our hope...

They make us stop in front of the building. By now we are basically accustomed to the shouting, which you must get used to. They know how to do nothing but yell, "Ruh! Ruh!" We understand that this means "silence." And that we must do everything in silence.

Our [female] guards order us to strip, to make a pile of the clothes that we have just taken off. After, we will be given new clothing. In small wicker bins, we must leave our jewelry, wedding rings, and any money that we may have on us. As soon as the bins are full, the *Kapos* take them and dump the contents into the great big pockets of their black aprons. The SS pretend not to see. They will share it all later.

So here we are, completely naked, as naked as the day we were born. It's already dark out and we are starting to get cold. We will later learn that it can get really cold at Auschwitz, even in the middle of summer.

We are beaten into the building with cudgels. We pass by another [female] guard, our clothing in hand, and we place it on the floor close to her. Another [female guard] has us open our mouths and directs those with gold teeth to the side. These women are pushed into a small room where the teeth will be pulled to extract the precious material.

They give me a small piece of "soap," but it's so hard that I think it's a piece of rock, one of those little pebbles I used to play hopscotch with my friends not so long ago.

The shower? What a joke, what an absolute joke! [Female] guards, prisoners like us, are waiting for us there with a cane in hand. It's a sickness, someone always has to be beating us! She makes us rush underneath a trickle of water that is falling from the ceiling, a trickle so fine that some of us don't even get wet. The water is either cold or very hot, which means that certain women are burned while others shiver from the cold. It's incredible how we have to rush, still and always rushing.

At the end of the shower room is a door. *Kapos* accompanied by female SS wait there to give us clothes that we must hold in our arms, and which we receive in exchange for the little bit of barely dampened soap. Our new rags, crumpled and damp, smell bad but they tell us that this is because they've been disinfected. As for me, try as I might, these clothes are either too big or too small and nothing fits. The undergarments, a canvas shirt and panties, are stained with long brown streaks, surely dried blood. What disgust we feel at this!

My dress is striped, like the pajamas of the man who waved at my mom, who was given an awful gray dress, whereas Jacqueline's is rather black. On the back of the "civilian" dresses are sewn little pieces of striped fabric. They also give us shoes, I receive espadrilles that I will keep until the end of the winter.

On the back of my dress there is a big, drawn-on cross. I must be a dangerous person seeing as this means I am a "target." This is how they single out the ones that they think might escape. To think I'm only thirteen years old!

Our new clothes in our arms, we are directed towards another hovel, rather squat, made of wood, that seems dreary in the twilight. There, men—also prisoners—are waiting for us. We are embarrassed by our nakedness, but they don't seem to see it, trying only to ask us questions, each one in her native language. Some of them speak French and we are happy to tell them about the landings in Normandy. They don't respond, but their eyes shine bright with tears. And yet how it seems so unreal to us, these landings in which we had placed so much hope. We wouldn't ever have believed that we would leave France, we who thought we'd be freed soon. Oh, how delusions hurt.

Next, we go in for disinfection since, as we will see, we mustn't have any lice at camp.

Men with hoses in hand spray us with liquid disinfectant and then, equipped with clippers, they begin their work. First the underarms, but not in my case as I don't yet have anything there, any more than in my pubic area, and then it's time to cut off our hair. When the first lock falls onto my knees, I can't stifle my cry, it's so horrible! I'm sobbing for hair? This solicits a laugh from the woman who is picking up my hair, gathering it, and keeping it, no doubt to make herself a wig. I cannot hold back my tears of shame, because now I am even more naked. It all seems so unthinkable, this total violation of human dignity!

This won't be the last time that I am humiliated. A bit later, a female *Kapo* will make me bend over to ensure that all of my body hair is indeed gone. Laughing at my humiliation, and no doubt to have a bit more fun, she takes the clippers to my body yet again. I feel the clippers' coldness as they squeak over my body and begin to shake, not knowing whether it it's due to cold, rage, anger, or hopelessness.

Timidly, I slowly look up and—what a surprise! I no longer recognize anyone! We are no longer the same. I don't see my mom and I start to cry. I'm embarrassed by my tears, but I can't help myself. I feel the great sorrow of a child, but am I even still a child?

Suddenly, my mom comes over to me, her hands tensely covering her lower belly. She is obviously uneasy, however she smiles at me, softly caressing my shaved head: "You know," she tells me, "hair grows back even more beautiful, you'll see. And it's cleaner this way because in prison, we might have gotten lice."

Two by two, we enter a small room lit by a single lightbulb hanging from the ceiling. Three women are waiting for us, seated on a bench. They are going to tattoo a number on our arms, something that I just can't bring myself to believe, because for all that has happened, we are not animals being led to the slaughter! Alas, soon we will no longer be anything but an ID number, forever etched onto our forearms; in very little time, we will no longer be anyone at all.

Getting a tattoo hurts, but what hurts me the most is that I feel dirtied by it. From that moment on, it is part of me, and will always be part of me.... Whereas for the previous several days I had believed myself to be weak like a child, suddenly this mark that I am going to have to keep forever relights my combative spark. I bear my claws, I do not accept the loss of my identity, that I will be nothing more than an ID number that I'll have to memorize. And in German! That, I utterly refuse! And with a sudden rage, I start to press down on the digits written on my arm, pushing the ink out. Too bad if it hurts, I am proud to stand up to those who want to turn me into someone who doesn't exist anymore. I want to get out this ink that contaminates me. My number is A8624, but soon the four is no longer recognizable. I succeeded in fighting this digit and I am proud, so proud of this. All of a sudden, I again find my lost spirits. They won't get me, that's for sure! I smile at my mom, who looks at me and smiles back, but that attracts the attention of a guard who comes over to me. Upon noticing the blurriness of the last digit of my number, she quickly understands and pulls me towards her, making me bend over on a stool close by. She yells, but what do I care, I don't understand.

Then, with a whip, she starts to lash my back. Oh, how it burns! And I start to scream in pain, but also out of anger because I simply cannot stand lashings. A deathly silence settles over the rows [of women], no one could have imagined that they would whip a child to such an extent.

One lash, two lashes. Painfully, I count them. Eight lashes, nine lashes, I don't even feel the pain anymore. After ten lashes, it's finally over!

With a brusque movement, my torturer lifts me back onto my feet and then it hurts, I hurt so terribly, to the point that I cannot even stand up straight. All the other women look at me, astonished because they don't understand why I was beaten. I go over to my mom, but slowly, discreetly, because I have just realized that if they notice I'm with her, I risk being separated from her. How quickly one learns!

During this time, other prisoners have finished sewing onto our dresses the number that corresponds to the tattoo we were given and we can therefore get dressed. We look at ourselves and while some women start to laugh, others cry. They no longer recognize themselves and this is exactly what the Germans want. Of course, we still have some dreams, but our guards will be sure to crush them; we can count on them for that.

Close to my sewn-on ID number there is a red triangle with an F on it.[1] As for my mom, she bears a star of David made up of two triangles, one red, the other yellow,[2] also with an F in the middle. As far as my friend Jacqueline is concerned, she in entitled to a yellow star, which doesn't change things for her as she wore one back in Paris. I'm curious, and want to know why we have all been differentiated from one another. I certainly do not want them to separate us, the idea terrifies me!

Then we receive the order to get into rows of five, a habit to which we will become accustomed. We take the camp road to Lager A.II,[3] Block 30. This will be our quarantine block and we'll stay there a long time.

Who could express the anxiety that suffocated us on the path that led us towards our block? Who could one day describe the night that began to fall, the tormented sky, purple, gray and red, the smoke that floated straight up to the firmament, the stench, bitter and sweet at the same time, that invaded our mouths and noses? I don't think that one could ever describe the hellish odor.

Along the way, we met lines of [female] prisoners carrying shovels and pickaxes on their skinny shoulders. All of them are dirty, sad, as if they exist outside of time. Yet through their empty eyes and dead stares, they seem to question us, maybe also to pity us. But quickly the *Kapos* who surround them issue the order to speed up. These [female] guards never forget to yell, to hit.

1. [Note in original text] "Leftist" prisoner of French nationality.
2. [Note in original text] Jewish prisoner, left-wing political party.
3. [Note in original text] Auschwitz, a massive Nazi concentration-camp complex, was composed of three camps: base camp (Lager A. I), Birkenau camp (Lager A. II) where the gas chambers were located, and Monowitz camp (Lager A. III) which held IG Farben's synthetic rubber production facilities.

It seems that nothing can ever happen here without beatings and shouting. It's truly hellish!

Lagrange, Simone. *Coupable d'être née: Adolescente à Auschwitz*. Paris: Harmattan, 1997. Selection from pages 52–57. Translated from French by Rebecca Glasberg.

59. OLYMPIAN, VICTIM, SURVIVOR (1942–1946)

Jews were well represented on interwar Europe's Olympic teams, for the allure of sports was as strong for Jews as non-Jews—and in some cases stronger still, as many Jewish athletes were motivated by the desire to challenge anti-Semitic fantasies about the weak Jewish body. It is estimated that thirty Jewish Olympians were murdered in the course of the Holocaust. Among them was Tunisia-born Victor "Young" Perez (1911–1945), a French boxing star who became, in 1931, the youngest flyweight campion in boxing history—only to be deported by the Nazis and annihilated in Auschwitz. Lesser known is the story of Alfred Nakache (1915–1983), who was born in Constantine, Algeria, and rose to fame in France as a record-setting swimmer and water-polo player. Nakache represented France in the 1936 Summer Olympic Games, notoriously hosted by the Nazi regime in Berlin. At that event, Nakache came in fourth as part of the French 4 × 200 relay team, losing out on a bronze medal by mere seconds. Five years later, Nakache surpassed a German competitor to set a world record for the 200-meter breaststroke. With the rise of the Vichy regime and the passage of anti-Jewish legislation, Nakache was barred from racing, a determination protested by some of France's leading swimmers, who refused to compete in protest. Nakache was among countless Jews of North African origin to be deported to the Nazi death camps from France. Working with the French police, the Nazi authorities deported him to Auschwitz in January 1944 with his wife and two-year-old daughter, both of whom perished there. Before the war's end, Nakache was transferred to the Nazi concentration camp of Buchenwald, a last-minute relocation that may explain the following mistaken reporting of his death, rumored after the liberation of Auschwitz. Astonishingly, less than a year after Nakache's return to France, he was again swimming, with a world-record-setting 3 × 100 relay team. He also triumphed as a national champion in butterfly stroke and in the 4 × 100 relay. Nakache is one of only two known Olympians to compete in the games after surviving the Nazi camps. In 1948, he represented France in the Olympic Summer Games in London, as part of a team that set a world record in the 3 × 100 relay, as a breaststroke swimmer, and on the water-polo team. Here, in a collection of articles drawn from the French press, Nakache's experience of the war years—and false rumors of his death in Auschwitz—are detailed. Strikingly, wartime and postwar French journalistic coverage of the athlete rarely heralded his North African roots, instead embracing him as a hero of France.

Nakache Shows Off His Form in Tunis

An event to promote swimming took place at the Tunis municipal pool with the participation of Alfred Nakache, world-record holder. Prince Raouf and General Barré, Senior Commander of the Tunisian troops, as well as several other civilian and military authorities attended the demonstration. Over the course of the evening, Nakache clocked a time of 1 minute 1.6 seconds in the 100-meter freestyle and 1 minute 12.6 seconds in the 100-meter breaststroke, breaking the pool record of 1 minute 14 seconds. Vadya, former European champion in diving, put on an amazing display, during which there were a great number of other feats for the *ondines* [water nymphs] and swimmers, which were enthusiastically received by a large crowd. To finish, the C. A. T. team, which has won the North African Water Polo Championship several times, easily beat the opposing team.

"Nakache, à Tunis, démontre sa forme." *Le Petit Journal* (Paris), July 20, 1942. Translated from French by Rebecca Glasberg.

With Nakache and the Tunisian Clubs Abstaining, France's Competitions Were Not What They Should Have Been

(From our special correspondent)
Toulouse, 15 August [1943]

These two big days of pure swimming were clearly a success, and the substantial number of swimmers gathered did not disappoint.

However, it should be noted that the majority of the best French swimmers from the Southern Zone belonging to the two Toulouse clubs, TOEC [Toulouse Olympique et le Toulouse Employés Club] and ROT, forfeited in solidarity with the former French champion and world record holder Alfred Nakache, [who was] prevented from participating in the competitions for unknown reasons. After these mass abstentions [of the finest athletes], the competitive swimmers had no trouble taking the lion's share and winning the majority of the trials [but the feat did not] earn them any glory. This [absence of real competition] is why no [standing] French championship times or those of previous competitions were ever in jeopardy.

Aside from the meets on Saturday afternoon and Sunday morning, yesterday afternoon's meet was the most spectacular: as a matter of fact, this last event of the national competition was presided over by Colonel Pascot, the Commissioner General for Sports, along with Mr. Driny, president of the PSN; the delegate of Toulouse; and numerous other notable figures.

The meeting began with the hoisting of the flag, which was raised by our prestigious champion Jean Taris. As with the preceding meetings, none of the times were worth mentioning and the recorded performances were hardly respectable.

"Nakache et les clubs toulousains s'abstenant, les critériums de France n'ont jamais été ce qu'ils devaient être." *Le Petit Provençal* (Marseille), August 16, 1943. Translated from French by Rebecca Glasberg.

Alfred Nakache Dies, Victim of German Torturers

Alfred Nakache, world recordholder for the 200-meter breaststroke, was killed alongside his wife and child by the Gestapo in Poland after having been deported last year.

"Alfred Nakache meurt victim des tortionnaires allemands." *L'Aube* (Paris), Aug. 31, 1944. Translated from French by Rebecca Glasberg.

Alfred Nakache, Victim of the Milice[1]

Newspapers have announced the death of Nakache, the best French swimmer. We are not certain, but it does seem that this news is unfortunately true. Tormented and marginalized since 1940, Nakache became a world record holder in July 1941. He was arrested by the Gestapo in September 1943 after being denounced by the father of the *milicien* Pallard, an unsuccessful [swimming] competitor. Deported to Poland with his wife and child, he worked in the salt mines in Silesia [Auschwitz] with [the Tunisian Jewish world flyweight champion Messaoud Hai Victor] "Young" Pérez. A repatriate maintains that he saw his [Nakache's] grave. Be that as it may, a horrible crime was committed and the French were involved. We highlight as well that Cartonnet[2] was not a friend of Nakache.

  1. The Milice was a fascist, French paramilitary organization.
  2. Jacques Cartonnet (1911–1967) was a French swimmer who competed in the 1932 Summer Olympic games in the men's two-hundred-meter breaststroke.

"Alfred Nakache victime de la milice." *L'Humanité* (Paris), sec. Sports, August 31, 1944. Translated from French by Rebecca Glasberg.

Alfred Nakache Reported Dead in a Concentration Camp in Poland

According to the *Populaire*,[1] the great swimming champion Alfred Nakache has reportedly died in a concentration camp in Poland.

"Alfred Nakache serait mort en Pologne dans un camp de concentration." *L'Écho d'Alger* (Algiers), October 8, 1944. Translated from French by Rebecca Glasberg.

What Has Become of Alfred Nakache? The Only French World-Record Holder in Swimming

News of the death of Alfred Nakache is persistently circulating in Toulouse, where he lived before his arrest. However, there has not yet been official confirmation.

Alfred Nakache, a native of Constantine and of the Jewish religion, found himself forbidden from participating in the French Swimming Championships in 1943. Many remember that the majority of his competitors refrained from participating in solidarity with him.

Hunted down by Vichy agents, Nakache was forced into hiding. He was finally arrested and deported, as were his wife and his young daughter. They were all deported separately.

Alfred Nakache always fulfilled his duties to France. He was in the French Air Force during the war. He was our best representative in international competitions from 1935–1939 and the only French swimmer whose name is on the list of world records, having bested the record for the 200-meter breaststroke in Marseille in 1942. He also held the European record for the 100-meter breaststroke, which he stole from the German [swimmer] Balke.

He was a champion of exemplary modesty, a conscientious sportsman who loved swimming for swimming's sake, an esteemed comrade who showed sincere fondness for his club, his friends, and his country, at every occasion.

None of these considerations mattered to his persecutors. They attacked him fiercely, with an idiotic blindness that was equaled only by their cruelty.

Despite everything, France's athletes still remain hopeful that they will not have to mourn the death of one of the most dignified and most representative among them, but will remember him fondly if they do.

Gérard BEAUSITE

1. *Le Populaire, journal revue hebdomadaire de propagande socialiste et internationaliste*, or *Populaire*, was a French socialist newspaper founded in May 1916.

Beausite, Gérard. "Qu'est devenu Alfred Nakache? Le seul français déteneur d'un record du monde de nage." *La Gazette Provençale* (Avignon), October 11, 1944. Translated from French by Rebecca Glasberg.

Nakache Returns, but Alas!

Alfred Nakache is alive. We had refused to believe in his death, and the good news was conveyed to the racer [Roger] Foucher-Créteau by a White Father[1] who saw his brother, who is also a prisoner, in Buchenwald.[2] The swimming word recordholder was chief nurse at the camp hospital and is reportedly in good health. Unfortunately, the same cannot be said for his young wife—a physical education teacher in Toulouse—or for his four-year-old daughter, both of whom were taken with him to Auschwitz. After falling ill, they were gassed by the Krauts.

"Nakache revient mais, hélas!" *Combat* (Paris), April 21, 1945. Translated from French by Rebecca Glasberg.

Nakache Waits for Repatriation in Weimar

Alfred Nakache, world recordholder in the 200-meter breaststroke, is very much alive and is waiting for the hour of his return in Weimar.

Alfred Nakache lost his wife and his daughter, [who were] both deported with him, and [who] died in Auschwitz, victims of the Nazis.

"Nakache attend à Weimar son rapatriement." *France-soir* (Paris), Apr. 21, 1945. Translated from French by Rebecca Glasberg.

Hardly Home, Nakache Is Back to Being a Star

Alfred Nakache, whom we thought lost to the sports world, has been back from Buchenwald for only a month and has already made his return [to sports].

His abilities do not seem dulled, and he swam the 100-meter breaststroke in 1' 16" Sunday at the Tourelles, thereby remaining our best "butterflier."

But what is even better is the value that Nakache brings to water polo.

1. The Missionaries of Africa, or "White Fathers," are a Roman Catholic apostolic order founded in Algeria in 1868 by the archbishop of Algeria.
2. Roger Foucher-Créteau (b. 1911), a French journalist, was deported to Buchenwald in 1943 for his public opposition to the Nazis. While imprisoned in the camp, he assembled a notebook of testimonies, including his own and that of sixty other prisoners. It is not clear, in this sentence, whether the brother in question is Foucher-Créteau's or Nakache's.

Without serious training, "Artem" has shown himself to be one of the best French players. Everything points to him as a dream for our future French national team.

Questioned about his plans, Nakache told us, "I am readapting bit by bit and I plan to settle down in Toulouse. I might go back to the gym that I directed before my deportation. Physically, I am back on top, but my spirits are still low."

"Will you return to international competitions?"

"I don't know yet. Water polo interests me the most. I think that the TOEC [Toulouse Olympique et le Toulouse Employés Club] can become a great team, and I am going to work on making that happen as best I can. With a bit more technique, we should be able to put an end to the reign of the Tourcoing team, whom we hope to see again soon."

On this justifiably hopeful note, we left the world record-holder to his friends, of which there are many.

Robert Vey

Vey, Robert. "À peine de retour, Nakache reprend rang de vedette." *Ce Soir* (Paris), June 21, 1945. Translated from French by Rebecca Glasberg.

Because He Robbed Him of All His Titles, Roland Pallard Denounced the Resistance Activities of Alfred Nakache

TOULOUSE—We remember that in 1943, the champion swimmers Krakowski, Nakache, his wife and daughter, and Foucher-Créteau, the swimmer's well-known brother, [all] refugees in Toulouse, were arrested and deported to Germany.

Only [F]oucher-Créteau and Nakache came back from the Nazi hell.

The police investigation permitted the identification of the men responsible for these deportations: Roland Pallard, his father, and an engineer from Toulouse, Saint-Blancart, currently on assignment in Germany.

Pallard was a local swimming star. Jealous of the athletic success of Nakache, who robbed him of all his titles, [Pallard] wanted to get rid of [Nakache] by alerting the police to his activity and that of his friends within the "Anti-Axis" resistance organization.

Referred to the military justice system, both the father and son Pallard have been released on bail.

"C'est parce qu'il le dépossédait de tous ses titres que Rolland Pallard denonça les activités de resistant d'Alfred Nakache." *La Gazette Provençale* (Avignon), March 20, 1946.

Alfred Nakache Receives the Gold Medal

Alex Jany had to beat a European record for us to remember that we have another world-record holder who was never officially recognized.

Commander Roux, director of sports, was keen to right this wrong and Alfred Nakache, whose exceptional courage we are all familiar with, will be honored Sunday at the Tourelles Stadium. Just like his comrades Alex Jany and Minville, he will receive the gold medal in Physical Education.

A.B.

A.B. "Alfred Nakache reçoit la médaille d'or." *France-soir* (Paris), June 16, 1946. Translated from French by Rebecca Glasberg.

PART III
The Late- and Postwar Era, 1943–1950

60. LMIRIKAN (1942)

During the 1930s and 1940s, Lḥussain Slawī ascended in the Moroccan popular music scene with his powerful, socially engaged songs that drew on popular ideas. Before his death in 1951 at the age of thirty-three, Slawī became the first Moroccan musician to record for Pathé-Marconi, the legendary international record company based in Paris. While his popular songs include "Yā al-Kaḥla" (O, black woman), among others, Slawī is primarily known in Moroccan musical history for his song "Lmirīkan"—also known as "El Marikan," or "The Americans" in English, and as "Zīn wa al-'ayn zarqā" (Beautiful and blue eyed) and "Tsma' ghir okay okay" (You just hear, OK, OK), which has been popular since it was first produced. "Lmirīkan" is a sonic snapshot of the social dynamics surrounding the arrival of American soldiers in Morocco with the Allies' landing in Casablanca and Safi in 1942. The song depicts the misogynist perceived moral decay of Moroccan women, who are represented as decadent and gullible dupes of American consumerism and colonialism. It also mocks the racist preferences of American soldiers (as well as Moroccan male urbanites) for light-skinned prostitutes. Slawī's remarkably enduring song sheds light on notions of beauty, colorism, social hierarchies, and patterns of materialism that crystallized with the American military presence in Morocco.

Lmirikan

Ayayayaya! New times are here.
The Americans are here.
People are empowered
Women have rebelled
Even the hags tore off their veils
And filled their mouths with chew gum
Married men waited in vain
For their wives
Handsome faces and green eyes
Have spirited them away
And the girls parted their hair
And wore French skirts
They wanted to be with the Americans
And all you heard was Okay okay! Bye bye!
On horse carriages or buses
I can no longer find a place
Wherever I turn I'm worthless
Okay, okay was all you heard
This is our life
Soldiers handed out cigarettes
They offered chocolates and cash
Even the oldest crones wore silk kerchiefs
When the American were here
And all you heard was Okay okay! Bye bye!
Soldiers gave mints and gum
Girls covered their faces
With powder from chickpeas
And ate bonbons
And even the hags sat drinking rum
With the Americans
And all you heard was Okay okay! Come on! Bye bye!
Money for everyone
The girls brought it back
They carried handbags
They wanted to be with the Americans

All you heard was Okay okay!
Give me dollar.
All you heard was Okay okay! Come on! Bye bye!

Lḥussain Slawī, *Dakhlou Lmirikan*, CD, original recording 1942. Translated from Moroccan Arabic by Aomar Boum.

61. HITLER'S HAGGADAH (C. 1945)

Written in Judeo-Arabic by Nessim ben Shimon, also known as Simon Coiffeur ("The Hairdresser") of Rabat, Hitler's Haggadah *was published with the approval of the Moroccan office of censorship to celebrate the American landing in Casablanca. The book offers a contemporary riff of the Haggadah, a text compiled during the Mishnaic and Talmudic periods that narrates the Jews' exodus from Egypt and establishes the order of the Passover seder, or ritual feast. While echoing the flow, purpose, and language of the original Haggadah,* Hitler's Haggadah *narrates the rise and threat of Adolf Hitler, the menacing spread of anti-Semitism, and the liberation of North Africa. Using humor and irony, it pokes fun at the forces that oppressed Jews during the war (including the Vichy, Italian, and German authorities); celebrates the liberation of North Africa by the Free French Forces and the British, Soviet, and American armies; and revels in the elimination of the Hitlerian threat to North African Jewish life and property. Ben Shimon's work can be understood as one example of a rich North African Jewish folk literature that is anchored in local Jewish conventions of prayer and ritual but boldly responsive to current events; it is also one of numerous Haggadot (written in myriad languages, during and after the Second World War) that liken Hitler to the biblical Pharaoh of Egypt.*

The Americans came in great haste:
That expression void of hope
Which our fathers' frightened faces wore
Due to Hitler
The hungry shall walk in fear
The needy shall flee in fright.
This year we are here
Next year may we have peace and calm.

This year on the black market
Next year may we be free men in Palestine.
What makes this night different
From any night in '39?
That on those nights, we couldn't utter a word
But tonight, we are not frightened.
For on those nights our sleep was disturbed,
But tonight, our hearts are filled with joy.
For on those nights we were afflicted
And burdened
But tonight, come and see;
For on those nights we hadn't eaten
Nor drunk
We only snuck away in fear.
And tonight we dine in peace.
Wicked Hitler enslaved us
And the Allied Forces rescued us,
With a great and mighty outstretched arm.
Had the Brits not come,
Nor the Yanks,
We would not have been saved
Neither us nor our children
Nor our grandchildren.
We were petrified by Hitler's might.
. . .
Once upon a time, in the days of Mussolini
The Great,
Hitler and that bastard Göring,
Ribbentrop and that Italian Ciano,[1]
Came to plan and plot,
In the course of that one night,
Until the Angels of Destruction came
And shook them, oh dear,
And threw them into dawn's furnace.
So spoke Roosevelt:
For I am like a man who's hit seventy,

---

1. Galeazzo Ciano served as foreign minister in Benito Mussolini's government.

Lucky enough to remember
The ruin of Germany by air raids at night.
Until Churchill came and taught,
As it is written:
"For ye shall remember
What the Eighth Army did unto them
On their way to Egypt."

...

Blessed is the All-present, blessed is He.
Blessed for bringing the Brits
And the Yanks, blessed is He.
The Torah speaks of four sons:
England, the wise one.
Hitler, the wicked one.
America, the good one.
And Mussolini, who isn't worthy of our words.

...

All the more so,
Was the favor shown us by God
Doubled, tripled, quadrupled, multiplied five times over.
The wicked ones were kicked out of Egypt,
And finished off,
And Tobruk was taken back from them,
And they were chased to Tunisia,
And pursued to Sicily,
And their cities were demolished,
And the Jews were granted the right to return to work,
And our fathers were saved,
And the anti-Jewish law was revoked,
And the Jews were reinstated in their positions
And they asked to bring all of us,
To Palestine,
To atone for our sins.

...

Therefore we must
Thank Russia,

Honor and Glorify Stalin,
Praise England,
Laud America,
...
The Allies took us out of enslavement
And gave us freedom.
We went from alarm to celebration,
From confining blackouts
To great light,
And so we should say to them
Hallelujah!

ben Shimon, Nissim ("Simon Coiffeur"). *The Hitler Haggadah* (Rabat, 1943). Translated from Judeo-Arabic by Adi and Schnytzer Jonnie Schnytzer as *The Hitler Haggadah: A Moroccan Jewish Piece from World War II*, edited by Eppie Bat-Ilan and Roz Elmaleh. N.p.: Mineged Publishing House, 2021.

62. A MOROCCAN ADOLESCENT'S VIEW OF OPERATION TORCH AND HIS AMERICAN EMPLOYERS {1942–1947}

A teenager during the Second World War, Sidney Chriqui had an up-close view of the Allied landing on North Africa, which took shape just outside his waterfront home in Casablanca. The Jewish adolescent writes in his memoir (an excerpt of which we present here) of watching Operation Torch unfold, and of his shocked, initial views of the American soldiers who arrived on North African shores. In interviews conducted with Aomar Boum in October 2019, Chriqui described how the encounter exposed him to African Americans for the first time, opening his eyes to the complexity of race in America. Chriqui worked closely with American military representatives once they were settled in his native city, serving as an interpreter for the army's legal department from 1942 to 1947. Following in the footsteps of the Europeans, American officials had, for over a century, hired North African Jews (along with some Muslims) as consular employees, and sometimes in return they granted those individuals and their family legal protection. In Chriqui's case, the experience gave him an intimate view of how the American military functioned, its soldiers, and the hopes and danger (including sexual violence) they brought to

Morocco. Through Chriqui's eyes, we can appreciate the many complex and lasting effects of the American military presence in Morocco, not least the marriages of Moroccan women (both Jewish and Muslim) to Allied soldiers. Like many of the translators who served the American army in North Africa after the war, Chriqui leveraged his professional contacts to obtain a visa to the United States in 1948. He passed through New York City before settling in Los Angeles, where his sister Claudia already lived. In Southern California he became a leader in Los Angeles's Moroccan Jewish community, over which he continues to preside as a distinguished elder today.

I was an eyewitness to the attack on Casablanca. My building was very close to the harbor and from our apartment on the fifth floor we had a bird's eye view of the entire battle. I was about 17 years old and it was an experience I will never forget.

I woke up that morning to the sound of big guns. The Vichy French had declined an earlier opportunity to surrender, so the Americans and British attacked from the sea and the air. The ocean was black with the great number of transport ships. From our balcony it was a spectacular view, as we watched allied planes dive and bomb the Vichy ships that were trying to get out of the harbor. We were so fascinated by what we were watching that it never occurred to us that we could be in danger from a bomb going astray, which did happen in other parts of the city. One French battle ship, the *Jean Bart* with its 15 mm guns, was shooting from the harbor and the noise was deafening.

As the battle was taking place in the harbor, American planes were dropping thousands of leaflets on Casablanca. The leaflets, in both French and Arabic, contains a message from President Roosevelt that said that the Americans were there to liberate us from German occupation, that they would do us no harm, and they would leave once the threat from Italy and Germany was removed. The message requested that we not stand in their way so that peace could return to the region. The leaflet was signed by Dwight D. Eisenhower, then Lieutenant General and Commander in Chief of the American Forces. My brother André, just 13 years old at the time, kept one of the leaflets and still has it to this day. . . .

In the end, the Vichy French gave up the fight and later, to our great satisfaction, they joined the Allied forces in their fight against Germany and Italy.

Because they landed miles away, it took the American soldiers a few days to make their way to Casablanca. We had been following the developments on the radio, so we knew that soldiers would soon be entering the city. I was very excited, believing that the American presence would change the course of the country for the better.

A large crowd of people, Jews, Arabs, Europeans, gathered in the Place de France, the city's central square, to await their arrival. We had never seen Americans so there was tremendous curiosity and a mood of anticipation. The first thing we saw was a jeep with four soldiers, sent ahead to makes sure there were no hostiles in the square. Then slowly but surely, the foot soldiers arrived from all directions.

For days I had thought about what they would look like, envisioning soldiers in crisp uniforms, walking in unison in a kind of grand military parade. Instead, the soldiers were bedraggled, muddy, unshaven and exhausted, dragging their feet like prisoners in a chain gang. To me, they looked like giants—big, burly and tall. The crowd's reaction was mixed—some were happy, others were wary, and many didn't know what to think. But the soldiers came in with smiles, waving and handing out chocolates and gum. One soldier, who had no candy, gave me his empty wallet instead. Moments later, another boy ran up to me and snatched it from my hands.

Though some newspaper articles spoke of the American's "invading" Morocco, the Jews greeted the Americans with an open heart and welcomed their presence. Even without fully knowing what would have happened on November 15th, we understood that the Americans had saved us from a terrible fate.

... After the landings, it was difficult for the US Army to find Moroccan citizens who could speak English, Arabic and French, so they relied on young men fresh from school who had some language skills.

I was barely 17 years old when I got a job with the US Army Contracting Office. Shortly after, I was transferred to the Civilian Personnel Office of the Air Transport Command or ATC (there was no US Air Force at the time) which was recruiting a large number of local personnel for assignment to various bases. We were hiring Arabs, French, Spanish and Portuguese workers, and every morning a large crowd of job seekers would gather outside the ATC personnel office at Camp Cazes, just outside of Casablanca. Together with an American Officer, I would stand in the middle of a very large circle of job seekers, all anxious to work for the Americans. My job was to assist in the selection process by using my knowledge of Arabic and French. We repeated this process daily for many months until we hired thousands of local workers to support the military at our base and others in Morocco.

Prior to working for the Americans, I had always gone by my given name, Salomon. But the Americans found it difficult, so I became Sidney, and have been so ever since.

Americans had a more open, casual way of social interaction that the more formal French. They also didn't have the class distinctions the French had. A French acquaintance would never say, "Hey Sid, how's the family?," something so common and ordinary among the Americans. This more casual interaction was foreign to me at first, but I took to it immediately.

In 1943 I was assigned to the US Army Judge Advocate Office. That Office was responsible for the investigation of local accidents and/or crimes involving American soldiers. My job consisted of coordinating with the French or Arabic courts when local residents were involved as victims and/or witnesses. I translated French and Arabic documents into English, and vice versa, and served as a sworn interpreter for the Army County Martials.

I vividly remember a particular case where an American Military Police sergeant was accused of raping an 18 year old Jewish girl. The girl had accepted a ride to her job on the base but instead of taking here to the base, the sergeant had driven to a deserted beach where he had raped her at gunpoint.

Afterwards, the girl went to the American Hospital to be examined and as a result, the soldier was charged. A General Court Martial was established to try the soldier. I interpreted the entire case, which was somewhat embarrassing at my young age, particularly because I knew the girl. The soldier was found guilty and given a prison sentence.

These tribunals were held at the Anfa Hotel in a suburb of Casablanca. In that same hotel and in that very same room where the above mentioned trial took place, a conference of world importance was held in 1943: the historic Casablanca Conference between US President Franklin Delano Roosevelt and British Prime Minister Winston Churchill. In that conference a joint declaration pledged that the war would end only with the unconditional surrender of the Axis states (Germany, Japan and Italy).

. . . Life in Casablanca improved after the landings, but many critical items were still hard to find. Clothing for instance was very scarce and we often relied on the US Merchant Marine whose members sold us most of their clothes when they visited the city. Because I was employed by the US Army, I was entitled to special weekly rations of sugar, rice, flour, soap and fabrics. This last item was particularly appreciated by my sisters Esther and Marie at the time of their weddings since they needed new clothes.

Around that time, big packages of goodies started arriving from America. Our sister Claudia, now living in New York, was spending much of her hard earned dollars to buy and send us critical foods and clothing packages on a regular basis.

I was fortunate to have great friends such as Henri Leb, Roger Harroch, Edouard Bendahan, Maurice Perez, Albert Assayag, Albert Nahon, Paul Harroch, Sammy Oiknine, Joe Bouzaglou, Henry Sibony and Henri Elkouby. I remained close with these childhood friends throughout my life and am still close with Henri Leb and Henri Elkouby to this day. Humor was extremely important and we all learned not to take things too seriously. Each one in my group of friends would tell jokes and try to top the other in who could get the biggest laugh. The laughter was infectious.

We loved everything about America—the food, clothes, music and singers. We learned how to dance the jitterbug, swings, rumbas etc. Each week, we would stage "surprise" parties in a different home, called such because everyone needed to bring a small "surprise," like a bottle of wine or something to eat.

When the parties were at my house, the living room and one of the adjacent bedroom (separated from the living room by French doors) would be the dance floor. My father would help me completely dismantle the bed to get it out of the way, then he and my mother would sit by the door waiting for my guests to arrive.

Our parties were always held in the afternoons because good Jewish girls did not go out at night. We all knew the lyrics of famous WWII era songs by Frank Sinatra, Bing Crosby, the Andrew sisters etc. For music, we had old 78 rpm records and phonographs with changeable needles. Only later were we introduced to 33 rpm records when an American friend got them from the base theater.

I would always tango with my preferred partner, Juliette Gabay. My love for Juliette was growing and I frequently took the lead in organizing these parties just so I could dance with Juliette.

Juliette was very hard to read—I surmised that she liked being with me because she always accepted my invitations, but she was not demonstrative in any way, which was typical for the girls at that time. It was not proper to show any affection without some kind of commitment.

I knew many soldiers from my work on the American base and soon discovered that some of them were good musicians. I invited a few to play for a group of friends, which was the beginning of a close collaboration. They formed a dynamic 5-piece band and would practice by playing for us every weekend. We would reciprocate with the best we could offer in food and wine. To our delight, they played all the American tunes we loved, and that I was so familiar with, having heard them on the American radio broadcast on the base, the ABS (Atlantic Base Section).

Chriqui, Sidney. *As Time Goes by: A Life's Journey from Casablanca*. CreateSpace Independent Publishing Platform, 2014. Selection from pages 33, 35–37, 41–42.

63. THE POLITICS OF COTTON AND THE POSTWAR STRUGGLE FOR POWER [1943]

Cotton is a potent symbol and commodity globally, its history inextricable from that of imperialism and colonialism. When Muslim merchants in Fez were arrested in the summer of 1943 for trading American cotton on the black market, the case quickly became explosive, for much more was involved than wartime profiteering. At stake was the question of who deserved to capitalize on the Allied victory against the Axis powers in North Africa. As Moroccan nationalists, the royal family, French colonial officials, and American representatives jockeyed for influence, individual merchants and consumers played out the same drama on a more modest scale. In this report by American authorities stationed in Fez, we learn of a number of Muslim merchants who were arrested by French authorities after selling modest quantities of American cotton in violation of French colonial quotas. The merchants involved, one of whom was a British protégé, bristled at being singled out while larger-scale sellers of the same goods went undisturbed: they were also outraged at the harsh and humiliating punishment French authorities meted out to them, which appeared an excessive flexing of authority. All told, the incident speaks to the delicacy of the political climate in 1943, when it was yet unclear who would reign politically ascendant following the end of Vichy rule.

July 14, 1943

Our own sources in FEZ, under date of July 9, report the following:

Nine arrests (names can be supplied if necessary) were made last week in the Kissaria (native cloth market of Fez) following an inspection by French authorities of the sale of American cotton goods. The retailers arrested, one of them a British protege, were all accused of fraud. Eight of them were tried before the Pacha and sent to prison for terms of varying length but the British protege will be tried in the French Tribunal de Paix.

This incident has had a *very bad* propaganda effect among Moslems of all classes and there is very much discontentment shown by pro-American natives who realize that once again the French officials are blaming the Americans for something which actually comes from their own corrupt administration.

The merchants implicated in this affair are all well-known respectable citizens of Fez and the fact that they have been sent to prison and had their heads shaved like criminals of the worst type, is causing angry comment throughout the city. For example, one man was in possession of only seven meters of American cloth which, according to the charge, he had hidden with the intention of selling it on the Black Market. Even if this were true, the fact cannot be denied that, in order to obtain any goods at all, the retail merchant must first promise to split the profit of his Black Market sales with the French official who issues the bons or distributes the goods from the Ravitaillement. The retailer buys at Black Market prices and must, therefore, sell at Black Market prices in order to make any profit at all and remain in business.

Many Moslems consider it very unfair to have made an example of these minor offenders when there are other exponents of the Black Market who have been and still are, dealing in thousands of meters of American goods and while the French officials themselves are aware of what is going on.

All Moslem informants say that the French authorities to whom they appealed or with whom they discussed the matter, replied that "American authorities were responsible for it all" Commandant Coget of the Pacha's court he himself a receiver of bribes according to former Fez reports, was one of the French officials to say that the French did not like performing such painful duties but that they were forced to by America.

Pro-American Moslems think that the French authorities, knowing that the Americans are amazed at the terrible Black Market situation all over

IMAGE 18. North Africans had a wide range of reactions to the Allied victory against the Axis powers in North Africa. Some greeted the British and American soldiers as liberators, while others harbored suspicions about the rise of (what would come to be called) neocolonialism in their region. American goods such as cigarettes, chewing gum, soap, and sweets, which reached North Africa with the Allied soldiers, symbolized and furthered these political contests. "Landing Operations of US Task Force in Algeria and Morocco, Nov. 1942," United States, Office of War Information, LOT 11582, Library of Congress Prints and Photographs Division, Washington, DC.

Morocco, feel obliged to make some show of trying to check it but have gone to the minor culprits while the ruthless traffikers [sic] who are dealing on a very large scale, are left alone, because to expose them would mean that a number of French officials would also be deeply involved.

Other intelligent Moslems think that the French are suffering from an acute "crise de jalousie" [jealous fit] and that at the present time they would do anything to counter-attack the increasing popularity of the Americans in Morocco. It is even thought that the arrest of these men is a direct result of the Sultan's visit to Oujda and the very friendly contacts established there between him and General Clark. The Moslems say that the French are vexed because the Americans gave the Sultan such a magnificent reception, and are giving him too much importance, and what is worse from the French point of view, is that American Moslem contacts are becoming just a little too direct.

To have arrested these men seems to be a very poor attempt at checking Black Market sales on such a large scale as they exist here, and it is suggested that the whole thing is just to cause strife between Moslems and the Americans especially when the blame is publicly put on America for what has happened.

It is thought that the case of the British protege which is to go to the French Tribunal will probably be hushed up as it would be going into far too much detail for the safety of the French officials.

This affair is being discussed, not only in Moslem business circles, but even in the streets of the native City where some Moslems are saying that it would be better for America not to send any goods at all to North Africa if they have to come through French officials and their corrupt channels which result in prison and fine for the retailers.

Unsigned American intelligence report of July 14, 1943, RG 226, Records of the Office of Strategic Services, 1942–1947, Entry 97, Algiers Station Files, Box 20, National Archives Record Administration, National Archives at College Park, MD.

64. A MOROCCAN SOLDIER SERVES THE COLONIAL, VICHY, FREE FRENCH, AND AMERICAN REGIMES {1906–1942}

Indigenous North African, Arab, Amazigh (Berber), and/or Black soldiers served in the French Army since the late nineteenth century, when they were recruited in Algeria and Tunisia, and later (as of 1908) in Morocco. The Moroccan recruits, many of whom were Black and enlisted under physical or economic coercion, were known as goumiers or goums. The French military considered these soldiers instrumental but lesser members of the military, "irregular" recruits who were dispensable. In general, these soldiers were tasked with assisting regular troops in combat or in the policing of newly occupied territories, frequently being positioned in the most dangerous situations, including battle front lines. During the Second World War, the Moroccan goumiers served under both Vichy and (later) Free

French officers, in auxiliary units known as tābūr (regiments). In this excerpt from an interview conducted with Aomar Boum, Al-Haj Ali Al-Ḥusayn Tliti remembers his varied experience as a goum. Tliti served first during the colonization of Ouarzazate (1928), during the so-called pacification of the southern Anti-Atlas (1931), and in a variety of stations and capacities during the Second World War. Tliti highlights how the goums were used to facilitate the last stages of the French military's colonization of Morocco's tribal communities, with the support of tribal leaders. This work put goumiers like Tliti, themselves marginalized subjects of colonial rule, in contact with other communities that experienced racialized violence—arguably laying the groundwork for the postwar struggle for independence and civil rights.

I was born in Taznakht in 1906, just a few years before the Great War. For a few years, I was one of Pasha Thami Glaoui's trusted messengers (*zatat*). I joined the *goum* unit of the French army on the order of the Pasha. He thought that the French commanders would benefit from my knowledge of the regions of Ouarzazate and Tata. In March 1931, I was asked to join *goum* unit number 35, under the command of colonel Chardon to control—what would later be known as the Foum Zguid Bureau of Indigenous Affairs. I later served under French colonels and lieutenants who supervised the post of Foum Zguid until 1939, occasionally being tasked to take letters to Thami in Telouet or Marrakesh.

In May 1940, I joined the *goumiers* to fight in the Libyan front, but our station was temporary because after Vichy signed the armistice with Hitler, we were relocated back to Morocco and I served in Marrakesh in the Kasbah mostly in charge of maintaining public [order].

In November 10, 1942, a group of *goums* in Marrakesh were ordered to head to Safi to fight the Americans. By the time we arrived, the Americans were in control of the city and we were held for a few days before our release and [before] enlisting in the French Free Army, Moroccan division, to fight on the Tunisian front. In Tunis, we were put under the supervision of an American general named Omar. We called him Lhaj si Omar l-mirikani, although he was not Christian as I recall. We could not believe that Americans could name someone Omar, although later I found out during my service in Casablanca that a few Black American soldiers were named Omar.

The Americans respected us in the battle and made fun of the French who lost so many soldiers in these conflicts. The American guns were much better than those the French used to give us, so with our new guns we destroyed the last German soldiers [in the] Zaghouan mountains and we were sent back to Casablanca.

I was happy to come back to the bled [countryside]. My father was dying of typhus. However, I was not allowed to visit with him for fear of infecting the *tābūr* of *goums* that I served with in Casablanca.

We were stationed not far from the port of Casablanca and tasked with maintaining public order. I remember being tasked a few times to guard the prostitutes' quarter of Bousbir. I hated that job. I could not believe that the French would allow our women to sell their bodies for the pleasure of soldiers. Many Jewish women were also in the quarter.

There was so much poverty and hunger that families had to do everything they could to eat. By late December and almost six months after my return from Tunisia, I received the news that my only child with my first wife, Izza, had died in Igrehm, where I left her with my in-laws. A few months later, Izza succumbed to famine, which affected most of the villages in the south. I remained in Casablanca until the end of the war when I was granted a release from service and returned to Telouet, where I remarried.

Interview in Arabic with Al-Haj Ali Al-Ḥusayn Tliti by Aomar Boum, Ighrem, Morocco, February 3–15, 2004.

65. SINGING THE PRAISES OF AMERICAN TROOPS IN TUNIS (c. 1943)

In November 1942, when the Americans landed in Algiers, locals had divergent perspectives on the event: some viewed the American soldiers as liberators, others saw them as enemies, and still others perceived them as capitalist overlords introducing a new form of colonialism to the region. The Tunisian Jewish composer and musician Simon di Yacoub Cohen analogizes the American entrance in Tunis to a bride who offers purity and sweetness. In his popular song "Khamous Zana," di Yacoub Cohen narrates the German's arrival in Tunisia and all the deprivations their rule inaugurated, including the confiscation of the radios of the Jews of Tunis. The song concludes with the Americans' triumphant routing of the Axis powers, heralding them as an offering of God. The title of "Khamous Zana" encapsulates the song's message. The word Zana [jana] *signals an arrival, while the word* Khamous *is derived from* khamsa *(literally, "five"), which refers to the palm-shaped amulet North African Jews use to ward off the evil eye; as a nickname, "Khamous" is given by Tunisian Jews to a beloved child. In Cohen's hands, "Khamous" stands for the Allies, here configured as a beloved savior and intimate. "Khamous Zana" was played widely in Tunisia after its production and in decades to come: still today Jews of Tunisian heritage sing it at celebrations. In recognition of the sustained importance of "Khamous Zana" to North African Jews and their descendants, the editors have worked with a number of distinguished members of the community in Israel to bring Cohen's song English translation.*

Khamous came for us and took out the Germans from our midst
On a Shabbat We got a shock
Tunis filled up with German soldiers
They spread their army and posted fliers all around,
Proclaiming: "Jews are our enemies"
In Tunis, there's a guard His heart is hard
He stole our money without compassion
They inhabited our houses looted our assets
Ruled over our elders and took them as hostages
They stole our radios and beds with mattresses
Even from our reserves laying us bare
Nasty and cruel They ambushed us
The sick with the weak none were left
The committee announces people are taken
While I am hidden above the alcove
Oh god, how they took me by force
They told me, "Jew follow behind us"
A large group they took us to school
Locked us up in it Our hearts afraid
They registered our names shovels in our hands
With stale bread and jam they gave us
We went on foot without beds
Blistered from the cold, fighting behind us
In Ksar Tyr we worked, digging
Old and young They took us all
Children of Zbibina How did we suffer!
There wasn't enough food Hunger overwhelmed us
Bombs dropped people were killed

Anti-aircraft defense destroyed
Married or single,
Trampled on the ground are
We cry, with our tears
On a Friday
With tanks, they entered
Their trucks
They arrived and made us happy
A lamb was slaughtered

[Khamous], like a bride, entered
The Germans were stunned
[Khamous] brought flour
Delicious chocolate
[Khamous] arrived
The money changed
Soap and sugar
Chewing gum and cigarettes
Living in Tunis
I fish and draw five [against the evil eye]
Berlin is destroyed
Germans are running away
Why not drink?
I don't like the Germans
We were scared
Now, we're full
De Gaulle, the Greatest
Left Pétain's words behind
Long live France
Her flag won't be debased
The evil will be removed from France
Her star is shining
Roosevelt is the light of our eye
De Gaulle and Stalin

houses ruined
children too, like dead bodies
our men and women
We melted like a candle
Khamous is near us
the night of Shabbat
were filled with goods
from the Germans, we were wrested
and the Bukha [alcoholic beverage]
    was shared among us
its flag planted
and raised their hands up
and distributed among us
and sweets were given to us
when we recited the Kaddish
and the banks filled
and the milk is flavored
American-made
accompanied by Khamous
and eat with appetite
from bomb strikes
barefoot, naked
Why not delight?
they fled from us
We were starved
We thank our Lord
May God the Great protect him
and entered with a brave army
and [may she] enter Paris, happily
and her friends are ours
for she gave us freedom
and her children make her joyful
and the compassionate Churchill
May the Lord Protect them!

Cohen, Simon de Yacoub. *Khamous Zana.* Tunis: Imprimerie Uzan, c. 1943. Translated from Judeo-Arabic by Rabbi Joshua Bittan and Joseph Chetrit, with help from members of the Jewish community of Tunisia in Israel.

66. AMERICAN "LIBERATORS" PERPETUATE SEXUAL VIOLENCE [1943]

The Anglo-American invasion of French Morocco and Algeria, conducted in November 1942 and known as Operation Torch, brought some 107,000 British and American troops to North Africa. Many accounts of this moment (especially those gathered by Allied representatives and their sympathizers) emphasize the joyousness with which American and other Allied troops were welcomed in North Africa, particularly by Jews. But the Americans did not bring political or social transformation to the region overnight. The Allied powers agreed that Vichy rule in North Africa did not officially end after Operation Torch (and would remain in place until 1943). Therefore, despite lobbying by international Jewish organizations, political prisoners, including many Jews, languished in Vichy camps for some time, and anti-Jewish Vichy legislation was not immediately abrogated. What's more, in North Africa as in Europe, the presence of Allied soldiers introduced danger for local communities, including the threat of sexual violence against women. This internal correspondence among American officials speaks to the at least occasional habit of American soldiers forcing their way into residents' homes and brutalizing men "if they will not let them play with their women." The thinly veiled allusion to sexual violence offers a powerful reminder. The Allied landing did not bring safety to the peoples of North Africa. Women, in particular, were especially vulnerable during the war and even in its supposedly peaceful aftermath.

March 18, 1943

Today, I have interviewed a few workers and asked them about their living conditions. They replied that things are good in every single way with the Americans. Every day they make 27 francs. Also, twice a week, [they get] half a kilogram of sugar with the corresponding amount of tea, plus half a kilogram of rice. Also, [they get] four meters of linen every month. Some get even more than that.

All in all, they are extremely happy for this and all of them praise the Unites States and hope this activity will last. They say that they haven't seen days like these, and haven't even dreamt of them.

March 14, 1943

At my place, there was a Jew making some repairs and I asked him about the situation since the American invasion. He answered by saying "We thank

God for this blessed hour for which He graced us with the entrance of the Americans and the English because they are people who love justice and despise injustice. And we are grateful that they provided us with all bounties and abundant work opportunities with them. Everyone started earning with them, especially the poor."

And he said: "However, American soldiers drink a lot of wine and when it splinters in their heads, they do bad things such as entering people's homes and threatening to beat them if they wouldn't let them do what they please with their wives."

He also said that "the English soldiers are polite and they only drink a little so they are joyful and don't do things that are disgraceful."

And I asked him what is his opinion on the French and whether they like the Americans. And he told me "Sir, that is impossible because the United States is better than France, so how would they like it. France simply tolerates it and that's it."

Handwritten note dated March 14, 1943, RG 226, Records of the Office of Strategic Services, 1942–1947, Entry 97, Algiers Station Files, Box 25, National Archives Record Administration, National Archives at College Park, MD. Translated from Arabic by Jessie Stoolman.

67. AMERICAN POWER AND THE POLITICS OF "SEDUCTION" [1943]

The Second World War left many civilians in North Africa poverty stricken, displaced, jobless, and socially isolated. In this postwar environment, women and girls were often forced into prostitution, found themselves vulnerable to rape or other forms of sexual violence, and at times entered into relationships with soldiers that hinged on an imbalance of power, capital, and social mobility. Sixteen-year-old Colette Marsol, an orphan living with her grandmother in her Casablanca guesthouse, was caught up in this perilous environment. Lieutenant Schneider, a representative of the American military, who was years (if not decades) Marsol's senior, began a sexual relationship with Marsol, later claiming to feel deep affection for the teenager. When Marsol became pregnant and had a child, Schneider protested that formalizing their relationship was impossible given that he had a wife and children at home. While the US military's priority was minimizing the damage to Schneider's reputation and to the United States, allies of Marsol argued that her financial security and reputation also deserved protection. Astonishingly, the matter reached the American consul in Casablanca. This episode reminds us that in North Africa (as in Europe) postwar sexual encounters between local women and soldiers were not so much private or intimate affairs as politicized struggles over power and influence. This case reinforces the precarities that indigenous women faced in a colonial and militarized context: although the legal category of statutory rape did not exist in Marsol's time, she was nonetheless vulnerable to sexual abuse at the hands of one with far more power.

Dear Sir,

I am writing to inform you of the following events. After the US Military Services dismissed this affair, and as a result of the disinterest shown by its leaders, I believe it is my duty to bring you up to date.

Before I do so, I would like to point out that your "Rue d'Algérie" offices promised me all of their support; unfortunately, there have been significant changes lately and the new directors maintain that this matter is none of their concern.

Here are the facts:

One year ago, Lieutenant USNR [United States Naval Reserve] Paul Schneider, an American army officer, met and began to court Miss Colette Marsol, a 16-year-old French orphan who lives with her grandmother in the boardinghouse her grandmother owns at 25 Rue Prom.

The result of this relationship (the numerous lodgers can testify to Lieutenant Schneider's attentions and feelings) are such that the young girl, currently seventeen years old, has just given birth to a boy in the maternity ward of Colombani Hospital.

It should be noted that as soon as Lieutenant Schneider realized the situation he was in, he informed the grandmother that it was impossible for him to set things right due to the fact that he was already married and had children.

Knowing the precarity of the family's situation, and in order to permit the young girl to avoid scandal and distance herself from Casablanca, Lieutenant Schneider handed over a sum of 5,000 francs, solemnly promising to never abandon the mother and her child, and regularly sends them maternal assistance.

In the meantime, the Lieutenant was moved to Agadir Base, and despite his visits to Casa, has refused to be interviewed.

As the due date approached, countless appeals were made to the US Military Service; unfortunately, these appeals, made by an older woman, only resulted in dismissals and empty promises. These appeals ceased following the response of the officers of the Naval Base, located at the Place de France: "Nothing to obtain from Mr. Schneider."

It is neither for us to judge nor to critique what has just been explained to you; it is, however, our duty to do the impossible, and find a solution.

On the one hand, we have a serious error committed by a man wearing the uniform of a country whose loyal traditions are beyond reproach; on the other, we have an honorable and well-known family that has become destitute, as both the authorities and charitable organizations refuse to help since the young woman is an unwed mother.

After offering this explanation, I would like to add that it is not the family's intention whatsoever to force the father to acknowledge the child as his, but only to request that he make an effort to provide for the mother's needs until the moment when she—given her young age—is able to start a new life honorably.

I hope, Sir, that this difficult case will pique your kind interest, and that after an investigation, this family will be able to obtain a bit of satisfaction.

I can only offer my apologies for the inconvenience that this may cause for you. Please accept, Sir, my best wishes along with my sincere thanks.

Casablanca, November 25, 1943
Ermanno Colombo
Ste Fortin-Moullot
12, boulevard de la Liberté
Casablanca

Ermanno Colombo, Casablanca, to US Consul, Casablanca, November 25, 1943, RG 67.008M, Box 2, Ermanno Colombo to American Consul, Casablanca, November 25, 1943, American Friends Service Committee Records Relating to Humanitarian Work in North Africa, 1942–1945, United States Holocaust Memorial Museum Archives, Washington, DC. Courtesy of American Friends Service Committee. Translated from French by Rebecca Glasberg.

68. THE POLITICS OF HUNGER [1943]

Hunger was long a manifestation and symbol of the inequities wrought by colonial rule in North Africa and across the globe: before the Second World War, this point was brought to the world through the work of writer Albert Camus, who grew up in a poor settler colonial family in Algeria. In serialized newspaper articles written in 1939, Camus narrated the devastating famine affecting Kabylia, Algeria. After the war, a generation of anti- and postcolonial writers (including Mohammed Dib and Frantz Fanon) dove deeper still into the politics of state-engineered famine under colonial rule. The following account, an internal exchange circulated between French officials in Morocco, details the scarcity felt by Muslim families in Rabat during the war, reflecting the food shortages and poverty that was ubiquitous across Morocco under Vichy rule and shedding light on local protests that were organized as an expression of locals' pain and outrage. Deprivation followed Morocco and Algeria into the postwar period, when the foundation of wartime scarcity was exacerbated by drought, widespread crop failure, and a typhus epidemic. These dynamics played a role in stoking anticolonial sentiment and consolidating the power of nationalist movements across the region.

His excellency, Mr. René Massigli
Ambassador of France, Commissioner of Foreign Affairs, Algiers

Following my telegram number 474 from 10 October 1943 concerning a demonstration that took place on 27 September in Rabat, I have the honor of informing Your Excellency of several clarifications that I was able to obtain regarding this incident, its origins, and its meaning.

1st. For some time, the difficulties surrounding food supplies have provoked an unease that translated into muffled and limited unrest in the Muslim neighborhoods. This dissatisfaction was due to two issues which are, in truth, essential: the inadequacy of the quality of wheat allotted to the urban population, and the bad quality of oil allocated to the natives.

As for the first issue, potentially excessive cautionary measures—in theory, justified by the insufficiency of grain stocks—were the root of the inadequate fixing of wheat provisions. This cause was aggravated by the fact that the wheat collections in the interior of the country had practically exhausted the familial and individual supplies that partially feed the cities.

As for the second issue, the shortage of good-tasting oil obligated [us] to resort to a mix of olive and linen oils which, although perfectly fit to eat, was not accepted without complaint by the Muslim population of Rabat.

2nd. The natives' dissatisfaction had not been expressed in any remarkable way when a minority of Rabat public figures decided to organize a dramatic collective appeal to His Majesty the Sultan.

Meetings were held in Rabat on this subject in which civil servants, rentiers, shopkeepers, and intellectuals—including a certain number of nationalists, but no party leaders—took part. It should be noted that some of the Pasha of Rabat's close associates participated in these discussions, proof that despite what he may have said, this leading figure could not have been unaware of what was in the works.

The demonstration was decided upon during the course of these meetings. On the evening of 26 September, the rallying cry was launched: close the stores and send a significant delegation to the Palace to hand over a formal written petition.

Indeed, on the morning of the 27th, all the Muslim artisan stores on the Medina's two main streets were closed and a procession of approximately four hundred people, composed of artisans and working people, arrived at Mechouar Palace. The demonstrators were peaceful.

The Sultan received a group of protesters who gave him their request. He spoke first with the Adviser to the Sharifian Government and with the Director of Political Affairs in the presence of Pasha Bargach. At the end of these conversations, the Sultan—who had not ceased supporting the demands of his subjects—peacefully assured them that he had just himself received triple the quota of wheat from the Protectorate Authorities, and promised better quality oil, with a slight reduction in rations, for October. In the afternoon, life went back to normal in the medina.

The next morning, the Sultan conveyed to the Resident General his gratitude for the speed with which his subjects' demands had been satisfied.

3rd. The genuine dissatisfaction provoked among the natives by the poorly adjusted measure of food supplies was exploited by a group of notables who are themselves free from want and who, in general, show little interest in the poorer classes.

In the demonstration that was triggered, we can see a gesture of protest against the organization of food supplies, which is often misunderstood, and which is opposed because incompatible with the development of clandestine trade.

This collective solicitation of His Majesty was acutely exacerbated by the mental jitteriness at the end of Ramadan; [the demonstrators] used the pretext of a grain shortage [which impinged upon] the "fetra"—charity traditionally given to the poor—to express their displeasure.

We can therefore conclude that the demonstration had only an indirect political character owing to the fact that the nationalists within reach abstained from participating publicly in it.

But it is important to stress the significance of this incident in which the Pasha of Rabat and city notables were involved, and also not to underestimate this clear indication of the possible reactions of an urban population anxious about food supplies during a winter expected to be difficult.

French Ambassador Gabriel Paux, Rabat, to French Ambassador René Massigli, Algiers, September 27, 1943, RG 43.006M, Reel 23, Ministère des affaires étrangères: Guerre (1939–1945), United States Holocaust Memorial Museum Archives, Washington, DC. Courtesy of Ministère de l'Europe et des affaires étrangères. Translated from French by Rebecca Glasberg.

69. THE APPEAL OF AN AUSTRIAN LIEUTENANT [1943]

The American Friends Service Committee (AFSC) was formed during the First World War to provide Quakers and other pacifists a means of serving the war effort while remaining nonviolent. During the Second World War, the AFSC worked to hide Jewish children in Europe, to assist Jewish and non-Jewish refugees, and to alleviate the suffering of those in French internment camps. It was the largest non-Jewish American organization to assist those escaping Nazi persecution through its Refugee Division, which by the early 1950s, had opened more than twenty-two thousand case files. The AFSC invested a great deal of labor into its North African office. Working out of Casablanca, representatives of the committee fielded appeals from desperate refugees across North Africa, and sometimes traced and aided such individuals or families over months, if not years. In this series of letters to a representative of the AFSC, the Austrian refugee (and retired Austro-Hungarian lieutenant) Erwin Sommer describes his extraordinary wartime travails—and the incomplete wartime story of his Czechoslovakian wife and two children—that carried him from Vienna to Paris to the labor camp of Bou Arfa and the (Third Republican-era) state coal mine in Jerada, both in Vichy-controlled Morocco. Poignantly, the last of these letters is written after the Allied landing in North Africa, at a time when Sommer expected liberation, but instead experienced sustained imprisonment, hardship, and legal limbo. His appeal to the AFSC asked whether the organization might help him locate the family from whom he had been separated for several years, and assist him in locating work in England.

February 2, 1943

Dear Sir,

I heard that the American Quakers have a Moroccan Committee, and I take the liberty to write to you hoping you would, even partially, help me in my distress.

I am an ex-Austria, married, born 8/6/1898 at Waidhofen o/d Ileles (Lower Austria). I have the *baccalauréat* and my diploma in Vienna. I am lieutenant in the reserve of [i.e., retired from] the old army Austrian-Hungarian. With my family (wife and two children of 4 and 2 years old respectively) I lived, before the war at Chelles s/Marne, 15 rue Pasteur. I was manager-partner of a rather important firm in Paris. When the war broke out I enlisted in the Légion Étrangère. I have left my family, my home, my social position. My wife was left alone with my two children. I did my service at 3rd REI [Régiment étranger d'infanterie, or Foreign Infantry Regiment] (Fez).

During the occupation of Paris by the Germans, my wife, who is Czechoslovakian, could not leave, for the two children were sick. Our house has been plundered, sacked, and later on my family was dispossessed by the Germans.

Nevertheless my wife tried to arrange living up till July 1942; when persecutions became worse in Paris, she could arrange to pass clandestinely the "ligne de demarcation," leaving our remaining belongings. She arrived with the two children in Marseille, where she has been the witness and victim of the persecutions ordered by the Germans. She had been arrested on Sept. 24th and sent in "residence force" at Centre Bompard, 4 Traverse Beaulieu, in Marseille, with the two children, to whom they even refused the authorisation to go to school. All this moving correspondence is at your disposal.

The American Friends Service Committee in Marseille generously intervene[d] in favour of my two children. A *commission de criblage* chose them for a children convoy which would be sent to the United States; convoy which should have left last November. Enclosed is the copy of a letter Mr. Richie, Quakers Delegate, wrote me on October 30th 1942.

The events which took place since that time had the consequence that I am without news of my family since Nov[ember] 2nd, and I do not know whether my children have left (as I hartily [*sic*] hope) or whether my wife with the two children have been deported. I add that my wife, chemical-engineer, has been invited by the authorities to go back to Germany, but she always refused.

If the children are in the USA, their uncle, Mr. Ferdinand Wind, 151 Fenimore Road, Mamaroneck, NY, will take care of them with great pleasure. Mr. Wind had sent affidavits in Marseille, documents which arrived too late...

Could you help me in trying to know where my children and my wife are? Hereunder are the dates of birth for the children, to help you in your investigations:

Michel Sommer, born 30/8/35, in Vienna (Austria),

Elisabeth Sommer, born 11/1/1938 at Zatec (Tchéco-Slovaquia [sic])

I take this opportunity to solicit your intervention in favor of the Austrians, ex-*engagés pour la durée de la guerre*, always interned, unjustly and unduly interned in camps of *travailleurs étrangers*.

Our situation is as follows: Demobilized after the Armistice, we have been placed in those famous *groupements de travailleurs*. We were sent from bled to bled; we were ignobly treated being under treatment of "surveillants" of the Foreign Legion, most of them being [N]azis, who did not hide their contemp[t] for us.

We have been working for two years, two summers under the very hot sunrays, to the constructions of the Bou-Arfa/Kenadza railroad. We have broken flint-stones, we have placed rails (fr. 1,25 per day!!) But we resisted to all those invitations more or less threatening to be sent back into our own country. Much of my compatriots prefer[r]ed to be sent back rather than to support such a treatment, it is true; but about ten of us remained inflexible, Austrians and Sarrois.

Then we have been hired to public, or private enterprises, for work. Just now, we are working at the state mine of Djerada. We are paid 50 frs. per working day, less 20 frs. for food.

Then the arrival of the Americans in Morocco happened. Our joy, our hope have been rather short: no freedom for us, ex-Austrians. Our Comrades: Czechs, Belgians, Polish, Yougu-Slavs [sic], who took part in our exile, left us one month ago. We have taken steps every place we could to leave for England. The reply has always been the same: it is fit to the French Authorities to free you. But is the interest of the French Authorities to let us at liberty? For we represent a main-d'oeuvre, precious and not expensive?

Can one give a better [proof] of dislike with the [N]azis than to enlist them against us? In spite of the "capital punishment" in case we are taken? Have we sacrificed everything in France as well as in Austria, to be treated that way? Are we not the first victims of the fury of the [N]azis? and however we are considered as being "Germans"—Austrians we are, Austrians we remain, no one has exchanged his passport, as they tried to have us did in 1938!

I heard that the Quakers are willing to be interested in our situation, and we feel very grateful toward them. I would ask you earnestly to intervene so that our mortifying and worthless situation ends; this as well as for us, former French soldiers, as for the State and the principle of livery proclaimed by the state. We are willing to leave for England, if France considers our presence in North-Africa as undesirable.

Among us are specialists, fitters, [mechanics], one Vienna Cook, electricians, etc . . . who would be pleased to work in England.

Hoping to be honored with a favorable answer, I beg you to believe . . .

For the Ex-Austrians of GT 11

Erwin Sommer

Erwin Sommer, Djerada, to American Friends Service Committee, Casablanca, February 2, 1943, RG 67.008M, Box 31, Folder 15, American Friends Service Committee Records Relating to Humanitarian Work in North Africa, 1942–1945, United States Holocaust Memorial Museum Archives, Washington, DC. Courtesy of American Friends Service Committee.

70. AN UNEQUAL "LIBERATION"— SUSTAINED INTERNMENT AFTER OPERATION TORCH [c. 1944]

The Vichy regime created varieties of internment in North Africa, in part to identify, confine, and force into labor different perceived enemies. Among those imprisoned and compelled into forced labor in Vichy camps across the region were "volunteers of the French Foreign Legion engaged for the duration of the war." The foreign volunteers included men who were Jewish and non-Jewish, European and non-European, German and Austrian, as well as citizens of nations conquered by the Third Reich—all measure of individuals who had dedicated themselves to serving France in opposition to the rise of Nazism, fascism, and Germany's wartime aggression. Many sources in this book speak to the experience of foreign volunteers in the course of their wartime imprisonment; this undated manifesto, sent to the American Friends Service Committee, addresses the outrage felt by the internees and their advocates at the fact that their imprisonment continued after the Allied victory in French-colonized Morocco and Algeria, and despite the avowals of President Franklin D. Roosevelt, who was not a consistent ally on the topic of camp liberation. Although internees had hoped that the Allied landing meant liberation, instead Great Britain and the United States signed an agreement with Admiral François Darlan that enabled him to prolong Vichy legislation and general rule. The prolonged functioning of Vichy labor camps was a profound insult to internees, their families, and their advocates. It took years before Vichy's brutal trans-Saharan railroad project was finally abandoned, Vichy camps dismantled, and the regime's thousands of prisoners released.

Case for engagés volontaires

"I asked for the liberation, in North-Africa, of all those persons who were imprisoned because they were opposed to the effort of the Nazis to rule the world, and I asked also for the abrogation of all laws and decree [sic] inspired by Nazi Governments and Nazi ideals.
(Comments of President Roosevelt on the situation in North-Africa, November 17th, 1943).

1.

To whom can such words be applied, if not to the former "Engagés Volontaires Etrangers pour la durée de la guerre dans l'Armée Française" (Foreign Volunteers in the French Army for the duration of the war), who are still kept in work camps, or concentration camps in Morocco, who have been suffering for more than two year [sic] who are awaiting their freedom at the hands of the Americans, and who will be only too pleased to volunteer for the Allied Forces?

The fact that they are awaiting their freedom at the hands of the Americans is easy to understand, as easy to understand as the request of President Roosevelt. It is not asking for an extraordinary request. The former Free Volunteers are not asking for a favor. President Roosevelt is not asking for a favor. It is right that both are requesting.

2.

To return once more to the problem of the former Engagés Volontaires who are in camps in Morocco:

In Morocco, in these camps are kept, "imprisoned persons who were opposed to the efforts of the Nazis to rule the world," and enlisted at the beginning of the war in 1939, in the French Army, to fight against the Nazi Government. These men, of various nationalities various creeds, the majority of them living in France a long time before the war, were not forced to enlist. Those who were citizens of neutral countries could have remained free. People of Axis origin could have remined in concentration camps, or they could have enlisted as civilian workers under military control to serve the Allied cause. They did not do so, and preferred to serve in the [French] Army. Many of them were over fifty years of age, others were under eighteen. Many of them remained in France, in the Foreign "Régiments de Marche," many died in the Battle of France, many died in the Norwegian Campaign. Those who did not remain in France were sent to North-Africa, to [serve in] the Foreign Legion. They did their military service, and were waiting to be sent to the front, a[n] event which did not take place on account of the signing of the Armistice. After the Armistice had been signed, they had the right to freedom due to the fact that they volunteered only for the duration of the war. The French did not let them go except under severe restrictions which most of those men could not meet. Those who could give proofs of having means, or labor contracts, or certificates of support by near relatives could leave only after long months of difficult negociations [sic], the conditions being continually changed with [consequent] lengthening of negociations [sic]. Those who could not meet all these stipulations, those whose money, parents, relatives, or certificates were in the Occupied Zone of France, were obliged to remain and were imprisoned in camps created by the Government where they were subjected to forced labor for more than two years.

3.

These men, after the arrival of the Americans in North-Africa, can be classified in three groups:

a) Citizens of countries at war against Germany, or Axix [sic] Countries;

b) Citizens of neutral countries;

c) Citizens of Axis countries.

IMAGE 19. During the Second World War, Donald Coster volunteered for the American Field Service, was briefly held as a prisoner of war by German troops, was conscripted into the US Navy, served as an American vice-consul in Casablanca, helped plan the D-Day Invasion in England, participated in Operation Torch (the Anglo-American landing in North Africa), and served as a member of the Joint Commission for Political Internees and Refugees in French North Africa. Here, Coster (seated, second from right) watches a celebration by former internees at the Djerba internment camp. Although internees hoped the Allied landing meant liberation, Great Britain and the United States allowed the prolonging of Vichy legislation and rule in North Africa, which in turn allowed for the ongoing functioning of Vichy labor camps. "Former internees celebrating, Djerba internment camp, Algeria," c. June 1943, Donald Q. Coster Collection, Accession No. 2016.394.1, p. 92, United States Holocaust Memorial Museum, Washington, DC.

a) With the intervention of the Americans, and having their Consular Representatives here, Poles, Czechs, and, generally speaking, all people of countries at war against the Axis, have been released from the camps. Russians, Greeks, Yugo-Slavs, have also been released for the greater part. The first have been incorporated in their National Armies at war against the Axis. The second seem to have been incorporated under labor contracts for military purposes under British Command.

Without any doubt, all those men can be considered as citizens of countries at war against the Axis; though their respective countries might not be directly at war, they have been invaded and oppressed, and their Governments in the Foreign countries are at war against the Axis.

b) Under this group are Spaniards, Turks, Armenians, etc. One cannot reasonably suppose that they have feelings of great sympathy for the Axis regime. For example, the Spaniards of that category are nearly all former soldiers of the Spanish Republican Army. The fact that *all* those men, Spaniards and others, volunteered to fight against the Axis, should be considered sufficient to remove all doubt if there is still any doubt—about their feelings of faithfulness towards the Allied Forces fighting against the Axis.

c) Now for the people belonging to Axis countries: Germans, Austrians, Hungarians, Roumanians [sic], and Baltese (the latter if placed in this category):

To say for example, that "these Germans are Germans and remain Germans, and are consequently the enemies of the Allied Forces" would be absurd and would only be an excuse to avoid taking up the question and to remain indifferent to their release from the camps, as asked by President Roosevelt. If would be shameful on the part of those who are in charge, to interpret President Roosevelt's demand in this way.

Can one believe that these men—amongst them are numerous Jews—who have been driven away, or have voluntarily left their countries, as they could not, or would not support conditions of the Nazior [sic] Fascist Governments, who, at the beginning of the war, volunteered to fight against these Governments, in spite of reprisals which might be taken against their parents and relatives remaining in those countries (who can say whether such measures or punishment have not already been taken since the Armistice, as both German and Italian Commissions have had all means of knowing the names of the ex-engagés volontaires?)—can one really believe that these men have friendly feelings towards these forms of Government?

Can one believe it, if one knows that German and Italian Commissions d'Armistice in Morocco went to the camps of these men, several times, to invite them to go back to their countries, and those men refused, preferring their miserable conditions in the camps, rather then [sic] to make a change in their opinions and principles?

Actually, they do not hate their people. It would be too much to ask them to do so as a proof of faithfulness towards the Allies. But they hate, more than the others, the form of Government which placed, and is still putting their people in both moral and physical misery.

And it is to help their countries that they volunteered against such forms of Government.

... All the above being said, why are all these men not released from the camps in which they have been interned, under pressure of German and Italian Commissions d'Armistice? Whether that has been done under their orders, or under the orders of the Vichy Government, does not matter. Now times have changed. Neither of them exists any longer since the arrival of the Americans in North Africa. Certainly, the Americans came here to fight, and not to take care of matters which do not concern them. That is true. But to whom can be applied then the words of President Roosevelt? And to whom did he entrust the application of his request? ...

Is it right, is human to leave in misery men who volunteered (one cannot insist too much on this point) when America was not yet at war, who, after the Armistice, were never released as was the right, who were treated like slaves, with forced labor, mortifications who were persecuted, imprisoned, earning a salary more than derisive for the work they were obliged to do, hygienic conditions often beyond imagination, food and clothing often bad an insufficient.

It would be too long to enter into details, to speak of the man whose feet were amputated because, as a punishment, he was left outside, in the cold, until his feet were frozen; of those two men who, punished in the same way, died because they refused to eat, as a protest against such inhuman punishment.

Here are facts.

Why has nothing been changed? Why?

4.

Are those men asking for their freedom in order to live normally and as civilians?

No.

They ask to be released to be able to help the Allied Forces to continue to serve the common cause.

If they cannot enter the American Army, there are numerous other fields in which they could be useful. They could work, for instance, as "civil soldiers."

If one mistrusts them, not knowing them: they ask to be examined one by one.

Examine them!

If, being employed as "civil soldiers" by the Americans, it is thought advisable to place them under strict surveillance, to place them among others: then examine them, place them among other! They all know that the above would be logical. And they also know that soon everybody will be convinced that they can be relied upon.

What they are asking is to be taken out of misery, in which they still remain. They would like to be treated as men who can be reproached for no crime against the Allies.

And they are in the hope that a better use will be made of their professional skill; that their numerous skilled people will not be utilized, as it has been done up till now, to break big stones work that any French workman, even unskilled, has never been obliged to do in Morocco.

Now we must state reasons for which these men (at least most of them) are not willing to volunteer in the Corps Francs d'Afrique, created since the arrival of the Americans in North Africa. This dislike—it is not a refusal, the engagement being voluntary—to enlist once again either in the Foreign Legion, on in the Corps Franc d'Afrique, would only be interpreted by the French Authorities as proof to the American Authorities in North Africa, that these men are dangerous, even contrari [sic] to the Allies, as they refuse to serve the Allied cause by not enlisting in such formations. If they say so, it is impudence on their part, or is the memory of the French Authorities so sort [sic] that they forget that these men volunteered once under the French flag?

Can one ask these men to be confident in a French Government, who, not only, did not keep promises and engagements with them, but has treated and is still treating its servants like slaves? Even at the time of the French Republican Government before the Armistice, the Engagés Volontaires have been treated by their "superiors" in a most mortifying way, not to say more.

This disregard shown by the French Authorities toward the Engagés

Volontaires has always been so well known, that it is very difficult to imagine that a change might occur.

To summarize the above, the former Engagés Volontaires cannot have confidence, and are not desirous to enlist once more under French command.

...

6.

Under the circumstances, a change in the situation of the former Engagés Volontaires, "imprisoned as being opposed to the efforts of the Nazis to rule the world," that is a change which would mean their release from the camps by the French Authorities, cannot be expected.

It is up to the Americans, who seem to have been entrusted by President Roosevelt, and have power to change the existing state of things, to do what is to be done.

"Case for Engagés volontaires," n.d., RG 67.008M, Box 1, Folder 15, "Case for Engages Volontaires," American Friends Service Committee Records Relating to Humanitarian Work in North Africa, 1942–1945, United States Holocaust Memorial Museum Archives, Washington, DC. Courtesy of American Friends Service Committee.

71. A MANIFESTO OF THE FORMERLY INTERNED [1943]

Although Anglo-American forces claimed victory after Operation Torch, in reality, they signed a power-sharing agreement with Vichy authorities, which meant that many internees continued to languish in camps, in many cases under the oversight of the same French officers who had previously supervised their cruel internment. This was a tremendous slight to those interned, as well as to their families and allies, for the internees had been assured of their release by the Allied leadership and found no logic—and great insult—in sustained captivity. As this adamant manifesto by German and Austrian refugees who remained interned in French hands after Operation Torch reveals, they and other internees found themselves prone to a particularly cruel logic at the time. The Vichy regime had earlier vilified these refugees because they were Jews or communists, socialists, or supporters of the Spanish Republican cause. In the wake of Operation Torch, erstwhile Vichy officials who remained in power continued to vilify them, ostensibly because they were Boches

(Germans or German sympathizers). In so doing, the French effectuated a subtle transformation in their own self- and public image. Those who had loyally served the Vichy regime were, even before the war's end, remaking themselves as unwitting victims of German aggression. This widely accepted mythology followed France long into the postwar period. It was not until 1995 that France's president Jacques Chirac admitted that the French people and government were culpable of the genocide of French Jewry at the hands of the Germans, having handed over thousands of people during the Vel d'Hiv roundup in 1942. Significantly, neither Chirac nor any subsequent president of France has recognized the government's role in the death of countless others, Jews and non-Jewish political prisoners, at the hands of French soldiers in Vichy-run camps.

For English and American Authorities

1. We refugees of the Hitlerian fashisme [sic]—belonging to the so-called 3° and 4° foreign de[m]obilised workers Companys, are nearly all interned by the order of Vichy (Darlan et Pétain). The fourth group is officially called the Company of doubtful elements (Compagnie des douteux). Most of us have families and friends in Great Britain and in the USA.

2. All of us are ex-volunteers for the duration of the war or members of the AMBC [*armement militaire des batiments de commerce*, i.e., military-armed merchant vessels] (RIP). The big majority of us are [J]ews.

3. Vichy's manners are going on here. Up to date we have been treated as dirty communists, dirty [J]ews; now they are trying to treat us as "Boches" [slang for Germans].

4. The authorities which we are depending on, do their utmost to prevent us from communicating directly with the American and British liberators. Our numerous letters and wires to the English and American authorities, posted these last days, have been intercepted.

5. All of us, we want to put our forces in the service of the English and Americans. In contrast you will perfectly understand that after an internment of two years and a half, the interest of being [enlisted] in any sort of French formation (exception made for the troups [sic] of the General de Gaulle) is rather small amongst us.

6. A special report will be sent on murders and [manslaughters], committed on [unfortunate] comrades of ours, interned in the so-called "group of discipline."

"For English and American Authorities," January 30, 1943, RG 67.008M, Box 1, Folder 15, American Friends Service Committee Records Relating to Humanitarian Work in North Africa, 1942–1945, United States Holocaust Memorial Museum Archives, Washington, DC. Courtesy of American Friends Service Committee.

72. POLISH INTERNEE, POLITICAL CHAMELEON [1943]

The convoluted wartime story of Karol Kormes (b. 1915) goes far to illustrate the extraordinary variety of histories that converged in North Africa during and after the Second World War. When his case came before the American Friends Service Committee in the autumn of 1943, Kormes declared himself to the organization as a Polish national who had served with the International Brigade during the Spanish Civil War (1936–1939). When the Nationalists emerged victorious in that struggle, Kormes was arrested and imprisoned in Miranda De Ebro, one of two hundred concentration and forced labor camps constructed by the Franco regime to house Spanish and foreign nationals who had supported the erstwhile Republican government during the civil war. Kormes languished in Miranda for three years, somehow finding his way into French territory (perhaps over the Pyrenees, an escape route used by some half a million refugees from Franco's Spain) and under the thumb of the Vichy regime. Kormes's next internment was in the Vichy camp of Mediouna, twelve kilometers southeast of Casablanca. There, he emerged as leader of ten other Polish internees, all former International Brigade volunteers in the Spanish Civil War. Kormes and his comrades were still in Mediouna after the Anglo-American landing in Morocco during Operation Torch. His imprisonment technically over, he found that the Polish consul in Morocco was either unwilling or unable to help him return home. Poland was awash in refugees, with much of its territory controlled by the Soviet Union—and in any case, the consul (whose voice is not represented here) denied that Kormes was Polish at all. Kormes, then legally stateless, expressed a fervent desire to serve the Soviet Union. He ultimately succeeded, but only after remaining two more years in the camp at which he had been earlier interned. When Kormes was finally released from Mediouna, in December 1945, he journeyed to the Soviet Union carrying documentation that labeled him "Ukrainian." Kormes's English-language, autobiographical account is reproduced here in its original form, inclusive of misspellings and grammatical errors of a nonnative speaker.

Soldier of the 11th International Brigade, I was captured at June 10th, 1937. From this date on I was considered prisoner of war by the "authorities" of Franco Spain and not released but July 31th, 1943, four years after the end of the Spanish Civil war. This fact was due to the refusel of the Polish Embassador in Madrid to take care of the polish former Internationals, meanwhile Americans, English and other prisoners left Spain already in 1939.

Finally I was evacuated by the [P]olish Red Cross, with several other comrades, to Gibralter. Contrary to other Poles, which were sent at once to England to join the Polish Forces, we former International Brigaders were informed that we had to sign an "engagement" otherwise we would be sent to North-Africa.

Then we defined our point of view:

If we were considered Polish citizens, it was our duty to serve in the Polish Army an "engagement" being superfluous. Any special "engagement" which can only be the expression of the doubt in our Citizenship we refused.

In a meeting with the Adjudant of the British Town Commander I exposed this point of view, asking him to send us to England. He regretted, basing himself of the (*false*) information furnished by the Polish Military Mission, that every Pole had to sign an engagement.

A cable sent to London to our "International Brigade Association" asking advice, was retained and delivered to the Polish Mission. (Evidentely was it considered dangerous and London probably confounded as ennemy territory)

On September 20th I arrived in Casablanca, after an air-travel on bord of [A]merican transport engine.

We had a letter with us, from the Polish Mission at Gibraltar, which referred to an agreement "between this Mission and the French High Commissar" of North Africa, permitting us to enter.

The Polish Consul at Casa conduced us to the "Caserne Malakoff." After he had a conversation with the Captain in Chief, we were told to have to stay until the finally solution of our situation" (I remember here the above mentioned letter and the fact, that we presented us [quite] voluntarily at Malakoff.) The process of the so-called "finally solution" of our situation lasted "only" two month!

During this time we were neither asked, what we had come to North-Africa for, not what we wanted to do here; not even the question if we perhaps wished to join the French Foreign Legion was not put to us.

Twice, during that time we were sent to the Camp of Mediouna. Meanwhile we goy [sic] from the Polish Consul a certificate, stating that we were no longer considered Polish Citizens.

At the our arrival at Casablanca, I had put myself in touch with the American Civil Affairs Department, where I had stated: We were considering us Sowyet-Citizens, being from these former Polish Territories, Incorporated in 1939 in the Sowyet-Union.

We wished to be repatriated to our country to join the Red Army.

In case of the impossibility of such repatriation we would be ready to join any Allied Army (except the French Foreign Legion).

A cable in this sense was sent to the International Brigades Association as well as several letters to the Sowyet-Representation at Algier.

In spite of these facts, which were exposed to the French Authorities by the American Civil Affairs Department and which proved our sympathie to the cause of the United Nations, we were no release until November (what was of cause also no "finally solution of our situation").

Kormes

Testimony of Kormes, n.d., RG 67.008M, Box 4, American Friends Service Committee Records Relating to Humanitarian Work in North Africa, 1942–1945, United States Holocaust Memorial Museum Archives, Washington, DC. Courtesy of American Friends Service Committee.

73. THE "INFINITE PROLONGING OF THEIR INTERNMENT"—FORCED LABOR AFTER OPERATION TORCH [1943]

The Vichy camp of Jerada, located 160 kilometers east of Fès, was situated near mines where forced laborers extracted coal that could be converted into electricity or produced into steel. Created in 1933 with funding from the World Bank, the Jerada mine functioned during the war under the oversight of the Vichy-run Directorate of Industrial Production and housed mostly European prisoners, half of whom worked within the mine and half of whom worked above it. While the labor was punishing, conditions and food at Jerada were considered decent. After the Anglo-American landing on Moroccan shores following Operation Torch, prisoners in the Vichy labor camps waited in vain for news of their release. Given the Anglo-American forces' tentative alliance with Vichy authorities in Morocco, in Jerada, as in many other camps, internees continued to be treated as prisoners, housed under the oversight of former Vichy representatives who remained (as the author of this source puts it) "fascist-leaning and anti-Semitic." Despite having received word of the ostensible liberation of North Africa from the grasp of the Vichy regime, internees such as the author of this letter, Étienne Niessner, continued to be subjected to forced labor and feared that their captivity could be, in their words, infinitely prolonged. Here, Niessner describes the Jerada camp and political limbo of its internees to Hélène Cazes Benatar, representative of the American Jewish Joint Distribution Committee in Casablanca, in advance of her visit to the site.

February 19, 1943

Dear Madam,

In response to your letter dated 10 February, which I acknowledge receiving, I thank you, dear Madam, for your understanding and offer to help me in my situation as well as my comrades.

I am sending you herewith the list of my compatriots who responded immediately to my suggestion. We are all stateless, formerly of Austrian nationality.

I am delighted about your upcoming visit and will be happy to be able to speak to you privately and to express my profound gratitude to you.

For practical purposes, I have taken the liberty of assembling a report on the premises and location for you:

Djerada is an agglomeration situated sixty kilometers from Oujda that belongs entirely to the Mine. Communication is established via a bus that leaves Djerada in the mornings for Oujda and returns in the evenings. It departs from Oujda at 5:00 p.m. every day except Tuesday and Friday. The return trip must be carried out the following day, unless you use a personal or official vehicle. Absence of hotels; there is no nightly lodging, but if needed, one can find [a room] in private households. The meals in the mine's two restaurants are acceptable.

Until 1942, the mine belonged to a Belgian company, which the French State relieved of its duties due to German influence. Ever since, despite the arrival of the Americans, the leadership circles remain fascist-leaning and anti-Semitic; the policies of the [Office of] Native Affairs are in the hands of the president of the French Legion and commander of the SOL [Service d'ordre légionnaire, a collaborationist group notorious for its hostility to Jews] of Djerada. People don't even bother to hide their true colors when discussing our camp, in which we are considered internees; created by an institution whose purpose is rather unknown, it resembles slavery and this is due to the fact that certain human beings unfortunately do not have national representation; they can thus be abused at will, and our captivity can be infinitely prolonged. In short, it's a lucrative enterprise that permits the owner to make, as in the present case, a profit of 200,000 fr in two years. Our 30,000 fr of leave, which was paid by the Mine to the Group of Foreign Workers, evaporated and we are not even allowed to know what has been done with this money that belonged to us.

Speaking of my future plans, as I lack any French diplomas, I would happily take a job as construction designer or specialized industrial designer. They're being sought daily in the newspapers. First-rate references from French and Moroccan companies are at the employer's disposition.

With the hope that I will have the honor of welcoming you here, I remain sincerely yours.

P.S. I would be pleased to know what has become of the Abergel family.

An Austrian comrade who would like to send a letter to the Joint in Lisbon and who doesn't know the exact address has taken the liberty of enclosing a letter [herein], which I beg you to transmit to this Committee if possible. Thank you in advance.

Étienne Niessner, Djerada, to Hélène Cazes Benatar, February 19, 1943, RG 68.115M, Reel 5, Private Collection Hélène Benatar (1936–1953), United States Holocaust Memorial Museum Archives, Washington, DC. Courtesy of Central Archives for the History of the Jewish People. Translated from French by Rebecca Glasberg.

74. A MOROCCAN JEWISH COMMUNITY SEEKS TO RESCUE JEWISH CHILDREN FROM OCCUPIED HUNGARY [1944]

Many of the sources in this book address events that unfolded in North Africa under Vichy French, Italian fascist, and Nazi occupation; this source, by contrast, explores the extent to which individuals and communities in North Africa were aware of the Nazi-directed genocide taking shape in Eastern Europe. The exchange concerns an attempt by the American Jewish Joint Distribution Committee and the Jewish community in Tangiers—which existed within the Spanish zone of Morocco during the Second World War—to obtain Spanish protection for at least five hundred Hungarian Jewish children and seventy Hungarian Jewish adults who were under temporary oversight of the Red Cross. The appeal took shape at the initiation of Renée Reichmann, a Hungarian Jewish refugee in Tangier, in March 1944, when the rapid genocide of Hungarian Jewry was well under way. (Although the Hungarian state had executed mass murder preceding Nazi German occupation, most notoriously in the Novi Sad massacre of 1942, with the installation of Nazi forces following March 1944 the situation continued to deteriorate for Jewish and vulnerable non-Jewish communities.) Despite the relentless thoroughness of the Nazi assault on Hungarian Jewry, German officials were determined to avoid alienating neutral and Allied nations such as Spain, and therefore allowed these countries to repatriate their foreign nationals from areas under German control. Selected Spanish and Portuguese representatives across Europe were heroic in working this loophole (at times against the explicit wishes of superiors at home), granting legal documents to Jews that allowed them to escape deportation and be repatriated instead to a country they had never lived in or visited. What is striking about this exchange is that a member of Tangier's Jewish community, herself a refugee from Hungary, knew enough about the timeline and nature of the Nazi assault on Hungarian Jewry to lobby her own community, heads of state, and multiple nongovernmental organizations in defense of the rescue effort. Tragically, the effort did not succeed. The Spanish government assented to the operation, but it appears from the source that the German Nazi government refused to grant exit visas. We can only assume that the Jewish children and adults targeted for rescue perished in Auschwitz along with the majority of Hungary's Jews.

Tangiers, May 30, 1944

Dear Mr. Childs,

I am enclosing herewith copies of the letters concerning the request of ten local Jews to the General of the Spanish zone asking for permission to allow 500 Jewish children to come to Tangier from Hungary.

The response of the General to Mr. Jacob Benmaman, a signer of the letter, and president of the Jewish Community in Tetuan is also included.

May I add, that this movement is being directed by Mrs. [Renée]

Reichman, a Hungarian refugee of Tangier, whose name does not appear because she herself is enjoying the hospitality of the city.

I will attempt to follow up on the matter and keep you informed concerning its status.

Sincerely yours,
Mordecai Kessler
delegate, American Joint Distribution Committee

Date: Sept. 5k [sic] 8 p.m., 1944

Following is our 3044 to Department, repeated to Tangier and Lisbon.

It is not clear from Dept.'s 2331 Aug. 24 to Lisbon whether War Refugee Board is interested in pursuing matter discussed in Dept.'s 2361 of Aug. 24 to Madrid. Pending clarification Embassy is taking no action. Spain's role in rescuing persecuted persons in German controlled territory has been changed considerably with the disappearance of a commong [sic] Spanish-German controlled frontier and related developments militarily. There would seem to be no need now for such persons to traverse Spanish territory.

Information from Intercross Budapest is that refusal of Germans to grant transit visas is holding up departure of 500 Jewish children and 70 adults accompanying them although Spanish visas have been granted. Foreign Office is endeavoring to obtain further information on this and the issuance of 1,500 other visas.

Hayes

September 21, 1944

My dear General Orgaz and distinguished friend:

Being fully aware of the deep humanitarian impulses of Your Excellency and appreciating the kind support which you have already accorded the appeals made to you on behalf of the Jewish refugee children in Hungary, I am writing to appeal for your further support in behalf of the 700 additional Jewish refugees who were the subject of a letter dated August 28, 1944, from the Jewish Community of Tangier. I do so not only in light of the kind consideration previously accorded me on this general subject, but also in view of the official instructions which I have had from my Government to do everything possible on behalf of the victims of oppression who are in imminent danger of death.

Although Your Excellency is no doubt already acquainted with the developments with respect to the 500 Jewish refugee children who have been the subject of discussion with you, it is desirable to inform you of the status of these according to information which the Legation has received. According to a telegram dated August 31, 1944, addressed by the International Red Cross at Budapest to the President of the local Jewish Community:

"Government authorized departure 500 children and 70 adults accompanying staff. Transit visas at present unobtainable. Gathering children in special camp under protection International Red Cross Committee around Spanish Legation here daily cost about 4,000 pengoes... Cable agreement..."

His Excellency
Lieutenant General Luiz Orgaz y Yoldi
High Commissariat of Spain in Morocco, Tetuan

In reply to this telegram the local Office of the Jewish Joint Distribution Committee cabled on September 3, 1944, agreeing to accept responsibility for this refugee group.

The local representative of the American Joint Distribution Committee has informed me that it is his belief that the 500 children and 70 adults will remain in Hungary under the protection of the Spanish Legation in Budapest pending the conclusion of hostilities when they will be free to resume their normal mode of living.

The interest which Your Excellency is now requested to take in extending protection to 700 additional persons will not involve, as I understand it, any actual removal of these persons from Hungary, but will mean merely that they will enjoy protection from the Spanish Government such as is afforded to the 500 children and 70 adults.

I feel confident, in view of our previous conversations and in view of your well known humanitarian ideals, that Your Excellency will do everything possible in behalf of these additional 700 persons. Any expenses incident to the further protection of these 700 persons will be borne by the agencies now occupying themselves with the 500 children and 70 adults in whose fate you have already taken so much interest.

Believe me, dear General Orgaz and distinguished friend, in the expression of my kind regards and highest consideration.

J. Rives Childs

Select correspondence pertaining to the rescue of Jewish children from Budapest, May–September 1944, RG 84, Records of the Foreign Service Posts of the Department of State, 1788–ca. 1991, US Legation, Tangier (1940–1954), Box 91, National Archives Record Administration, National Archives at College Park, MD.

75. DIRECTOR OF THE FREE FRENCH COLONIAL TROOPS RECOMMENDS DEPORTATION OF MIXED-RACE COUPLES TO MADAGASCAR [1945]

The French military—like French society writ large—had long maintained a racist and ambivalent stance toward its "colonial soldiers," the boys and young men conscripted from France's territories in North, West, and Central Africa and Indochina to serve under the French flag. The conscription of colonial soldiers by the French state dated to the mid-nineteenth century; by the era of the Second World War, the population of these infantrymen had swelled to nearly two hundred thousand, with many serving in pivotal front-line engagements and/or becoming German prisoners of war. The fact that the so-called colonial soldiers were more likely to be stationed on dangerous front lines was part and parcel of the state's disregard for their lives. Other sources in this volume speak to the harsher violence (including eugenicist medical experimentation) and more precarious conditions in forced labor camps that colonial prisoners of war experienced. Here, we learn that even after leaving the camps, French and other Allied forces were intent on erasing their contribution to the war effort. Specifically, with the explicit goal of whitening the so-called liberation of Paris in August 1944, French, British, and American commanders (including the highest-ranking officials, like de Gaulle) pushed Black troops to the background so that spectators would not know of their essential role in the Second World War. Simultaneously, the French war ministry mulled over the following proposal by the director of the Free French colonial troops, General François Ingold, who uses eugenicist notions to support his plan to deport all mixed-race couples of a Black colonial soldier and a white French wife to the colonies. For the director, like the top-level commanders who deliberately whitewashed the Allied victory, the bodies of interracial children and their parents were a threat to white supremacy. This proposal serves as a powerful reminder that the Second World War did not result in an unmitigated victory against racism and colonialism. Fascist and liberal forces alike shared a racist and colonial agenda that predated and endured after the war.

May 9, 1945
To: The Minister of the Colonies

A certain number of Colonial Natives have married French women during the occupation with or without the permission of their military chiefs. Still others have had children with French women and would like to marry the mothers. All of them request to be allowed to stay in France.

The Colonial Troops Administration has taken an intransigent position and has refused authorization for marriage as well as for continued residence in the Metropole [France] even in the case of married men.

We are faced with two possibilities, both of which have serious consequences:

Allowing native men married to European women to remain in Europe.

Sending European women married to native men to the Colonies.

We have to determine which solution has the most serious consequences.

Allowing native men married to European women to remain in Europe:

This solution is more serious. Indeed, its repercussions will be felt for centuries. Within one generation, a coupling of this sort will generally result in four new black offspring and, within two generations, sixteen new black offspring. One should only read the American studies on this subject. This is not a matter of treating the races unequally, but it is completely evident that the creation of a mixed race in France is undesirable for reasons of health, psychology, and prestige.

Sending European women married to native men to the Colonies:

This solution is less serious. As a matter of fact, it is serious only for a short while. Over time, this temporary problem turns into a true advantage for the colony through the support of mixed-race people who are well-adapted to the country. Understandably, administrators may be against this because they only see the temporary effects, namely the undeniable loss of prestige this solution entails. But a member of the colonial leadership has to see the broader framework and the future.

If we accept the principle of sending European women married to natives to the colonies, we certainly have to conduct deeper studies, for we cannot pursue this solution in its simplest form: natives returning to their homes with European wives. It might be possible to create some sort of colony, that would benefit from generous government support, in a particularly favorable region on the margins [of civilization], on the high plateaus of Madagascar, for example.

Under Louis XIV, five French women, married to white men, created the significant white population that today lives in La Réunion. In the same vein, one hundred French women married to native men could create a significant core of mixed-race [individuals] that would be invaluable for the future of the colony.

This problem is a very important one; we have to address it with firmness and without excessive sentimentality.

For the Minister and on his order:
General Ingold
Director of Colonial Troops

General François Ingold, Director of the Colonial Troops to the Minister of War, May 2, 1945, "Direction des Troupes Coloniales" (December 1943–December 1945), Service historique de la Défense, D, 6 P 6, Dossier 5. Translated by Rebecca Glasberg and Raffael Scheck.

76. A MEMORIAL TO THE "MARTYRS" OF TUNIS (1946)

Gaston Guez's Our Martyrs under the German Boot *closely resembles the Yiddish-language* yizker-bikher *(memory books) published after the Second World War to commemorate Jewish communities destroyed during the Holocaust in Poland and Eastern Europe. Guez, a mohel (one who performs ritual circumcisions) for the Tunisian Jewish community, intended his book to list those killed in the course of occupation and internment, to catalog the existence of forced labor camps in German-occupied Tunisia, and to detail the experiences of Tunisia's Jewish forced laborers. Even more, he imagined it as a kind of memorial of its own, a "living summary of life" that would honor not only the Tunisian Jewish community as a whole but more specifically Guez's brother Simon Chalom Guez, who died from injuries sustained during the Allied bombing of the El-Aouina air base near Tunis in early 1943. Guez opens his book with a dedication "in memory of the poor fallen martyrs," inviting readers to "pray for the peace of their souls" and concluding "Amen." He clarifies that he deliberately chose to write the majority of the book in Judeo-Arabic because his intended audience was, first and foremost, his community—the Jews of the ḥāra. These words of prayer, and the language Guez prioritizes, set his account off from so many other narrations of the Second World War, written by secular-minded authors and in Western European languages. This point is reinforced by the signature Guez affixed to his dedication: "F.H.G. Guez, mohel." In the following selection, we encounter two firsthand accounts of internment drawn from Guez's book—one by Guez himself, the other by a fellow prisoner, David-André Uzan.*

One time, our work consisted of each lifting an eighty- to hundred-kilogram piece of timber and transporting it five hundred meters. I made the effort for a first one, a second, and then a third; as for the fourth, I started to walk, but after ten meters I lost consciousness. I woke later in the infirmary, near the camp doctor who was giving me an injection. Incidentally, this brought about some dizzy spells and urinary troubles that required more leave.

Would you believe that I had the unpleasant surprise, following a serious visit to the medical center, to find myself ordered to take a rather long leave and prescribed strict bed rest, as it had become clear that my hemorrhagic nephritis had gotten worse?

The excess of zeal, jealousy, misunderstanding, deceit, and the sense of self-importance that enveloped certain civil servants at the barracks led one of them, motivated by an unknown force or unidentified reason, to confiscate my leave slip—or rather, to rip it from my hands—and to order me to immediately join the workers leaving for Mateur (an incident that occurred at my home while I was on bed rest)!

Understanding that trying to argue with such a brute would do nothing but waste my time and create bad blood, I took it upon myself to play hide and seek. You should know only that his goal was not met, and after my wife took certain steps, I received a second slip that clarified the following:

"The laborer Guez Fragi Gaston spent this afternoon at a follow-up inspection and was recognized as ill. His suspension from work was upheld, so there is no need to worry him."

Sadly, I was soon forced to get back on my feet in order to attend the funeral of my dear, poor brother Simon Chalom.

Guez, Gaston. "Résumé de ma captivité sous les allemands, étant travailleur juif à Gammarth, Grombalia, et El-Aouina." In *Nos martyrs sous la botte allemande: Où les ex-travailleurs juifs de Tunisie racontent leurs souffrances*, edited by Gaston Guez. Tunis: Presses typo-litho du journal "La Presse," 1946. Translated from French by Rebecca Glasberg.

In Djebebina

We have suffered no less than the other Jewish laborers, keeping in mind that it [Djebebina] was finally the last camp to which we had been moved after Mohamdia, Mograne, Pont du Fahs, Djouggar, Saouaf, Bir halim'a, Zachouan ... Djebebina.

I will never be able to detail the suffering endured since December 9 when we were rounded up, as each minute seemed years to us. That is to say, dear readers, that it would take me a whole book. But happily, I have the chance to speak about a man of exemplary courage and devotion, the charming Mr. Robert Bellaïche. The renowned M. Bellaïche was able to raise our spirits and encourage us with his pleasant speech.

Our company's state of mind was the most hopeless.

We were without Jewish leadership, without provisions, without news, with neither liaison nor contact with our families and friends.

Below, I will tell you about a work day in the camp.

Working under the Italian authority, which was more bearable than the German, protected by our friend Robert Bellaïche and inattentively supported (if at all) by our doctors, we started our labor at 4:00 a.m. To wake us up, the soldiers would hit the lot of us with their rifle butts. Only those who were sick (and God knows in what state), did not leave for work after presenting a pass obtained in exchange for myriad sacrifices.

How many bare feet, how many REAL invalids, were coerced into getting in line and leaving for work under the tremendous threat of the authorities and the cynical gaze of the camp doctor?

From there, you had to pass by the canteen to get your rations.

Many times, our friend Bellaïche was able to obtain a bit of relief for us in the realm of food provisions and leadership.

At its best, the menu was made up of ... a quarter of bread, approximately two hundred grams, and two scoops of jam. Keep in mind that it is only once one is able to have them that one can savor them.

Finally comes the moment of departure to a place unknown to us, for work.

From our arrival on the premises until noon, we fell trees, from noon to one we eat, starting at one, picks and shovels begin to gleam under the reflection of the beautiful sun, this protecting and beneficial sun during the glacial month of December, during this terrible month that we spent felling trees in the mountains.

At 6:00, work ends, return to the *gourbis*. Exhausted by fatigue, we arrive at our *gourbis* only around 9:00 p.m., with no desire to eat, as we would have to do so in complete darkness.

One hour later, the moaning would begin. At times the crying of parents thinking of their kids, at others the groaning of invalids, at others, cries of nervousness and distress, and finally the voice of the stubborn criticizing this thing or that, unhappy with such and such an event.

Could one call in "sick," even if the scenario is possible? No! It was something else that made you "sick and excused from work." You are not believed, even when speaking the truth, because the "truth" in the camps meant something other than the definition in the French dictionaries.

Perhaps I am insisting a bit on this point, but such is my intention as this was the reason for our greatest hopes and our greatest suffering.

Would you permit me to mention a troublesome memory in speaking to you about our dear, deceased friend André Assuied, who died under lax medical supervision due to the negligence of the camp doctors? ("Doctor"? What did that mean?)

Assuied suffered from a throat infection, a feverous infection that ate away at him. He died from it, abandoned and poorly tended, like a dog. I still see him, on a bit of straw, knees folded, wrapped up in his military greatcoat, panting.

Poor Assuied... poor martyr...

I can still see our friend Bellaïche with his black glasses arriving one morning to announce the sad news.

He came each morning to say hello, to fill us with courage and bring us pleasant news from Tunis. But that particular morning, with a pale face and a serious expression, he walked in silence to the middle of the *gourbi*: "Children," he said. "I have bad news to tell you. Our dear friend André Assuied has died."

Poor André Assuied, whom I had as a schoolmate. Full of action and courage, supported by his parents throughout the December 9 round up, on our path towards the unknown, he had distributed a number of supplies to those who did not have any, he had encouraged us as best he could. Very kind, and with a joke always at the ready, he amused us despite all our pain and our great despair. A charming boy who left much sorrow in his wake . . .

May God rest his soul.

Sometime after, Mr. Robert Bellaïche obtained quarantine . . . for the workers . . . under the pretense that typhus was threatening the camp.

After forty-five days of captivity, I was evacuated because I was sick. I was unaware of other developments. This did not prevent me from noting that, although rare, there are selfish people among us.

Uzan, David-André. "In Djebebina." In *Nos martyrs sous la botte allemande: Où les ex-travailleurs juifs de Tunisie racontent leurs souffrances*, edited by Gaston Guez. Tunis: Presses typo-litho du journal "La Presse," 1946. Translated from French by Rebecca Glasberg.

77. A YOM KIPPUR PRAYER FOR TUNISIAN VICTIMS OF THE THIRD REICH (1946)

The Ashkava is a centuries-old memorial prayer traditionally recited at burials and in the Yizkhor memorial service on Yom Kippur, the holiest day of the Jewish calendar, which is devoted to atonement, confession, and fasting. The following Tunisian Ashkava, written in the postwar period, customizes the prayer to honor Tunisian Jewish victims of Nazi terror. Still today, the prayer is offered by Tunisian Jews during the Yom Kippur memorial service of Yizkhor. The lament provides evidence of the myriad forms North African Jewish Holocaust memory and memorialization have assumed in the postwar era—here, in a religious and intimate vein.

Memorial Prayer

To be read every evening of Yom Kippur in memory of our laborers, who died as martyrs at the hands of the Germans.

But wisdom, where shall it be found? And where is the place of understanding? [Job 28:12]. Happy is the man who finds wisdom, and the man who obtains understanding [Proverbs 3:13]. How great is Your goodness, which You have reserved for those who fear You, which You have wrought for them who trust in You, before the eyes of the sons of men! [Psalm 31:20]. How precious is Your benevolence, oh God, and the children of men take refuge in the shadow of Your wings. They are abundantly satisfied with the riches of Your house; and you let them drink from the stream of Your delights

[Psalm 36:8–11]. A good name is better than precious oil; and the day of death is better than the day of one's birth [Ecclesiastes 7:1]. The end of the matter, after all has been heard is to fear God and keep His commandments, for this is the whole duty of man [Ecclesiastes 12:13]. Let the pious exult in glory; let them sing for joy upon lying down in their beds [Psalm 149:5].

May the rest established in the heavenly dwelling, under the wings of the holy presence, in the ascendance of those holy and pure, that shine and are radiant as the radiance of the heavens, a renewal of strength, a forgiveness sins, a removal of transgressions, a drawing near of salvation, compassion and mercy, from he who dwells there, and a good lot in life in the world to come, and the resting place of the souls of the deceased brothers.

These are the good names of the deceased young men who passed: Rabbi Haïm (Victor) Nataf; also the souls of Simon Chalom Guez, Isaac Gozlan, Lili (Émile) Hababou, Mordékhaï (Gilbert) Mazouz, Eliaou (Elie) Saâdoun, Haïm (Victor) Lelouche, Yacoub (Kiki) Attal, Edmond Azria, Abraham (Robert) Amran, Yéchoua (Sauveur) Assous, Fraji (Gaston) Bokobsa, Itshak (Jacques Kakou) Cohen, Simon Cohen, Aaron (Henri) Cohen, Yossef (Joseph) Chelly, Aaron (Henri) Darmouni, Abraham (Albert) Fitoussi, Khamous Guetta, Haï Victor Guez, Abraham (Albert) Guez, Saloman Houri, Mordékhaï (Mardochée) Hacoun, David (André) Haddad, Meyer (Emile) Jaoui, Itshak (Jacques) Meimoun, Yossef (André) Naccache, Abraham (Albert) Slama, David Smadja, Yossef (André) Suied, Nessim (Ernest) Sâada, Abraham (Albert) Tibi, Moché (Maurice) Kalfon, David (Edouard) Zeitoun, Nessim (Simon) Allali, Abraham (Robert) Cohen, Moché (Maurice) Kharoubi, Acher (Gino) Uzan, Haï (André) Naccache, Moïse Sberro, Elie Dadi, Yossef Sâada, Elie (Lucien) Bokobsa, Albert de Aaron Temam.

May the spirit of God guide us into the Garden of Eden, he who departed from this world according to the will of God, the Lord of heaven and earth. May the supreme King of Kings in his infinite mercy, have compassion on him. May the supreme King of Kings cover him in the shade of his wings, and in the secret place of his tabernacle, to behold the graciousness of God and to visit early in his temple [Psalm 27:4]. May he raise him at the end of his days and cause him to drink of the stream of his delights. May he cause his soul to be bound up in the bond of life, and his rest to be honorable. May God be his inheritance and bring him peace, and may his rest be in peace, as it is written, "He enters into peace, they rest in their beds, each one that walks in his uprightness" [Isaiah 57:2]. May he and all the people of Israel who lie in the dust, be included in compassion and forgiveness. So may it be God's will and let us say amen.

The End.

"Achcava." *Nos martyrs sous la botte allemande: Où Les ex-travailleurs juifs de Tunisie racontent leurs souffrances*, edited by Gaston Guez. Tunis: Presses typo-litho du journal "La Presse," 1946. Translated from Hebrew by Rachel Smith.

78. THE LONG SHADOW OF COLONIALISM— SEEKING LEGAL RIGHTS IN THE SAHARA [1948]

It took a controversial year after the Allied occupation of North Africa for the French state to revoke the Vichy state's abrogation of the Crémieux Decree, the nineteenth-century law that granted French citizenship to Jews of Algeria's northern departments. The relevant law, passed in October 1943, applied to Jews of Algeria's northern and Muslim benefactors of French citizenship. The legal, civil status of Algerian Muslims and Jews born in the southern territories, however, remained unchanged by the 1943 legislation because the Crémieux Decree had never extended to Algeria's south. As they possessed no prior French naturalization, the Jews of southern Algeria had no French citizenship to be restored by the state. Indeed, at the war's end, the ascendant French Fourth Republic fortified the legal distinctions between Algerian and European French territory, on the one hand, and Muslim subjects of France from Algeria and French citizens, on the other hand. These legislative shifts granted neither Algerian Muslims nor southern Algerian Jews common civil status, such as was held by non-Muslim French citizens, including northern Algerian Jews. This distinction was reaffirmed in 1947, when male Algerians were divided into two electoral colleges designed to protect the dominance of citizens with common civil status. The first college was reserved for Europeans, northern Algerian Jews, and a token number of Muslims with French citizenship; the second was available to the vast majority of Algerian Muslims and Jews from Algeria's south. In the letter that follows, 125 Jewish men from the town of Ghardaïa, in southern Algeria's Mzab Valley, demand to be classified as French citizens with common civil status, like their coreligionists in the north. The petitioners' appeal was denied, as legal distinctions born of racialized imaginaries of the colonial order persisted into the second half of the twentieth century.

March 26, 1948

Represented by the Rabbi Jacob Ben Meyer Partouche, Vice President of the Consistory of Ghardaia

Mr. Governor-General [of Algeria],

We the undersigned, native Israelites of the Mzab currently residing there, hereby give full authority to Rabbi Jacob Meyer Partouche, Vice President of the Consistory of the Mzab community in Ghardaia, to serve as our representative before your lofty authority.

We hereby ask you, in your great benevolence, to grant us full naturalization to French citizenship for all of us, as well as for our families.

In hopes of a favorable response,

Sincerely,

125 Jewish heads of households.

Petition of March 26, 1948, 10H/47, "Statut des Israélites du Mzab, 1952," Les Archives nationales d'outre-mer, Aix-en-Provence, France. Translated from French by Amber Sackett.

79. A LIBYAN JEWISH RABBINICAL STUDENT TRIES TO EMIGRATE TO PALESTINE (1949)

A native of Tripoli, Mosé Habib was seventeen years old when he sought the assistance of the International Refugee Organization (IRO, subsequently renamed the International Tracing Bureau) in the spring of 1949. Two years earlier, the IRO had been vested with the task of tracing civilian survivors of Second World War concentration camps and labor detachments, inheriting the job from the United Nations Relief and Rehabilitation Administration's Central Tracing Bureau. Habib's petition describes an adolescence pocked by war. A Jewish Italian subject, Habib's education in an Italian high school was cut short by the introduction of fascist Italian race laws. To avoid the reach of these laws and the threat of internment or deportation, Habib, his eight siblings, and his parents fled to Gharyan, a city eighty kilometers south of Tripoli, where they lived (in his words) "in hiding" until Tripoli fell to British rule in the late summer of 1943. Habib's father died in Gharyan and his mother soon after, leaving the young man head of a prodigious household. For three years, Habib worked as a mechanic to support his family. He then resumed his education in a British school in Tripoli and then a rabbinical school in Rome. The immediate postwar years were painful for the Libyan Jewish community. Between 1945 and 1948, Muslim Libyans initiated a wave of anti-Semitic violence against Tripoli's Jews—whom they paradoxically identified with their European occupiers—and the British occupying forces did little to protect the victims. Libya's Jews began to emigrate in ever-greater numbers to Palestine, Habib's eldest brother among them. When Mosé Habib approached the IRO for assistance, it was with the intention of doing the same with his remaining brothers and sisters. (By the time of his appeal, the state of Israel had existed for fully a year, but still the IRO representative recorded that Habib wished to emigrate to "Palestine," because the applicant chose the term or the bureaucrat did.) Strikingly, the IRO determined Habib's case to be outside its purview, Habib being (in the IRO's eyes) neither a displaced person nor a refugee. The organization's rigid definition failed to appreciate that these terms had distinct histories, timelines, and definitions when it came to North African Jews.

Application for IRO Assistance

1. Family Name in block capitals: HABIB
2. Other spellings or aliases by which family is known: none
3. RELIGION: *Check with an "X"*
    a. Roman Catholic _____
    b. Protestant _____
    c. Orthodox _____
    d. Jewish ____X____
    e. Other (specify) _____ None _____ None reported __
4. Date of Completion of Form CM/1: 27.5.49
5. MARITAL STATUS: *Check one with an "X"*
    a. Married _____
    b. Single ____X____
    c. Separated _____
    d. Divorced _____
    e. Widowed _____
    f. Unaccompanied child _____

...

6. a) Country of Citizenship: Libia (Arabian)
    a. *Check one with an "X"*
        i. Claimed _____
        ii. Former _____

iii. Established _____X_____
iv. Presumed
b. Country of last habitual residence prior to displacement: Libia
c. Ethnic or National group such as Ukrainian, Jewish, Volksdeutsche, etc.: Arabain-Jewish [sic]
d. NANSEN [STATELESS PERSONS] STATUS: *Check one* Yes ____ No __X__

8. Names of all members of family living together
   a. Man: Mosè
   b. Male of female: M
   c. Relationship to head: head
   d. Date of birth, Day, Month, Year: 19.8.31
   e. Country of citizenship: Libia
   f. Check one: C ____ E ____ X __ F ____ LR ____
      i. Abbreviations: C = claimed/ E = established / F = former / LR = last habitual residence prior to displacement
   g. Town, province, and country of birth: Tripoli, Libia
9. Other members of family living with applicant: None
10. PLACES OF RESIDENCE FOR LAST 12 YEARS (account for entire period and all members of family)
    a. 1938 Oct. [19]47: Tripoli, Giama Mahmud II. N. 17., Libia
    b. May [19]49: Rome, via Cesare Balbo, N. 33
11. employment FOR LAST 12 YEARS, INCLUDING PRESENT (account for entire period for any member who is or has been employed)
    a. 1938–40: pupil, Italian school, Tripoli
       i. Reason for change: because of war school got closed and applicant escaped to avoid fascist
    b. [19]43: in hiding, Garian (by Tripoli)
       i. Reason for change: British occup[ation]
    c. Oct. [19]44: with family, Tripoli
       i. Reason for change: end of war
    d. Oct. [19]47: student school, under Brit[ish] control, Tripoli
       i. Reason for change: to emigrate
    e. May [19]49: student, Rabin school, Rome

    f. Present Wages: none
12. Education (for all members of family of school age or older)
    a. 1938–1940: Elementary school, Tripoli
    b. 1944–1947: [Elementary] & Secondary [school], Tripoli
13. languages (for all members not infants)
    a. Arabian: speak, read and write fluently
    b. Hebrew: speak, read, and write fluently
    c. Italian: speak, read, and write fluently
14. FINANCIAL resources (for all members who have any present re sources): None
15. RELATIVES (any who are closely related or with whom family wishes to be reunited; list *all* relatives of unaccompanied child)
    a. Habib Gina: sister, Tripoli, Gianna Mahmud, N. 17
    b. Viola, Margaret, Liliana: sisters [same address as above]
    c. Habib Saul: brother, Tel Aviv, Israel, str. Hayaroon N. 91
    d. prospective employers or friends who might be of assistance to applicant (Names and addresses): None
16. ASSISTANCE (Including care and maintenance in assembly centre)
    a. ...
    b. If assistance has been received, number of months: None
    c. ...
17. DOCUMENTS (list all in family's possession including birth and marriage certificates, passports, identity, employment, ration cards, affidavits, statements or witnesses, etc.)
    a. Laissez passer N. 10415
      i. Date 27.9.43
      ii. Place of Issue: Rome
      iii. By whom issued: Ministry of Africa Italiana
    b. Temporary travel docum[ent] 8417
      i. Date: 16.10.47
      ii. Place of Issue: Tripoli
      iii. By whom issued: Brit[ish] Milit[ary] Admin[istration] in Tripoli
    c. Extension of travel docum[ent] P2/2448/21
      i. Date: 16.9.48

  ii. Place of Issue: Rome
  iii. By whom issued: until 17.1.49; W.A. Anderson by Brit[ish] Embassy

18. ORGANIZATIONS OF WHICH MEMBERS OF FAMILY HAVE BEEN MEMBERS (political, religious, social, pre-war and post-war): None

19. present address of family:
  a. Date: May [19]49
  b. Street address or name of camp: via Cesare Balbo, N. 33, Rabbin College, tel. 43927
  c. Town or city: Rome
  d. Country: Italy

...

20. REMARKS USE FOR ANY ADDITIONAL INFORMATION:

Applicant has never been registered with IRO before. Wishes to emigrate to PALESTINE (has brother there).

Wishes O.C.C. and travel expenses.

Profession: Student (*Rabbin* [Rabbinical] school). Brother in Palestine wrote him to come.

References: Rector of *rabbin* college (via Cesare Balbo, N. 33).

Received on 27.5.49. Registertion [*sic*] certificate N. 5331.

...

Activities and position held from beginning of the war until arrival in Italy. Give dates and places:

Applicant born in Tripoli as Arabian, Italian subj[ect] like his parents where in 1911 the Italians occupied Libia [*sic*]. Before Italian occupation there were the Turks and applic[ant]'s parents were Turkis[h] subj[ect].

Applic[ant] in

1938 attended Italian school. He lived with father and mother and 9 brothers.

June 1940 When War broke out, the schools got closed an[d] applic[ant] with whole family escaped from Tripoli to Garian Village (100 km from Tripoli) for racial reasons, when racial law was issued under Fascism.

Aug. 1943 When British troops occupied Tripoli, applic[ant] with family returned to Tripoli, previous address. In this year also mother died.

1944 Applic[ant] to help mother worked as mechanic, until

1946 When he returned to school (English, French, Hebrew, Arabian languages) In this year the elder brother (Saul) escaped to Palestine but reached it only one year later, as got caught and sent to Cyprus, from where escaped again and reached Palestine in 1948.[1]

Oct. [19]47 Came to Italy with regular laissez-passer with the pretext to study in Italy, but the very reason was to emigrate to Palestine. He could not do it directly from Tripoli. When reached Italy he preferred to stay here and attend school and wait until could go regularly, as refugee, not to meet same troubles as brother, who finished in Cyprus island for more than a year. Now that got news from brother from Tel Aviv, that is waiting for applicant, he referred to IRO to get registered and leave with regular transport. Is without means and wishes also travel expenses.

...

What organization did you belong to? None

When, why and how did you leave our home? Applicant left Tripoli in Oct. [19]47 with the intention to emigrate to Palestine as elder brother did. He came first to Italy with Brit[ish] laissez-passer as could not emigrate directly from Tripoli.

Do you want to return there? No

      a. Willing to be repatriated __No__

      b. Undecided _____

      c. Determined against repatriation __Yes__

If not, why? First of all, all my brothers and sisters will emigrate to Palestine, it is only question of time. I wish to stay in Palestine, I consider [it] my country. I don't know why we have to stay under foreign dominium when there is a State for the Jews.

In what country do you wish to settle permanently? Palestine

CLASSIFICATION

By interrogator: Eligible _____ Ineligible _____

Reasons for suggested classification: Story true-sounding, but seems more an emigrant than refugee.

Signature of Interrogator: [signature] MORINI

Comments by the supervising officer: [stamp] NOT WITHIN THE MANDATE OF IRO

---

1. Habib's brother's time in Cyprus was likely in one of a dozen internment camps run by the British government designed to intern roughly fifty thousand Jews who had immigrated or sought to immigrate to Mandatory Palestine in violation of British policy.

Not a Refugee or DP [Displaced Person]—not within the mandate of IRO—not eligible for any services.

Mosé Habib, CM/1 files from Italy A-Z, Reference Code 03020102 oS/ITS Digital Archive, Arolsen Archives, Bad Arolsen, Germany.

80. BEARING A "WEIRD" TATTOO—A SURVIVOR OF THE NAZI CAMPS RETURNS TO TLEMCEN {1950}

We have already encountered the extraordinary wartime journeys of Gabriel Bénichou, a young Jewish man from Tlemcen who fled Vichy restrictions in Algeria for Marseilles, was deported by the Nazis and French police to the Drancy internment camp and thence to Auschwitz, where he was subjected to forced labor. Bénichou was compelled to assist with the erasure of the Warsaw ghetto (after its violent destruction by German troops) and was driven northward, toward Germany, as part of a ruthless death march. Here, in his recently released memoir, we read of Bénichou's return to his native city after the war's end. The account is a rare one, as so few Jews from North Africa were deported to the Nazi death camps, let alone returned to their home after the war. (Larger numbers of North African Jews living in France were deported to Drancy and the death camps.) In this painful selection, Bénichou recounts his disorienting return: the joy surrounding his reunion with family and friends; his post-traumatic stress (then not a medical category) that manifested in anorexia, avoidance, nightmares, and anxiety; the inability of others to accept or absorb the nature of his trauma; and his attempts to return to something resembling a normal life. While the account bears some resemblance to the memoirs written by European Jewish survivors of the Nazi death camps, the fact that Bénichou's experiences played out in Algeria, isolated from other survivors, renders it staggeringly unique.

The House

Peace, Serenity, the Calm after the Storm

Lyon-Bron military airport. Instead of bombs, we eight or ten repatriates board the bomber towards an unknown destination in North Africa. We should land in either Tunis, Algiers, or Oran. As I don't know anyone in any of these cities, David gave me the address of an old friend in Oran and [the address of] a war buddy in Algiers with whom he had fought in the war, and who had been discharged due to age. As for Tunis, I had the address of Jules's relatives.

The bomb bay had been fitted out: [there were] two benches along the fuselage for passengers to sit, and the flaps through which bombs used to be dropped were half-opened so that we wouldn't be in the dark. During the journey, the copilot opens the shutters below us a bit wider and asks us whether we think we see the sea or the clouds. The question is written down on a piece of slate since we can't hear each other. We are clinging to our benches because below us, there is only emptiness, and our legs are floating in the air. It was only much later, when I traveled by plane, that I found out that what we were seeing were clouds.

We landed in Algiers. Mister El Kouby, Boulevard Bugeaud, was the Algiers address. I get dropped off not very far with my stuff. I had brought back a big burlap bag, a bit like a flour sack but much larger, with an eagle sitting atop a big swastika stamped on each side. I had stuffed everything in it: clothes, food, shoes, everything I gathered during my stay in Paris. It was full, virtually as tall as me, tied at the end, I carried it on my shoulders.

It must have been around 1:00 or 2:00 p.m. The address was that of a store, with a door and a window, below which was a sort of stone bench, where I sat to wait. Around 3:00 p.m. the store was opened by an employee, "Salah," who told me that the owners lived just at the corner of rue Mac Mahon on the sixth floor. I didn't find anyone, so I sat in the stairs in front of the door to wait. Once they arrived, they were greatly surprised because they didn't expect to find this kid on his way back from the war at their doorstep.

I was dressed in Tyrol pants, authentic ones that I got in Munich when I bartered a bike for a wheel of parmesan cheese. The guy from Munich offered me one of his pairs of pants before I left. I had a fairly lightweight yellow jacket that I had gotten in Dachau when they allowed us to access the clothing stores right before we were evacuated. And on my head, I was wearing the striped cap that I had kept. Gabriel takes care of me and indicates me where to go in order to get a place in the train going to Tlemcen. I hadn't decided to leave immediately. I wanted to stay a few days to visit Algiers, but he almost forced me to leave, and so I went to see the local army officer to get a ticket. Our conversation was rather surprising. I showed him my repatriation ID with my destination. Despite the transportation shortage and the large number of travelers, I had priority.

"For what reason do you possess this repatriation ID?"
"I was deported."
"But what is this, it's not military?"
"It's like for prisoners of war."
"Then you are entitled [to a ticket], what is your identification number?"
"I don't have one. I wasn't in the army."
"If you don't have one, then you are not eligible for [a ticket]."

The discussion, which lasted a quarter of an hour, consisted of us repeatedly telling one another that, as a prisoner of war, I was qualified for a ticket, but not being a military, I was not allowed one. As far as deportees were concerned, he hadn't the slightest idea. Finally, I gave him my Auschwitz number, which he ended up accepting before giving me a requisition voucher for the train to Tlemcen. This surprised me at first, then it really sunk in. How was it possible that a rather high-ranking military officer, in charge of the Place d'Alger, didn't know what a deportee was? (I had gotten through as a prisoner of war.) I have often thought back on this. If an officer whose profession is war is unaware of such an important fact, it is no surprise that the civilians living in Algeria were particularly ill informed of the horrors of the concentration camps and of what the Jews have been through. . . .

The train is crowded. There are no free seats, and with my swastika-bearing burlap bag, I settle down in the corridor and sleep. Passengers step over or walk on me, I don't move or even react. The trip from Algiers to Oran lasts all night, and that of Oran to Tlemcen lasts the following morning. Despite the Algerians' lack of knowledge about the war, there was a "patriot" who denounced me to the train chief because of my bag with a swastika. This was solved quickly. My casual manner and the way I dismissed them cut short their suspicions.

There was a great commotion in Tlemcen's train station. They were all there waiting for me, kissing me. It was my aunt Rica who first noticed my tattoo while I had my arms around my mom's neck. She was surprised to see such a thing. . . . I took a shower and here I am within the family, as if I have not left at all.

Life Starts Again

What Is Freedom? What Is Life?

. . . After the war that had wreaked such havoc, and in which everyone had suffered and had been frustrated, each person believed they had it worse than everyone else. Life conditions being normalized gradually, the past had to be dealt with. For us, who had rubbed shoulders with death, all these efforts were superficial. We were subconsciously still in hell.

Expressing my parents' concern and attention is hard; to say that they were attentive to my every need is an understatement. I was seeing my relatives and friends again; everyone was happy to see me, yet I wasn't living in the real world. . . .

We were in the midst of the summer, on holiday, and were only thinking about having fun, going out, and joking around. One day, I wore my Tyrol pants (those that had been given to me by the man from Munich), put a feather in my hat, and went for a walk with friends on rue de France, the main thoroughfare where we used to stroll every evening. We laughed a lot and this did not go unnoticed. The day after, my aunt, my mom's sister, came to visit and asked me "Why did you do that?" as if I had done something foolish. A few days later, she told me, "It seems that they beat you." This simple and innocent question provoked a strong internal reaction in me. . . . I contained myself and replied "Not at all!" but I was deeply annoyed. For me, the question was so ridiculous that it didn't even merit an answer.

And to say that we were beaten to death would have seemed so enormous and implausible that it would have only made them doubt me more. Whereas in my mind, the blows we received were permanent, beaten for not working fast enough, beaten for having tried to swipe a piece of bread, beaten for not having seen or not having stood at attention in front of a SS [officer], beaten because a *Kapo* was in a bad mood, beaten for having moved during roll call. For me, such a question was an affront, an insult to our suffering, our memory, and our feelings.

Multiple small moments like this were the reason I have spoken less and less about that time. For a long time, I didn't say anything; I did not discuss it, I trapped myself in my past. Obviously, whatever I would have said would have been so implausible, so monstrous, that no one would have believed me. Even when I mentioned what I considered something trivial, but which was terrible for them, certain people would consider me a braggart who was showing off. This demoralized me so much that I would immediately stop. There were also those who thought that war is a terrible thing that leaves lasting damage and that I wasn't quite right in the head.

And [there were] those who were scared to bother me with questions that would make me relive bad moments, those who were sick of the war and wanted to be done with this nightmare, stop talking about it, and avoid being killjoys like the veterans of the First World War. Not to mention that I had come back in one piece and seemingly in good health, while there were combatants who had returned wounded. I'd add that my appearance didn't inspire pity; I hadn't stopped eating since [my] liberation, [and I was eating] much more than usual. Which means that when I arrived to Tlemcen, I wasn't skinny, but rather slightly plump. So, I decided to be quiet.

Life in Tlemcen resumed its [normal] course, my parents didn't know what to do to make me happy. Friends came to see me, and we had fun as best we could. Despite the restrictions, food was abundant and we had a wine cellar that I visited copiously. I would drink almost an entire bottle a meal and would nap until almost four in the afternoon. I used to fall asleep quickly because of the heat. I went to see a doctor, Dr. Ayache, who gave out disability claim certificates that allowed veterans to have double rations. Food supply cards were still used at that time. He was very friendly, and didn't even want to make me pay for the visits, since he had been in the war and understood the suffering of others. Nevertheless, when I was in Paris a few years later, I wrote to him to ask for a copy of the disability claim certificate. He refused, on the pretext that he didn't give out sympathy certificates. So, I never received my convalescence pay.

With the coming of October, I decided to return to school, not without difficulty because I had forgotten everything during the turmoil. I no longer knew how to read or write, so I started [to work on this] seriously before school started again. I thought that I would be in eleventh grade, so as not to lose a year, but the principal was not of the same opinion. He needed proof of my schooling. We wrote to the Lycée Saint Charles in Marseille, which immediately sent a certificate confirming I had completed tenth grade. This was not enough for the principal; he wanted to test my abilities with an exam. Naturally, I was in no shape to take an exam. I had forgotten everything. And so it was only the certificate from the Lycée Saint Charles that confirmed that I was enrolled in eleventh grade and that I was supposed to continue my schooling, that allowed me to enter eleventh grade at the school in Tlemcen.

I started studying intensely. It was a haven for me, an evasion from the life of freedom that hadn't brought me the answers to captivity or the satisfaction of being free, or any other impression I didn't achieve in myself. . . . I shut myself away and took refuge in my studies, except for Saturday. [On this] holiday, the day of rest, I had to vacate the large dining room, which I had requisitioned as my office during the week, so that it could once again serve as a dining room on festive days.

As a veteran, I was allowed special privileges, and I took both of my baccalaureate [exams] in the same year. [I took] the first exam in February and the second in June, but I only earned a passing score on the second one in October.... During my schooling, I had learned English as my modern language, but I had forgotten everything and it was too complicated to pick it back up. However, I was fluent in German, so I had a few lessons in grammar and syntax. That is how, during the German exam, I had a really easy time translating into French, and I quickly wrote out the text that we were given.... German, which I had learned in insane conditions, came in very handy at this time.

On the surface, I had a normal life, that of a young man of my age who went to school, spent time with friends, and tried to flirt with girls. Nevertheless, I had nightmares every night. I was running away from the Nazis, and I managed to escape and hide in incredible situations. Fortunately, I pulled through. Sometimes I had other dreams, but always of the same kind.

In addition, sometimes I would act in a certain, seemingly bizarre way. [My behavior] was explained by the fact that this experience had forced me to grow up while I was still a child; in fact, I had been robbed of my adolescence. This is why I could hardly stand certain rules at school....

Likewise, after the first baccalaureate [exam], I butted heads with almost all of the teachers and the principal who were trying to make me take philosophy when I wanted to take math. I was called down for a quiz in which all the math teachers who were present tried to prove to me that I wasn't good enough in this subject. This was a trying experience; I was called to the principal's office every day, as he wanted to prove to me that I'd made a mistake, but knowing that they could not force me [to take philosophy], and that the exams took place in Oran, not Tlemcen, I refused to give in and remained in math. Yet again, I believe that I was mature enough to do what seemed right for me, and to resist giving into rules that I didn't agree with....

And then, I lost my appetite. I was eating barely anything. Despite the restrictions, almost every lunch my mother served me a huge steak that my father bought on the black-market. However, seeing this meat made me sick to my stomach. My mom begged me to eat at least half of it, but to no avail.

I started to lose weight, but this only really became apparent a bit later, once I had become nothing more than the shadow of a human being. One day, I received a letter from my friend George Chebbat, who told me that he had found the SS commanding officer of the Marseille prison, the one we had nicknamed "Sacsac." He was in Alsace now, a colonel in the French army, and George was asking for my testimony in order to put an end to such an aberration. Having lost all contact with everything related to that awful period, being in conditions that were very far away from all that, and maybe because of my personality, I didn't answer. Sometime later, I received an incendiary letter, filled with insults and criticism; I was embarrassed by my [earlier] attitude, so I responded eagerly.

On the surface, I led a normal life, both in the eyes of others as well my own. But I worked a lot, I ate less and less, and every night I went back to Auschwitz or had similar nightmares. However, in my nightmares, I always escaped at the last moment....

I kept losing weight. I consulted professors at the medical school, I had treatments, particularly oil injections. I was injecting myself in the thigh, but unsuccessfully. I wasn't feeling weak, quite the opposite, I was rather strong. I could even say that I was in good shape. But I was losing weight. I had become the walking dead. I was forcing myself to eat but was quickly full. When we went to the beach, I didn't dare to wear a swimsuit, since I was nothing but skin and bones. So, I always kept my shirt on. Not to mention that my tattoo provoked many unsolicited comments, some of them weird or nasty. In an attempt to make a joke, a rather nice girl once asked me if it was my phone number that I had tattooed on my arm. I was already used to people not knowing about what had happened, so I didn't answer. My shirt would ward off further stupid comments.

Bénichou, Gabriel. *L'adolescence d'un juif d'Algérie: Récit autobiographique.* Collection Graveurs de mémoire. Paris: L'Harmattan, 2004. Selection from pages 127–37, 164. Translated from French by Rebecca Glasberg and Jessie Stoolman.

Acknowledgments

We wrote this book to fill a void. To date, there has existed no sourcebook in English that explores the impact of the Second World War on the people, cultures, and landscape of North Africa. It is our hope that with this volume, this complex topic will be opened up to scholars, students, and general readers.

This book exists as a complement to our coedited volume *Holocaust and North Africa* (Stanford University Press, with the cooperation of the United States Holocaust Memorial Museum, 2018), and we remain inspired by the brilliant contributors to that volume.

Wartime North Africa was born out of casual conversation during a graduate seminar at the University of California, Los Angeles, between us and a number of students who later became directly involved in this volume's production. This book—and more generally, our intellectual drive, curiosity, and growth—owes much to our partnership with these students, and our first debt of thanks is to them.

One budding scholar in particular was at the forefront of this monumental project. Rebecca Glasberg anchored our research process with skillful, meticulous, lightning-fast efficiency. Not only was she primary translator of our sources; she also managed the project from its outset: organizing a complex system of files, overseeing the preparation of hundreds of emails to individuals and institutions in French and English, securing permissions to publish primary sources from institutional and family archives, partnering with us in the editing process—in general, keeping us and this project moving forward at a regular hum. We are so grateful to her.

We also owe a debt of thanks to our graduate student Jessie Stoolman, who served as a translator, research assistant, and wise editor of our introductory materials. Jessie's keen knowledge of the intricacies of the political and cultural landscape of North Africa, combined with her hallmark critical acumen, enriched our writing to no end.

Thanks are also owed to our other translators, including Rachel Smith, Amber Sackett, and Ben Ratskoff. These UCLA graduate students (along with Rebecca and Jessie) spent hours ably poring over original sources from French, Arabic, Hebrew, and Yiddish and translating them into English.

The monumental task of creating an English-language canon of primary sources on wartime North Africa would not have been accomplished without the incalculable patience, guidance, and assistance of many students, colleagues, and friends across the globe. We are fortunate to be part of a generous community of scholars willing to share knowledge, contacts, and archival fruits, and throughout our research journey, we benefited from their collegiality and friendship.

Susan Gilson Miller, Chris Silver, and Jürgen Matthäus generously took part in a manuscript review process, offering all measure of erudite suggestions and saving us from embarrassing errors and omissions. At every stage of book research and writing, Daniel Schroeter contributed to the improvement of the manuscript.

We are additionally indebted to Jamaâ Baida, Khalid Ben-Srhir, Lia Brozgal, Joseph Chetrit, Alioune Deme, Brahim El Guabli, Ruth Ginio, Harvey Goldberg, Emily B. Gottreich, Mohammed Hatimi, Laurie Kain Hart, Alma Rachel Heckman, Magueye Kasse, Ethan Katz, Habib Kazdaghli, Mohammed Kenbib, Jessica Marglin, Susan Gilson Miller, Thomas Park, Haim Saadoun, Robert Satloff, Raffael Scheck, Susan Slyomovics, Lior Sternfeld, and Orit Yekutieli.

At UCLA, we are thankful for the support of our colleagues Ali Behdad, Philippe Bourgois, Lia Brozgal, David Myers, Todd Presner, Michael Rothberg, Susan Slyomovics, and Jason Throop. Our warmest appreciation goes to the staff of the Center for Jewish Studies, who always make us look better and more polished than we are: Reina Chung, Vivian Holenbeck, Caroline Luce, Chelsea White, and David Wu. Sarah owes an enormous debt to the fabulous team at UCLA's Department of History, and Aomar to the staff at UCLA's Department of Anthropology.

This project would not have seen the light of day without the support of a global array of community members who helped us acquire, decipher, and interpret rare and difficult documents. In particular, we thank Abderrahman Aouad, Rabbi Joshua Bittan, David Bensimon, Sidney Chriqui, Sidney Corcos, Al-Husin Al-Gedari, and Driss El Yazami, as well as the many friends mentioned by name in the paragraphs that follow.

Many archives, libraries, publishing houses, and holders of private papers granted us permission to translate and publish materials featured in this volume. Special thanks to the library and archives of the Alliance Israélite Universelle, especially Director Jean-Claude Kuperminc; the Archives du Maroc; and Yad Vashem for their help securing documents.

This book, as well as our first coedited volume, was published in partnership with the United States Holocaust Memorial Museum, where both of us have spent countless hours conducting research and engaging with colleagues. We owe an enormous debt of thanks to this institution and its staff, especially Suzanne Brown-Fleming, Robert Ehrenreich, Krista Hegburg, Lisa Leff, and Leah Wolfson.

Bill Nelson once again left an indelible mark on our scholarship by producing elegant maps, and Nancy Zibman a most thorough index. Terry and Marilyn Diamond provided us generous financial support to defray the cost of rights and permissions.

The project would not have been possible without the generous support of UCLA, including the Maurice Amado Chair in Sephardic Studies, the Viterbi Family Chair in Mediterranean Jewish Studies, and the Alan D. Leve Center for Jewish Studies. Support also came from a Faculty Research Grant from the Academic Senate.

We are endlessly in awe of Kate Wahl, our editor at Stanford University Press, who has offered unlimited guidance through the many stages of book writing. Thanks, too, to the press's anonymous reviewers and staff for their instrumental aid.

Last but not least, we have thrived thanks to the support and wisdom offered by Norma Mendoza-Denton, Fred Zimmerman, Majdouline, Ira, and Julius.

Index

Abbou Ben Abbou, 54–55
Aboulker, Henri, 40
Abravanel, Marie, 8, 38–39
Adler, Camillo, 58–62
African American soldiers, 286, 295
Aïn al-Ouraq camp, 218
Aïn-Zammit, 14map2, 150
al-Fassi, Allal, 26
Al-Geddari, Al-ḥusin, 15, 75, 76(image 6)
Algerian Committee for Social Science, 40–42
Algerian Communist Party (PCA), 175
Algerian Jews: antiracist manifesto, 40–42; athletes, 15, 263, 271–77; campaigns against anti-Semitism, 40–42; civil status of, 333; French citizenship of, 4, 9, 40–42, 112, 333; racism of, 43
Algerian Muslims: civil status of, 4, 333; as communists, 175; internment of, 175–87; Mohammed Arezki Berkani, 174–87; support for Jewish doctors, 101–3
Algerian People's Party (Parti du peuple algérien, PPA), 174–75, 176
Algerian Saharan Jews, 9, 192–98
Algiers (Alger), 40–42, 146, 186, 340, 341

Al- Ḥusayn, Ali Tliti, Al-Haj (goumier), 295–96
Alliance Israélite Universelle (AIU), 23, 27–28, 39, 56–57, 132, 162
Allied armies: anti-fascists in, 257; and children in camps, 248; erasure of Black troops, 325; in Hitler's Haggadah (Nessim ben Shimon), 284; as liberators, 283–86, 289, 298, 299–300; Moroccan women's relations with, 281–82; Operation Torch, 1, 15–16, 214, 216, 286, 299–300, 311(image 19), 315, 320
al-Qarawīyin University, 26
Al-Qrishī, Yaʿqub, 121–22
al-Sayyid, Ḥamīda, 259–60
American army: antifascist refugees employed by, 257–58; attack on Casablanca, 287; clothing sold by, 290; consumer goods distributed by, 282, 288, 290, 293(image 18), 298; employment for refugees, 220, 256; food rations, 290; goumiers and, 295–96; "Khamous Zana" (Simon di Yacoub Cohen), 296–98; as liberators, 283, 286, 288, 298, 299–300; Moroccans employed by, 257–59, 288;

352   INDEX

reactions to, 228–29, 296–98; sexual violence against women, 16, 286–87, 289, 300–302
American Friends Service Committee (AFSC), 11, 13, 104, 224–32, 256, 257, 305–8
American Joint Distribution Committee (JDC), 11, 13, 43, 117–19, 200, 216–17, 321–24
American soldiers: appearance in Casablanca, 288; court martial of, 289; Moroccan women's relations with, 281–82; music of, 291; presence in Morocco, 55–56; racial preferences of, 281–82; sexual violence against women, 16, 286–87, 289, 300–302
amputations, 109, 216, 218, 219, 220, 313
Anti-Atlas Mountains (Morocco), 75–76
anti-fascism, 1–2, 7, 11, 60, 188, 192–93, 222–23, 226, 256–58, 317–21
anti-Jewish legislation, 2, 216; Aryanization of the economy, 90, 98; Dahir decrees, 3, 91–92, 96–99, 116, 122, 123, 125; on education, 90, 334; evictions, 91–92; exemptions from, 9, 96–97, 98–101, 110–21; on exportation of Jewish financial assets, 94–96; Jewish challenges to, 9, 98–101; Jewish quotas in business, 98, 116, 121–22; Leggi per la Difesa della Razza, 241; in professions, 91, 94, 99; racial definition of Jews, 123; Statut des Juifs, 9, 112, 122–23, 145, 168; Viziriel decrees, 91–92, 93
anti-Semitism: abrogation of Crémieux Decree (1870), 333; in Algeria, 40; anti-Jewish exhibitions, 93; campaigns against, 40; conspiracy against doctors, 239–40; economic sanctions, 9, 90, 96, 97, 98–101, 116–17, 121–23, 159; harassment of Tunisian Jews by SS, 131–32; Italian policies, 128n, 241; mob violence against Jews, 94–95; riots in Constantine, 40; SOL (French right-wing party), 175, 176, 320–21; spoliation,

57, 90, 94, 133, 134, 136–37, 144, 211, 241–43; Statut des Juifs, 9, 112, 122–23, 145, 168; stereotypes of the Jewish body, 271
Aouad, Abderrahman, 75
Aouina airfield, 148, 327
Aquilina, Frederick, 252
Arsalan, Shakib, 26
Arviv, Shoshana (Giado), 241–49
Aryans, 8, 90, 98, 129–30
Ashkenazis, 52
Ashkeva (memorial prayer), 2, 331–33
Association of Algerian Ulamas (AUA), 175
Assuied, André, 154, 330–31
Assuied, Rabbi, 205, 209
athletes, Jewish, 15, 263, 271–77
Aub, Max (Mohrenwitz), 171–74
Auschwitz-Birkenau, 261
Auschwitz concentration camp: colored labels on clothing, 270; deaths in, 55, 251, 271, 273–75; deportations to, 254, 266, 340; disinfection, 268; families murdered in, 271, 273; gas chambers, 266, 275; genocide, 263, 275; Hungarian Jews in, 322; living conditions, 267, 270; nightmares of, 346; prison uniforms, 267–68; tattoos, 1–2, 269–70, 342, 346; teeth extractions, 267; torture of children, 269–70
Ayache, Eugène, 264
Azemmour, 110, 199–202

Bahri, Yunes, 25–26
ballili [Italian youth fascists], 147
Balsi, Mohamed, 175
bank accounts, 94, 95
Barberousse prison, 186
Barbie, Nikolaus "Klaus," 266
Barqah (Cyrenaica), Libya, 4, 202, 241–49
Bawden, Edward, 221(image 14)
Béchar forced labor camp, 10map1, 179, 220, 233
Bedeau internment camp, 10map1, 224, 229
Bekerman, Chil, 109–10

INDEX 353

Belafrej, Ahmed, 26
Bellaïche, Robert, 152, 153, 329, 330, 331
Benatar, Hélène Cazes, 11, 108–10, 200–202, 214, 216–17, 233, 238–40, 320–21
Bendayan, Elie, 122–26
Bendelac, Alegria, 47(image 4); Ashkenazi refugees, 52–53; food rationing, 52; Pétainist administration in schools, 51–52, 53; religious observances, 46; school attendance in Tangier, 46, 52
Bénichou, Gabriel, 260–65, 340–46. *See also* Drancy internment camp
Bensimhon, Juda, 98
Bensimhon, Raymond, 9, 98–101. *See also* Fez (Fès), Morocco
Bensimon, David, 8, 9, 55
Berbers, 3, 4, 162, 238, 294
Berdah, Max, 139
Bergen-Belsen, 8, 250, 254
Berkani, Mohammed Arezki, 174–87
Bernou, Maamar ben, 175
Berrouaghia concentration camp, 10map1, 87, 193
Biberach, Bavaria, 254–55
Big Mountain [djebel Kebir], 152
Birkenau, 261, 263
Bir-M'Cherga camp, 14 map2, 149
Bizerte camp, 14map2; boats visible from, 206–7; camp surveillance, 148, 206; defiance of prisoners, 152; deportations to, 151–52; escapes from, 142, 212; food, 206, 207, 211–12; interactions with local residents, 207; labor in, 148, 151–52; living conditions, 151–53, 205–6, 207, 212; medical care, 139, 206, 211; morale in, 139, 146, 147–48, 152, 205, 206, 208–9; population of, 134, 138–39, 148, 206, 207–8, 212; Purim in, 204–5, 209–10; roundups, 148; tensions between Arabs and Jews, 207–9; vermin, 151–53, 205–6; weather, 207, 209, 210, 212; work assignments, 207–8
Black American soldiers, 295
Black intellectuals, 39, 66–67

black markets, 50, 143, 175, 178, 215, 220, 291–94, 292–93
blackness: anti-black rhetoric, 43, 45; black intellectuals, 39, 66–67; segregation of Black populations, 63, 241; soldiers, 5, 63, 65, 73, 286, 294, 295, 325; terms for, 39
Black soldiers, 5, 65, 286, 294, 295, 325
Boghar camp, 224, 226, 227, 228, 229
bombings, 142, 166–67, 210, 253, 298
Bonan, Alex, 150
Bonnafous, Max, 111
Bordeaux. *See* Saint Médard camp
Boretz, Eugène, 9, 126–30
Borgel, Robert, 145–58, 168–71
Bossuet camp, 186, 188–89, 195
Bou Arfa forced labor camp, Morocco, 110, 218–19, 235, 305, 307
Bou Azzer labor camp, 10map 1, 77, 238–40
Bouhali, Larbi, 175
British citizenship: of Libyan Jews, 8, 28, 241–48, 249–55
British military, 226, 287, 335
Buchenwald concentration camp, 271, 275
Buchris, Pinchas, 141
Bulletin of the Federation of Jewish Societies of Algeria, 43
Buqbuq (Bakbuk) labor camp, 14map 2, 202, 203–4, 241, 249
Burbea, Sion, 250–55
burial of the dead, 15, 155, 195–97, 207, 252
businesses, Jewish, 90; forced sales of, 116–17, 121–22, 123; sale of, to non-Jews, 96, 97, 121–22, 123, 159; sales to foreign nationals, 117

Caboche, Julius Caesar, 173(image 12)
cadavers, 209, 212
Caillaud, Paul (d'Hérama, Paul), 81–90, 187–91
call to prayers (muzzeins), 182–83
Camp Cazes (Casablanca), 288
camp commanders, 179–81, 182–86, 227, 228–29

Camus, Albert, 303–5
Casablanca, Morocco, 9, 10map1, 10map 1; Allied forces in, 146, 287; American consul general in, 90–97; American presence in, 214, 257, 287–88, 290–91; cinemas, 93, 122–26; clothing shortages in, 289–90; declaration of assets by Jews, 94–95; Jewish students expelled from high schools, 51–52; mellah of, 92; Refugee Aid Committee (Casablanca), 11; refugees in, 52, 255–59; restrictions on Jews from professions, 98, 116, 121–26; sanctions against Jews, 51–52, 98, 122–26; Vichy French surrender at, 287. *See also* Chriqui, Sidney (Casablanca memoir)
Casa Migliorata, 250
cemeteries, 192, 195–96, 207, 209, 252
Centre Bompard (Marseille), 306
Chanukah, 253
Chemla, Moïse, 150
childbirth, 246, 248–49
children: American Friends Service Committee (AFSC) interventions for, 306; American soldiers as fathers of, 300–302; arrest of parents in place of, 167–68; convoy to the United States, 306; deaths of, 34, 246, 248–49; deportation of, 306; education denied to, 306; graves of, 196; heads shaved, 244, 245, 268; hospitalization of, 200–202; humanitarian aid for, 110, 119, 200–202, 227, 232; humanitarian interventions on behalf o, 306; illnesses of interned children, 119; on imprisonment, 241–49; in internment camps, 109, 117, 119; interracial children, 325, 326; as Jewish foreign born, 260–65; memories of deportations, 242–44; murder of, 34; Pétainist propaganda, 56, 57; physical punishment of, 269; recreation in the camps, 246, 263–64; as refugees from Nazi persecution, 52; request for Spanish protection for Hungarian children, 322–25; trauma, 132, 143, 269

Chirac, Jacques, 316
Chriqui, Sidney (Casablanca memoir), 286–91; on American culture, 290, 291; on American soldiers' entrance to Casablanca, 288; attack on Casablanca, 287; employed by American army, 288–89, 290; friendships, 290–91; impressions of American soldiers, 288, 289, 291; language skills, 288–89
Christians, 112–15, 224–32, 250
Christmas celebrations, 61–62, 155
Churchill, Winston, 285, 289, 298
cinemas, 62, 95, 122–25, 122–26, 128
circumcisions, 252, 327
citizenship: Crémieux Decree (1870), 4, 333; of engagés volontaires étrangers (foreign volunteers), 311–12; indigenous subjects of France designations, 4, 9; of Libyan Jews, 335–36; Libyan Jews with British citizenship, 8, 28, 241–48, 249–55; of Muslims, 4, 333; North African Jews, 90; Spanish citizenship, 4, 333; Statut des Juifs, 9, 112, 122–23, 145, 168
civil service: Jews excluded from, 115–16
Civitella del Tronto internment camp: accommodations for the ill, 250; arrival of Germans, 252; Bergen-Belsen, 254; births in, 251–52; deaths in, 252; deportations from, 254–55; food supplies, 253; help from local residents, 250–51, 253; population of, 252; treatment of prisoners, 250–51; work assignments, 253
classrooms: portraits of Pétain in, 56, 57; presence of Pétain, Philippe, Marshal in, 4, 8, 9, 51–52, 53
clothing, 64, 68, 141, 153; distribution of, 139, 257; shoes, 13, 17, 98, 109, 110, 238, 267; shortages, 77, 289–90; sold by American military, 289–90; striped prison uniforms, 267–68; worn by survivors, 341, 343
Cohen, Prosper, 6, 23–25
Cohen, Simon di Yacoub, 296–98

INDEX 355

Colomb-Béchar forced labor camp, 10map1, 179, 220, 231, 233, 235
Comité d'assistance aux réfugiés, 234
Committee against Fascism and War, 188
communists, 81, 175, 176, 188
Como displacement camp, 252
concentration camps. *See* individual headings (e.g. Auschwitz)
Constantine riots (1934), 3, 40
consumer goods, American, 282, 288, 290, 293(image 18), 298
Contrôleur Civil de la Région de Casablanca, 94–95
Corps Francs d'Afrique, 314
Corso Mazzini, 250
Coster, Donald, 311(image 19)
cotton, 291–94
Crampel labor camp, 10map1, 220, 224, 227–28
Crémieux Decree (1870), 4, 112, 333
Cyrenaica (Barqah), Libya, 4, 202, 241–49

Dachau concentration camp, 158, 160–61, 233, 234, 261, 341
Dahir decrees, 3, 91–92, 96–99, 116, 122, 123, 125
Dahomey, 11, 65
Dambrowski Brigade, 192
dam construction project, 240(image 15)
Dammert, Hans, 219–24
Darlan, François, Admiral, 309, 316
D'Ascaio, Fioravante, Don, 250
DCA [Défense contre les aéronefs], 210
deceased inmate (Shpilgarn), 192–94
de Gaulle, Charles, 49, 58, 179, 298.325
delousing, 64, 268
dental care, 198–99, 214
Department of Indigenous Affairs, 26
Deriko (commander of Djenien Bou Rezg labor camp), 182–83, 184, 185, 186
Diary of Djelfa (Mohrenwitz), 171–74
Djebebina labor camp, 142, 153–55, 329–31
djebel Kebir, 152

Djelfa internment camp, 10map1, 173(image 12); deportations to, 171, 192; disease in, 194–95, 226–27; interactions with local residents, 195–98; living conditions, 171, 173, 188–90, 226–27; medical care in, 190–91, 194–95, 224, 226–27; Paul Caillaud in, 81, 188; in poetry, 171–74; population of, 171, 188, 191–98, 226; trans-Saharan railroad project, 11, 81, 104, 173, 188; work assignments, 195–98
Djellouli, Aziz, 159–60
Djenien Bou Rezg labor camp, 10map1; commanders at, 180–86; educational opportunities in, 177; food supplies in, 176, 178, 180, 185; geography of, 176, 184; *goumiers* (Moroccan infantry) at, 180, 181; Jewish-Muslim relations in, 184–85; labor in, 178; liberation of prisoners, 178–79; Muslim religious observances in, 176–80, 182–83, 186–87; political climate in, 174–77, 178; population of, 175–76, 178, 180, 182, 184, 186, 191–98; suffering of prisoners, 180, 181–82, 185–86
Djerada internment camp (Jerada), 307, 319–21
Djerba internment camp, 307, 311(image 19)
Djouggar, 14map 2, 153, 154
doctors, 136, 165; Christian doctors, 224–32; expertise of, 225; humanitarian interventions by, 67, 218, 219; in internment camps, 190, 229, 251; Italian army doctors, 153–54; in labor camps, 186, 206, 224, 227–29, 238–40; Muslim Algerian doctors' support for Jewish doctors, 101–3; psychiatrists, 120–21; sanctions against, 9, 101–3, 112, 225–26, 228–29, 239–40
dogs, 171–73, 173(image 12)
Drancy internment camp: deportations from, 261, 265, 266; families at, 264, 265; food, 262, 264, 265; German occupation of, 265; Jewish athletes in, 15, 263, 271–77; living conditions, 261–62,

263–66; population of, 262–64; reunions at, 262–63, 264; women at, 262, 263, 266; work assignments, 265; yellow star worn at, 265
Drezdner, Chana, 117–19

education: Alliance Israélite Universelle (AIU), 23, 27–28, 39, 56–57, 132, 162; in Arabic language, 264; coed education, 47; denial of, 306; in Djenien Bou Rezg (labor camp), 177; Jewish quotas in, 90; and religious observance, 46, 176–78; of survivors, 344–45; in Tangier, 46–47, 52; Vichy propaganda in, 4, 8–9, 51–52, 53; of women, 46
Eid El-Kebir, 186–87
Eid-Seghu, 180
Eisenhower, Dwight D., 287
electoral colleges, 333
El-Fassi, Allal, 175
El Fassi, Si Allal, 26
ElGrichi, Jacob (Al-Qrishī, Yaʿqub), 121–22
El Jadida (Mazagan), Morocco, 8, 55
El Squelli, 27
El-Wazzani, Hassan, 26
Enfidaville, 148, 158
engagés volontaires étrangers (foreign volunteers): character of, 314; citizenship of, 311–12; imprisonment of, 219–24, 308–10, 316–17; International Brigade, 1, 2, 7, 11, 12(image 3), 106(image 7), 188, 192–93, 194, 256, 317–21; interventions for, 309–15; Jews as, 216–17, 233, 312; military service of, 310–12, 314, 316; professional skills of, 314; repatriation of, 312–13
escapes from camps, 66, 70, 71, 89, 137, 163, 171, 207, 212, 217–19, 253, 256, 317
espionage, 66, 67, 70
Essaouira (Mogador), Morocco, 1, 6–7, 29, 266
eugenic policies, 325–27
European refugees in North Africa, 52, 118(image 8), 219–24, 251, 306

euthanasia in Nazi Germany, 120

families: American sponsors for, 307; application for immigration to Palestine, 337; attendance at funerals, 326; communication with, 110, 232, 236, 237, 262, 290, 305–7, 306–7, 322; deaths from starvation, 296; deportations of, 265; of engagés volontaires étrangers (foreign volunteers), 312; extortion of Jewish families, 159–60; fathers, 35, 180, 182, 204, 207, 223, 242, 254, 266, 296; incarceration of, 199, 200, 213–15, 261–63, 271, 273, 275; reprisals against, 312; reunions with, 237, 266, 305–6, 340, 342, 344; sisters, 234, 236, 290; treatment of survivors by, 344; violence against, 35, 169, 265, 275, 296
family background, 98–101, 235–36
famine, 15, 303–5
fascism: anti-Jewish legislation, 241; Benito Mussolini, 4, 8, 27–29, 202, 249, 284; Jewish support for Italian fascist movement, 27; National Fascist Party (PNF), 4, 27; racial laws, 334, 338. *See also* Vichy regime
fathers, 35, 180, 182, 207, 223, 242, 254, 266, 296
Feldgendarmerie, 170
female guards, 266–67, 268, 269, 270–71
Ferjani, Hassan, 158, 159
Fez (Fès), Morocco, 9, 10map1, 26, 97–100, 291–94
food and food supplies, 228, 254; demonstrations about, 304; food packages, 65–66, 69, 74, 161, 262, 265; in French camps, 178; as humanitarian aid, 119, 201, 214–15, 253, 262; kosher food, 200, 201, 210, 214–15; malnutrition, 15, 30, 75; of Muslims, 179–80, 303–5; POW camps, 64, 65, 67–68; quality of, 64–65, 67–68, 82, 178, 253, 254, 303; rationing of, 49–50, 65, 75–76, 344; shortages, 60, 71, 143, 247, 303–5; starvation, 15,

71, 75, 76(image 6), 185, 229, 296; water shortages, 186, 203; weight loss, 346
forced labor camps. *See* individual headings (e.g. Djelfa prison camp)
Foreign Workers (Traveilleurs Etrangers), 229
Foucauld, Charles de, 98, 99, 101
Foucher-Créteau, Roger, 275
Foum Zguid Bureau of Indigenous Affairs, 295
Foundation for the Memory of the Shoah, 145
France: citizenship, 4, 9, 44–45, 112, 122–23, 130, 145, 168, 249, 250, 333–34; Crémieux Decree (1870), 4, 112, 333; culpable of genocide, 316; French Resistance, 49, 58, 298.325; German occupation of, 8; International Brigade volunteers in, 7; Jewish loyalty to, 112–15; Jews' service to, 98–101; Muslim loyalty to, 44–45; North African Jewish émigrés in, 2; Operation Torch, 1, 15–16, 214, 216, 286, 299–300, 311(image 19), 315, 320; opposition to, 54–55; POW camps, 1; POW internment camps in, 2; Tunisian camps maintained by, 13; Viziriel decrees, 91–92, 93. *See also* engagés volontaires étrangers (foreign volunteers); French Foreign Legion; Pétain, Philippe, Marshal; Vichy regime; individual headings for camps (e.g. Poitiers Camp)
Franco, Francisco, General, 7, 171, 21996
French army: Jewish volunteers, 216–17; in the popular imagination, 48
French citizenship, 9, 44–45, 130, 249, 250, 333–34
French Foreign Legion, 193; Christmas celebrations, 61–62; coercion in, 62; foreign volunteers in, 308; Germans in, 61; incarceration of volunteers, 233; Jewish volunteers in, 7, 217–19; Jews in, 58–62; living conditions, 59–61; nationalities in, 60; Polish volunteers in, 318; recruitment to, 57–58; romantic image of, 58–59; Sidi Bel Abbès, 58–62, 233
French Fourth Republic: distinctions between Algerian and European French territory, 333
French-German Armistice (June 22, 1940), 8
French government: forced disposal of merchandise, 56; French Resistance, 266
French Guinea, 11, 65
French Jews: military service of, 274
French military, 274, 325–26; racism of, 325–27
French Ministry of Industrial Production and Labor, 11
French nationals: sales of Jewish businesses to, 116, 122
French Resistance, 49, 58, 298.325
French soldiers: knitting projects for, 48–49, 56
"French subject, Algerian Jewish native," 260
French Zone of Morocco: Spanish influence in, 95
Freud, Esti, 118(image 8)
Freud, Sophie, 118(image 8)
Fronstalags, 63, 71, 73
funerals, 195, 196, 209
Furcolow, M. L, Major, 255

gas chambers, 263, 266, 270, 273, 275
Gasquet, Frédéric, 158–62
Gasquet family (Scemla): arrest of men, 159; betrayal of, 159; courage of women, 160; deportation of men to Dachau, 160–61
General Association of Students of Algiers, 40
General Commission for Jewish Affairs (Vichy), 8, 98, 121
General Commission on Jewish Questions, 121–22
German army: anti-Semitic propaganda in Tunis, 279; arrival in Tunis, 146; demands for Christmas celebrations,

155; destruction of Jewish homes by, 128, 169; in French Foreign Legion, 61; requisition of properties by, 127; sexual violence against Jewish women, 128, 169; social tensions created by, 163; surveillance of citizens, 127–30; tensions with Italian army, 126

German Jews, 192–93

German soldiers, 165(image 11); abuse of prisoners, 253; atrocities of, 244–45; executions of prisoners, 212–13; extortion by, 169; harassment by, 129–30; humiliation of Libyan Jews, 244; rape of Jewish women, 168, 169; SS (Schutzstaffel), 15, 131–35, 164, 236, 254, 261, 265, 343

Gestapo, 66, 134, 147, 261, 266, 273

Ghardaïa (southern Algeria), 333–34

Gharyan labor camp, Libya, 202, 241, 335

Ghez, Paul, 130–40, 157

Giado labor and internment camp: aid to prisoners of, 246, 247; arrival of Allied forces, 248; children's lives in, 243, 246; contact with outside world, 246–47; food distribution, 243, 247–48; head-shaving in, 244–45; infanticide, 248–49; Libyan Jews in, 202, 241–49; living conditions in, 241, 243, 247–48, 249; population of, 241, 248–49

Giraud, Henri, General, 16, 257

girls: interrogation of, 266; memories of camps, 241–49, 266–71; memories of deportation, 241–49; social restrictions on, 290; torture of, 266

"Gnayet Madloumin" (Song of the Oppressed), 140–44

gold teeth extractions, 267

Goubellat, 14map2, 149

goumiers (Moroccan infantry), 11, 63, 171, 181(image 13); at Djenien Bou Rezg (labor camp), 180, 181; forced recruitment of, 11, 63, 65(image 5), 294; interactions with American soldiers, 295–96; surveillance of Muslim prisoners, 180, 181–82, 187

Gozlan, Elie, 42–45

grandmothers, 242, 246, 247

grave digging, 207, 216

Grynszpan Affair, 234

GTE (groupes de travailleurs étrangers (groups of foreign workers)), 229, 233, 235, 236, 237, 307

guards: female Kapos, 266–67, 268, 269, 270–71; torture by, 31–32. *See also goumiers* (Moroccan infantry)

Guedj, Maurice/Moïse, 112–15

Guetta, Amishaddai, 202–4

Guetta, Amishaddai (Sidi Aziz camp), 202–4

Guez, Gaston, 327–31

Guez, Jacob André (Bizerte prisoner), 205–13

Guez, Simon Chalom, 327, 333

Gurs (internment camp), 60

Habib, Haim, 243(image 16)

Habib, Hlafo, 252

Habib, Mino, 254

Habib, Mosé, 334–40

Hacker, Samuel, 254

Hadji, Messali, 174

Hagège, Émile, 155

Haman, 7, 24–25

Hammanet, 161

ḥāra, 3, 90, 136, 168, 169

headshaving, 244–45, 268

headstones in cemeteries, 196

Hebrew Immigrant Aid Society, 11, 218

Hebrew Immigration/Jewish Colonization Association (HICEM), 233

Hebrew language, 198

HICEM (Hebrew Immigration/Jewish Colonization Association), 11, 13, 171, 233. *See also* Benatar, Hélène Cazes

Hitler, Adolf: as Haman, 23–25, 283–86; Hitler's Haggadah (Nessim ben Shimon), 283–86; megalomania of,

34–36; as murderer and criminal, 34–36; as Pharaoh, 283; in poetry, 29–36; support for, 54–55
Hitler's Haggadah (Nessim ben Shimon), 283–86
hospitals, 34, 68, 117–18, 119, 138–39, 200–202, 218, 235, 250, 258
hostages, imprisonment of, 134
"Hosties noires" (Senghor), 63
houses: confiscation of, 128, 141, 144
humanitarian aid: American Friends Service Committee (AFSC), 11, 13, 104, 224–32, 256, 257, 305–8; American Joint Distribution Committee (JDC), 11, 13, 43, 117–19, 200, 216–17, 321; applications for refuge, 224; camp visits by aid workers, 43, 320–21; censorship of requests for, 254; for children, 110, 119, 200–202, 227, 232; clothing, 64, 107–9, 139; for dental care, 198–99, 214; doctor's request for reassignment, 238–40; financial aid, 227, 232, 251; food, 119, 201, 214–15, 253, 262; from foreign governments, 251; Hélène Cazes Benatar, 11, 108–10, 200–202, 214, 216–17, 233, 238–40, 320–21; hospital visits, 139; human rights violations, 216–17, 218–19; interventions for internees, 73–74, 145, 150–51, 154, 223–24, 246; limits of, 200–201; from local residents, 250–51, 253, 259–60; for medical care, 117–19, 139, 190, 200–202, 218–19, 233–38; missing persons, 110; packages, 65–66, 69, 74, 161, 262, 265; Red Cross, 64, 70, 109–10, 160–61, 217, 251, 252, 254, 318, 324; religious aspects of, 201, 214–15; for rescue of Hungarian children and adults, 322–25
humiliations: delousing, 268; headshaving, 244–45; loss of identity, 268, 269, 270; resistance to, 168–69, 269; Star of David, 149(image 10), 157, 158, 265, 270; tattoos, 1–2, 269–70, 342, 346; of women prisoners, 266–67, 268, 269, 270–71

Hungarian Jews, 321–25, 322

ʿId al-Aḍḥā, 175
Il Duce. See Mussolini, Benito
Im Fout forced labor camp, 240(image 15)
indigenous Moroccan infantry. See goumiers (Moroccan infantry)
Industrial Production, 219
infants: in internment camps, 109, 248–49
infirmaries, 194, 211, 216, 217
Ingold, François, 325–27
International Brigade, 1, 2, 7, 11, 12(image 3), 106(image 7), 188, 192–93, 194, 256, 317–21
International Refugee Organization (IRO), 334, 335–39
International Tracing Bureau, 334
inventor scandal, 53
Italian Antifascists, 222–23
Italian army: Jews protected by, 126–27
Italian Republican party, 223
Italian Socialist Party, 222
Italy: Benito Mussolini, 4, 8, 27–29, 202, 249, 284; deportations of Jews, 1, 8, 241; internment camps in, 2, 8, 154, 249–55; political parties in, 222–23; rabbinical school, 338; Tunisian camps maintained by, 13. *See also* Libya
Ivory Coast, 11, 65

Jacobson, Herbert, 250–51, 252
Jean Bart (French battleship), 53–54
Jefna labor camp, 14map2, 150–51
Jenn, Jean-Tony, 160–61
Jerada (Djerada internment camp), 307, 319–21
Jeren labor camp: internment of Libyan Jews in, 202, 241
Jewish burial rites, 195, 196, 197–98
Jewish cemetery, 195
Jewish Colonization Association, 218
Jewish Council of Tunisia, 146
Jewish girls: Arab girlfriends, 242; detention

of, 132; humiliation of, 244–45, 268; imprisonment of, 132; Jewish identity of, 38–39. *See also* individual headings (e.g. Arviv, Shoshana)
Jewish identity: of camp inmates, 193; denial of, 110–12, 120–21, 160; documentation of, 132; physical characteristics, 130; social privilege, 163; women, 8, 38–39
Jewish neighborhoods. *See* ḥāra; mellāḥ
Jewish observances: food preparation for, 210, 211, 250; kosher food, 200, 201, 210, 214–15; Passover, 150, 156; Purim celebrations, 23–24, 204–5, 209–12; Shavuot, 214
Jewish Scouts of France, 262
Jewish students: ostracism of, 51, 53; sanctions against, 51–52; in schools, 51–52
Jewish women: detention of, 132; German soldiers' sexual violence against, 128; sexual violence against, 1, 9, 128
Johnson, Eric W. (memorandum), 255–59
Jordanbad, 255
Judeo-Arabic, 264, 325–27
Justice (Tunisian Jewish newspaper), 130

kaddish prayer, recital of, 198, 298
Kapo, female, 266–67, 268, 269, 270–71
Katach-Baya, 14map2, 150
Kenadsa forced labor camp, 10map1, 231, 235
Kersas forced labor camp, 235
"Khamous Zana" (Simon di Yacoub Cohen), 296–98
khevra kadisha, 195, 196
Knafo, Isaac, 6–7, 29–32
knitting projects, 48–49, 56
Kormes, Karol, 317–21
kosher food, 200, 201, 210, 214–15
Krief, Georges, 132, 135, 138, 164
Krief, Jacques, 153
Kristallnacht, 234
Ksar-Tyr, 14 map 2, 148, 149, 297
Kutno, death march to, 261

Labi, Alfredo, 250
labor camps: children in, 238; colonial soldiers in, 325; construction of, 9; continued operation of, 16; despair in, 166; doctors in, 186; evacuation of sick men, 151, 153, 154; evacuations from, 163; illness in, 163; Legionnaires in, 58; living conditions, 13, 107–8, 151–52, 166, 228, 238; populations of, 256; Purim celebrations, 204–5, 209–12; roundups for, 167–68; sanitary conditions, 166; social stratification in, 163; transfers between, 153–54; vermin, 166; water shortages, 186
labor camps, Vichy: prolonged functioning of, 309
laborers: clothing for, 139; memorial prayer for, 331–33; payment of, 207; protests in support of, 134; sabotage by, 152; torture of, 152; Women's protests on behalf of, 137–38
laborers, Jewish: dead bodies of, 138, 212; executions of, 212
La Goulette, 148
Lagrange, Rachel, 266
Lagrange, Simon, 266
Lagrange, Simone (Drancy and Auschwitz), 266–71
La Marsa: deportations to, 250
Lamḥamid: death in, 15, 75, 76(image 6)
la Mornaghia, 148
Languai, Jacob, 204
La Redoute, 188, 189
Leclerc, Philippe François, 158, 159
Left Republicans (RG), 176
legal professions: Jews barred from, 145, 168
Leggi per la Difesa della Razza, 241
Legion des Combattants (Vichy guard), 228–29
Le Kef internment camp, 14map2, 258(image 17)
Lellouche (prisoner): execution of, 212
Les Hitlériques (poem by Isaac Knafo), 29–31

Le Vernet d'Ariège (Vichy penal camp), 171
Libya, 2; camps in, 14map2; fascist rule in, 8; German citizens in, 2; internment camps in, 8; Italian citizenship, 4; Italian labor camps, 28; Jewish identity in, 38–40; Mussolini's race laws, 28. *See also* Tripoli
Libyan Italian Citizens, 4
Libyan Jews: British citizenship of, 8, 241–48, 249–55; confiscation of property, 243; deportations of, 8, 202, 241–49, 249–50; education, 336; internment of, 2, 202, 241–49; Jewish-Muslim relations, 259–60; language knowledge, 337; legal status of, 249–50, 335–36; mixed marriages, 8; Muslim anti-Semitic violence against, 335; in Palestine, 335, 338; return to Libya, 255. *See also* Giado labor and internment camp; Tripoli
Libyan Muslims: anti-Semitic violence of, 335; deportations of, 241, 249–50; Jewish-Muslim relations, 259–60
lice, 13, 64, 68, 136, 142, 149, 151–53, 166, 205–6, 241, 244–45, 248
"Lmirīkan" (song by Lḥussain Slawī), 281–82
Lubelski, Benjamin, 191–98
Lūfranī, Marcel, 102–3
lumberjacks, 188
Luzon, Joseph, 259

Maa-Abiod, 150
marabout tents, 173(image 12)
Marechal nous voilà (ode to Marshal Pétain), 55, 56
marriages, 8, 112–15, 287, 325–27, 335
Marseilles, 306
Marsol, Colette, 300–302
Martigny-les-Bains (Vosges), 234
Massicault, 148, 149
materialism, 55, 281, 282, 298
Mateur camp, 14map2, 148, 151, 152, 328
matzah baking, 156
Méchéria (internment camp), 220–21, 222–23

medical care: dental care, 198–99, 214; evacuations for, 151, 153; hospitals, 34, 68, 119, 138–39, 200–202, 235, 250, 258; labor camps, 224, 227–28; pharmacists, 112–15, 151–52, 250, 251; women's requests for, 110, 117–19; for work injuries, 234–35. *See also* doctors
medical experimentation, 73, 325–27
Mediouna Internment Camp, 10map 1, 221(image 14), 317, 319
Megilat Ester, 23, 109
Megrine, 142
Meknes, Morocco, 6, 7, 23–25
Melca, Haïm, 29
Melca, Meïr, 29
mellāḥ, 3, 90–92
Memmi, Albert, 15, 162–68
memorial books, 325–31
memorial prayers (ashkeva), 2, 331–33
mental illness, 162, 330
Mersane (neighborhood in El Jadida), 55–56
Mexico, asylum in, 11, 13, 171, 224
Migliorati, Giovannina, 250
Migliorati, Rivo, 250
millstones, 242, 246
mines, 77, 178, 238–40, 305, 307, 319, 320–21
Miranda De Ebro, 317
mixed-race couples, 325–27
Mizrahi, Asher Shimon, 141
Moatti, Dr., 132, 137, 138, 154
Mohrenwitz, Max Aub, 171–74
Montagard, André, 55
Morlay, Gaby, 110–12
Moroccan Jews: on American soldiers' entrance to Casablanca, 288; arrival of Allies welcomed by, 15; assimilation of, 46; citizenship of, 9, 44; Dahir decrees, 3, 91–92, 96–99, 116, 122, 123, 125; of Fez, 97–100; forced disposal of merchandise, 56; forced purchases of Pétain portraits, 56, 57; French nationalism, 9, 44; as indigenous subjects of France designations, 9; language skills, 288; military

service of, 44; mobilization of men, 48; occupations of, 23; persecution by French authorities, 56; reactions to rise on Nazism, 7; in United States, 287
Moroccan Muslims: arrests of cotton merchants, 291, 292, 294; food supplies, 303–5; on French authority, 292–94; loyalty of, 71; marriages to Allied soldiers, 287; relations with Jews, 90
Moroccan nationalist movement, 175
Moroccan women: American soldiers' relations with, 281–82; exploitation of, 282, 300–301; "Lmirīkan" (song by Lḥussain Slawī), 281–82; materialism of, 282
mothers, 110, 136, 140, 142, 200–201
moussem Alamiyne (pilgrimage ceremony), 27
Msallata, Libya, 259–60
Müller, Erwin, 224–32
music, 140–44, 211, 220, 233–38, 251, 281–82, 290
Muslims: as American consular employees, 286; cemeteries, 195; as cotton merchants, 291–94; food supplies, 179–80, 303–5; French citizenship, 44–45, 130, 250, 333; internment of, 15, 174–87, 175, 176–80, 181–82, 182–83, 186–87; Jewish-Muslim relations, 90, 101–3, 184–85, 259–60; military service of, 44, 58; Nazi associations with, 25–27; neighborhoods, 168, 303–5; patriotism, 44–45; perceptions of current events, 37–38; prayers of, 177, 180, 182–83, 186–87; relations with Jews, 40–42, 55, 101–3, 157–58, 184–85, 259–60, 335; religious observances of, 176–80
Mussolini, Benito, 4, 8, 27–29, 202, 249, 284
muzzeins, 182–83

Naftali Brigade, 192
Nakache, Alfred, 271–77
nakedness, 266–68
Nataf, Victor, 155, 156, 333

National Fascist Party (PNF), 4, 27
Nazism, 5(image 1), 6(image 2); Adolf Hitler, 1, 6, 23–25, 29–36, 54–55, 283–86; cruelty of, 156, 266; euthanasia in, 120; Gestapo, 66, 134, 147, 261, 266, 273; Jewish community negotiations with Nazi occupiers, 130–40, 145–58; kapos, 266–67, 268, 269, 270–71; memorial prayer for Nazi victims, 327, 331–33; opposition to, 7, 137–38; propaganda, 25–27, 63, 66, 71, 279; refusal to grant transit visas, 323; SS (Schutzstaffel), 15, 131–35, 155, 164, 236, 254, 261, 265, 343; violence in Tunis Jewish community, 130–40, 145–58. See also fascism; Vichy regime; individual headings for camps (e.g. Auschwitz)
Negro (use of term), 39
Nemni, David, 252–53
Niessner, Étienne, 319–21
Noguès, Charles, General, 54
non-Jews: as doctors, 224–32; humanitarian aid for, 224–25; Jewish businesses sold to, 96, 97, 121–22, 123, 159
North African Jews: anti-Semitic attacks on, 90; anxiety of, 93, 94; arrival of Allies welcomed by, 15; citizenship, 90; as colonial subjects, 90; dhimma status, 90; embourgeoisement of, 90; in Nazi camps in Europe, 15; in Paris, 15; reactions to Allied landing, 299–300; resistance against Nazi ideology, 7; social mobility of, 90
Novi Sad massacre, 322
Nuremberg Laws, 9

Oberfeld, Kazimierz, 55
OFRRO [Office of Foreign Relief and Rehabilitation Operations], 257–59
oil shortages, 300
Olympic Games, 271–72
Operation Torch, 1, 15–16, 214, 216, 286, 299–300, 311(image 19), 315, 320

Oran, Algeria, 7, 37–38, 146, 222, 340
Oued Akreuch labor camp, Morocco, 10map1, 107–9, 216–17, 233, 235, 236
Our Martyrs under the German Boot (Gaston Guez), 327–31
Oyf Gots Barot (Lubelski), 191–98

Pack family (Moses, Macha, Samuel), 213–15
Palestine, 198, 204, 335–39
Paris, 15, 325
Parti du peuple algérien, PPA, 174–75
Partouche, Jacob Ben Meyer, Rabbi, 334
Passover, 150, 156, 250, 283–86
passports, 8, 28, 50, 249, 254
patriotic performances, 48–49, 55, 56, 57, 62, 179
PCF (French Communist Party), 176
Perez, Victor "Young," 15, 263, 273
Pétain, Philippe, Marshal: *Marechal nous voilà* (ode to Marshal Pétain), 55, 56; opposition to, 160, 298; Pétainist administration in schools, 51–52; portraits of, 56, 179; propaganda, 4, 8, 9, 51, 55, 56, 178, 179. See also individual camp headings (e.g. Djenien bou Rezg)
Petliura, Symon Vasylyovye, 25
pharmacists, 112–15, 152, 250, 251
photojournalism, 103–7
pianists, 233–38
pickpockets, 59–60
poetry, 6–7, 29–30, 30–32, 63, 171–74, 259–60
Poitiers camp, 63, 64, 66–67, 69, 71, 72
Poitrot, Robert, 110–21
Poland, 7, 43–44, 140, 213–15, 261, 317–21, 340
police, 132, 138, 170, 259–60, 262
political climate in camps, 175–77, 226, 256
post-traumatic stress of survivors, 340–43
POW camps: barbed wire systems, 70; Black African POWs in, 73; Black intellectuals in, 66; clothing, 64, 68; community relations with, 69; diet in, 68–69; division of prisoners in, 72–73; escapes from, 66, 70; favoritism in, 69–70; food in, 64, 65, 67–69; labor in, 69, 71, 72, 108; leadership, 64, 66, 67–68; Léopold Senghor in, 11, 13, 63–72; living conditions in, 64, 65, 67–70, 89; medical care, 67, 68; morale in, 67, 71; mortality rates in, 73; nutrition, 64–65; prisoner relations, 66, 69–70; propaganda in, 66–67, 69; racism in, 69–70, 72; theft in, 69, 72. See also Poitiers camp
PPA (Parti du peuple algérien), 174–75, 176, 177
PPF (ex-communist), 175, 176
prayers, 2, 177, 180, 182–83, 186–87, 197–98, 250, 331–33
pregnancy, 300–301
priests, as aids to Jews, 250
Prisoner of War Diplomatic Service (Scampini Mission), 63
prisoners, 12(image 3); advocacy for, 329–31; burial of, 192, 195–96; corporal punishments, 216–17, 217–19, 229; correspondence with outside world, 227–28, 232, 235–36; defiance of, 152; dehumanization of, 269–70; deportations of, 218, 219; despair of, 204; entrepreneurship of, 254; escapes by, 66, 70–71, 89, 137, 163, 171, 207, 212, 217–19; executions of, 212–13; families of, 234, 236–37; financial aid requested by, 107–8; as financial support for, 251; French conscripts as, 72–73; humanitarian aid for, 73–74, 145, 150–51, 154, 223–24, 246; identification by number, 269; information networks, 186; inhumane treatment of, 216–17, 217–19; interactions with local residents, 207, 247, 248, 250–51, 253; interrogations of, 265; liberation of, 71, 74, 204, 254–55; markings of, 268; petitions for visas, 233–38; postwar lives, 264, 334–46; preferential release of, 71, 73, 311–12; prolonged imprisonment of, 310–15, 320; racism against, 70; reaction to Americans' arrival in Algeria, 228–29;

requests for French naturalization, 231–32; reunions of, 252–53, 254; surveillance of, 180, 181–82, 187, 206, 254, 258(image 17), 262; *tombeau* (punishment), 216–17, 217–19; torture of, 152, 216–17; tradesmen among, 223–24; train journeys of, 77; transfers of, 231, 261–62; triage of prisoners according to race, 63; wages of, 71, 72, 108, 214, 231, 238, 307, 321; women prisoners, 266–67, 268, 269, 270–71; work assignments, 151, 207–8, 212, 235, 238, 240(image 15), 253, 265, 307. *See also* families; food and food supplies; humiliations; medical care; trauma

prison uniforms, 267–68

propaganda: from American military, 287; anti-Hitler poetry, 29–30; anti-Semitic propaganda in Tunis, 279; Arabs and, 7, 66–67; arrests of Muslim cotton merchants, 292; Black intellectuals' resistance to, 66–67; in camps, 66–67, 69, 70, 71, 178; exploitation of personal relationships, 25–26; Fez as target of, 26–27; in films, 67, 128; French intelligence, 37; German propaganda, 25–27, 63, 66, 70, 71, 279; languages of, 7, 26, 54; Mussolini's visit to Tripoli Jewish community, 4, 27–28; Nazi propaganda, 25–29, 33, 54–55; newspapers as, 66, 70; Pétainist propaganda, 4, 8, 9, 51, 55, 56, 178–79; in popular imagination, 36–37; prisoner solidarity used in, 69; pro-Spanish propaganda by Jews, 96; radio broadcasts, 7, 26; resistance literature, 266; Vichy propaganda in schools, 4, 8, 9, 51–52, 53

property, Jewish: Aryanization of, 9, 90; confiscation of, 9, 116, 141, 144, 243; objections to seizure of, 9, 98–101; restitution of, 123–26

property sales, 9, 96, 97, 116–17, 121–22, 123, 159

prostitution, 61, 281, 296, 300

protests against sanctions against Jewish athletes, 274

psychiatry, 120–21

Public Welfare and Relief Division (North African Economic Board), 255

Purim celebrations, 23–24, 109, 204–5, 209–12

Quakers. *See* American Friends Service Committee (AFSC)

Quaraouiyine Madrasa, 26–27

Quargla labor camp, 58

Rabat, Morocco, 303–5

rabbis: aid requested by, 200–202; authority of, 28, 90, 94, 131, 334; as bringing hope, 197, 198, 205, 209; deaths of, 155, 156; funerals, 195, 197, 198; in internment camps, 152, 197, 198, 200, 205, 209, 211; preparation of kosher food, 210; rabbinical school, 334

race and racism: African American soldiers, 286, 295; of American soldiers, 281–82; anti-black rhetoric, 43, 45; eugenic policies, 325–27; exclusion from public spaces, 130; interrogation of citizens, 129–30; Leggi per la Difesa della Razza, 241; mixed-race couples, 325–27; prostitutes, 281; race laws, 7, 28, 241; religious identity compared with racial identity, 39; segregation, 241; Statut des Juifs, 9, 112, 122–23, 145, 168; treatment determined by, 32, 63, 71, 72–73

radio broadcasts, 25–26, 49, 54, 140

radios, confiscation of, 279, 296, 297

railroad construction, 1, 11, 81, 104, 128, 173, 188, 307, 309

Ramadan, 176, 177–78, 180, 304

rape, 168, 169, 289, 300–302

Rauff, Colonel, 131, 133, 140, 160

Recruitment Committee for Jewish Labor, 130

Red Cross, 64, 70, 109–10, 160–61, 217, 251, 252, 254, 318, 324

INDEX 365

Refugee Aid Committee (Casablanca), 11
refugees: American sponsors for, 307; army service of, 306, 308; assistance to, 257, 266; character references, 236–38; clothing, distribution of, 257; displacements of, 266; employment by the French, 257–58; Hungarian Jews as, 321–25; lack of news from families, 236, 306–7; legal identity of, 260; migration of, 52–53; patriotism of, 306, 308; physical characteristics of, 52–53; political allegiances, 256; professional skills of, 307; separation from families, 305–8; as skilled labor, 307; skills of, 236, 237, 307, 314, 321, 338; as stateless, 317
Reginiano, Abraham, 250
Reginiano, Jacob, 253
Reginiano, Shalom, 251, 254
Reichmann, Renée, 322–23
religious observances, 143; burial of Jewish prisoners, 195, 196; call to prayers (muzzeins), 182–83; Chanukah, 253; Christmas celebrations, 61–62, 155; circumcisions, 252, 327; Days of Awe, 202–4; Eid El-Kebir, 186–87; interference with, 46, 215; *kaddish* prayer, recital of, 198, 298; kosher food, 200, 201, 210, 214–15; memorial prayers *(ashkeva)*, 2, 331–33; moussem Alamiyne (pilgrimage ceremony), 27; Muslim prayers, 177, 180, 182–83, 186–87; Passover, 150, 156, 283–86; Purim celebrations, 23–24, 109, 204–5, 209–12; Ramadan, 176, 177–78, 180, 304; Sabbath observance, 46, 205, 215, 297, 298; separation from families, 203; Shavuot, 214; Yom Kippur, 204, 331–33
Republican army. *See* International Brigade
Reuter, Walter, 12 image 3, 103–7, 181(image 13)
Roosevelt, Franklin D., 284, 287, 289, 298, 309, 313, 315
Rothschild vocational retraining camp, 234

Sabbath observance, 46, 205, 215, 297, 298

Safi, Morocco, 10map 1, 55, 117–18, 281, 295
Saïda (El Kheiter) camp, 224, 226, 234–35
Saïda internment camp, 10 map1, 220, 224, 226, 229, 233–34
Saint Médard camp, 63; Arabs in, 69, 70; exercise routines, 72; living conditions in, 67–68, 69, 71, 72; medical care, 68; Poitiers (camp) compared with, 67–68; propaganda in, 69, 70; theft in, 69, 72; work assignments, 72
Samuele, Zieg, 254
Santé prison (Paris), 261
Saouaf camp, 153, 154
Saraf, Michal, 141
Sbikha, 153, 154
Scampini Mission (Prisoner of War Diplomatic Service), 63
Scemla family, 159–61
Schneider, Paul, Lieutenant, 300–302
schools: Ashkenazi refugees in, 52; as barracks, 127; expulsion from, 51–52, 260, 334; high schools, 47–48, 51–52; patriotic performances in, 48, 55, 56, 57; prisoners in, 167; survivors' return to, 344–45; Vichy propaganda in, 8–9, 55, 56, 57. *See also* Alliance Israélite Universelle (AIU)
Sello, Ernest, 217–19
Senegal, 1, 11, 63, 65, 67, 71–72
Senghor, Léopold, 11, 13, 63–72
sewing machines, 241, 242
sexual violence against women: American soldiers, 16, 286–87, 289, 300–302; experiences of captivity, 241–49; by female kapos, 266–67, 268, 269, 270–71; French military, 296; identification of perpetrators, 168, 169; Jewish women protected by Muslim neighbors, 259–60; politics of, 300–302; prostitution, 61, 281, 296, 300; rape, 168–69, 289, 300–302; by soldiers, 16, 129(image 9), 286–87, 289, 300–302; support for victims of, 170; women prisoners at Auschwitz concentration camp, 266–68

Sfez, Henry, 137, 151, 153
SFIO Socialists, 176
Shalom, Haim "Mino," 252
Shapir, Bibi, 259–60
Shavuot, 214
shoes, 13, 17, 98, 109, 110, 238, 267
Shpilgarn (deceased inmate), 192–98
Sidi Ahmed, 14 map2, 143, 150
Sidi Aziz labor camp: Days of Awe observance in, 202–4; deaths of prisoners, 204; deportations to Bakbuk, 203–4; food supplies, 200, 203; Libyan Jews in, 202, 241, 249; water shortages, 203
Sidi Bel Abbès, 58–62, 190, 233
Sidi El Ayachi camp, 104, 106(image 7); dental care, 198–99, 214; families in, 199, 200, 213–15; food supplies, 214–15; living conditions in, 109–10, 117; medical care in, 117; population of, 109, 213–15; rabbis in, 200
Slawī, Lḥussain, 281–82
Smeets, Intendant, 155
"soap," 267
SOL (French right-wing party), 175, 176, 320–21
soldiers: sexual violence against women, 1, 16, 128, 129(image 9), 168–69, 286–87, 289, 300–302
SOL [Service d'ordre légionnaire], 320–21
Sommer, Erwin, 305–8
songs, 48, 58–59, 264, 281–82
southern Algerian Jews: in electoral colleges, 333
southern Algerian Muslims: in electoral colleges, 333
Soviet Union, 317
spahis, 65
Spain, 26, 50, 53, 96, 256, 323–24. *See also* International Brigade
Spanish Civil War, 106(image 7), 171, 192, 226, 317. *See also* International Brigade
Spanish Republicans, 171, 316
spoliation, 57, 90, 94, 133, 134, 136–37, 144, 211, 241–43

sports, 1, 15, 211, 263, 271–76
SS (Schutzstaffel), 15, 131–35, 155, 164, 236, 254, 261, 265, 343
Star of David, 149(image 10), 157, 158, 265, 270
starvation, 1, 15, 75–76, 76(image 6), 143
Statut des Juifs, 9, 112, 122–23, 145, 168
Statute of Moroccan Jews (Dahir, 5 August 1941), 98–99, 112, 116, 122–23, 125
striped prison uniforms, 267–68
Strössler, Karl, 233–38
Surgères, France, 188
surveillance of prisoners, 180, 181–82, 187, 206, 258(image 17), 262
survivors: descriptions of train journeys by, 77; language fluency, 345; medical interventions for, 344; memories of, 343–44; poems of thanksgiving, 259–60; repatriation ID, 342; reunions with, 266, 305–6, 340, 344; tracing of, 334; trauma of, 16, 340–43, 345, 346; treatment of, 307, 344; weight loss, 346
swimmers, Jewish, 1, 271–76
synagogues, 131, 132

Taïeb, Gilbert, 211
Taïeb, Maurice, 150, 151
Tangiers: education in, 47–48, 51; Hungarian Jews in, 322–23; Spanish government in, 50, 53; wartime life in, 49–50. *See also* Bendelac, Alegria
tattoos, 1–2, 269–70, 342, 346
teenaged girls: advocacy on behalf of, 300–302; rape by American soldiers, 300; sexual abuse of, 300–302; as unwed mothers, 300–302
Thumim, Pinkas Josef, 200–202
Tiger 1 (tank), 5(image 1)
Tigrinna labor camp: internment of Libyan Jews in, 202, 241
tirailleurs, 11, 13, 63–65
Tlemcen, Algeria, 1–2, 10map 1, 16, 260–65, 340–46. *See also* Bénichou, Gabriel

tombeau (punishment), 216–19, 313
Torah scrolls, 203
Torres, Abd el-Khalek (National Reform Party), 26
Trabelssy, Alush, 140–44
train transports, 77, 81–90, 227–28, 261
trans-Saharan railway, 11, 81, 104, 173, 188, 309
trauma: expressions of, 330, 343; headshaving, 244–45, 268; post-traumatic stress of survivors, 340–43; recognition of, 342; tattoos, 1–2, 269–70, 342, 346; *tombeau* (punishment), 216–17, 217–19, 313
Trenner, Maximilien, 168, 169
Tripoli: British army in, 335; expulsion of Jews from, 241–49, 334; Jewish flight to Gharyan, 334; Jewish neighborhood in, 4; Mussolini's visit to Jewish community, 4, 27–29
Tripolitania, Libya, 1, 3–4, 252
Tucci, Eugenio, 251
Tunis: aircraft bombings of, 146; American army in, 296–98; forced recruitment of labor, 133, 207; German army in, 127–28, 146–47, 168–69; ḥāra in, 168–69; Jewish flight from, 148; memorial book of, 327–31; military presence in, 127; morale in, 152, 296–98; radios, theft of, 296, 297; rape of Jewish women by German soldiers in, 168, 169; round-ups in, 212; SS (Schutzstaffel) harassment of Jewish community, 131–32; survivor's return to, 340–41
Tunisian Jews: Albert Memmi, 15, 162–68; assimilation into French society, 163; citizenship of, 9, 14, 44, 130; Jewish Council of Tunisia, 146; Jewish identity of, 163; languages of, 162, 327–28; mediation with Nazi occupiers, 130–40, 145–58; memorial prayer for Nazi victims, 327, 331–33; military service of, 44, 158; reactions to American soldiers in Algiers, 296–98; reaction to arrival of German army, 147–48, 168–70; songs of, 141–44

typhoid epidemics, 9, 15, 102
typhus, 75, 77, 154, 186, 244, 248, 261, 296

Ullman, Julius, 238–40
Union of Friends of the Algerian Manifesto and Liberty (ULEMA), 175–76
Union of Monotheistic Believers, 42–43
Upper Volta (Burkina Faso), 11, 65
US Army Contracting Office, 288
Uzan, David-André, 328
Uzan, Maurice, Dr., 154

Valensi, Victor, 157, 163
Vallat, Xavier, 8
Vichy regime: abrogation of Crémieux Decree (1870), 333; Algerian Saharan Jews under, 9, 192–98; Anglo-American agreement with, 315–17; anti-Semitic laws of, 8, 16, 41–42, 90–91, 98, 115–16; Commissariat-General for Jewish Affairs, 8, 99; food supply, 75–76, 303–5; Gaby Morlay (actress) in, 110–12; incarceration of Spanish refugees, 256; Operation Torch, 1, 15–16, 214, 216, 286, 299–300, 311(image 19), 315, 320; propaganda of, 4, 8–9, 51, 54, 55, 56, 178–79; resistance to, 40–42, 43; restrictions on Jewish professionals, 98, 101–2, 115–17, 122–26, 153; Statut des Juifs, 9, 112, 122–23, 145, 168; trans-Saharan railway, 11, 81, 104, 173, 188, 309. *See also* Pétain, Philippe, Marshal
Vichy regime camps: 10map1. *See* individual camp headings (e.g. Djenien bou Rezg)
visa applications, 226, 230, 232, 233
Viziriel decrees, 91–92, 93

Warsaw ghetto, 261, 340
wartime correspondents, 219–24
water shortages, 186, 203
weather conditions, 1, 15, 75, 98, 148, 207, 209, 210
whippings, 244, 245, 269

Winckler, Peter, 216–17
women, 118(image 8); abuse by prison guards, 246, 266–67, 268, 269, 270–71; advocacy on behalf of, 300–302; American soldiers, 16, 286–87, 289, 300–302; Ashkenazi refugees, 52; careers of, 162, 307; childbirth, 246, 248–49; clothing for, 290; as cooks, 251, 254; courage, 160; deportation of, 188, 254, 306; European women married to Black colonial soldiers, 325–27; graves of, 196; interventions for husbands, 202–3, 252, 326; Jewish identity of, 8, 38–39, 111; Jewish women protected by Muslim neighbors, 259–60; khevra kadisha members, 196; as legionnaires, 189; prostitution, 61, 281, 296, 300; protests of, 134–35, 136, 137–38, 160–61, 167, 247; psychological trauma of, 161, 162; repatriation of, 307; sales of Jewish businesses to, 121–22; vulnerability of, 129(image 9), 130, 207, 300–302; as widows, 35; wives of prisoners, 207, 212–13. *See also* children; families; sexual violence against women; individual headings (e.g. Arviv, Shoshana (Giado)); individual women (e.g. Bendelac, Alegria)

yellow star, 149(image 10), 157, 158, 265, 270
Yom Kippur, 204, 331–33

Zaghouan, 14map2, 136, 142, 148, 152–53, 159, 296
Zano, Camus, 204
Zionism, 43, 202, 204, 285

The authorized representative in the EU for product safety and compliance is:
Mare Nostrum Group
B.V Doelen 72
4831 GR Breda
The Netherlands

www.ingramcontent.com/pod-product-compliance
Lightning Source LLC
Chambersburg PA
CBHW031845220426
43663CB00006B/506